When Flying Was Fun!

An Autobiographical Compilation of Aviation Anecdotes

BILL EADS

NAVAL AVIATOR AND AIRLINE PILOT

PublishAmerica
Baltimore

First printing

At the specific preference of the author, PublishAmerica allowed this work to remain exactly as the author intended, verbatim, without editorial input.

ISBN: 1-4241-6407-9
PUBLISHED BY PUBLISHAMERICA, LLLP
www.publishamerica.com
Baltimore

Printed in the United States of America

Preface

Forty years of flying airplanes for the U. S. Navy and United Airlines have provided me with many memories of my life in aviation. Most of these anecdotes are funny, some are serious, a few are tragic, but all are true. Of course, literary license gives me the right to embellish these tales just a wee bit!

Not wanting to embarrass any of my buddies who might be included in these stories, I have omitted last names. However, I am sure that many will recognize themselves should they take the time to read these attempts to relate interesting events with interesting people in a humorous vein.

On a more somber note, I believe that commercial aviation in America was changed forever by the tragic events that occurred on September 11, 2001. Americans in general and aviation managers in particular were not prepared for terrorists to hijack our airliners and, after murdering the crews, fly our planes into buildings in order to murder innocent people. Airline crews had been taught for over thirty years (when hijackings began) that the typical hijacker wanted a free flight to Cuba, was trying to exhort money, or was making a political statement. We were told to try to calm the hijacker, get the airplane on the ground and delay, delay, delay until we got help from ground forces. Crews were not prepared for the psychotic fanatic willing to commit suicide in the name of his religion.

I consider myself so very fortunate to have been in aviation during what I call the Fun Years—basically the four decades starting with the sixties and ending with the turn of the century. This is the time frame that this book is about.

Chapter One

"It's better to be down here wishing you were up there than be up there wishing you were down here."

It was a dark and stormy night (most tales in aviation start this way) up and down the entire West Coast but especially in the Los Angeles area. Our flight that day had originated in Vancouver, Canada after another delightful layover in that beautiful city. Our Boeing 727 cockpit crew was based in Denver and this was the last day of a three day trip—we would get to sleep in our own beds that night. The last day of a multi-day sequence was always interesting and this would be no exception. Airline managers did not like to use the word that all crews knew so well: *get-home-itis!* I do not have the statistics to prove it but I would bet that most crew-related incidents happen on the last leg of the day and especially the last leg going home. It is very easy to cut corners just a bit if one is flying that last trip home after a long sequence.

We departed Vancouver late that afternoon for a short flight to Seattle, continuing to LAX and then on to Denver. The good news was that we would have the same airplane all day—all too often we changed airplanes at each major hub and both SEA and LAX were West coast hubs for United Airlines. I was the copilot (First Officer with UAL) as I did not yet have the seniority to get a Captain bid but I was getting close to getting that exalted position and was probably considered one of those "crusty old copilots" that Captains hated to fly with. I believe we were called "crusty" because we did not want to purchase a new copilot hat when we would get a "free" Captain's hat from the company upon successful completion of Captain School. Therefore you could always judge how long a copilot had been in that seat by how worn out or salty his hat was. When I became a new Captain I would cringe each time I had to fly with a copilot whose hat was not new and shiny.

The Captain of our crew was a good friend of mine and a fine aviator with great leadership qualities. Normal procedure was for the Captain and copilot to alternate flying duties with the other pilot handling the communication part of the job. It was my turn to be the "flying pilot" for the first leg. I always enjoyed the short legs such as that one between Vancouver and Seattle—especially if the weather was nice and we could fly low and enjoy the beautiful scenery by Whidbey Island and the Straits of Juan de Fuca. Today was not one of those sightseeing days as we were in the clouds all the way to SEA. We did depart on time and arrived within five minutes of our scheduled ETA—good enough for airline work as we used to say. We had less than an hour on the ground in Seattle which was just enough time for my routine. The UAL mechanics had a lunch room under the terminal where they had a popcorn machine that made some of the best popcorn in the entire system—I knew where every popcorn machine was at every airport we flew to. There were only a very few airports that did not have popcorn—San Francisco was one of the major airports that fell in that bad category. I often wondered why?

After a couple of bags of popcorn (25 cents per bag) I stopped by my next favorite spot in the SEA-TAC airport—the Washington apple booth—to pick up a granny smith for the next leg. Although we were actually fed quite well on our trips we never knew if our scheduled meal was needed to feed a hungry passenger whose meal was missing. Most of the pilots did not complain if this was the case. Anyway, it often paid off to have a snack available in the cockpit in case of such emergencies.

The next leg, SEA-LAX, flown by the Captain, was essentially routine with a few delays in the L.A. area due to traffic and the worsening weather. Probably ninety percent of the time airplanes take off and land to the west at LAX. When this is not the case it is because of two possibilities. Either the weather is really rotten and the winds are quite strong from the east or it is nighttime and noise abatement procedures are in effect. Situation number two can be a bit hairy to say the least. During these "noise abatement" periods aircraft depart, as usual, to the west, but arriving aircraft land in the opposite direction, to the east. Obviously if the wind was 10 knots or greater from the west, planes could not land to the east. During conditions when the tailwinds are less than ten knots it really does decrease the noise over land as departures and arrivals are over the ocean. Many late night arrivals from Hawaii and Japan are grateful for this procedure as it allows the pilots to land straight in as opposed to a circling approach. The disconcerting part is that on a clear night with unlimited visibility the arriving plane can see the runway from 20 miles or more—and the pilots watch planes taking off and heading directly towards them as they maneuver for landing. Departing airplanes have their landing lights on for departure and the illusion can be a bit startling.

On the evening in question it was a case of the first possibility—planes were taking off and landing to the east because the weather was lousy and the winds were definitely from the east with strong gusts from thunderstorm activity. We made a few laps in a holding pattern awaiting our turn then commenced our approach to runway 7 left. Most of the thunderstorms were to the east of the airport so the approach and landing were pretty much routine although the runway was wet and slippery.

As we were now a bit behind schedule we off-loaded the passengers and as soon as cabin service had finished their chores we began loading the new passengers for our final flight to Denver. We contacted flight dispatch to update our weather briefing and were told that there was a line of thunderstorms to the east of LAX but that departing aircraft were able to "pick their way through" with use of the onboard weather radar and help from departure control. It just so happens that at this time in history United Airlines was introducing a new radar to the fleet—a fancy new COLOR radar! Most of the 727's were still equipped with the old style black and white tubes that we were very familiar with, but tonight we had one of the new type sets. None of the cockpit crew, including the second officer, had ever flown with this new radar, but we had operated it the last two legs and were impressed with the pretty colors! Green was okay, just light rainfall; yellow meant heavier rain; red was bad stuff to be avoided and then they threw in a new color called MAGENTA! None of us knew the definition of magenta but were not going to admit it to ourselves, much less to each other.

As we taxied out for takeoff—runway 6 Right (the only time in my career to take off from that runway) the Captain briefed for the departure. The airplane was completely full, a face at every window and a fanny in every seat, and the two observer seats in the cockpit were occupied by deadheading pilots, making the cockpit very crowded with a total of five pilots onboard. It was my turn to be the flying pilot and the Captain briefed that after takeoff he would operate the radar and give me headings to fly to avoid the weather in our flight path. This made good sense to me and it became a procedure that I used when I moved to the left seat—whenever taking off in thunderstorms I would have the copilot fly (even if it was not his/her turn) and I would act as a controller to avoid the bad stuff. We lined up on the runway when it became our turn and focused on what was on the radar screen—I have often said that one look out the windshield was worth several looks at the radar screen—and observed a lot of red returns straight ahead. Previous departures had reported moderate turbulence on climbout but that they were able to navigate around the thunderstorms. The tower issued us our takeoff clearance with instructions to contact departure control when airborne—then added "good luck!" Did they know something that we didn't?

As I released the brakes and started the takeoff roll I noticed that it was very dark ahead with moderate rainfall—then lightning in the distance revealed several huge thunderstorms within five miles of the airport. Acceleration was normal for a heavy aircraft with water on the runway but I knew that we had a long runway to work with that night. I subconsciously added a few knots to rotation speed and we were soon airborne into the black soup. "Positive rate, gear up" were my commands as soon as I was sure that we were safely aloft. The Captain raised the gear lever and switched to departure control. After checking in with L.A. Departure Control we were cleared to deviate as necessary to avoid the weather and advised that a large cell was directly ahead. The Captain was fiddling with the weather radar at this time and I was looking out the windshield—I said, "I think I need to turn left" and the Captain said, "Look at this, I think this is MAGENTA"—when the loudest boom I have ever heard vibrated not only the cockpit but the entire airframe! The nose of the aircraft appeared to explode in a brilliant flash of lightning which blinded everyone in the cockpit for a few seconds. The Captain reacted very quickly and turned on the thunderstorm light switch— a switch that was rarely used for the purpose it was designed, to turn on all the white lights in the cockpit in the event that the pilots were blinded by a lightning flash. We often used that switch at night at the gate when we needed lots of light to do our cockpit setup procedures—I believe that this was the only time this switch was used in flight during my career! Now there were five sets of bulging eyeballs scanning the engine and flight instrument gauges to see what had happened to our aircraft. With my hands on the controls I felt a lurch when the lightning hit but I now felt that the plane was powered normally by the three aft-mounted engines and the controls seemed to be responding properly. I completed my left turn and it appeared that we were at least out of the dreaded MAGENTA!

Probably less than ten seconds went by after the lightning strike (although it seemed a lifetime) before a word was uttered. All five pilots in the cockpit were checking to see if their pants were soiled and saying a silent prayer that they would survive this night! Then we heard a quiet knocking on the cockpit door—obviously from the first flight attendant who was strapped in facing aft in the jumpseat just to the left of the cockpit door. The Captain said: "What the hell—open the door to see what she wants"—or words to that effect. The deadheading pilot in the rearmost jumpseat opened the door just a crack and the senior flight attendant—a very professional lady who also had a great sense of humor—stuck her head in and said "I just learned a very important thing a few seconds ago." The Captain, not wanting to spend any time with trivial matters, said "What is it—quick—we're a bit busy right now!" She said, "Well, I have decided not to put my shoulder harness on for takeoff with you fellows ever again. When I heard that explosion, I bent over to kiss my ass goodbye and couldn't reach it!" Then she quietly closed the cockpit door.

Again silence lasted for about five seconds—then we all burst out laughing, almost uncontrolled, until we were brought back to reality with a transmission from departure control: "United 496, are you OK?" The Captain, now perfectly composed, responded that we had experienced a lightning strike but everything appeared to be okay. Following normal procedures, departure control asked what our intentions were and could they be of assistance. At that time I looked around the cockpit for the first time— we were still brightly illuminated with the thunderstorm lights—and noticed four pale faces (I am sure that my face was equally pale) with very bright eyes. I asked the Captain to dim the lights so that we could regain our night vision and stated that the controls seemed normal. After the lights were dimmed we again scanned all the instruments and ascertained that everything did seem to be okay. We were now breaking out of the squall line and clear skies appeared ahead. The decision was up to the Captain, as it should be, but we all seemed to agree that we should continue to Denver (get-home-itis) as we surely did not want to return to LAX and penetrate that wall of MAGENTA again.

Aviation has been described as hours of boredom interspersed by moments of stark terror, and there were surely more than a few seconds of uncertainty and terror when that lightning bolt hit—but the levity of that flight attendant cleared the air, relieved the tension and brought us back to reality faster than any training could have provided. We did continue to DEN and once on the ground we all exited the cockpit, departed the jetway via the stairs to the ramp and went to look at the nose of the aircraft. Not a word was said as all five pilots looked at the nose cone of this beautiful B-727 and saw three small holes, less than the diameter of a dime each, burned into the paint of the radar dome—the color around those burned holes—MAGENTA!

After discussing the incident with maintenance and a short debrief, the crew departed the airport to our individual homes. I arrived at my townhouse in Southeast Denver about one hour after landing—at the time I was a bachelor living alone—and followed my usual routine after a long trip. I opened a Coors Light and stood up while perusing my mail—after many hours sitting in a cockpit seat I would always stand or walk for an hour or so before sitting or lying down. As I opened my mail I noticed that my hands were still a bit shaky—something that had not happened before, even though I had experienced many really scary events in my aviation career. I began to think back on the events that had led me to this point in my life.

Chapter Two

**"Those who hoot with the owls by night cannot fly
with the eagles by day!"**

Most of the pilots that I have met and befriended over the years are basically average guys and gals who have only one thing in common—love of flying. There is the old saying that **"flying is the second greatest thrill known to man, landing is first!"** However you look at it, most pilots chose aviation because of the challenge and the thrill that only comes with events such as one's first solo flight or that really great grease job landing after a difficult approach. Pilots used to be stereotyped, ala Chuck Yeager, the swaggering good old boy from the hills of West Virginia who was in the right place at the right time and had the "right stuff." The fact that he was gifted with outstanding vision and motor skills certainly helped.

In reality, pilots come from all walks of life and from every part of our country. The movie industry used to portray aviators as quiet, unassuming heroes from the farmlands of middle America who rose to perform outstanding aerial feats in defending our country from our enemies far away—Gary Cooper, Jimmy Stewart, Clark Gable and the likes. Now our movie heroes in aviation are cocky young bucks such as Tom Cruise's portrayal of the fighter pilot hero in Top Gun.

Pilots that I have known seem to fall somewhere in between—they come from big cities like Chicago and San Francisco, small towns throughout middle America, farms in the South and ranches out West. Young pilots are prone to ego problems; they are the best of the best, the cream of the crop and if you don't believe that, just ask them! Self confidence such as this is exactly what we want from Navy carrier pilots and Air Force fighter pilots. The airline passenger, however, wants to see a steely-eyed, ramrod-straight, mature aviator with just a bit of gray around the edges. Another aviation axiom is: **There are bold pilots and there are old pilots, but there are no old, bold pilots!**

I must admit that growing up in a small town in Virginia after World War II, my hero was Chuck Yeager—not only was he from the part of Appalachia that I called home but he had set every conceivable record in aviation following an illustrious career as a fighter pilot in WW II and the Korean War. I met that gentleman a few years ago at an airshow where he was signing autographs—he still has a twinkle in his eye that says: I did it all and I had a great time doing it! I wanted to relate a personal story to him but did not want to take more of his time than I was entitled—if I had it to do over I would have told my story and I bet he would have chuckled. Here is that story.

I was a young Naval Aviator on my second cruise aboard an aircraft carrier in the early sixties. The ship was in port for liberty in Yokosuka, Japan and I was enjoying an evening with my fellow squadron pilots at the Navy Officers Club. About a month earlier, we had enjoyed liberty in Hong Kong where I met a lovely young lady vacationing from her job as a school teacher at Clark Air Force Base in the Philippines. She was a graduate of Ole Miss and a very proper southern belle—except that she could out drink every pilot in our squadron! We had formed a close relationship in Hong Kong and I couldn't wait until our ship arrived in the Philippines so that we could be together again. After quite a few beers at the O'Club, I decided to give her a call, although I had no idea how to call the Philippines from Japan. On the way to the men's room I spotted a phone on a desk in a small unoccupied room which was probably the mess officer's private office. I thought: Why not try that phone to make my call!

The fact that the phone in question was RED did not trigger any alarms, so I picked up the receiver—there was not a dial on that phone—and instantly a male voice said, "Yes Sir!" I responded that I would like to make a call to Clark Air Force Base in the Philippines. The male voice said, "Yes sir—what priority, sir?" I had no idea what to say to that question so I replied, "Priority One." I could hear an audible gasp at the other end of the line before the operator repeated, "Priority One—yessir, right away, sir." In a few seconds another male voice came on—this time obviously an officer with a great deal of authority. He said, in a calm, mature, deep voice, "May I have your name and rank, sir?" Grasping for something to say as I could see myself getting into something more serious than a frivolous call to a girl friend, I gave the first name that came to mind: "This is Chuck Yeager." The authoritative voice instantly turned to one of respect: "Yes sir, Colonel Yeager, I will be happy to connect your call—just give me the number." I read the number from a crumpled piece of napkin from the Hotel Merlin in Hong Kong and in just a few minutes heard the phone ring. Since it was a bit late, it took several rings before a sleepy voice that I recognized answered, "Hello?" I was laughing so hard at this time that it took a few seconds before I said, "Hi, this is Chuck Yeager." A long pause, then: "Is this a joke?" Then I gave her my real name, asked for her forgiveness for calling so late, gave her a date that I would be in the Philippines, and promised to explain this phone call when we got together. Then I quickly hung up and returned to the bar where my cronies thought that I had probably passed out in the john. This was my one night of fame as "Chuck Yeager."

When I was born, my parents were living in a small, unincorporated area called Yards, Virginia—located about halfway between Bluefield, West Virginia and Pocahontas, Virginia. These two towns were nine miles apart by road, probably about five miles apart as the crow flies, but you crossed the state line seven times in those nine miles. The only hospital was located in Bluefield, so my birth certificate shows that West Virginia is my state of record— although our family resided in Virginia at this time. In those days there was a lot of rivalry between the two states—something about which side was supported in the Civil War—and I never enjoyed relating that I was from West (By-God) Virginia when my allegiance was always with the South.

My parents did move to the big city of Bluefield, W. Va. a few years later (my father worked for the railroad at this time but it is not clear exactly what he did there) and I attended the first grade at Whitethorn school. When my parents met, my Dad was running a "speakeasy" on a mountain top near Bluefield and I believe that this was his true calling. He was, without a doubt, the most outgoing and gregarious person I have ever known. He never met a stranger and if he couldn't remember a person's name, he simply made one up. The man who lived near the tracks that went through town was called "Railroad," the shell-shocked veteran was called "Hardrock," and the man who always looked like he had a bad hangover was called "Redeye." In many cases these names stuck and the poor guys had to go through life with the moniker given to them by my father.

I remember when World War II was over—actually it was when Japan surrendered in August 1945—and my sister and I were given pots to pound

13

with metal spoons as we ran through the neighborhood. I had turned six years old in June and would start the first grade in September. My mother walked me to school the first day, about a half mile, and met me when school was over. After that first day, my dog "Blacky" took me to school and was always waiting for me when I finished. One day my faithful companion was not there when I walked out of the school—it turned out that someone shot my dog as he was on the way to the school. It was a very tearful day for me, my sister and Mom as Blacky (a mixture of half English Bulldog and half Chow) was the kind of dog that every kid wanted in his/her childhood. When my Dad came home from work that day, he found a very sad family. When we explained what happened, my Dad became very quiet, and then said, "I'll take care of it." As he left the house, we assumed that he was going to bury our pet, but he did not return for quite a while. When he did return home he had a firm but pleased look on his face. I also noticed that the knuckles on his right hand seemed a bit bruised—he took care of it alright! A few weeks later the man who mistakenly shot our dog knocked on our door, introduced himself, apologized for his mistake and presented us with a new pup that we quickly named "Blacky." My Dad really did know how to "take care of it."

During the summer of 1946 we moved to Pocahontas, Virginia and that was the last move for our family. Pocahontas was a small coal mining town nestled in the hills of the western tip of the state of Virginia. This was the type of town that Tennessee Ernie Ford was talking about when he sang, "I owe my soul to the Company store." The only reason for the existence of this town was the enormous deposits of accessible bituminous coal in the nearby hills. Also in those hills and hollers were many moonshine stills! My father had purchased a beer joint (you could call it a restaurant but in reality it was simply a place where the coal miners spent a lot of time and money drinking large quantities of beer) in this town that boasted twice as many saloons as churches. Some of the residents called this town "Little Reno" as it had the reputation of a wild and wicked frontier town. In 1946 it was still a boomtown with Pocahontas Coal Company the second largest producer of coal in the nation. Later this company merged with Pittsburg Coal Company to become Pittsburg Consolidated, which then became the largest coal company in the U.S.

Pocahontas had a population of around 2,000 when we moved there and over the next ten years the population slowly dwindled to less than 1,500— I believe that there are fewer than 500 souls presently occupying this community. The main claim to fame for Pocahontas is the fact (rumor?) that the town is listed in Ripley's "Believe It Or Not" as the only incorporated community in America where there are more dead people than live people! The reason for this strange but true fact is the very large graveyard located on the outskirts of Pocahontas that contains over three thousand markers mostly for the many miners killed in mine explosions and disasters over the lifetime of the town. Coal mining was considered the most dangerous occupation in America, and during the boom years that started in the late 1800's and continued through the 1950's, Pocahontas was the only burial site for the numerous deaths in the local mines.

Thirteen years of my life were spent in this quaint little town and I would not exchange those years for anything. We did not have a lot of amenities but since we did not know the difference we certainly did not miss them. There was no McDonald's, no mall to hang around, no television to watch and nothing to do on Saturday night but sit on the bridge and watch the few cars drive by. My father did get one of the first TV's in our village when one of our more farsighted citizens ran a cable across the mountain to bring us into the twentieth century. The first memory I have of watching TV was the inauguration of President Eisenhower in 1952 and the picture was so grainy it was difficult to make out just who was who. Instead of watching TV as we were growing up, my sister and I read books, played cards and games and spent a lot of time outdoors. When the weather was good (most of the time) I was out "exploring." I hiked into the surrounding hills, climbed trees, camped out and later did my share of hunting and fishing.

When school started in September 1946 I was rightfully placed in the second grade. My mother had been a schoolteacher in South Carolina and had provided my sister and I with a bit of "home schooling" before we entered the formal education process. The first grade had been very easy for me in West Virginia and now the second grade seemed a repeat of what I had been taught the previous year. After about two weeks I was promoted to the third grade— and I arrived at my new class as not only the youngest and smallest kid in the class, but the only one wearing short pants! Years later this double promotion would be beneficial to my career, but at this time it was a difficult transition to be in the third grade with kids two years older. In retrospect it all worked out and I enjoyed a typical childhood filled with learning, playing and growing that produced many lifelong friends with whom I stay in contact to this day. By the time I was a senior in High School I had discovered what at that time I considered the three greatest thrills in life: **Smoking, Drinking and Screwing**! I had not yet been introduced to flying which would soon replace my only bad habit—smoking! My only exposure to aviation was the occasional Sunday afternoon drive that my parents forced on my sister and myself when we would drive to the town of Princeton, West Virginia, about twenty miles from home. There was an airport in Princeton that we drove by and once or twice my Dad pulled over to the side of the road and we would watch the small airplanes taking off and landing. There seemed to be a random chaos to the whole process that I found fascinating—but I never dared to think that one day I could become a pilot. I had never even met a pilot or talked to anyone who knew anything about aviation.

My first flight on an airplane came in June 1955, just after I graduated from Pocahontas High School at the age of fifteen. Tazewell County, where Pocahontas was located, was probably one of the last counties in the country to still operate on an eleven year system—seven years of grade school and four years of high school, so with one grade skipped, I really attended school only ten years. During that last school year, my grandfather (my Dad's father) had passed away and my father had received a small inheritance—around seven thousand dollars, I believe. That was a large sum of money to my Dad, who never had a savings account in his life and never owned a stock or bond! Whatever money our family had was in my father's pocket (he always had a huge wad of bills) or in his business checking account that also served as the family checking account. For the past several years the economic climate in Pocahontas had been declining as the coal mines were becoming mechanized. More coal was produced but fewer miners were required as one large machine could do the work of dozens of pick and shovel miners. My father recognized that conditions were changing as many small businesses in town had closed and there were now only three beer joints to choose from in town! My Dad's place, named "The Anchor" was still the most popular spot in town but business was definitely on the decline. Instead of several shooting and stabbings each weekend, there were now mostly just fist fights and drunk and disorderly arrests. My father decided to take the money he had received as an inheritance and buy a business in Florida—naturally a beer joint!

No way was my mother going to leave our home in Pocahontas for the uncertainty of an excursion to a far away place such as Florida! So my Dad left by himself to test the financial waters of South Miami. When I finished high school my father wanted me to come to help him with his new business and I was eager for a little traveling and adventure. My graduation present was a ticket to fly from Bluefield, WV to Miami, FL—which was just the gift I wanted. I departed Bluefield's Mercer County Airport early one June morning and arrived in Miami late that afternoon. The first flight was on Piedmont Airlines, a finely run Mom and Pop type airline that later was absorbed by the US Airways System. I flew on what I considered a very large propeller driven aircraft—actually it was quite small—nonstop to Atlanta, Georgia. There I switched to a Delta flight (I believe it was called Delta C & S at that time), a larger aircraft but still a prop job as the age of jet powered commercial aviation was just dawning. The first flight had been in rainy weather and it was quite a bumpy ride with little or no view of the ground. I was a bit "green around the gills" as I stepped off that first airplane, but the next leg was under clear and smooth skies and I began to realize what a great thrill it must be to pilot such a powerful beast and have it under your control.

I spent that summer helping my Dad—part of the beer joint he bought on Bird Road in South Miami consisted of a small grocery with a deli counter—and I learned a lot about that type of business. The main lesson I learned was that I wanted no part of this kind of job for the rest of my life—there had to be a better way to make a living. At the end of summer I returned to Pocahontas, this time driving a new 1955 Ford that my father had purchased while in Florida. The distance to drive was about 900 miles and it was difficult to average more than forty five miles an hour with mostly two-lane roads and many small and large towns to pass through. I had planned two days to complete the trip (I had just turned sixteen and was certainly no experienced driver) but after navigating through the traffic of Miami I found it smooth sailing once on US Highway 1 north. The freedom of the road as I drove solo toward home was a surprisingly pleasant experience and perhaps explains the fact that to this day I still enjoy being "on the road again." I did not check into a motel for the night as planned but continued non-stop home—perhaps my first case of "get-home-itis." Before going home I stopped at my favorite swimming hole, a small lake at Falls Mills, Va., where my two best friends were working as lifeguards. Falls Mills is exactly 7.2 miles from Pocahontas—I know because I not only drove it many times but I also walked it a few times! My two pals, Stuart and Jimmy, found it hard to believe that I had driven for almost 24 hours without sleep to get home from Miami. Stuart was my best friend as we had been in the same class throughout my school years and Jimmy was a bit of role model for me as he had graduated from our high school two years before me as the valedictorian of his class and had been admitted to the University of Virginia, where I aspired to attend. Unfortunately, as bright as Jimmy was, he was not prepared for the quantum leap from our small high school to "The University" as we called it, where academics were emphasized in class but fun and frivolity were the norm after school. Jimmy flunked out of UVa his first year and returned to Pocahontas with his tail between his legs. Partly because of this fact I had decided to attend a local Junior College in Bluefield, Va. in September and if things worked out okay I would transfer to UVA for my second year.

The other reason for not attending UVA for my first year was the fact that my sister was away attending Virginia Intermont in Bristol, Va. Incidentally, there are two twin cities in that part of the country: Bristol, divided down the middle by Virginia and Tennessee, and Bluefield, the larger city being in West Virginia but the smaller on the Virginia side. My sister would complete VI in the spring of 1956 and that would be the end of her formal education. As my folks were not really financially able for the two of us to be away in college at the same time, it was the best solution for me to attend that small Southern Baptist Junior College as a day student for my first year in higher education.

That year at Bluefield College was quite an experience, both socially and spiritually—notice that I did not include academics as part of that experience. The education I received was really not far removed from high school but required a bit more memorization—especially the religion part, as courses in the Bible were required as well as mandatory chapel attendance three days a week. There were four of us from the 1955 Pocahontas graduating class to attend Bluefield College that year and we rapidly gained the reputation of being a bit on the wild side. We took turns driving the nine miles each way to class and had a lot of fun in spite of bad weather, slick roads and unreliable automobiles. The classrooms were conducted under very strict rules as most of the professors were also Baptist ministers and it was forbidden for the students to smoke, drink, or, heaven forbid, DANCE! Those of us who gave in to these weaknesses of the flesh were listed prominently each week on the bulletin board as sinners whom were to be prayed for by the more proper students. Soon it became a badge of honor for those of us to make the list each week. There were many really nice students there who were simply seeking an education but there were also quite a few who were taking advantage of the system. The vast majority of the live-in students were from far away places like New Jersey, Kansas and even California—why would these kids come from so far away to attend a small two year college such as this? The answer was simple: tuition as well as room and board was free for those who declared their lives dedicated to full time Christian service in the Baptist religion. Turns out that most of these types transferred to four year colleges after their two free years at Bluefield College to become engineers, dentists, CPA's and the like.

Although my parents were not overly religious, my sister and I were raised in the Methodist Church. I attended Sunday school, joined the MYF (Methodist Youth Fellowship), sang in the church choir and eagerly went to church camp in the summertime. Church camp (sometime called bible school) was a great place to meet girls and I do believe there is some truth to the rumor that the wildest girls of all were the minister's daughters! There is simply no way to prevent adolescent teenagers with raging hormones from getting together—even at a closely chaperoned event such as church camp. What I was not prepared for at Bluefield College was the aggressive manner that religion was force-fed to the students. The course titled Bible 101 that was required for freshmen was nothing but memorizing most of the New Testament—I suppose Bible 102 was for the Old Testament which I missed out on, thank you very much! Mandatory chapel three times a week was a bit like an old time holy-roller tent meeting with repeated calls for those of us sinners to repent and step up to the altar to be saved. Needless to say, I left Bluefield College with a bit of a bitter taste for religion.

That summer, 1956, I worked as a lifeguard with my friend Jimmy at Falls Mills Lake. It was the first time I actually had a job that paid a salary. Previous jobs had been mowing lawns (push mowers, not power) or working for my Dad—not really getting paid for the latter. Not that I would ever complain about working for my Dad—he was really a dear man who was more tolerant and forgiving that I will ever be—and there is no way that I could ever repay him and my Mother for all they did for me. The job as a lifeguard paid $120 each month for three months. I will never forget receiving my first paycheck—for the amount of $105.60—and wondered what happened to the $14.40? No one had told me about taxes and other such withholdings! We worked (if you call it work) seven days a week and never had a day off for the three months of the summer. Each morning at eight o'clock my friend Jimmy and I would walk to the outskirts of town, stick out our thumbs and hitch a ride to Falls Mills. Usually we were able to get a ride quickly as there were many

19

working people who lived in Pocahontas and drove to Bluefield each day. We were usually dropped off at the turnoff to Falls Mills and we walked the last 1.2 miles to the lake. In reality, this walk was fun as we passed several apple trees where we picked off a few pieces of fruit and also grabbed a few grapes from some wild grape vines (maybe they were not wild but there was no one watching). The swimming area—actually part of the lake defined by a gate that led to a small sandy beach and two long wooden piers—did not officially open until ten o'clock each morning and we normally arrived by nine. We changed into our swim trunks, raced to the end of the pier, dove into the cool waters of the lake, raced across to the other side and back (a distance of just over one mile) and then started our day. We were the only two employees and had a lot of freedom in running this small business. The lake was actually owned by the Falls Mills Fishing Club, made up of a group of men who got together to manage the man-made lake as a private, members only fishing club. My father, an avid fisherman most of his life, was a member of this club so our entire family had access to all the facilities, which consisted of the lake for fishing, covered docks for boats, a picnic area and the swimming area. Members and their families were given free access to the swimming area— later (after my tenure as a lifeguard) it became available to the public for a daily fee.

In addition to our salary as lifeguards we operated a snack bar that sold soft drinks, candy, potato chips, etc. and any profits were ours to keep. Jimmy had been a lifeguard here for several years so he knew the ropes. Remember, he had flunked out of UVA two years previously and was now ready to try Charlottesville again after completing two years of junior college. I had been accepted to transfer to UVA after my one year at Bluefield College and Jimmy was now giving me valuable information as to what was in store for me in September. We spent many hours discussing why he had busted out after such a promising finish to his high school education. Basically, he had partied too much and had found that the lack of discipline at The University was more than he could handle. At least he did not lose his enthusiasm for a fun time as a lifeguard and we got along famously—we decided to keep a bottle of vodka and a bottle of gin in the soda pop cooler, just for emergencies! Occasionally we would have a bored housewife show up for some fun and sun at our little swimming area and it was nice to get a ride home with a lady looking for a few moments thrill. This was my introduction to the pilot's axiom: **candy is dandy, but liquor is quicker!**

During that summer, Jimmy and I pulled a sunken, abandoned row boat from the bottom of the lake and spent lots of rainy days making it seaworthy. We painted that boat in UVA colors (blue and orange) and christened it the "Virginian." We formed a friendship that lasted only until we arrived at Charlottesville the next September. He had learned his lesson from his previous experience at UVA and became a serious student and scholar—on the other hand I needed to find for myself just what this University life was all about.

Chapter Three

**"What's the difference between God and a fighter pilot?
God doesn't think he's a fighter pilot!"**

As a transfer student I was required to spend at least the first semester of my first year in a dormitory. At The University you were not a freshman or sophomore—you were a first yearman, second yearman, etc. The reason for this was the fact that most Virginia attendees did not graduate in the customary four year span that defined most college educations. It was not unusual to meet a classmate who was in his fifth, sixth, seventh year and still an undergraduate—many students attended for a year or two, flunked out and later returned to complete their education. The day I arrived at The University I met my dorm roommate who introduced himself as Francis—as I shook his limp, moist hand, I said, "Nice to meet you, Frank" and he was always Frank to me. One of the application forms sent to me by The University was a psychological profile that I filled out in order to properly connect me with a suitable roommate, based on common interests. I often wondered, just what did that profile have that would match me with this flaming homosexual? Well, Frank became a caring mother type to me, as he would take care of me when I staggered into our room and cleaned up for me when I threw up from too many beers. I do not know whatever happened to "Frank" but he was truly a caring soul—and he never made a single advance to me of an offensive kind. I suppose that I was just not his type.

Charlottesville was my kind of town. The University of Thomas Jefferson was, and still is, a marvelous institution of higher learning for young men and women—although during the time I attended, it was an all-men's university with no female undergraduates. There were a few exceptions, I believe, such as some females in the School of Education who had transferred to the

University from other colleges and a few daughters of University professors. Basically, UVA was a southern Ivy League University with style—we wore coats and ties to class each day and behaved like idiots each weekend. In 1956 there were fewer than 4500 students enrolled at UVA, and this included the graduate schools. There was a small nursing school called McKim Hall, connected to The University geographically but not academically, that contained a group of females, but the main source of feminine companionship was located throughout the state in numerous all-female colleges such as Mary Washington College, Madison College, Randolph-Macon, Mary Baldwin, Hollings, etc. The distance to each of these girl's schools was measured in the number of beers to get there, not in miles. It was probably true that it was impossible to get lost between Charlottesville and Fredericksburg (home of Mary Washington College) because all one had to do was follow the discarded beer cans along the road.

After getting moved into my dorm room on that first day I walked to what was called The Corner—a long block of buildings just off the grounds of The University. There the student could find just about everything he needed for school and after school. There was Mincer's Pipe Shop which sold everything but pipes—you could get your UVA insignia drinking mugs, buy your class ring, pick up supplies of all types, etc. Then there was Eljo's University Clothing Store where one bought the customary uniform for all the students—a $70 Harris Tweed sport coat, several button down dress shirts, a couple of rep ties and at least two pairs of wash khaki trousers. There was Anderson Brothers Book Store where you purchased all your schoolbooks, either new or used. The following year I would get a part time job working for Jim and Bill Anderson at that bookstore. My third and final year at UVA I basically worked full time there. The pay was $1.25 per hour so I could make ten dollars for a full day's work of eight hours. About enough to support my beer habit during that last year! There were also several eating establishments on The Corner, all of which sold beer. Hard liquor had to be purchased at the Virginia ABC (Alcoholic Beverage Control) store a few blocks away—a very busy place every day but especially on Friday and Saturday. That first evening I ate at one of the restaurants called The Virginian which was mostly a tavern with a long row of booths along one side and a bar down the other side.

I had just turned seventeen and here I was away from home for the first time and starting my second year of college. The legal age for buying beer in the state of Virginia was 21—I would not reach that legal age until long after my UVA days were over. As I sat down for my first meal at The Virginian, the waitress asked, "Would you like something to drink?" In my deepest, most mature voice I said, "Yes, I'd like a Falls City beer, please." Falls City beer was the cheap, local beer that we drank in Pocahontas and over the state line in West Virginia, where the legal age was only 18. Without batting an eye, or even looking closely at me, the waitress said, "All we have is Bud, Miller or Schlitz." I tried not to display my relief as I blurted out, "I'll take a Bud!" Now I knew that I was going to love this town.

My friend Jimmy had explained to me The University Honor System and I knew that it was a dismissal offence to lie, cheat or steal while enrolled as a student here. Had the waitress asked my age or asked if I were 21, I would have had to respond truthfully—and end up drinking coke at the Virginian for the next three years. Most of the places in Charlottesville that catered to University students were quite lax—if you looked, talked and acted like a student they rarely questioned you about your age. The Honor System was not a problem for me as my parents had raised me to always be truthful and it certainly never occurred to me to cheat or steal. I hope that the Honor Code at Virginia is still intact and respected by all the students to this day. The ABC store was a bit different. Since it was operated by the state, the clerks were very careful about selling hard liquor to underage students. Many times I waited in a long line at the ABC store to be asked by the sharp-eyed clerk, "Are you 21?" I would say no, go outside, get into another line for a different clerk and try again. There were usually four clerks on duty and chances were that one clerk was too busy to really look me in the eye as I ordered my bottle of Virginia Gentleman bourbon. If all else failed you could always get a local wino to buy a bottle for you for a buck—but I thought this was in reality a dishonest act and possibly a violation of the Honor Code. Maybe I'm wrong but it did not seem dishonest to purchase a bottle of booze under age if the clerk did not question your age.

I had to declare a major subject of study when I enrolled at The University. My previous year at Bluefield College had been spent taking general academic subjects plus the Bible 101—which was not transferable to UVA. All other courses were transferred as a grade of C even though I received an A in every subject—so I started out as a second yearman with a "C" average at The University. I also graduated with what was called a "gentleman's C average." I really did not know what I wanted to do with my life at this time—

not unusual for a seventeen year old more interested in girls and parties than academics. I had enjoyed science and chemistry in high school so I decided to major in chemistry. One problem: at The University it was required that in order to receive a BS in chemistry one had to take three years of German! Not aware of this when I attended Bluefield College; I started French, liked it and wanted to continue with two more years of it. I just did not want to start over with a new foreign language that required three years to finish. I found out that English Literature was one major that required only eighteen hours of advanced courses to receive a Bachelor of Arts degree. Therefore, I declared my major as English Lit but took all the required courses for a BS in Chemistry except for German. Since I had always enjoyed reading, I actually liked the English courses that I took.

After the first semester at The University I was eligible to join a fraternity—and there were 28 different ones to choose from—in reality I suppose the fraternity actually chose you, not the other way around, after a frenzied rush campaign that involved many drunken parties. There was a fraternity (never called a frat at UVA) for every type of student, from the most studious to the biggest goof-off, from straight-laced to true "Animal House." I trended toward the latter but stopped just short of the wildest of the wild. I narrowed my choices to three, received bids from all three and chose the ATO (Alpha Tau Omega) house. My three best friends at that time, Dan, Chops and Matt, all went to the ATO house too, so we were happy campers. By the time we finished Hell Week we were not sure that we had made the right choice. At the start of that week we were each issued a large wooden paddle and the object was to get the signature of each fraternity member on that paddle to successfully complete the initiation process. Of course each member got one whack at the rear end of every pledge before affixing his signature. Each time the paddle was broken the pledge started anew with a fresh paddle and by the time I was on my sixth paddle I was about ready to say uncle. Thankfully I was able to acquire all the necessary signatures on this last paddle—I believe my record of six paddles still stands!

I moved into the ATO house at 502 Rugby Road after initiation week and there I resided for the next two and one half years. Fraternities at The University were not exactly as depicted in the media at that time. We did not have a "house mother" or anyone else living in our house except our own fraternity members and it was basically a group of male college students living together in a large house with no supervision. There were approximately 60 undergraduate members in our fraternity but only about half of those actually lived in the fraternity house. The others were smarter and lived off the "grounds" in small apartment buildings where a saner environment prevailed. Those of us who chose to live in the "house" rarely had more than a few minutes each day to study, be alone or resist the temptations of doing something stupid! There were only two employees at the ATO house: Drury and his wife Lydia—a great couple who cooked for us, cleaned our rooms, and nursed us all through the travails of undergraduate life at The University. Drury later became very active in the local civil rights movement in Charlottesville and I believe even ran for Mayor of that great city.

We had our very own bar in the cellar of the house where we sold beer to anyone who wanted a beer—mostly our own members, but on weekends there was a profit to be made. Beer was twenty five cents a bottle (or can) and we often did a road trip to Washington, D.C. to buy cases of "Happy Hal's" beer for $1.95 a case. Therefore, we sold the beer for three times our cost— not too different from the bars and taverns of today. Everything was on the honor system—you drank a beer, you put a quarter in the box—or if you lived in the house you could sign a chit and settle at the end of the month. There were times when a member's bar tab was higher than his food bill each month. By my last year living in the house, I had cut down my meals to only dinner each day—skipping breakfast and lunch provided me with more money for important things such as beer and party time.

Dinner at the fraternity house each evening during the week was a ritual. Most of the members would show up for dinner, including several graduate students who were rarely seen around the house. We all wore coats and ties and arrived about five o'clock to enjoy cocktails (mostly beer) and play bridge until dinner was announced at six PM. The type of bridge played here was different—we played very quickly and if you did not make your contract you were replaced by the next two waiting their turn. If you and your partner made your contract then the defenders were replaced by the next two. It was a fun and challenging game that left me with a lifelong interest in the game of bridge. At six o'clock we all gathered around the tables in the dining room for very reasonably priced, wholesome food prepared by Drury and Lydia. After dinner there was always a bit of socializing and more beer drinking until someone would say, "Let's make a run to Mary Washington" (or Madison, or Mary Baldwin, etc.) Although I never had an automobile during my college years there were quite a few of our members who owned some form of transportation—usually a piece of junk that was unreliable to say the least. We would pile into two or three vehicles—usually four to each car—and head down the road with a case or two of beer. Someone always had a girl friend or a phone number so getting fixed up with dates was never a problem. I just wonder why those nice young ladies were willing to go out with such a group of boozed-up guys such as our motley lot! If the weather was nice we took our "dates" to a park, threw down a blanket or two and proceeded to drink more beer. If the weather was not conducive to this type of activity we usually went to some sleazy joint where we could drink cheap beer and act like idiots as usual. Come to think of it—I do not recall any of the girls complaining; I think they were as lonely and horny as we were!

There were four big weekends at The University: Opening, Homecoming, Midwinters and Spring. Each of these major party weekends involved a name band or musical personality such as Satchmo (Louis Armstrong) who was my favorite of all the groups that appeared at The U while I was there. For these weekends we imported our dates from the surrounding girl's schools and they arrived in droves, usually via Greyhound bus, on Friday afternoon or evening. The first major party weekend for me as a fraternity member was the Spring celebration and my date was a really neat gal I had met a month or so earlier who attended Mary Washington College as a freshman. She was Miss Chesterfield County (near Richmond) for 1956 and we were later to become "pinned" when I asked her to wear my fraternity pin. At the time this was considered a sure way to get into a young girl's panties! The Thursday night before this big event, as usual, a group of us decided to take a little road trip after dinner at the ATO house. Eight of us loaded into two cars with lots of beer and took off over the mountain to Staunton, Virginia, the home of Mary Baldwin College, a fine institute of higher learning full of eager young ladies in their prime. All went well until the return trip.

I was in the first car with three of my buddies when we had a blowout about halfway to Charlottesville. Naturally, there was no spare tire—but the second car came along in just a few minutes so we all crammed into the one auto and continued the trip toward home. It was now approaching three o'clock in the morning—but we still had a few beers among the eight of us to keep us happy for the rest of the journey. As we reached the suburbs of our town, about three miles from the fraternity house, this second vehicle ran out of gas! We had no choice but to walk the rest of the way, as there were simply no fueling stations open at that time of night. We took what few beers were left and started walking. As we proceeded along the highway someone decided that it would be fun to turn some of the directional signs around to confuse drivers—very dumb looking back on it but it seemed to be a harmless prank at the time. Then we came upon a small public park with swings and slides and stopped to enjoy some childish games. Two of our group did not stop and continued on to the fraternity house—they were the lucky ones as it turned out. The rest of us were enjoying our kindergarten games when suddenly we were hit with searchlights and loud speakers—we were surrounded by the police who rounded us up and hauled us all to the police station. We were still in a jovial mood as the police put us all in one large cell—obviously a "drunk tank." To the best of my recollection we were not charged with a crime and we figured that the police would let us "sleep it off" and release us the following morning. We certainly were not booked or even searched as my friend Dan had two beers in his pocket after we were locked up—we passed one around for the six of us and decided to save the last to celebrate when we were released.

As it was almost dawn when we arrived at the Charlottesville jail, we had only a couple hours of fitful sleep before we were rudely awakened and taken directly to court. What a shock as we staggered into the courtroom to see not only the judge and the usual court employees but also a rather large contingent of reporters. Seems that we had messed up big time! The judge read the charges—displacing state and county road signs—and immediately sentenced us to thirty days in the county jail! I was about to faint when he added that all but three days of that sentence were to be suspended and there was no fine—case over! We were to spend the weekend in jail and would be released on Monday morning in time to make our scheduled classes. We were taken in a paddy wagon to the county jail where we were searched and issued prison garb. Dan still had that last beer in his jacket pocket which was now discovered and confiscated!

Our dates for the weekend arrived later that day as we had no way to notify them about our incarceration and were picked up by other fraternity brothers (those with no dates) who took **very good care** of our girlfriends! The local Charlottesville newspaper put our story on the front page: "Students Plan Cooler Weekend." We had attained a bit of notoriety that none of us wanted. The ATO fraternity at Virginia had a tradition of having a Sunday morning party on big weekends, called "a knee-walking by noon party," complete with a band and the usual refreshments. Many of the other fraternity parties held on Saturday night would last all night and we usually had many of those party-goers arrive already pretty much "knee-walking." On this Sunday morning, our last day in jail, we were notified by our guards, most of whom we had befriended by this time, that we had some visitors. We were taken outside to a large exercise yard which was part of the county jail. We heard music and raucous cheering from a rowdy group outside the chain wire fence—the "knee-walking party" had been moved for our benefit! We certainly could not participate but it was great to watch our fraternity brothers, our dates and the whole gang having fun—but in a way rubbing salt in our wounds.

After my first year at UVA I returned home to Pocahontas to find a summer job. The lifeguard position was certainly fun but just did not pay enough to provide the funds I needed to supplement my costs at The University. Tuition was quite reasonable for state students and all expenses, including room and board, cost my parents less than one thousand dollars per year—a far cry from today's sky high bills for higher education. Nevertheless, I needed to make as much money as possible to help out and the only available jobs for the summer were working in the coal mines. Luckily, I managed to get on with a survey crew at the local coal company and we did most of our work on the surface. The few times that we were required to actually enter a working coal mine was very revealing—convinced me that I wanted to get as far above that hole in the ground as possible! The mines were cold, dark and scary—with an odor that can only be described as the smell of potential disaster. Our crew consisted of a civil engineer, a nice guy named Ray, his full time assistant and two of us young summer workers—basically gofers, though my official title was "apprentice rodsman." We worked long hours and the job consisted mainly of manual labor such as cutting brush—at least we were outside in the fresh air most of the time. The salary I received was $250 per month.

I turned eighteen that summer and was now legally able to purchase beer across the state line in West Virginia. There were at least ten roadhouses within a ten mile radius of my hometown, all located in unincorporated areas sprinkled throughout Mercer County, West Virginia. Some of these watering holes were almost like nightclubs, with decent music and edible food but most were joints that served beer to anyone tall enough to reach the bar. Music at these places came from a jukebox and any food served was questionable to say the least. I spent a lot of time in those sleazy places that summer with my buddies that included Stuart, Norman, Big Ben, and Louie—the fact that the five of us survived is remarkable. We were not troublemakers but there were a lot of bad guys who frequented the same places we did who were looking for a rumble. My friends and I were looking for cold beer and loose women but we did not shy away from a good fist fight. Norman was the best boxer in our little group but Big Ben, as his name would indicate, was the biggest and most feared. He later became the Chief of Police in Pocahontas—a position he held for many years mainly because he was considered the toughest guy in town. Our favorite spot was called The Villa, basically a beer joint that advertised Italian food because it was operated by an Italian couple. The wife did the cooking and served the absolute worst pizza I have ever tasted, a deep-dish watery mess that included fish heads and other disgusting leftovers! I think the real reason we liked that place was because this nice Italian couple had three lovely daughters that were ripe and ready. Anita, Vassitta, and Florissa (probably not the correct spelling) were twenty, eighteen and sixteen years old and, as far as the parents were concerned, ready for marriage. Our group was considered eligible since we were either in college or holding a steady job. I was attracted to the youngest but our relationship never progressed beyond a bit of kissing and petting. I hope that those nice young ladies married well and had successful and happy lives.

Sometimes, usually on a Saturday night, we would go to one of the better roadhouses located about a mile from The Villa, a place called Club 52. Obviously the name came from the fact that it was located on US Highway 52 about five miles north of Bluefield, W.Va. There was a cover charge to get in but no one ever checked ID's. Once inside and your vision adjusted to the darkness, it was a very large room with several dozen tables and booths surrounding a small, always crowded, dance floor. Music was loud and frenzied but not ear-splitting to the point of pain—just slightly quieter than a jet fighter with afterburner taking off! The last night I ever went to this place was a night I will never forget.

There were four of us from Pocahontas that evening—myself, Big Ben, Norman and another pal of ours whose name was Wes—who stopped in at Club 52 about ten PM. When we arrived at the entrance (actually on the side of the building) and paid our cover charges of $3 each, we noticed the usual small group of malcontents hanging around who either did not have the money to get in or had been turned away for various reasons. As usual, these tough guys were drinking cheap booze from brown paper bags and making surly comments that we ignored. My friend Wes had been our local football hero a few years ago and was now in the U.S. Marines and home on a short leave that summer. Wes was the kind of guy the gals fell in love with at first sight—he was handsome, witty and charming. He was also a big, tough guy who did not take any crap from anybody! We entered the "nightclub" and had our usual fun time drinking and trying to pick up girls. After a while Big Ben departed with a gal he met—most likely to the parking lot for some fun and games in the back seat of her automobile—and later Norman left with his "date for the evening". Wes and I soon found two young lovelies and the four of us departed through the same entrance that we had entered a few hours earlier. A smaller but meaner group of "bad guys" still lingered outside near the parking lot and one was letting his liquor control his mouth when he made a really nasty comment about the lady on the arm of my friend Wes. I tried to get him to ignore the remarks but Wes had had enough. He said, "Hold my jacket—this won't take long" and challenged the wise guy to step out into the parking lot. I took my friend's jacket and stood back to watch the fun—as Wes surely would have no problem taking care of this bum! Sure enough, the creepy guy took one wild swing that missed and Wes hit him between the eyes with a wicked right that knocked him to the ground. Wes turned to me to retrieve his jacket when I saw the downed fighter get to his feet and charge toward my friend. I yelled for Wes to watch out and as he turned it seemed that the attacker merely slapped at my friend and hit him lightly near his shoulder. Wes took a couple of steps back and I saw a very surprised look on his face—then he dropped to his knees. What's going on, I'm thinking, when the bad ass then stepped up and again hit my friend with what appeared to be a light blow on his back. Then I saw the knife withdrawn from Wes's back, covered in blood, as the assailant started running into the darkness. Oh, my God, he's been stabbed! In slow motion, it seemed, Wes went from a kneeling position to lying on the ground face down.

Suddenly, my friend Norman appeared from nowhere and we tried to get Wes to his feet—not aware of how badly he had been injured. Everyone else disappeared as if by magic and then there were just the three of us in the parking lot. We could not get Wes to his feet and he never said a single word. I was yelling for help when a stranger stepped out of a pick-up truck and offered to take Wes to the hospital in Bluefield. This Good Samaritan apparently had pulled off the highway to get some rest when he saw what happened. His wife and child were in the front seat so we loaded Wes into the back bed of the truck. There was a lot of farming equipment in that truck bed so there was room only for Wes and one other person. Norman, who was holding his hand over the deepest wound to stop the bleeding, was the only friend to accompany Wes to the hospital. Wes died in his arms before they got there.

Chapter Four

**"Always remember that you fly an airplane with
your head, not your hands."**

The following year at The University was a very busy one for me as I was
now taking a heavy load of difficult subjects such as qualitative and
quantitative analysis, physical chemistry and other advanced courses in the
sciences. It was also a fun year of friendships and good times with my buddies
in the fraternity. I needed to take physics, which was a course with the
reputation for having the most failures of all classes at UVa. I could not
squeeze physics into my schedule that year and did not want to take such a
difficult subject during my final year, which I had already planned to be a year
of fun with minimum time spent on academic matters. Therefore, I decided to
stay in school through the summer months to take a shortened but more
intense course and get it over with! Since I was able to work in the book store
during the summer, I would be able to make enough money to pay my
expenses.

Usually the fraternity house was shut down for the summer but I was able
to talk my way into staying in the house if I kept everything in good shape—
in other words, I would be the custodian for those three months. I was
spending about eight hours daily either attending physics classes or studying
for the next session—it seemed that if you dropped your pencil you were a
day behind. Maybe taking physics in summer school was not such a good idea
after all. However, there were few distractions during the summer months in
Charlottesville and the time moved very swiftly. One evening as I was
studying in my room, which was on the third floor of the house, a stranger
suddenly walked in and said, "Hello." Since I never locked the doors, it was
not a problem for someone to come in unannounced but I was a bit shocked

that this guy found his way to my room without my hearing a single sound. He was a young man about my age who introduced himself as Jack O'Hara and stated that he was a college student attending the University of Maryland. He told me that he had been spending that summer hitchhiking around the country and spending the nights at fraternity houses at various colleges and universities. He seemed to be a very nice guy and we went downstairs to the bar and had a couple of beers together—he insisted on paying for my beers and seemed to have plenty of money. He told several very interesting and humorous stories about his travels that summer and I envied him a bit because of his adventurous nature.

I told Jack that he was welcome to spend the night in the fraternity house and he thanked me and said that he would sleep on the couch in the living room. The next morning I left for my physics class and did not disturb my new guest who was still sound asleep on that couch. When I returned to the house that afternoon, Jack was gone—and so were many of my clothes and personal possessions! He had ransacked my room and taken sport jackets, shirts, sweaters and the only piece of jewelry I owned, my high school class ring from Pocahontas. I was pissed that this person whom I befriended had violated my personal space and taken my belongings—and I was even more pissed at myself for being such an easy target. This was the first time in my life to meet someone who was dishonest. The only phone in the fraternity house was a pay phone and the thief had even taken all my change—so I could not even call the police right away. I walked to the police station, just a few blocks away, and made my report to the desk sergeant. When the officer asked if I could describe the suspect, I responded, "I can do better than that—I even know his name, he said it was Jack O'Hara." The officer's eyes got very large and he looked over his shoulder to the chief's office and yelled, "Chief, you better come here, looks like O'Hara has struck again!"

The Police Chief, a big burly Irishman, rushed up to me and asked if I knew where this guy O'Hara was presently. I said that I did not know where he was but that he had spent the night at the ATO fraternity house. The Chief looked at me and said, "Son, you are lucky to be alive! This person has been going around the east coast all summer setting fires to fraternity houses and at least one person has died because of his arsons!" I was shocked to say the least and my anger at being robbed soon turned to a feeling of great relief that no real harm had come to me and our fraternity house. Several months later I was notified by the police department that the suspect had been captured and they had recovered some items that might belong to me. When I went to the station I was given a brand new suitcase which indeed did contain some of the items that were stolen from me. There was also a note in that suitcase written to me from Jack. He apologized for taking my things and thanked me for being nice to him! Unfortunately, my high school class ring was not part of the items that were returned. I never learned what happened to Jack O'Hara, if that was his real name, and, for all I know, he may still be in prison.

Summer school was finally over and I survived that tough course in physics—I managed to get one B and one C for the two semesters credit, which I considered quite generous of the professor. I had now decided that I would not become a physicist and maybe my true calling was not in the sciences after all. Just what that calling might be was still undecided. Since I would now be entering my final year of college, time was running out for making a decision. There was a break of only a week or two between the summer session and the start of the fall term so I remained in Charlottesville and worked full time in the book store. One day after work I arrived at the fraternity house to find a beautiful powder blue Oldsmobile convertible in the parking lot. Since I was the only resident at the house I wondered just who this new arrival might be—not another O'Hara I hoped! Inside was a tall, deeply tanned gentleman who introduced himself as Dick—he was to become one of my very best friends as it turned out. Dick was 28 years old, almost ten years older than me, and had spent the last eight years as a professional lifeguard. He worked his summers at Virginia Beach, where he had been raised and presently lived, and his winters were spent in Miami Beach working for one of the large hotels there. Dick had attended The University previously but had dropped out in his third year before earning his degree. He had been a member of the ATO fraternity and had lived in the house before and was now returning to finish his undergraduate work.

There was a definite seniority system within the fraternity. Your seniority started when you became a fully initiated member after surviving Hell Week and there were a few perks to being senior. One was that the most senior brother got his choice of rooms in the house and some rooms were definitely more desirable than others. Since I was living alone in the house that summer I had moved into the best room of all—called the "pink room" because of its paint scheme of course—with the hope that I would be able to remain there during my final year. The pink room was also the only room in the house that had a fire escape—useful not only to escape in the event of a fire but to slip someone into your room without the knowledge of all the other brothers! Dick, who was super senior because of the fact that he had become a member so many years ago, announced that he was moving into my room—the only one in the entire house presently occupied! As there were two men to each room, I quickly asked if I could be his roommate. He agreed to that arrangement and I did not have to move—just share. We became good friends and drinking buddies and I could not have found a better roommate.

The week before the start of the fall semester was a very busy time at the book store as we received tons of new books each day. These shipments had to be unloaded, unpacked, sorted and placed in bins or put on shelves to prepare for the onrush of new and returning students. I believe that Anderson Bros. Book Store was the only source for graduate and undergraduate student's books and supplies at this time. This yearly ritual required the hiring of several additional part time clerks; students such as myself for the most part. One of the new employees hired in September 1958 was someone who would change the direction of my life. Scott was a bit older and more mature than the average clerk—the median age was probably about 21—and he had a quiet "been there, done that" air about him. One of the sharpest individuals that I had ever met, Scott and I bonded quickly and he became sort of a mentor for me during my last year in college. He had graduated from The University some five years earlier and was now returning to attend Law School. Those past five years had been spent on active duty with the U.S. Navy as a Naval Aviator and he was still involved with the Naval Air Reserves. Scott was certainly more stable than most of my buddies at the fraternity. He was married and the father of a lovely baby about one year of age. His wife was a knock-dead beauty who could have been a model or movie star—she was also kind, considerate, intelligent and a **great cook!** I became a frequent guest at their home for dinner and I listened intently as Scott related his stories about flying as a carrier pilot.

One day Scott invited me to attend a party being held at the home of one of his neighbors, a divorced lady who worked as a legal secretary for a law office in Charlottesville. I did not know any of the people at this party, except for Scott and his wife, as this group consisted mostly of young professionals, and I felt a bit out of place as a nineteen year old undergraduate student. A good time was had by all, however, and as the party ended and the guests were leaving, the hostess, Sharon, whispered to me to stay. And stay I did—not only for the evening but the next day and the following evening! I had enjoyed several sexual encounters with young ladies of my approximate age and considered myself "experienced". What followed was a true "experience".

After the last guest departed, Sharon turned to me and we embraced into a deep lingering open-mouthed kiss that left me breathless. She reached to gently touch my manhood and I thought I would explode. She said, "You're really ready, don't come yet, we have only begun" and led me into her bedroom. We were halfway undressed by the time we reached that room—she told me to slow down—and we finished undressing while facing each other. I tried to keep looking into her eyes but I was unable to not notice her incredible breasts—large but firm with the most beautiful pink nipples I had seen to this time in my life. I finished removing the last item of my clothing and Sharon was down to her panties when she stopped. I stepped forward and said, "Let me help you" but she said, "No, I want you to watch." She then pulled the covers from the bed, arranged the pillows and laid down on her back. She looked me directly in the eyes and with a very wicked grin began to slowly remove her panties—it seemed to take forever as she writhed seductively in the most sexually stimulating maneuvers my eyes had ever seen. To watch a beautiful woman remove her panties while on her back is still the most erotic thing in life for a man to experience—perhaps because you know that she is doing it just for you! When Sharon finally slipped those panties over her feet she threw them to me and said, "Now come to me."

I needed no encouragement and leaped onto the bed with a most urgent desire. Before I could enter her she stopped me again and said, "I want you in my mouth first." I was on my knees between her legs as she bent forward and engulfed my penis into her mouth. I climaxed almost instantly and thought that she would probably cough and spit as most of my female companions had done in my previous encounters of oral sex. Not Sharon—she swallowed! Then she smiled and said, "That was for you, the next is for **me** and you!" My real education had begun.

The next 36 hours or so were incredible. We took breaks only for food, showers and a little bit of sleep as Sharon introduced me to every manner of sexual activity and every position known to man or beast. She delivered me back to the fraternity house on Monday morning before she went to work— I cut classes that day and slept for the next twelve hours. That was my first proof that the female gender has much more sexual stamina and endurance than their male counterparts. Nothing that happened during the rest of my life would change that sage revelation!

Sharon and I continued our relationship for several months—it was purely a sexual relationship as we really never dated, never went to a movie, or never went out to a nice restaurant. She would call me at the fraternity house, tell me when she would pick me up and I would be waiting when she honked her horn. Usually we had sex of one kind or another before we left the parking lot—she did not wear any underclothes on these encounters and when I touched her between the legs she would climax immediately. Then she would take me in her mouth and our evening would begin. When we were not able to be together or she was in her period we would have phone sex—at least that is what I would call it today. She would call me, tell me how much she wanted me and describe just what she was doing with her fingers. After she climaxed she would bid me a good night! The relationship simply faded away—Sharon probably moved on to a new lover and I returned to the typical fraternity life of booze and debauchery. The first chapter of my sexual education had been completed, thanks to Sharon, who was truly the clinical definition of a nymphomaniac, just what every red-blooded American male teenager dreamed of!

My final year in college was, as I had planned, a very easy one. However, Sharon had been a major distraction from my studies and I found myself in peril of flunking out. I needed to devote a little time and effort to my classwork in order to graduate on time in May, 1959. Fortunately, by this time I knew just how little I needed to study in order to pass with the minimum grade point average. I had completed all the difficult courses and needed only a few advanced English Literature classes to obtain the required hours for my degree. I only carried twelve hours that year and even had the opportunity to take an easy elective—previously there was just not time for any frivolous courses. I chose a course called Greek 21/22, that was considered the easiest class in the entire University. Most of my classmates were football players but they rarely attended any of the sessions. The professor did not take roll call and had only one test for each semester—and a copy of this test was passed out on day one. I missed most of those classes and never opened a book but was awarded a B. I actually enjoyed the class and found it interesting that there were some few courses out there that were easy—not typical at The University. With fewer classes I had more time to pursue other activities—but working at the book store was now almost a full time job.

My friend Scott and I were spending more time talking about flying. I began to think that I would like to do just what he had done—graduate from The University, enter the flight program in the Navy, and eventually return to UVA for Law School. He encouraged me to apply for a program called Aviation Officer Candidate School (AOCS). This was a flight training program available to college graduates that recognized the fact that the applicant had already completed college and would be commissioned as a Naval Officer even if he did not complete the flight program. Scott wanted to show me what Naval Aviation was all about so he invited me to attend a drill or two with him. He was required to spend one weekend each month with his reserve unit in order to maintain his flying proficiency. The first time I went with him to Oceana Naval Air Station, near Norfolk, Va., for one of his weekend drills was surely a turning point in my life. We departed Charlottesville early one Friday afternoon and arrived at the Oceana Officer's Club just in time for "happy hour." Scott was greeted by his squadron buddies like one of my fraternity brothers returning to the fraternity house after a long absence. His friends were sincerely happy to see him again and I immediately recognized the fact that there was true camaraderie in this group. This gathering of Naval Aviators was not too different from my fraternity brothers at a weekly meeting—they were just a bit older and wiser. This was definitely the kind of people that I wanted to be involved with. I did not always follow exactly what they were talking about as the aviation terms were still unfamiliar to me, but I could feel their enthusiasm and joy as they told their stories and jokes!

We spent the night in the BOQ (Bachelor Officer Quarters) and the next morning Scott went flying. I accompanied him to the flight line and watched as he took off in formation with three other pilots in their F9F Panther jets— the same type of plane that William Holden flew in the classic movie, "Bridges of Toko-Ri." As I watched those jets blast off and disappear into the sky, I was hooked—where do I sign up?

Chapter Five

"Flying is not dangerous; Crashing is dangerous!"

Upon returning to Charlottesville I visited the U.S. Navy recruiting office and started the process of applying for AOCS. There were forms to fill out, tests to take and a background check was conducted to make sure that I was not a convicted felon or psycho of some sort. I was concerned that my college prank episode that led to three days in jail would cause me to be rejected. The interviewer winked and said not to worry—I had the feeling that Naval Aviation was looking for men who were on the "adventuresome" side. There was also a very thorough physical exam, the most complete I had ever had, and I was basically found to be fit for duty. I had never had an eye exam before and was told that my vision was 20-15, considerably better than the norm of 20-20. I would not require glasses for reading until well into my fifties. A month or so later, I believe it was April, 1959, I was notified that I had been accepted into the Aviation Officer Candidate program and was to report to NAS Oceana the first week of August to be swore in.

My college days were rapidly drawing to a close and my excitement for the future was starting to mount. My parents were making the trip to Charlottesville to attend my graduation—they had not been to The University since dropping me off there almost three years previously—and I was hoping to make their visit an enjoyable one. They had never been to the fraternity house and would probably be a bit shocked if they attended one of our parties. My concern was unwarranted as my fraternity brothers were on their best behavior and the graduation weekend went without a hitch. My folks were more open-minded than I thought as they seemed not to notice the persistent smell of stale beer and spilled booze that permeated our house. Although both of my parents drank and my Mother smoked, I had never smoked or had a drink in their presence. My Dad took pride in the fact that no male member of his family had ever smoked—I broke that tradition but never smoked in his presence throughout his lifetime. I started smoking at the age of fourteen but quit forever about the age of twenty six. Drinking, however, would be something I would probably continue for the rest of my life. I suppose that I have been part of the "drinking generation" as we were never introduced to drugs and none of my contemporaries (to the best of my knowledge) ever had the least interest or problem with drugs of any sort. Booze, however, was always available and seemed to be socially accepted, at least in my circle of friends. After the graduation ceremony my parents took me to a very nice restaurant and my Dad asked if I wanted to join him in having a beer! I had finally grown up.

My graduation present was $100, a lot of money to me at that time. I had also saved a bit from working at the book store so after graduation I went with my friend and roommate, Dick, to Virginia Beach. He had his usual job as a lifeguard but I was not able to be hired as I would not be available for the entire summer. I basically bummed around for over a month—until my money ran out—then it was time to go home to Pocahontas. I hitchhiked home with only loose change in my pocket. My last quarter was spent on a shoe shine in Richmond, Va. as I did not want to return home looking like a total bum. My folks were very understanding and I enjoyed a relaxing month at home with them until it was time to report to the U.S. Navy.

I received a voucher in the mail that I could exchange for an airline ticket so I made my arrangements to fly from Bluefield, WVa. to Norfolk, Va. where I was picked up at the airport in an official Navy vehicle, berthed in the BOQ and treated like a high ranking officer. Then the next day I was sworn in as a cadet (with no real ranking) and handed a train ticket from Norfolk to Pensacola, Florida! The party was over before it began.

Three of us newly sworn in cadets boarded the train that afternoon. My fellow travelers were Tom, great guy from William & Mary University, and Coogie (real name Carl) from the University of West Virginia. We were on that train for two long days that included lengthy layovers in Atlanta, Georgia and Foley, Alabama. When we arrived at the train station in Pensacola late the next afternoon there was no one to meet us or take us to the Naval Air Station. My new buddies thought that we should go directly to the Navy base and check in. I persuaded them that our orders said to report before midnight and that we should not waste our last night of freedom. We went downtown to Pensacola, really just a small town in the panhandle of Florida that prided itself as being the "Cradle of Naval Aviation." We hit several bars before we were directed to the real hangout for Navy pilots and student pilots: **Trader John's!** This place was incredible—a huge, dirty, smelly beer joint/bar that was the kind of place where you drank from the bottle because the glasses were not to be trusted. It was packed with boisterous half drunk Naval Aviators or students and an equal number of local females trying to snag one of the former. Hanging from the ceilings were countless pieces of aviation memorabilia that one could spend hours looking at and there were hundreds of portraits and photos on every square inch of the walls—walls that had not been cleaned or dusted in years. We stayed at Trader John's until it was time to leave in order to check in at the base a few minutes before midnight.

We were feeling pretty good when we arrived at the front gate of NAS Pensacola and were taken to what was called the Indoctrination Battalion. There we were issued a few pieces of clothing and assigned to our bunks. It seemed that I had just placed my head on the pillow when I was rudely awaked by a loud-mouthed, surly Drill Sergeant who insisted that I "hit the deck and fall out!" Given tennis shoes, shorts and t-shirts we were soon outside and taken on a short run of three miles. It was barely sunup and at least three of us were in pretty bad shape—each time I caught the eyes of Tom or Coogie I was given the "it's your fault, asshole" look. I managed to complete the run with only throwing up twice and knew that we were in for a really rough week. Obviously, we all survived and looked back at that first week as quite a revelation for aspiring young Naval Aviators. We spent a total of sixteen weeks in what was called "Pre-flight" which was a combination of OCS (Officer Candidate School) and academic studies pre-requisite to starting flight training. Our Drill Sergeants (you never forget their names for the rest of your life—Sergeant Elm and Sergeant Penney) controlled us for about two hours each day and instructed us in basic military drills such as marching and handling firearms. Another two hours each day were spent in physical training such as running the obstacle course, weight training, boxing, wrestling, and swimming. At the end of the sixteen weeks we were in top condition—as Sergeant Elm would say—"the best shape you future pilots will ever be in for the rest of your lives."

The movie "An Officer and a Gentleman" was actually a fair portrayal of the training that the Aviation Officer Candidate receives. At least four hours each day were spent in classrooms—taking courses in basic aerodynamics, navigation, meteorology, engines, hydraulics, etc. Very little time was left for recreation but by the fourth week we were able to relax a bit and start looking for some fun and games. At any given time there were about 300 cadets at NAS Pensacola in various phases of their pre-flight training and they needed some relief from the stresses of that training. We were provided with a place called the AcRec Club where we could go for snacks and beer. As we were not enlisted personnel with access to the EM Club, not Petty Officers with access to the CPO Club, and not yet Commissioned Officers with access to the O'Club we had the AcRec Club that stood for the Aviation Cadets Recreation Club. This place was like a mini O'Club in that young ladies from the local area were allowed to enter the base by telling the posted guards that they were "invited guests" to the AcRec Club. Security was very loose in those days and there was little to fear from these young girls, mostly between the ages of 18 and 23, except, perhaps, the low risk of contracting a social disease which was easily cured with a shot of penicillin. This was long before herpes and AIDS, and the main concern was to not "knock up" your girlfriend and be forced into marriage. I believe that there were only a very few of these ladies who were calculating enough to try to get pregnant so that they could marry a future Naval Aviator.

I was more interested in drinking beer with my new buddies and talking about our training which was leading up to what we all really wanted—the start of flight training. We would not get into the cockpit of a real airplane or even a simulator until after the successful completion of pre-flight—a sixteen week course. Only one person in my class, AOC 29-59, failed to complete, not because of academic or physical training failure but because of a strange accident on the obstacle course. He tripped and fell while running to set a new course record—this was my friend Tom who accompanied me on the train trip to Pensacola—severely breaking his ankle with a compound fracture that was beyond repair. Tom was without a doubt the best athlete in our group and it was ironic that he would be the one to wash out because of such bad luck. The rest of us managed to finish the sixteen weeks which culminated in a formal dance at the Officer's Club, followed by the graduation and commissioning ceremony the next day.

Somehow I had been selected to escort the daughter of the Commanding Officer of NAS Pensacola to this formal dance. I was very nervous as I knocked on the front door to what looked like a mansion—the largest and finest quarters on the entire base. The C.O. had addressed our class at one time during our training but I had never actually met Captain Pack, a very distinguished career officer whose picture should have been on every recruiting poster. He opened the door, shook my hand, invited me in and quickly put me at ease by asking, "Would you like a beer or a glass of wine?" He and his wife were hosting a small cocktail party that consisted of four high ranking officers and their wives. The ladies were in their long gowns and the men were all dressed in the white formal dress uniform with the stiff collar and shoulder boards. My shoulder boards were bare with only a cadet insignia on each one—the other officers had many stripes, lots of medals and each wore the Naval Aviator wings of gold. The next day I would get the single stripe as an Ensign, USNR. I was in awe in the presence of such a group of senior officers but soon found that they were really regular guys who had all been in my position at the start of their careers. They spent more time talking about my future than their past and I left with a deepening appreciation of this band of brothers—Naval Aviators.

My date that evening, the daughter of the Captain, was a knockout. She was gorgeous, witty and intelligent and we had a very nice time at the dance. Unfortunately, that was the only time we were together as after the next day's ceremony it was time for me to start the inevitable frequent moves of a Navy Pilot. My parents attended the ceremony which included a parade formation and the usual speeches before we were commissioned. As soon as we walked off the review stand as new Ensigns we were met by our drill sergeants, Penney and Elm, who extended the first official salute to each one of us in that time-honored ritual of the Naval Service. As we returned that salute we each presented a silver dollar to our task masters turned friends and shook hands with these men who are the backbone of the service. There were a few moist eyes as we had gone from being awkward young college students to "Officers and Gentlemen" in a relative short amount of time. The roles had changed now—we had been addressing our drill sergeants as "sir" for those past four months and now we were "Mister" and "Sir" to them. These professional soldiers had seen it happen many times before and were justifiably proud of the contribution they had made to our budding careers.

I had a mission to accomplish as soon as the commissioning ceremony was complete. I took my parents (in their automobile) to the first foreign sports car dealer outside the main gate of NAS Pensacola. There were several to choose from as it was also a ritual of sorts for new Ensigns starting flight training to buy a spiffy little convertible to signify their new status. The first

44

car I looked at was a peach colored, brand new, 1960 MGA with red leather interior—I would look no further. It was important for my father to be with me as he had to co-sign for the loan as I had not yet reached the age of 21. The price of the car was $2995 and my payments to the Navy Federal Credit Union were about $95 each month for the next three years. My pay as an Ensign was over $300 a month and I would soon start drawing flight pay of $50—not a problem! Housing, food and uniforms were provided by the Navy so a car payment and entertainment were my only expenses. This was the first automobile I owned.

I moved from the Cadet barracks of NAS Pensacola to the BOQ of NAAS Saufley Field. This was a Naval Auxiliary Air Station located to the north and east of Pensacola and part of a complex of outlying airfields used for various stages of flight training. Primary flight training was conducted here in the T-34, a single-engine tandem cockpit trainer built by Beechcraft. First we were issued flight gear—flight suits, flight boots, gloves, sunglasses, a flight helmet, a knee board and that great leather flight jacket that I still have to this day. We were ready to fly! One small problem, however—we had been commissioned at the end of November, 1959 and the Navy did not want to start our actual flight training until the first of the year. This was because there would be a holiday break over the Christmas season and it was not wise to start our flying unless there could be an uninterrupted period for this important initial training. Therefore, we were used as guinea pigs for the medical staff for a couple of weeks. Each day was spent with physical exams, mental tests and various prodding and poking until we were about ready to say "uncle." Finally it ended, the Christmas break came and went, the New Year was upon us and it really was time to fly!

Chapter Six

"Success in aviation is having the number of landings in one's logbook equal to the number of takeoffs!"

My first flight as a student Naval Aviator was January 8, 1960 and I soloed about two weeks later after twelve flights and about 17 hours aloft. It was new, it was different, it was exciting and it was not always easy. Most of my fellow trainees had previous flight experience—some had quite a bit of flight time and had already earned their private pilot's license. I had never been inside the cockpit of an airplane and had flown as a passenger in a commercial airliner only twice. I was in the forward cockpit with the instructor in the aft cockpit for that first flight and the view was incredible as we lifted off. The instructor flew the aircraft for takeoff and the first 30 minutes or so as he demonstrated various maneuvers—then he said, "Okay, you take it for awhile, just fly straight and level." With the stick in my right hand and my left hand on the throttle, I began to fly that aircraft under my own control. I thought I was doing a great job when suddenly someone grabbed me by the shoulders and pushed me to the right! The instructor had unstrapped his belt and harness, stood on his seat to reach forward and straightened me in my seat—a maneuver I did not know was even possible! When he sat back down he calmly said over the intercom radio, "You were leaning to the left and starting to go into a slow left turn." I sat up straight for the rest of that flight and ever since I have tried to "Straighten up and fly right!"

One thing that you will never forget for the rest of your life if you were a Naval Aviator who went through primary flight training in the T-34: **"CHOP, PROP, 110 DROP!"** That was the litany we memorized as we entered the landing pattern—**CHOP** the throttle, push the **PROP** lever full forward, and when the airspeed reached **110, DROP** the landing gear! This was the first of hundreds of rote memory items and acronyms that I would learn over the course of my flying career.

The twelfth flight in the T-34 was a check ride to see if the student was safe for solo. This was the first of hundreds of "check rides" that professional aviators must endure throughout their careers. Too bad surgeons and attorneys are not also subject to those frequent and sometime unannounced "check rides." On my first check ride I completed several touch and go landings at a small strip without a tower controller—one of those many outlying fields that the Navy owned. Finally the instructor told me to make a full stop landing, after which he climbed out of the back seat and told me to fly around the pattern and make a few landings then pick him up where he got off. At last I was all alone in an airplane—excited but most of all hoping that I would not screw up. After two touch and goes I made that full stop and the instructor got back aboard. He said, "The only reason I got off was that I was about to throw up and I really needed to take a leak!" I never knew if he was serious or if that was the way he handled all of his student pilots for their first solo. Nevertheless, I was thrilled and on top of the world—I was now a pilot!

After completing the primary flying syllabus in the T-34, a period of about two months, it was time to start basic training in the bigger and more powerful T-28 at Whiting Field, another NAAS a bit closer to the Alabama state line. I moved into the BOQ at Whiting but felt far removed from the night lights of Pensacola. It was time for a change in lifestyle. Three of my best buddies agreed and we decided to rent a beach house on Pensacola Beach—at the time it was called a "snake ranch." We rented a small two bedroom cinder block house that was probably less than 1200 square feet, not counting the single carport. Not much room for four bachelor officers with four sports cars—my MG, a TR-3, one Austin-Healey and a Corvette owned by our one Marine Corps pal. It was early springtime and in reality we were only spending the weekends on the beach as during the week we remained on the base busy with ground and flight training. The rent for this beach paradise was $50 per month but it would triple to $150 in June. We figured that if we had one more roommate it would be easier to divide the rent so we found a fifth student who turned out to be a great guy named Temple. It was a coincidence that Temple graduated from The University of Virginia the same time that I did, but we did not know each other—he belonged to the Beta house fraternity and we did not meet while in school. We became close friends for many years.

One day someone suggested that we go to New Orleans for Mardi Gras weekend. I had never been any further west than my present location and having heard so much about the goings-on in that wicked city, I was raring to go. We rented a large four door sedan so that we could all go together and share the driving—the total rental charge was less than forty dollars for the whole weekend. We piled into that car late Friday afternoon with enough beer to get us there with only stops for gas and bladder relief. Someone in our group knew that there was a small Army Base near New Orleans and we figured that we could get rooms at the Visiting Officers Quarters. We arrived in the middle of the night and went directly to the French Quarter—it was as wild and crazy as we expected and we fit right in with the rowdy crowds on Bourbon Street. When the sky to the East began to get rosy we headed for the Army Base. We were able to get rooms and hit the sack for about four hours. We agreed to meet at the Officers Club at 10:00 AM to get a bite to eat and plan our day. The only thing open was the bar at the O'Club as the food facilities were closed for the holiday—so our breakfast consisted of Bloody Marys and popcorn! The bartender, probably an enlisted man working at the Club on his day off, obviously did not recognize the four of us as some of the usual clientele, so he asked to see our ID's. After looking at our Naval Officer identification cards, he served us without question; however I noticed that he took a long look at my ID. When we paid the tab and started to leave he leaned over to me and said, "Sir, could I speak with you in private?" Of course I agreed and we walked to the other end of the bar away from my friends. I had a feeling what this was all about! He spoke to me in a low voice: "I noticed when I looked at your ID that even though you are a commissioned officer, you are not yet 21, the legal drinking age in the club. Did I do the right thing by serving you? You're not going to report me, I hope!" I tried to keep a straight face as I responded, "You did exactly the correct thing—don't worry, this will stay between just the two of us!" Then I slipped him two bucks and we were both happy.

We were back in the French Quarter by noon and parked our rental as close to Bourbon Street as possible. We agreed that if we became separated we would meet at the car no later than noon Sunday—about 24 hours—as we decided not to return to the Army Base. We all managed to arrive by the appointed hour and selected the more sober one to start the drive back to Pensacola. It was a remarkable trip over all but we arrived back at Whiting Field Sunday night and reported for duty the next morning in halfway decent shape.

By the time summer arrived I was spending more time at the beach and less in the BOQ at Whiting. The weekends were beginning on Thursday and ending Monday night—sort of like California weekends today. Each weekend was a new adventure with tourists pouring into the resort area and the full time residents trying to maintain some sense of normalcy. We spent the days on the beach or out on a boat close to the beach—none of us owned a boat but many of our neighbors and friends were happy to share. One young lady from Mobile, Alabama would arrive each weekend towing a large pleasure craft that seemed to be at our disposal. No one knew just how this proper school teacher came into possession of such an expensive boat—was she from a wealthy family, did she acquire it in a divorce settlement, or did she win the Irish Sweepstakes? Her name was Dot—Dot the Spot we nicknamed her—and she was a sweet southern lass who always said, "I just want to have a good time!"

Dot and I began a relationship—when she arrived with that beautiful boat my buddies would take it out to sea and Dot would be alone with me, an arrangement that worked for all of us. Once the boat and my roommates were out of sight, Dot and I headed to the bedroom. She had a very heavy southern accent and would never use any type of profanity when in a crowd, but in the privacy of the bedroom it was a different story. The first time that we made love she did not say a word until we were finished—I was thinking that she was certainly not impressed with my performance when she looked at me and said, "That was a good fuck, can we do it again?" Her Alabama accent was so heavy I almost laughed until I realized that she was quite serious. Then the school teacher training came to the fore and she began instructing me on just how we should "do it." Her instructions became quite graphic and it became a game we played—show me how you like it and I will try to please you! Once a school teacher always a school teacher...

Flight training in the T-28 was fun and challenging. After we were cleared to solo we began learning to fly in formation, which I really enjoyed, then it was gunnery practice and on to instrument training. Flying by use of the instrument panel alone was not easy but we all knew that it was as essential part of every aviator's training and it would save your ass one day! The first time that I flew from take off to landing under "the bag"—without ever seeing outside the cockpit—I was thoroughly impressed that such a feat was possible. This was before the advanced electronic instrumentation and automation of today—we did not have an auto-pilot or auto-land system. The instructor would start the takeoff roll and give control to the student in the back seat (literally under the bag) at about 60 knots. The student then flew with reference only to the flight and navigation instruments until about 100 feet from landing when the instructor would again take control. The purpose of this type training was obviously to build confidence in the student pilot that he was able to fly in all weather conditions—and it worked! The final part of flight training at Whiting was what we all knew was the essence of Naval Aviation—landing aboard an aircraft carrier!

The student Naval Aviator spent many hours in the FCLP pattern (field carrier landing practice) before actually landing aboard a carrier for the first time. We trained to arrive over the aircraft carrier at 350 feet above the flight deck—410 feet mean sea level (MSL) as the deck was basically 60 feet above the surface—much lower than the usual landing pattern altitude of 1000 feet. The secret was to get the aircraft stable at about 95 knots with gear, flaps and hook down. Once you were trimmed for this speed (able to fly hands off) it became fairly easy to start down to a landing position with small reductions in power. It became routine to fly this type of pattern over a stationary runway on land but we all knew it would be much more difficult when it was a moving carrier on an unsteady ocean. The day finally arrived when our instructors felt that we were ready to go to the carrier, the USS Antietam, a ship used exclusively for such training in the Gulf of Mexico. My group consisting of six student aviators (chased by one instructor) headed out to sea to find the carrier for the first time. The instructor circled over the ship as we entered the pattern for landing. We each made two touch-and-go landings (no hook) followed by eight arrested landings. After the first six arrested landings we were "deck launched"—taking off without use of a catapult—then the last two take-offs were catapult shots. The first arrested landing was a real jolt—I thought that I was prepared for such a quick stop but when the hook caught the wire I thought that my eyeballs were going to continue down the flight deck without me!

As soon as the hook was raised and the flaps repositioned I was launched by the flight deck officer (everything was by hand signals) and headed for the front of the ship with full power. I was airborne well before reaching the end of the deck and marveled with how easy it was to fly off such a short deck. The ship was making probably close to thirty knots on her own power and there was another twenty knots of wind—so it was like starting the take-off roll with fifty knots at brake release. Flying speed was about 95 knots so the aircraft was airborne after about 600 feet of roll. The rest was like a blur—fly around the pattern, catch a wire, launch again, then repeat. The first catapult shot was also a bit more than I was expecting as the airplane was rather slung into the air and the pilot was just a spectator hanging on for dear life! It was all over in what seemed like a New York minute and we joined up in formation for the return trip back to land at Whiting Field. The instructor had briefed that we would fly in loose formation until in the vicinity of the field then enter the break low and fast in a seven plane echelon! That in itself was not an easy task as we were really student pilots and formation flying was still very new to us. Nevertheless, we arrived over the runway of intended landing in a gaggle of aircraft that certainly did not resemble the Blue Angels. The instructor was in the lead and I was somewhere in the middle of this group as we broke formation for landing (when the plane ahead of you rolled into a hard left turn you counted to three then pulled into a turn to follow). We were still full of adrenalin from our first carrier experience and hoping to impress anyone on the ground who might be watching—probably no one except other students. As I rolled out on final to land on the runway I was not lined up on the proper heading, I was too fast, and I was way behind the "power curve"— I swallowed my pride and waved off. Suddenly I noticed that other planes were doing similar maneuvers—I was not the only pilot that was screwed up.

I was able to land on the second approach but the landing itself was certainly nothing to brag about. After parking and shutting down the aircraft I joined my fellow aviators—CARRIER PILOTS—to the ready room for our debrief. We were still sky high and grinning from ear to ear as we approached the instructor waiting for us. He looked us over and said, "Congratulations on getting carrier qualified, but that was one sorry-assed performance landing here at Whiting." We all felt a bit guilty that there were several wave-offs and lousy landings here on land—usually routine even for students. Then he laughed and said, "It happens every time—you guys are so pumped up after carrier quals that you forget how to do the ordinary. Let this be a lesson—no matter how difficult the mission, do not let your guard down until the aircraft is safely on the ground or flight deck and the parking checklist is complete." Sage advice that I remembered for the rest of my flying career.

It just so happened that our carrier qualification day was on a Friday so we all met—instructor included—at the Officer's Club for Happy Hour that afternoon. We were a boisterous group for sure as we had occasion to celebrate. After a few beers—maybe more than a few—I headed for the beach house to spend the weekend. Pensacola Beach was accessible from the mainland primarily via a two lane bridge that was controlled by a toll booth. The toll to go to the beach was 25 cents and there was no charge to return to the mainland. The operator of the toll booth would sit inside his very small hut and watch for automobiles approaching to go to the beach. As a car neared, he would go outside this booth and manually lower a wooden arm to alert the driver that he/she must stop to pay the toll. My buddies and I had a game that we played at night with this toll booth. We would turn off our headlights about a half mile from the toll gate, speed up and roar through the gate before the operator had time to lower the arm! Usually the operator was a bit slow or sleepy when this happened so we slipped through without a problem. This night I could not resist the temptation to run the gate as I was still on cloud nine. I doused my lights and hit the accelerator as I approached the toll booth and roared through without a problem. Then I noticed a car sitting just beyond the booth—a police car of course—and as I looked in my rear view mirror the lights came on and I knew that I was in a bit of trouble. Since I had a good head start and our house was quite close I made it to the driveway and ran into our little "snake ranch." Two of my buddies were there playing gin—it was a bit late by this time—and as I burst through the door I said, "I think the police are following me—tell them that I'm not here—I'm heading out the back." One of my pals looked at me and said, "Bill, we don't have a back door."

He was right. I ran into the back room just as the policeman arrived at the front, knocked politely on the screen door (we never closed the main door) and said, "I would like to talk to Ensign Eads." Trying to keep a straight face, my buddy Temple said, "What makes you think he's here?" The officer said, "Well, the last car in the driveway belongs to him and the engine is still hot." I heard this exchange and thought—he not only knows my name but he has figured out which car belongs to me—I am in trouble. One of my "pals" pointed toward the back room and then went back to playing gin. As the policeman approached my sanctuary I decided to jump out the window! Not a big deal as everything was on ground level and all I had to do was remove the screen and step out. As I made my exit I heard the cop say, "Hold it, son, we need to talk!" I was already outside so I ran across the sand to the next street, roughly a block away. When I got there, guess what—the police car was waiting for me! I did a u-turn and ran back toward the beach house (running in the fine sand of Pensacola Beach was not easy) and when I arrived the police car was waiting again. My friends and neighbors were now outside rooting for their favorite—I think it was 50-50—and as I approached I held my hands up high and said, "I surrender!" The police officer was standing with hands on hips and said, "Can we talk now?"

My reply was, "Can I get you a beer?" He chuckled and said, "Not just now, I'm still on duty—you have a beer and I'll have something non-alcoholic, if there is anything in this place that is non-alcoholic." I grabbed a beer, found a cola type mixer for the policeman and we sat down at the kitchen table. He introduced himself as "Bob" and admitted that he was a retired Navy Chief Petty Officer spending his "golden years" on the beach trying to keep aspiring Navy pilots out of trouble until they were able to defend our country. I felt very small as he related the admiration he felt for Naval Aviators that he had served with during his twenty year career. I apologized for my behavior that evening and he readily accepted my apology—stating that it was nothing new for our ilk to be a bit reckless. He drew the line at serious misbehavior—I guess that I had not yet crossed that line—and made me promise to not "run the toll booth" again. I gave him my word, we shook hands, and he took off his badge and said, "I'm now off duty, how about that beer?"

It was not easy to leave the life we enjoyed in Pensacola. The weather was great, the flying was fun, girls were plentiful on the beach and life was GOOD! Several of my buddies did not want to leave and therefore opted to stay in Pensacola for multi-engine or helicopter training. I wanted nothing to do with that type flying (never thinking that airline flying would be in my future) so I was focused toward single-engine fighter type training. I would be going to Texas for advanced training. Most of us aspired to flying the fastest and newest planes that the Navy had to offer—obviously the jet pipeline— and the start was in Beeville or Kingsville, Texas. Something happened that changed my mind. On one of the last days of my training at Whiting Field I was waiting for my turn to go flying when I heard the sound of two fast approaching planes—not the whine of jets but the roar of mighty reciprocating engines that I had never heard before. Two huge single-engine, single cockpit propeller planes swooped over the airfield, broke left and made a very tight pattern to land in front of a group of us gaping student pilots. As these big, powerful airplanes taxied to a halt and the aviators climbed out of their cockpits I could only ask: "What kind of planes are those?" Someone responded, "Those are AD's, the last of the great prop planes in the fleet."

I walked over to look at one of those God-awful ugly airplanes—dripping with oil and covered with burned marks from the engine stack gases along each side of the fuselage—and thought, I've got to fly that bird! As I walked around that beast I was amazed at the fourteen foot diameter four-bladed prop and the tiny bubble canopy that enclosed the single pilot cockpit. One of the pilots who had just climbed down from the cockpit was removing his helmet when I asked him, "How did you end up flying that plane?" He looked at me as if I had asked a very stupid question and responded, "I asked for it."

It was time to leave Whiting Field and continue to advanced flight training. I had been assigned to the jet pipeline and was ordered to report to Kingsville, Texas—just what most of us prayed for. My prayers had changed. I asked for a meeting with the Commanding Officer of the training squadron at Whiting and met with him in his office. He was a very busy person and brusquely asked why I was wasting his time. I responded that I wanted to change my assignment from jets to the AD advanced training program. He looked at me incredulously and asked why I would not want to go to jet training as I had very high grades and jets were what every red-blooded young Naval Aviator hoped for. I could only reply, that, yes, I wanted to fly the fastest planes in the fleet, but first I really wanted to fly the last of the great recip aircraft—surely I would fly the jets later. The C.O. rolled his eyes and said that he would check on it but for me not to hold my breath. A few days later the Executive Officer, the C.O.'s assistant and a much more understanding individual, called me into his office. He respected my request but informed me that there were no openings at the time in the AD program, which was conducted in Corpus Christi, Texas. He added, with a twinkle in his eye, that since I had a few days leave on the books, maybe before reporting to Kingsville I should "hang around" the AD training squadron before reporting to jet school.

I took the X.O.'s advice and bid my farewells to my friends at Whiting Field and Pensacola Beach. I tried to load all my belongings in my little MGA and found that it was like trying to stuff ten pounds of crap into a five pound bag. I was very fastidious about my uniforms so I rented a U-Haul trailer that was large enough to hang my clothing—about eight feet long, four feet wide and six feet high. After I hooked this trailer on the back of my sports car I realized that the trailer was much bigger than the vehicle pulling it! A strange sight, I'm sure, to follow a large trailer pushing a small car down the road from Pensacola, Florida to Corpus Christi, Texas! After bouncing over a few railroad tracks and having all my hangers fall off, I decided to abandon my bad decision and exchanged that large trailer for a more manageable one in Mobile, Alabama. Two days later I arrived in the beautiful city of Corpus Christi. After getting settled in the Bachelor Officer Quarters I visited the AD training squadron, VT-30. The officer on duty introduced me to the Operations Officer and I told him about my desire to go through AD training instead of reporting to jet training in Kingsville. The Ops Officer said, "I believe that we might be able to work something out—this is your lucky day!" Turns out that one of the students due to start in the next class, just a few days away, had been involved in an automobile accident and sustained a broken leg. There was a spot for me!

Before starting training in the AD, (the "A" stood for Attack and the "D" stood for the Douglas Aircraft Company) we had several weeks of more instrument training in the T-28. After that instrument refresher training it was time for ground school to learn all about the AD. The AD had more nicknames than any other airplane I ever flew. It was called the "Spad", the "Skyraider", the "Able Dog", and the "Flying Dump Truck". It was later redesignated the A-1. There were no tandem cockpit trainers for the AD so the first flight was solo with the instructor flying chase in another aircraft. That huge engine, a Pratt & Whitney R-3350, developed over 2700 horsepower on takeoff. That much power meant a lot of torque—the airplane wanted to yaw to the left—so the pilot was required to put in a lot of right rudder. The saying was that you could always tell a Skyraider pilot by looking at his muscular right leg! Because of this unique torque problem, the student first was required to accomplish taxi training! The Spad was probably the only plane in the Navy that required proficiency in taxiing before flight. The pilot's view while taxiing was restricted by the high nose as this was a tail wheel ("tail dragger") aircraft, different from the other trainers with the more traditional nose wheel. After taxiing around a bit and becoming familiar with turning by brakes at low speeds and use of rudder at high speeds it was time to line up for an aborted takeoff. The student would position the aircraft at the end of the runway and the instructor would be on the ground just off to the left with a radio to give instructions. The instructor would call for the student to hold the brakes (there was not a parking brake) slowly push the throttle to 30 inches of manifold pressure, release the brakes and increase the throttle to 45 inches (about 75% of normal takeoff power). Almost full right rudder was required at this time to keep the aircraft pointed straight down the runway. As the airspeed increased and the tail wheel became airborne (about 80 knots) the instructor would yell, "Abort!" The student then chopped the power and fought with the rudder pedals to keep the aircraft on the runway as left rudder was now required. This drill before the first flight was an important reminder of the different rudder inputs necessary to control this powerful beast on the ground.

The AD was the first plane I flew with folding wings—most Navy carrier planes had wings that folded so they could be parked on the ship with minimum space being wasted. The planes we flew in training were always parked with the wings folded and after engine start we taxied forward under control of a guideman until we were cleared to spread our wings. The story we all heard was that a Skyraider actually took off and got airborne with the wings in the folded position—obviously at night! Since the Marine Corps flew the Skyraider in Korea and later in Vietnam, we assumed that it must have been a Marine pilot that accomplished this remarkable feat! That engine was so powerful that the aircraft carried its own weight in armament—more payload that the famous B-17 of World War II. The empty weight of the plane was about 12,000 pounds and the maximum takeoff weight was 25,000. Every mission that I later flew in Vietnam was at that maximum allowable weight.

It was now early 1961 and the war in Southeast Asia was starting to heat up. About halfway through AD training in Corpus Christi, my class was put on hold as a group of South Vietnamese pilots arrived for priority training. There were eight in the first group and they were seasoned combat pilots who had been flying various fighter-bomber aircraft in their war for several years. The U.S. government was now going to provide the Vietnamese with AD aircraft and they required training right away. This group had very few problems making the transition to the more powerful AD and finished in just a few weeks. They were followed by a second group of relatively inexperienced pilots who had received training by the U.S. Air Force in their version of the T-28, a very underpowered, docile trainer when compared to the Navy T-28. The Vietnamese pilots were housed separately and we had very little contact with them—however, we heard lots of rumors. It seems that this second group of "pilots" consisted of sons of high ranking politicians in South Vietnam who were going through flight training in order to avoid the draft and having to serve in the ground forces. The instructors all felt that these "pilots" were neither qualified not motivated to be trained to fly the

Skyraider. Nevertheless, the rumor was that they would be trained at whatever cost and they could not be busted or washed out.

When the day arrived for this group to do the taxi and aborted takeoff training you could have sold tickets as we all wanted to watch! The Vietnamese pilots were smaller than their American counterparts and they had problems seeing over the glare shield, much less over the high nose during taxi. The solution was to add a cushion or two to the pilot's seat so they were sitting higher. This, however, created a new problem—now the pilots could barely reach the rudder pedals, much less have full throw as required by the torque of the engine. This problem was solved by putting wooden blocks on the rudder pedals which were removed after each flight. Only one in this group spoke English and when the American instructor briefed the procedures, this person would interpret for his fellow aviators. As we all know—something is always lost in the translation! As the four Skyraiders taxied out we were watching from inside the hangar, on the ramp and even on top of buildings. After taxi practice the leader (the one who spoke a bit of English) lined up on the runway for the aborted takeoff while the other three planes waited in the run-up area. The aircraft roared down the runway and as the pilot cut the power the plane swerved right, ran off the runway through a grass strip and impacted a hangar on the other side of the airport. Major damage but no one was hurt!

After a short delay, it was time for the next pilot to do his aborted takeoff. The instructor ordered, "Hold your brakes and go to 30 inches on the throttle." Then, "Release your brakes and go to 45 inches." We could hear the power increase and the nose of the aircraft began to drop down but the plane did not move—the pilot did not release the brakes! Slowly the nose dropped even more and the propeller started hitting the runway—sparks were flying and pieces of asphalt were hurling through the air. The instructor started running but he was still talking on the portable radio, "Cut the power, cut the fuel lever—the red one!" The fuel control was red but so was the gear lever— suddenly the gear folded and the engine came off its mounts! The airplane erupted in a ball of flames and was completely destroyed within what seemed like a few seconds. The pilot made no attempt to get out and was killed instantly. The crash crew and fire engines were on the scene quickly but nothing could be done to save the pilot. Meanwhile, the other two aircraft awaiting their turn were abandoned by their Vietnamese pilots who jumped out of the cockpits and began running across the tarmac. Each pilot had shut down his engine but as there were no chocks to hold the planes one slowly rolled forward then turned right to impact the other aircraft which was also slowly moving. I did not read the accident report but it may have been the first and only time ever that there was an accident where the aircraft was destroyed and the pilot killed before the plane moved a single inch! Major damage was done to the other three aircraft. I believe that the remaining Vietnamese pilots were sent back to the Air Force for more training. My training now continued uninterrupted.

My first flight in the Skyraider was all I hoped for and more. As ungainly as it may have been on the ground, once airborne it was a real pleasure to fly, with plenty of power and very responsive controls. I took off first followed by the instructor in the chase aircraft. As briefed, I entered a shallow right turn after cleaning up (raising gear and flaps) and the instructor rendezvoused and joined on my right wing. When we later debriefed, the instructor said that he had never seen such a big grin on the face of a student pilot on his first flight in the Spad! I loved this airplane and to this day it remains the favorite of all the different aircraft that I flew throughout my career. I later wrote a poem about the Skyraider—a parody on the famous poem "High Flight" by John Gillespie Magee, Jr.

Low Flight

Oh, I have slipped beneath the clouds so low
And blown sand where others fear to go.
Skimmed over the waves of Monterey Bay
Waving at cars above on Coastal Highway!

I have flown under the bridge that spans the bay
Drilled holes in tule fog that lasts all day.
Done a hundred things unfamiliar to you,
Things most prudent pilots would never do!

I remember the feeling, so very sweet—
To fly over the carrier at 410 feet,
The highest I've flown that entire day—
Grant me the three wire, that's what I pray!

Oh, of all the airplanes that I have flown,
Without any doubt, the truth be known—
None can match the venerable Skyraider—
Made me proud to be a Naval Aviator!

Chapter Seven

**"You know you've landed with the wheels up
when it takes full power to taxi."**

Corpus Christi was a great town—my first introduction to Texas and those great Americans who are "Texans" first, Americans second. Night clubs were called saloons or watering holes and it was necessary that one bring one's own booze to such spots unless one wanted to drink beer from long-necked bottles. I usually stayed with the beer so that I did not have to carry a brown bag around when bar hopping. One evening I met a lovely, dark eyed lady by the name of Marilee—actually I was introduced to her by a friend—and I was smitten at once. She was bright, sassy and full of self-confidence. She was also quite a looker with a sexy smile that said—I'm game if you are! We made a date for the following weekend and she surprised me by saying that she would pick me up! I was living in the B.O.Q. at the Naval Air Station and she worked as a civilian secretary on the base, so I agreed to this unusual arrangement. She picked me up after work on Friday afternoon and we grabbed a fast bite to eat and then went to a movie.

I don't remember the movie but what I do remember is that we started holding hands, then her breast was pressing against my arm and suddenly we were touching each other in very intimate places. She breathed into my ear, "There's a motel just down the block." That was all the encouragement I needed and we practically ran from the theatre to her car. I checked us into the motel as man and wife and we entered the room with great anticipation. She said, "I need to take a shower—can you get us something to drink?" I'm thinking, what a dummy she must think I am—but I had not planned for things to progress so rapidly—so I ran out to the desk clerk and asked where I could get something to drink. He directed me a nearby joint where I was able to buy a cheap bottle of wine. When I got back to the room she was waiting on the bed with just a bath towel wrapped around her bountiful treasures. I opened the wine and poured a glass for each of us in the motel plastic glasses and she demurely asked, "Do you have anything to use—I don't want to get pregnant!" I'm even a bigger dummy as I mumbled, "I don't have anything but maybe I can go find a place to get a rubber." She rolled her eyes as she said, "Thank God I came prepared—I have my diaphragm in my purse." I had heard about that thing called a diaphragm but had never seen one. She grabbed her purse and started for the bathroom—I stopped her and said, "Can I look at it—I don't even know what one of those things looks like!" She stopped and said, "Sure," then pulled a huge rubber disc out of her purse!

I looked at this monstrous thing and asked, "How in the world do you get that thing inside your vagina?" Again, she rolled her eyes and said, "It folds over and is very easy to insert—not a problem." I was more than curious and I looked her in the eye and said, "May I watch you put it in?" She looked at me as if I had really lost my mind then said, "I suppose you can watch— maybe you would like to help?" I followed her into the bathroom and she sat down on the toilet—she said that was the only way she had ever put in the diaphragm—and proceeded to make that thing disappear between her legs. I was amazed that when folded it seemed to slip into her vagina without a problem. By this time I was no longer aroused—mainly because of the clinical nature of what was going on. Then she stood up from the toilet and dropped the bath towel—wow, what a gorgeous body this young lady had, beautiful breasts, small waist, long lovely legs, and suddenly I was interested again. She smiled and said, "Looks like you are happy to see me!" I pole-vaulted back into the bedroom and was pleasantly surprised that no matter how hard I tried I was unable to find that diaphragm!

After this first encounter, Marilee would end up spending the night with me in the B.O.Q. Finally I had to ask the question—why can't we go to your place—and the answer was obvious. She admitted that she was married but insisted that she and her husband were "separated" and planning to be divorced. In the meantime she and the "husband" continued to live under the same roof! I was not comfortable with this situation so I ended that relationship—my first realization that not everyone was truthful and sincere in this complicated world we live in. The rest of my time in Corpus was spent living in the B.O.Q. and enjoying the training in the AD. Weekends were spent going to the beach on Padre Island or tasting the Spanish flavors available in Nuevo Laredo, a border town about two hours away. One night a group of us student Naval Aviators returned to the base and we were not able to awaken one of our buddies, my good pal, Dave, who always had the habit of falling asleep (passing out) on the way home. We decided that it would be funny to put him into the Dempsey dumpster to let him sleep it off. The Dempsey dumpster was a large metal trash container located outside our B.O.Q. We managed to carry him from the car and tossed him into this huge container and closed the heavy metal cover. The next morning I was awakened by a loud banging noise coming from outside my window—it was almost ten AM and the sun was high in the sky and it was already getting very warm. It took a few minutes for me to focus on that banging to remember what we had done the evening before—Holy Shit—Dave was still in the Dempsey dumpster! I ran outside and rescued my friend who was not able to lift the cover high enough to get out of that smelly tomb! It was already about 100 degrees in that dumpster and the fumes were overwhelming. Dave was pissed but very forgiving once he realized that I had probably saved his life.

Flight training was coming to an end. I carrier qualified in the AD on the ides of April, 1961 and was designated a Naval Aviator on the 28th of that month. My orders were to report to NAS North Island for more training before joining my fleet squadron, VA-25—the "V" stands for fixed wing and the "A" for attack. NAS North Island was located in Coronado, California which was just across the bay from San Diego. I thought that my training was complete now that I had those coveted Golden Wings of a Navy pilot—not quite! It seemed that the real training was just beginning. I would report to VA-122, a RAG squadron for fleet specific training. RAG stood for Retraining Air Group—where new pilots and older pilots training for a new type aircraft were sent before they deployed to fleet squadrons aboard aircraft carriers. This training would take about two months and consist of more instrument training, intensive weapons training, and more carrier work.

I was really looking forward to being based in California and the timing seemed to be perfect as spring was in full bloom and summer would be spent in southern California, the land of sunny beaches and beautiful women! At least that was what I had been led to believe. I departed Texas and headed west in my loaded little sports car—this time I was a bit smarter and shipped my uniforms and flight gear separately. All I had in the auto were enough clothes and toiletries to get me to the promised land. I decided to take a leisurely drive through the Southwest and visit some of the natural attractions. The second day of my drive was spent taking a tour through Carlsbad Caverns in New Mexico. I didn't realize that the tour I signed up for was over three hours in duration and after the first 60 minutes I had seen all the stalactites and stalagmites I ever wanted to see. I became more interested in a young lady who was obviously traveling with her parents. We introduced ourselves and enjoyed getting acquainted more than listening to the tour guide. It seems that this young lady, I believe that her name was Sherrie, was a college student from California on spring break visiting the Grand Canyon and other scenic areas in the Southwest. She and her family were heading back home after their stop at the Carlsbad Caverns. Her Dad had been a pilot in WW II so we bonded a bit with our common interest in aviation. When we finished touring the caves we decided to travel west together—the Dad had reservations at a motel in Las Cruces for that evening and I decided to stop there also. Sherrie looked at my peach-colored MG and wanted to ride with me—I certainly would not argue with that! The parents agreed and I unloaded my luggage from the front seat of my vehicle into the back seat of their sedan. We gave the "old folks" a big head start, took down the top on the MG, and started down the road—off on another adventure.

We took the back roads and enjoyed a scenic drive of about three hours before arriving at the motel on the outskirts of Las Cruces. Her parents had checked in and had a separate room for Sherrie. I rented a room of my own, near, but not adjoining, their rooms. I was invited to the parent's room for cocktails and we enjoyed a pleasant social hour. Then the Dad took me aside and suggested that I take Sherrie out to dinner so that he could spend the evening alone with his wife—sounded like a fine idea to me! Then he slipped me twenty dollars to help pay for the meal that his daughter and I would enjoy—I did not want to accept that money, but he insisted, saying that I was doing him a favor. Sherrie and I went to a decent Mexican restaurant, enjoyed good food chased down with drinks I had only recently been introduced to—something called Margaritas—then returned to the motel. I invited her to my room for a nightcap—I only had beer and one bottle of wine—but she readily agreed. After a drink or two and several lingering kisses, things started to get a bit warmer. Sherrie seemed quite nervous and unsure about her feelings. Then she admitted that she was a virgin and not sure what she was supposed to do next. I slowed down and told her that it was completely her decision as to what happened that night—I would never force her to do anything against her will. She took a deep breath, looked me in the eye, and said, "I'm nineteen years old and I think it's time—please be gentle and please don't get me pregnant."

I slowly began to undress this lovely young lady and kissed each new part of her body that I revealed—when I reached that special place between her legs I gently touched her with my fingers but was careful not to penetrate. I was happy to find that she was quite moist and obviously ready. I then removed my clothing and she watched with a bit of trepidation as my underwear dropped to the floor. She admitted that she had never seen a man naked and had only looked at pictures in books of the male genitalia. Her only comment was, "Are you sure that this won't hurt?" As much as I wanted my own sexual gratification, I realized that this was a special occasion for Sherrie and I certainly did not want it to be an unpleasant experience. I sat down on the bed beside her and assured her that we would go very slowly and that if she was under any discomfort I would stop immediately. I then asked her, "When was your last period?" She responded, "Just a couple of days ago, why?" I replied, "Then there's nothing to worry about—you won't get pregnant."

We started with long slow kisses on the mouth, then I began to kiss each breast until the nipples were hard and bright red and she was moaning with pleasure. It was now time to complete this journey that we had started such a short time ago. I was also about to explode! I placed a pillow under her hips and got into position to enter her when I noticed that she had closed her eyes and was starting to tense up. I hesitated long enough to place two pillows beneath her head, told her to open her eyes and watch—I wanted her to see my penis poised at the entrance to her vagina and watch as I slowly pushed into her wetness. She gasped as she watched my manhood disappear completely—with very little resistance, I might add—and then we began to make love. Several strokes into this most natural act between a male and female she began to make noises—I can only describe these "noises" as barking like a dog—and it became louder until she was howling at the moon! I was startled but amused that she had let herself go with her feelings and was probably unaware that she was making such strange sounds. I was also happy that my room was not close to her parent's room as we continued our loud, boisterous tryst that lasted late into the night. I returned Sherrie to her room before dawn and stumbled back to my bed for some much needed rest and sleep—for a virgin she was certainly a handful! When I arose the next morning, Sherrie and her folks were long gone—I never saw or heard from them again. I only hope that lovely Sherrie had memories of that night as fond as mine.

I drove all the way to Yuma, Arizona that day—a beautiful, sunny, warm day that was perfect for driving a sports car with the top down. By late afternoon I was beginning to feel the sun but the wind generated by my car kept me deceptively cool. I stopped at a roadside bar that had advertised "ICE COLD BEER AHEAD" for several miles on large billboards and picked up a six pack and a small cooler that just fit between my feet. I was feeling on top of the world—I was now a Naval Aviator, heading for California, driving a nice sports car, and reveling in the memory of a great evening with a lovely lady. And those cold beers tasted so good—I was surely the most fortunate person in the world! I pulled into a motel near Yuma just at sunset and as I stepped out of the MG I could not keep my balance and fell face down. The combination of sitting cramped up in that small cockpit of a sports car and drinking several beers on an empty stomach in the blistering sun was more than I could handle. I stumbled into the motel office wiping dirt from my face and was immediately told by the clerk that no rooms were available. After I explained that I was really not a drunken bum, the clerk reluctantly rented me a room for the night. Another lesson learned—be careful when drinking beer in the heat of the full sun on an empty stomach.

The next day I arrived in San Diego and took the ferry over to Coronado where the Naval Air Station was located. I drove by the famous Hotel Del Coronado but could barely make it out in the cool fog that engulfed the whole area. This is sunny southern California? The beaches were nothing like I had enjoyed in Florida and Texas and there seemed to be little or no surf. Maybe I had arrived at an unusual time when the weather was particularly unpleasant? It was a rude awakening to the fact that most of the coast in California is foggy and cold for the best part of the year. I checked into the B.O.Q. and then contacted a couple of my buddies from Pensacola Beach who were now based in the San Diego area. Temple and Dave (not the Dave of Dempsey dumpster fame) were helicopter pilots based at one of the outlying fields and shared an apartment in Coronado. We agreed to meet that first evening at the Mexican Village, a bar/restaurant that was famous with Naval Aviators—the beer was warm, the drinks were watered down, the music was horrible and the food was lousy. Just the perfect spot for Navy pilots—one of those few places in the world where if you sat long enough you would eventually see everyone that you had ever known pass through those doors! My pals invited me to share their apartment and I moved in the next day.

A few days later I reported aboard NAS North Island and was informed that the first thing I was scheduled for was *SURVIVAL SCHOOL!* All new pilots reporting to their first fleet squadron assignments had to go through this ritual. We all knew it would be tough but it was necessary and would prepare us for escape and evasion in the event that we were shot down or had to land in enemy territory. There were about 25 men in my survival class—officers of various ranks and a few enlisted flight crew members—and we started with two days of classroom instruction to prepare us for the week ahead. After the two days of ground school we were taken to a secluded beach and placed on small rafts in groups of two or three. After rowing out to sea for about a mile we were "rescued" by a navy helicopter and dropped off once again on the beach. We spent the night on the beach foraging for food and trying to stay warm. The next day we were taken, by bus, to the desert near Warner Springs, CA, where we were released and told to "try to make it to safety" about five miles across the desert. If we were not captured before reaching the safe zone we would be rewarded with water and special treatment in the POW camp. Almost everyone in my group ran as fast as they could to the safe area and were all captured. I hung back and hid until the captors passed me by and watched as they caught each of my fellow evaders. I waited until the time allotted for the exercise was about to expire before I strolled into the safe area—feeling very proud and quite cocky that I had managed to not be captured. As I turned myself in, I was taken "prisoner," stripped of all my clothes, beaten by the guards, and finally given my reward—a cup of boiling water. I had not had a drop of water all day and burned my hands when I grabbed the cup that was offered. I almost put the cup to my mouth but was not quite that desperate—yet! We were treated worse than any of us had imagined—stuffed into small wooden boxes that were way too small for even a child to fit into—and exposed to every type of humiliation and torture conceivable. We all learned to hate those guards and vowed to get our revenge once this drill was over. Most importantly, however, we began to bond together as a group and worked as a unit to make plans for escape. Obviously, before we were able to escape, the exercise was over and we were brought back to reality before we could take our revenge. Our hated guards reappeared during the debriefing, not in their prison camp uniforms but in their real uniforms as U.S. Navy Officers and senior enlisted men. They explained that they had played their roles not to make us suffer but to strengthen our resolve to survive—we half-way believed they were telling the truth! All in all, it was a very dramatic enactment of what we might be subjected to if and when we were shot down behind enemy lines.

After Survival School I checked into the Retraining Air Group (RAG) and was informed that since my orders were to VA-25, a squadron based at Alameda Naval Air Station in the Bay Area near Oakland, I was entitled to receive TAD. This was extra pay for "Temporary Additional Duty" when a Naval Officer was separated from his duty station. I had never heard of this special pay before but was happy to receive such a windfall—it was $180 per month and was paid in advance **in cash!** I had just been promoted to Lieutenant (Junior Grade) which increased my pay and I was now receiving $100 per month for flight pay. Now I was to receive another, completely unexpected windfall. I was beginning to love this Navy life! The next three months were the best times of my life—up to that point. The flying was great, the social life outstanding, and the weather became acceptable. I was introduced to low-level navigation routes, commonly called "sand blowers" where we flew our planes at very low altitudes (mostly below 500 feet AGL). This was what flying the AD was all about—we were training to fly under enemy radar to penetrate deep into hostile terrain to find and destroy our assigned targets. We planned these missions with reference to sectional charts—maps that displayed terrain and visual landmarks such as water towers, bridges, towns and highways. We joked that we could never get lost as we could get low enough to read the highway signs.

Usually these "sand blowers" started out with flying out to sea for a hundred miles or so, turning to parallel the coast for at least fifty miles, and then plotting a course to arrive over the coastal-in point that was the same as the coastal-out point. The purpose of this exercise was for the pilot to read the winds on the ocean below and determine the drift—then to fly a course to arrive back where he left land. Not as easy as one might imagine when flying a single seat aircraft without an autopilot at altitudes of less than 500 feet (usually less than 200 feet). Once we were back over land (called "feet dry") we would fly for several hours following the track we had plotted on our maps. We would plan to arrive over our "target"—usually a landmark such as an intersection or a bridge—make our "attack" and then return to base. As we became more proficient flying these long range training missions, we were able to arrive over the target within seconds of our planned TOT (Time Over

Target). We usually flew as a "section" which consisted of two aircraft and sometimes flew as a "division" which was made up of two sections or four aircraft. As I was the "student" I always flew with an instructor—either I flew on his wing or I led and he "chased" me in loose formation.

These low-level navigation hops were really legalized "flathatting"—a term whose origin is unknown to me—but to the Navy pilot, flathatting was an offense that could get you kicked out of the service. If you flew too low and endangered innocent civilians it was considered flathatting. In Naval legalese it did not matter that a civilian was not in danger from a low-flying aircraft— if the civilian **perceived** that he/she was in danger, it was sufficient to complete the offense. Because these sand blowers were authorized training missions we were pretty much exempt from complaints about low flying airplanes. In reality the routes were flown over sparsely populated areas and very few complaints were received. We flew over some of the most spectacular terrain imaginable on these flights—along the coastline up and down California, over the beautiful snow capped Sierras, and even into the Grand Canyon. In those days we were allowed to fly below the rim of the Canyon, being aware of several cables that were marked on our maps as hazards to aerial navigation! The real hazard was other aircraft in the Canyon as there was no control and we were not "talking to each other." It was easy to be so wrapped up in enjoying the view that the pilots were not always looking out for other aircraft. One day I was flying down the river at 200 feet with my "chase" behind and above me by another 200 feet. I was gawking at the scenery when I caught something in the corner of my eye pass just above me to my right. I hit the mike button and said to my chase, "What the hell was that?" He replied, "I think it was an Air Force jet—he went right between us!" It was amazing that we did not have mid-air collisions more often—a few years later those low-level flights were no longer permitted in the Grand Canyon. At least I was able to enjoy several—when "flying was fun."

The apartment that I shared with Temple and Dave in Coronado was actually a duplex. We had the upstairs three bedroom unit and below were three gals in a similar apartment. These fine working ladies were: Nan, the blonde; Sheila, the brunette; and Undine, the redhead—true story! We had lots of parties together on the weekends but there was very little hanky-panky. The six of us would hit the local bars on Coronado, starting of course with the Mexican Village, and when the bars closed at 2:00 AM we would head down to Tijuana, where the bars never closed. Occasionally we would take in some of the local sex shows at places like The Blue Fox. There was a two dollar cover charge to enter these filthy "clubs" and nothing was left to the imagination. There was no artistic talent with these shows—a man and woman would walk out onto the center stage that was circled by a guard rail to keep the spectators from getting too close, disrobe if they were not already naked, and start engaging in various forms of copulation. Sometimes two females would perform their sex act together, but the real show involved one girl and one donkey! These places were filled mostly with U.S. sailors on liberty who were loud and very drunk. Often one or more of the drunkest in the crowd would lean over the railing with a dollar or two between his teeth. One of the naked girls would take the money and squat down on the sailor's face for oral sex. Sheila and Nan both said that this was disgusting and wanted to leave—I looked at Undine and saw excitement in her eyes. I asked her, "What do you think about it, Undine?" Without hesitation, she said, "I think that she should be paying the men, not the other way around!"

One night (actually about 3:00 AM) we were walking to our vehicle to drive back to Coronado when we were stopped by two Mexican policemen. These two "cops" were sitting in their police car with the doors open as we walked by—naturally we had a bottle of cheap wine in a brown paper bag that was being passed around—but this was not unusual and the cops had never bothered us before. They usually were very friendly, waved and said hello with big toothy grins. This time was different. One of the officers walked in front of our group, held up his hand and said, "Stop, amigos!" As we came to a halt he stated in broken English that drinking in public was against the law. We laughed and offered him the brown bag but he shook his head and said, "I must take all of you to jail!" We recognized the Mexican "border town shake down" and asked, "How much do you want?" He rubbed his chin and said, "Fifty dollars, American." We looked at each other and started to pool our money—among the six of us we came up with a grand total of $17 and some change. We had learned that you took only the amount of money you planned to spend, or could afford to lose, when you went to Tijuana. We never took credit cards or any I.D. except our military cards—if the Navy I.D. was lost you could get a replacement without question. I never had more than $20, usually only about $10, on these jaunts across the border. We began to bargain with the cop but he would not take less than $25—still more than we had with us. Finally the officer said that he would take just one of us to jail until the others could return with at least twenty five dollars. Since I was currently holding the bag, so to speak, he pointed to me and told me to get into the police car.

I bid farewell to my friends and told them to hurry back with the money as I was not looking forward to a Mexican jail. This jail was just a few blocks away—actually it was sort of a tourist attraction as passers-by could look into this circular adobe block building and watch the "prisoners." A guard at the entrance opened the huge barred gate and I stepped into another world. No one had taken my name, asked to see my I.D., or explained what I was charged with. This dirt floored room (more like a pit) was about forty feet in diameter with a single guard sitting in the middle on a small folding type chair. On the far side, away from the street, two tunnels disappeared into the darkness. I found out that down those tunnels were individual cells where they kept the most violent and dangerous criminals. I estimated that there were about thirty people in the main room—both men and women—and most were curled up on the bare floor asleep. I decided that the safest place was to be as close to the guard in the middle as possible. This guard appeared to be dozing but as I approached to within ten feet he held up his hand in an obvious gesture that indicated I was as close as he would permit. He had his other hand on a large shotgun lying across his lap. Several of my fellow "detainees" were following my every move— finally one smallish Mexican male approached me and advised that I needed "protection" from some of the other prisoners. He showed me a small pocket knife that he had cupped in his palm and stated in broken English that he would be my bodyguard, for a price of course! I indicated that I was broke—if I had any money I certainly would not be in this hell-hole! He did not seem to believe me but finally he left me alone. Next I was approached by a very rough looking woman who appeared to be in her thirties and was obviously a prostitute. She propositioned me right away, saying that she would give me a blow job for five dollars! I laughed and asked just where she was planning to perform this act. She indicated that she and I could go over against the wall and no one would be the least bit interested in whatever we did. I'm sure that she was correct and have no doubt that such acts were quite common in this facility. I politely refused her offer and she returned to her spot against the wall to accost the next newcomer to enter her place of business. I asked the guard, "Where is the restroom?" He smiled and pointed to one of those dark tunnels. The whole place smelled of urine and feces and it was evident from the pools of liquid and wet stains on the walls that most of the residents here were relieving themselves wherever they wanted.

I could not bring myself to urinate on the wall so I reluctantly headed down the nearest tunnel. There appeared to be three cells on each side of this narrow path that led to an open latrine at the end. As I walked past these cells the occupants all started screaming and reaching through the bars at me—some were just begging me to help, others were hoping to do me harm. I reached the end of this gauntlet, did my business quickly, and turned to head back out—then I noticed the silhouette of a large male figure blocking the end of the tunnel. I quickly looked at my options—not many! I did not want to get stuck in that tunnel and there was only one way out—through that guy blocking the end. I tried to swallow but my mouth was too dry—I started running as hard as I could toward the light at the end of the tunnel, hoping that maybe I could knock him over before he was too deep into the tunnel. I was almost to the end when the big man stepped back a few steps and into the light—Thank God, it was the guard with the shotgun! He saw the frightened look in my eyes, grinned and said, "Just checking to see if you were okay, Gringo." The next hour or so I stayed as close to that guard as he would allow. I was almost asleep on my feet when the guard got my attention and pointed to the front gate. My buddies were there and the outside guard was opening the doors to let me out. I looked at the big guy sitting in the middle and stuck out my hand. He stood up, walked toward me and shook my hand, saying with that toothy grin, "Next time be more careful, Gringo."

After the twenty five dollars was passed into the hand of the front entry guard we were on our way back to the good old USA! After this episode I made it my personal rule that I would never again let the sun set while I was in a Mexican border town and the only times I returned to Tijuana were to watch the Sunday afternoon bullfights. On the way back to Coronado, Dave and Temple wanted to hear all about my stay in the notorious Tijuana jail. I had spent less than three hours in that pit but it felt more like days. I told my buddies that I would tell them all about it over a cold beer—my mouth was still quite dry. There was a joint called "The Hub" near the Mexican Village that had a large sign outside that advertised, "Open at Six AM." I had never been inside this bar and had wondered who would frequent such a place at 0600. When we stepped inside "The Hub" it was about 0630 on a Saturday morning—the place was jumping with standing room only at the bar! Almost all of the clientele were in uniform, Chief Petty Officers and senior enlisted men. There was a shuffleboard table and a pool table—both in use with spirited games with other men awaiting their turn. I decided that since this was the closest bar to the main entrance to the Naval Air Station, these sailors were just getting off duty and this was their "happy hour." After talking to a few of these men at the bar I found that I was half right—many were finishing an all night duty stint but others were stopping by the pub **before work** to have an eye-opener or two! Where did we get such men? After two beers it was time for me to call it a day, forget about Tijuana, go home, take a shower and get some much needed sleep.

My training in San Diego was coming to an end. The final part of this flight training was night carrier qualification. By this time I had amassed over thirty day traps and was beginning to be a bit more comfortable around the carrier—nevertheless, it was with some anxiety that I approached that first night approach and landing. We had been practicing night FCLPs (field carrier landing patterns) for several nights and felt that we were ready for the real thing—realizing of course that our training did not replicate the moving, pitching deck of an aircraft carrier. I sincerely believe to this day that the absolute most dangerous place on earth is the flight deck of an aircraft carrier during night operations. There are literally dozens of men (now women also) scurrying around in the dark while airplanes of all types are landing, taxiing, being launched or towed all over that dark, slippery, heaving deck! There was a reddish, eerie glow to the scene as white lights of any type were forbidden during night operations—only red lights were allowed so as to not ruin the pilots' night vision. Our ready room aboard the carrier was outfitted with red lights so that the pilots could brief their flights and at the same time let their eyes adapt to the darkness. We had red lenses in our flashlights and we wore red goggles when we left the ready room in case we were exposed to white light which would make us "night blind". Once we were in our cockpits and the instrument lights had been adjusted for night flying we could take off our red goggles.

For my night carrier qualification I flew out to the USS Hornet which was operating off the southern coast of California. I arrived during daylight and completed ten landings and launches before sundown. Then I stayed aboard, had dinner, and later briefed in the ready room for the night part of the training. I managed to get into the cockpit wearing my red goggles without any mishaps and had the lights adjusted before I removed those uncomfortable glasses. The plane captain was helping me strap in when I dropped my knee board (a cleverly designed devise that held briefing sheets with frequencies, rendezvous points and other important info). I was trying to find it on the dark floor of the cockpit when the helpful plane captain said, "Let me help, sir, I have a flashlight." He then stuck his flashlight into the cockpit and clicked it on just as I turned my head towards him. Yep, he did not have a red lens and I was hit in the eyes with a blinding light that wiped out my two hours of night adaptation! I was pissed and he was very apologetic—but there was no way that I was going to cancel or delay this flight as I was as ready as I would ever be for night quals. The first takeoff was to be a deck launch—no catapult shot—but luckily I was number three in line and my eyes had about five minutes to adjust back to darkness. It was at this time that I noticed just how dark it was—a solid cloud layer at around 1000 feet kept even the stars from being visible, and there was no moon that night. We were in moderate swells, not unusual for the Pacific Ocean off the southern California coast, and there were a few whitecaps visible on that dark, cold surface below. It was now my turn to take off. Just as we had practiced many times, the launching officer gave his signals with lighted wands. He signaled for me to add power, check my gauges, and if everything looked good I would turn on a small light on the side of the aircraft when ready. Then he pointed his wand to the bow of the ship and dropped it toward the deck. I released the brakes and added full power. I looked forward and found a single red light at the center of the bow—that was my aim point. The control stick was pulled full aft toward my stomach and my right leg was locked with full right rudder to compensate for the engine torque. The take off roll was started aft of the island which is located on the starboard side of the ship and I was prepared for the "burble" as I rolled forward of this structure. Suddenly it took almost full left rudder to keep the aircraft pointed towards that tiny light. Then the light disappeared—I was airborne—and now I had to make a quick transition to instrument flying. The easy part of the flight was over!

I joined up with three other airplanes and we were sent to a holding point to await our turn in the landing pattern. The ceiling was dropping so we would be required to fly a CCA for the first landing. A CCA is a Carrier Controlled Approach similar to the GCA or Ground Controlled Approach that was used to land in instrument conditions at airports on land. All went as planned and my turn was without incident—I broke out of the clouds at 800 feet and saw that I was lined up behind the carrier in perfect position for landing. Once visual contact was made the LSO (Landing Signal Officer) took over control with verbal instructions such as, watch your line-up, you're going high, you're slow or the dreaded, **power, power, power**—usually followed by a profanity or two. The lights on the flight deck were clearly visible but the pitching deck made the landing area alternately small and smaller! The object was to disregard the deck and fly the "meatball" which controlled your angle of descent. The meatball was the term used for the light that appeared in the center of a mirror just to the left of the landing area. When that light was centered it had a green glow which meant that you were on the proper glide path. If the "ball" drifted high it would turn white, meaning that you were going above the proper path, when it started to sink it would become pink and finally red which meant that you were dangerously low. Before that ball turned red the LSO was calling for more power. Another carrier aviator saying was: **Ball's turning pink, you're starting to sink; ball's turning red, you'll soon be dead!**

After the fourth landing it was time for a night catapult shot. I had experienced several shots off the catapult before and thought that I was ready for that first night blast. What they forgot to tell us was the fact that the USS Hornet was one of the last carriers that was equipped with hydraulic catapults—as opposed to the more modern steam catapults that were the norm. The steam catapult was a real "kick in the ass" but not all at once, whereas the hydraulic shot was like a shotgun blast that was a massive initial jolt that was so powerful that the aircraft actually slowed down before it reached the end of the carrier! It was almost like an ejection seat with a rocket attached. Once you were able to move your head forward and uncage your eyeballs you realized that you were airborne and now it was time to recover from an unusual attitude! Our group managed to successfully complete our night carrier qualifications in less than thirty minutes and we were now considered fleet pilots!

My buddies threw a party for me on my last night in San Diego—they did not need much of a reason to throw a party—and I was sorry to leave such a fun group. The next day I planned to drive to Moffett Field, a Naval Air Station located between San Jose and San Francisco in the Bay Area of Northern California. This was where I would now be based with my squadron, VA-25, the "Fist of the Fleet." Nan, the blonde who lived below us and a good friend, approached me with an idea. She was from the San Francisco area and wanted to visit with her parents—so she offered to share expenses if she could accompany me on this trip. Nan did not have a romantic attachment with any of us and she was a fun gal, so I said, "Sure, why not?" Our little party lasted until quite late and soon it was time to pack for the trip.

We departed just at sunrise with my fully loaded MG, which now had a luggage rack on the back. A few hours into this journey we decided to take the scenic coastal route and managed to stop at several "watering holes" as we slowly progressed northward. As a twenty two year old Naval Aviator I suppose I considered myself invincible and thought that I could complete the 500 mile road trip without stopping for sleep—not very smart! About halfway between L.A. and San Francisco, close to San Luis Obispo, Nan was asleep and I also drifted off. I woke up to the sound of gravel flying and I was off the highway and driving through an artichoke field. I recall someone opening the driver's side door and asking was I OK? Of course, what was the problem? With a little help I was able to get the vehicle back on the highway (no police were involved) and we were back on our way! I realized that it was impossible to continue our drive nonstop and after looking at my ashen faced passenger I knew it was time to call it a night.

We stopped at the first motel we found and jumped in bed with our underwear still on. We awoke the next morning in the bed together and Nan got up first and used the bathroom. When she returned to the bed I noticed that she was now braless but still was wearing her panties. I took my turn in the bathroom and after brushing my teeth and throwing some cold water on my face I returned to the bed. I noticed that those panties that I had last seen on Nan's fine frame were now lying on the floor and she was snuggled under the covers. I took her lead, left my underwear next to hers and slipped between the sheets to see what happened next. Nan was lying on her side with her back to me as I nestled next to her warm body. My erection was impossible for her to ignore and she giggled and said, "I think you have a problem!" I mumbled something about what should we do about it when she suddenly threw back the covers, pushed me over onto my back and straddled me backwards! Before I knew what happened she lowered herself down onto my manhood and began furiously pumping up and down. This was a position that was new to me. She had a boyish figure with small breasts but a really cute little butt that was almost in my face as she bobbed up and down for what I figured was less than one minute. I was now in a position to observe what I had never seen before—she was in complete control and would lift up to where only the tip of my penis was still embedded, then slide down to completely engulf me. These motions were alternately painfully slow and then with a force that took my breath away. I was enthralled at the incredible adaptability of that wonderful female organ that seemed to be able to both delight and amaze when encasing its male counterpart. No wonder we are such putty in their hands! I was only able to hold her around the waist and provide what little assistance was required—then she heaved a loud sigh, more like a groan, and rolled off. She was finished and fell over on her side, breathing hard and a bit sweaty. She gave me a cute little grin and said, "That was great, I'm going to take a shower now." I had not yet climaxed and as she walked to the bathroom, I felt as though I had been used as a *dildo!* She had turned the table on me— I now realized just what women go through so often, a selfish lover who takes his satisfaction then rolls over and proceeds to snore! It was so fitting that I laughed out loud and suddenly had a great deal of respect, not only for Nan, but for all of those wonderful ladies who deserve more than we men usually provide. The dawn of feminism had begun—sex would never again be for male enjoyment alone, at least not where I was concerned.

When I heard the shower running, I yelled to Nan, "Want some company in there?" She replied, "Sure, there's room for two—and we can conserve water!" As I stepped into the shower I said, "Nan, I'm afraid that I still have a 'problem'—what can we do about it?" She laughed and said, "I'll take care of it." She soaped her hands then took a firm grip on my erection—in less than a minute I no longer had a "problem." After I caught my breath I commented, "That was quite a hand job, where did you learn to do that?" She said, "I used to watch my brother masturbate, I know what you guys like."

Later, as we continued our drive northward, I wanted to learn more about feminine sexuality. Nan was a very down-to-earth person and the first female that I had ever met who seemed completely comfortable discussing that subject. Although we had just enjoyed intimacy together, it occurred to me that we had never kissed or even held hands before. She seemed to be more of a buddy to me than a girlfriend. I think she felt the same about me. I asked her if her brother had been aware that she was watching when he masturbated. She started talking and did not stop for at least thirty minutes—it was as if she wanted to tell someone about her early childhood. She related that one day when she was about ten years old she walked by the bedroom of her brother who was five years older and heard some moaning. The bedroom door was open a couple of inches and she peeped in to see if he was okay or maybe in pain. She observed her brother naked on his bed with his hand pumping frantically on his erect penis. She had seen her brother without clothes before but had never seen a hard-on. She was fascinated and watched until the conclusion when ejaculation occurred. She said that she did not think at that time that he was aware she was watching, but now felt that he had planned for her to see what he did in private. During the next year or two she watched several times when she noticed that his bedroom door was cracked just so. She said that she and her brother never discussed these things and she had never told anyone but one girl friend about those experiences. I asked her what effect this had on her at such an early age. She said that she would cry herself to sleep at night because she did not have one of "those things" to play with. Nan read my mind and said, "Yes, it was penis envy, but I think all young girls go through that to some extent or another. You men have it so convenient, one minute it's just hanging there and the next thing you know, it's sticking out as though waiting for a hand to grab it. Sure, girls masturbate too, but it's not as easy for us as we don't have anything to grab hold of like you guys do."

After she finished relating those intimate facts about her childhood, she began to get quite playful. She reached between my legs and began to fondle me. Then she unzipped my trousers and delicately took out my penis. She giggled again and said, "I know something else that you boys like!" Without further ado she put her head in my lap and proceeded to do a masterful blowjob! This was not easy in a tiny MGA while we were driving down the highway heading to San Francisco but she acted like it was something that she did every day. After she finished her "artful therapy" and everything was tidied up and tucked away she patted me on the knee and said, "Now then, don't you feel a lot better?" It was as if she had just performed a necessary medical act of mercy—maybe it was therapeutic! She was right; I did feel a lot better.

I dropped Nan off at her parent's home in one of the suburbs just south of San Francisco and she agreed to show me the nightlights of that famous city. We made a "date" for two nights later and she took me to the North Beach area where all the action seemed to be. We stood in line to watch the well-endowed Carol Doda perform her strip tease—I believe that she started the whole topless craze that soon followed. I had parked my car in a small nearby parking lot but did not read the small print on the ticket stub that I received. We bar-hopped until the bars closed and returned to get my car at about 2:15 AM. The lot was empty except for my little MG and there were two large chains across the only exit! Then I noticed the small print that said, "We close at 2 AM—no overnight parking allowed!" There was no way that I could get my car through those chains so we were stuck. We walked around for about an hour until we found an all night coffee shop where we sat and talked until it started to get light outside. We returned to the car around 5 AM, but the lot was still not open. After a very uncomfortable hour of dozing I was aroused by a tapping on the window—someone had arrived to open the lot for the morning business. My first visit to San Francisco had turned out to be a memorable one! I never saw Nan again but did receive a nice letter from her thanking me for the ride and expressing her enjoyment of our adventures together.

Chapter Eight

"Things which do you no good in aviation: Altitude above you, Runway behind you, Fuel in the truck, Airspeed you don't have."

When I reported to my fleet squadron, VA-25, at NAS Moffett Field, I found the place almost deserted. It seemed that everyone but a skeleton crew was on leave as the squadron had just returned from a long cruise aboard the USS Midway to the Far East, called a WestPac cruise. When I checked in with the Squadron Duty Officer (SDO) he casually said to take some time off to get settled into a place to live and come back in a few days. This sounded like a great plan to me so I asked him if he knew of any apartments in the local area. He replied that most of the bachelor pilots were living in the BOQ or in a complex called Del Charro Apartments in nearby Mountain View. I had already acquired a room in the BOQ but did not wish to stay there on a permanent basis, so I went to the place he recommended. I talked to the apartment manager about renting a small apartment and she said there were several available. I filled out a rental form and when she saw my name she said, "I show that you are already renting a two bedroom unit here with another pilot!" This was certainly news to me as I did not even know any other pilots in the squadron. I asked if I could see "my apartment" and she handed me the key and gave directions how to get there. I proceeded to that apartment and politely knocked on the door—I was a bit apprehensive about using the key and walking into a strange place unannounced. After a short wait the door was opened by a bleary-eyed young man about my age (it was around ten o'clock in the morning) who looked like he really did not want to be bothered at that moment. I told him my name and he brightened up, stuck out his hand and said, "Glad to meet you, welcome to our new apartment."

He introduced himself as Bob but said that everyone called him "Bum," invited me in and said, "Want a beer?" I nodded and took a quick look around—a little messy but certainly livable, with a nice balcony overlooking a large swimming pool. As I opened the beer, Bum started to explain the situation with an apology. Seems that he had seen my name as a new pilot that would be reporting into the outfit and since I was listed as having no dependents, he made the assumption that I would need a place to live and he needed a roommate. Without hesitation I agreed to this arrangement and asked if it was okay to move in that day. He said, "No problem, I'll show you your bedroom—sorry that it's the small one but I got here first!" He pointed to my room and I felt that it was perfect—it even had its own bathroom. I was about to leave when the door to the other bedroom opened and out stepped a sleepy-eyed young lady who was clad only in a bath towel. She looked surprised, excused herself, and went back into the bedroom and closed the door. I looked at "Bum" and said, "Looks like you already have a roommate!" He grinned and said, "Naw, she's just something I picked up at a bar last night, she'll be gone in an hour or two."

Bum and I roomed together at what we began to call the Del Charro Sex Village until the next deployment of the squadron, about eight months away. This shore period was considered the training cycle to prepare for the next WestPac cruise—it seemed that the Navy was always training and pilots especially had to maintain proficiency with instrument flying, long range navigation, weapons delivery, and carrier operations. This training cycle started slowly as was customary for squadrons returning from deployment but we began to accelerate so as to reach peak performance just before the carrier put out to sea. Moffett Field was a great place to be based—it was where all light attack squadrons on the West coast were located. Fighter squadrons were located at NAS Miramar near San Diego, heavy attack groups were at NAS Whidbey Island near Seattle, and anti-submarine outfits were at NAS North Island. Moffett had been designed and built to support blimps, or airships, in the twenties or thirties and there were two huge hangars that were big enough to park and maintain those huge dirigibles. We joked that on rainy days we could conduct flight operations indoors. There were several AD squadrons located at Moffett as well as A4 (Skyhawk) and FJ4B (Fury) units. I was not the most junior pilot in the squadron but I was still considered a "nugget". This was the designation of a new pilot who had not yet made a cruise aboard a carrier. The squadron consisted of about twenty pilots and one hundred twenty enlisted men. There were also two or three non-flying officers—an Air Intelligence Officer (AIO) and one or two maintenance officers.

Each pilot had several "collateral" duties in addition to flying airplanes. This had not been adequately explained to me during my flight training. The day after I reported aboard, a very senior Chief Petty Officer approached me, introduced himself and stated, "I understand that you are the new gun boss." I had not the slightest idea what a gun boss was so just looked at him and asked, "What does a gun boss do?" He laughed and said, "Don't worry; I've got everything under control." I knew that the CPO's ran the Navy and I was not about to change that tradition. The Executive Officer, whom I had not yet met as he was still on leave, had assigned me duties as Weapons Officer and Navigation Officer. The Weapons Division consisted of over twenty sailors, headed by the Chief and several Petty Officers. Their duties were to assemble, arm and load the ordinance that our airplanes were to deliver to assigned targets. Even during peacetime we expended huge amounts of bombs, rockets and ammo as we carried quite an assortment of weapons on our single engine, single pilot Skyraider. I was starting to realize that in the U.S. Navy, a pilot was first and foremost an Officer—with all the responsibilities and duties thereof—and secondarily an Aviator!

Squadron flying was completely different from what I had been exposed to in the training command and the RAG. My first couple of flights were flown as wingman to the Commanding Officer (the C.O. or affectionately "the Skipper") or Operations Officer (usually the third in command) to check me out on squadron procedures. After that I was scheduled to fly with various pilots until I became experienced enough to be designated a section leader (about one year) and later a division leader (usually at least two years). The flying was great! We flew lots of "sand blower" navigation hops, dropped lots of bombs, fired many rockets, and strafed with our 20 millimeter air to ground cannons. Almost every month we would be involved in carrier operations somewhere off the coast of California and I started to accumulate more and more carrier landings. I was becoming comfortable with shipboard operations and was really looking forward to that first cruise. After about six months in the squadron I was designated a "Test Pilot." That sounded very impressive until I found out that most "test hops" were the most boring flights imaginable—usually consisting of breaking in a new engine. On these flights, the pilot was required to fly the airplane for about four hours using various engine and propeller settings, usually directly over the air base in case anything went wrong. After five minutes you knew if anything was going to go wrong or not, so the rest of the flight was routine. However, the "test flight" was the only time a pilot got to go aloft by himself! We always flew as a two or four plane formation during all our training missions. As a junior officer I was required to stand duty as the SDO and since I was a bachelor I often volunteered to be on duty on weekends so the married pilots could spend time with their families. One of the perks of being the weekend duty officer was that he was allowed to take up test hops if there were any needing to be flown. One beautiful crisp Saturday morning the Maintenance Chief informed me, the duty officer, that he had an aircraft requiring a test hop. I was ready to go in fifteen minutes.

This was one of those routine flight tests that would require more patience than skill and after the first hour I was getting bored. I decided that I could perform the required procedures and enjoy some different scenery at the same time so I departed the normal pattern over the airport and flew over to the coast. In five minutes I was flying over Santa Cruz and then down the coast to Monterey and Big Sur. What a beautiful day and I was all alone in this fantastic aircraft with the entire California coast at my disposal. I was getting paid to do this? It was not a problem to fly the required speeds and power settings required by the test hop and I discovered that altitude was not one of the parameters so I decided to fly a bit lower to really enjoy the views. Soon I was flying over the water at 100 feet or less and paralleling the coast—The Pacific Coast Highway was winding along the same route and I noticed that often I was actually lower than those automobiles on the roadway! I could see people in convertibles waving to me and I would rock my wings to wave back. I continued flying the "green and blue" airway (green grass on one side and blue ocean on the other) down the coast past Morro Rock and almost to Santa Barbara before it was time to reverse my course and head home. The flight back was just as exciting with views from a different angle of some of the most beautiful parts of America. After I landed the Maintenance Chief asked, "Everything okay with the airplane?" I assured him that it was just perfect, and then added, "Maybe I should take it up again tomorrow to be sure!" He did a double take and commented that I was the first squadron pilot he had met who seemed to actually enjoy these test flights. I subsequently flew several such weekend test hops and explored the north coast all the way to the Washington border as well as revisiting the south coast.

My roommate, Bum, and I were enjoying our apartment in Mountain View—there were lots of parties and female companionship was readily available. One evening Bum and his "flavor of the week" came to the apartment and brought her roommate—a delightful, cute and vivacious young lady with whom I began an "on again, off again" relationship. We began to date and I was starting to fear that it could turn into a serious affair, not exactly what I wanted at this stage in my life. She was an undergraduate student at San Jose State University in her last year and was one of the nicest ladies I had met in my young lifetime. On this first "date"—a Saturday night, someone mentioned that the Kingston Trio, a new in-group of entertainers, was appearing at one of the showrooms in a Casino at South Lake Tahoe. I had never been to Lake Tahoe nor had I ever seen a big time show. The four of us decided, after several bottles of wine I believe, that it would be fun to rent a small plane the next day, fly to Tahoe for the show and return the same evening. Although I had never flown a small airplane, my buddy, Bum, assured me that it was easy and we would have no problems getting checked out. The next afternoon we went to a small airport in San Jose, Bum got checked out, and we took off for Lake Tahoe before dark. The weather was fine but cold and windy by the time we reached our destination. It was the dead of winter and we were not prepared for the extreme temperature difference from San Jose to Lake Tahoe, an elevation of 6000 feet. The runway was plowed and clear but there were mounds of snow on either side which made it feel and look like we were landing in a tunnel. Bum did all the flying and I helped with navigation—it seemed pretty simple to me. After landing, Bum said that he would make arrangements for taking care of the airplane and I headed to the small terminal to acquire transportation to the Casino. Soon we were having a great time with a few drinks, a nice dinner and watching the fabulous Kingston Trio! We all had to be back in the Bay Area the next morning for school or work and the plan was to fly back at dawn as neither Bum nor I felt comfortable flying that small, unfamiliar Cessna across the Sierras in the black of night. I stopped drinking after the show but everyone else remained in a party mood. I also thought it would be a good idea to get a room for a few hours sleep but was voted down on that idea right away. As it ended up, we departed the Casino for the airport after we all ran out of money—as I recall close to 4:00 AM.

It was just starting to get pink to the east as we arrived at our cold-soaked little airplane which was now covered with frost. The skies were clear but the temperature was well below freezing as we huddled in the small cockpit to try to stay warm. Bum immediately jumped into the back seat with his date and fell asleep—my new lady friend, who had never been in a small airplane, was now my navigator. I scraped the frost off a small part of the windshield so that I could see forward and we took off down through that tunnel of snow that seemed higher than the plane itself. I took into account the fact that the control surfaces and wings were covered with a thin layer of frost but the take-off roll was much longer than I anticipated. We finally staggered into the air and flew over the southern part of the lake until I reached enough airspeed to start a slow climb. I made three 360 degree turns before gaining enough altitude to start heading to the West and over the high Sierras. We were now in the sunshine and the frost began to slowly dissipate through the process known as sublimation, where a solid changes to a gaseous state without going through an intermediate liquid state. I later learned that just a tiny layer of frost on an aircraft could change the aerodynamics considerably and consider myself lucky that all went well on this adventuresome flight. Almost well! About halfway across the mountain range I finally located the fuel quantity gauge and discovered the needle in the red area that said: **DO NOT FLY!** I woke up my buddy in the back and asked him, "You arranged for the plane to be fueled in Tahoe, didn't you?" He confessed that he forgot but thought that we had enough fuel for the return trip. I pointed to the quantity gauge and we all swallowed hard and started looking for gas stations! We made it to a small airport in Tracy, a town just southwest of Stockton, and were able to get fuel because I had a Shell Gas Station credit card—we had less than five dollars between the four of us. We took off again and headed for San Jose—plenty of time for everyone to get to their appointed place that morning. One problem—we arrived at the airport in San Jose and found that it was socked in with fog. Even if this airplane was equipped with the proper instruments we were not able to land in such dense fog. We returned to Tracy and spent about three hours on the ground waiting for the fog to lift. We each made the necessary phone calls to notify our superiors that we would be a bit late for work or class and resigned ourselves to making the best of our situation. After pooling all our money we were able to buy soft drinks and snacks from vending machines and spent the time sitting on the grass and enjoying the warm sunshine. This was the first time I had really just talked to my new lady friend and I discovered that she was an intelligent, witty young lady who was fun to be with. After this adventure we began to date on a fairly steady basis and I was starting to ask myself: **COULD THIS BE THE ONE?** As usual, the Navy took care to interrupt these types of relationships by sending us on long deployments or changing our duty stations. It was time for me to go on my first WestPac cruise.

Our squadron consisted of twelve aircraft—all AD-7's, the latest and last version of the single seated Skyraider. I believe that VA-25 was the only squadron in the Navy to possess only that version—most squadrons were made up of the earlier AD-6 aircraft. When the time came for us to go aboard the carrier for this scheduled eight month cruise I discovered how important it was to be senior—the twelve highest ranking pilots would fly aboard several days after the ship left port. The rest of the pilots and all the other members of our squadron would have to walk aboard at Alameda Naval Air Station and sail with the ship when she left port. Unfortunately, I was in the latter group. My lady friend dropped me off at the dock on the morning of our departure and after a tearful farewell I stepped onto the Officers gangway for a new chapter in my life. I had arranged to leave my automobile, that peach colored MGA, with my girl friend, a decision that perhaps I would later regret!

Life aboard an aircraft carrier in the sixties was an incredible experience. There were 4500 officers and men on that huge floating airfield and it was a city into itself. I shared a "stateroom" in officer's country with another pilot, my good friend Rex, who was probably the best roommate I ever had. There was enough room for our uniforms, a few civilian clothes for liberty, our flight suits and very little else. The major part of our time aboard ship revolved around the Ready Room—we briefed and debriefed there, we watched movies there, and we spent all of our non-flying, non-eating, non-sleeping hours there! It was the operational and social center of our lives.

When the USS Midway departed the dock at Alameda Naval Air Station (just north of Oakland) we all stood on the flight deck and waved to our loved ones that we knew would not be seen again for many months. Soon we slipped beneath the Golden Gate Bridge and watched the mainland of the U.S.A. slowly disappear. Now it was time to start training for the ORI (Operational Readiness Inspection) that each carrier with its Air Group must pass before leaving Hawaii for the WestPac cruise. Our airplanes and those of our sister squadrons arrived and landed aboard three days after we were out to sea. Soon we would start the exercises that were graded by observers who were aboard but departed the ship in Hawaii—not a bad duty assignment, I thought! While we were still several hundred miles from the islands we started bombing exercises—the carrier would tow a target raft on a cable about 500 meters behind the ship and we made bombing and strafing runs—trying to hit the raft and not the carrier! We used Mark-76 practice bombs, weighing 25 pounds each and having a small explosive charge equivalent to a shotgun shell which marked the hit with smoke. We also used live ammo, 20 Millimeter, for strafing runs. When we were about 600 miles from the big island of Hawaii the ship launched almost every aircraft that was flyable to simulate a major strike against the enemy. After we successfully "hit" our targets and returned safely to the ship, the inspection was over and we were cleared to continue the cruise to the Western Pacific. First, however, we would enjoy liberty in Hawaii!

The day before the Midway berthed at Pearl Harbor, the airplanes were flown to NAS Barber's Point—about thirty minutes from Honolulu and the famed Waikiki Beach. Again the twelve senior pilots flew ashore and those of us junior pilots walked ashore! We were able to enjoy several days in Hawaii and a good time was had by all. There was a small Army Base located on Waikiki Beach called Fort Derussy and part of this base consisted of an Officer's Club and a BOQ. Before we went into town, we would stop at this O'Club and load up on ten cent beers and twenty-five cent mixed drinks—a small fraction of what we would pay in the tourist bars on the beach. Rooms were available at the BOQ but were not often used by the pilots—we usually returned to the ship each evening or to the nicer quarters at Barber's Point. An exception was made by one of our Maintenance Officers who had just been married before the ship departed CONUS (Continental U.S.). He had arranged for his new bride to meet him in Honolulu where they were planning to enjoy their honeymoon. Being a bit of a cheapskate, Frank rented a room at the Ft. Derussy BOQ (three bucks a night), where the honeymoon was held. Three days later, Frank and his new bride both came down with "crabs"—and each accused the other of being unfaithful and passing these body parasites to their partner. The marriage almost ended before they concluded that the bed sheets in that cheap BOQ room had been the problem!

When we departed Hawaii for the Far East we sailed with a "locked deck" for about two weeks—this meant that there were no flight operations and time was spent on repairs, maintenance and the usual training. The attack pilots were now introduced to SIOP (Single Integrated Operational Procedures) which involved planning for long range nuclear missions deep into enemy territory (Russia and Communist China). Even the name SIOP was Top Secret at this time and the fact that the carrier had nuclear weapons was denied when we arrived in Japanese waters. Each Nuclear Weapons Delivery Pilot spent dozens of hours planning his primary, secondary and tertiary missions. My primary target was another pilot's secondary target and a third pilot's tertiary target—there was redundancy that prepared for any and every eventuality. After this intense period of mission planning it was time to get back to flying.

Two thirds of the pilots in our squadron were married and their wives were truly remarkable in their support of all the squadron personnel, especially when we were away on cruise. When we were close enough to Japan to receive mail and packages via the COD (Carrier Onboard Delivery) aircraft we were presented with a huge package addressed to the Officers and Men of Attack Squadron 25. We opened this container to find 24 extra large (size 44 D) brassieres stuffed with cotton to fill them out and dyed bright green, our squadron color! Each had been sewn so as to fit over every ready room chair in such a manner that someone sitting in that seat would be able to rest his head between those beauties! Not only did the pilots get to enjoy this treat but the enlisted men were allowed to sit in any unoccupied pilot's seat—except for the Skipper's, of course. Spirits were high among the enlisted men and the camaraderie between the pilots was exceptional. After the ORI there was little pressure with inspections and the flying once again was fun and rewarding. There was a lot of competition among squadrons as to landing intervals, bombing scores, and particularly landing grades. Each squadron had one pilot whose primary duty was that of the LSO (Landing Signal Officer) but all of the LSOs had to be qualified to "wave" every type of aircraft onboard. These special people were on the platform just to the port side of the landing area during each and every recovery and they were instrumental in bringing all the planes back to the carrier safely. The LSOs had a vocabulary of their own and wrote down a shorthand critique of each landing. After all planes were recovered, the LSO would stop in each squadron's ready room and debrief each pilot on his landing. He would pull out his little notebook and say things like: LLU (late line up), DNIG (dropped nose in groove), DFD (dove for deck) or the worst of all, DNKUA (damn near killed us all)! Each landing was graded with a color code—Green was basically OK-3 (good approach and caught the number three wire), Yellow was okay with a minor problem or two, Brown was as the color might indicate—shitty, and Red meant that it was dangerous and came close to wiping out the aircraft and pilot. Each squadron kept a chart with each pilot's name and it was quite easy to see which pilots were doing okay and which ones needed some work by looking at the string of colors beside their name. I don't believe that any pilot had all "greenies" but we strived to at least never get a red square next to our name.

Our squadron, VA-25, known as The Fist of the Fleet, had a proud heritage. It was formed before World War II and had served honorably in each war or skirmish since its founding. We were also a colorful group! Each pilot had a long green scarf—reminiscent of World War I aviators—and we would throw that scarf out into the slip stream when we deck-launched (took off without the aid of a catapult). This became our trademark until one day my friend Abe tossed his scarf out as he launched and a visiting Admiral observed this flamboyant maneuver and decreed that this behavior would cease immediately! What an old stick-in-the-mud we all said—but that was the end of our colorful takeoffs.

The AD was the only aircraft aboard the carrier that launched with the canopy open—probably because it was easier to get out of the cockpit in the event of a crash with the canopy not closed. We did not have an ejection seat nor were we able to jettison the canopy if a crash was imminent. In the 1960's probably ninety percent of Navy carrier pilots smoked—today it's less than five percent. I smoked Chesterfields—a carton cost 90 cents aboard the ship—and I lit those cigarettes with my trusty Zippo lighter. I kept my pack of smokes and my lighter in the small pocket on the left upper sleeve of my flight suit. As we became more relaxed with shipboard operations we started to become a bit cocky. We bragged that we could get a cigarette out of that pocket and get it lighted by the time the gear was up! It became a challenge to see just how fast one could get that cigarette lit. One day it almost caused me to—aviator's terminology—buy the farm or bust my ass! I deck launched and was successfully airborne when I closed the canopy with the lever on the left hand side of the cockpit. As I reached forward to raise the landing gear—that lever was to the right—I was suddenly pulled forward and my face was now down into the instrument panel. This caused me to push forward on the stick which was in my right hand and the aircraft headed for the ocean! I heard the Air Boss yell on my frequency, "Pull up, pull up!" I tried to pull back on the stick but my body's forward motion was preventing me from pulling aft. Suddenly I realized that the closing canopy had caught my Zippo lighter and my left arm was useless in trying to reach the lever to reopen the canopy. If I let go of the stick to use my right hand to reach the canopy lever I would probably impact the ocean. My head was now down below the instrument shield and I could not see anything outside—but I could hear the Air Boss yelling to eject! He forgot that my airplane did not have an ejection seat! I pulled my left arm back as hard as I could and suddenly the pocket that contained the cigarette pack and lighter ripped off—I could now pull back on the stick and look outside the cockpit. All I saw in front of me was water and I was heading into it! The engine was still at full power and I'm sure I grunted as I pulled as hard as I could—that reliable Pratt & Whitney saved my life as I skimmed over the surface then soared almost straight up. Later I was told that my airplane disappeared completely when I left the ship and water was splashed on both sides of my wings as I missed the water by inches.

When I later landed on the carrier the Skipper did not know whether to chew me out or give me a hug. He just looked at me and said; "You've used up one of your nine lives!" I decided to quit smoking. I should have kept that bent up old lighter as a souvenir but I sent it back to the Zippo factory because they had a "life time guarantee." I received a brand new lighter in a few months but I never carried it on another flight.

Probably the most dangerous thing in carrier aviation was the dreaded **night deck launch**. None of the pilots wanted to be launched at night without using the catapult and it really made no sense for us to continue this practice. The last time that one of our squadron pilots made a deck launch at night was a memorable one. It was a "dark and stormy night" when Chuck began his takeoff roll—the winds were swirling, there was no visible horizon and that tiny little red light at the forward end of the ship was BURNED OUT! As his aircraft passed the island the wind shifted severely and he drifted to the starboard—then his right gear caught the edge of the flight deck and he flipped over and crashed into the sea upside down! He later recalled that he thought that he could roll the plane and pull out before impact, but suddenly water was in the cockpit and everything was very dark. As he was struggling to release his harness he could hear the screws of the carrier's propulsion system getting closer and his airplane was starting to bump along the underside of the ship. Suddenly he popped up to the surface—again, his recollections—and inflated his Mae West. At night we did not have the helicopters operating for pilot rescue, instead we had a Destroyer that stayed just aft of our ship to recover downed pilots. Chuck now saw that Destroyer bearing down on him as he bobbed along on the surface and was afraid that he was now going to be run down by his own Navy! He pulled out his .38 revolver and started shooting at the approaching vessel. At night we loaded our handguns with tracer ammo and Chuck says that several of his shots bounced off the rescue ship before they changed directions to miss running him over. Nevertheless, my friend was successfully rescued and returned to our carrier the next day via "highline," perhaps almost as scary as a night ditching at sea.

We were elated when Chuck was returned to the ship but we were unified in insisting that night deck launches must stop. The Skipper backed up his pilots and convinced the CAG (Commander Air Group) that this practice was unsafe and really not practical. Everyone listened to reason as night deck launches were cancelled thereafter. The next scariest thing in carrier operations was the night arrested landing. Another Naval Aviation axiom: **The three best things in a pilot's life are 1) a good landing, 2) a good bowel movement, and 3) a good orgasm. The night carrier landing is the only opportunity in life where you can experience all three at the same time!** My logbook shows over 100 night carrier landings and I can honestly say that each one was unique and memorable. Perhaps the most memorable was the first flight off the carrier at night after I was designated a section leader. My wingman was a good friend and the squadron LSO—the only reason that I was the leader was because I was a few months senior to Bob. His experience and great airmanship probably saved my life. Shortly after Bob joined on my wing I lost my radios and I passed the lead to him. I now flew on his wing and was completely dependent on his skills to safely bring me back to the carrier. The weather was bad and getting worse and we were required to fly a CCA. We held above the overcast for over an hour until it became our turn to be vectored into the pattern for radar control that would put us into position to land visually. We were trained for this predicament and the lead aircraft would fly down to a position where the carrier was visible, then break off and let the disabled plane land. All went as planned until we entered the clouds. I was used to flying on my leader's wing and in instrument conditions the wingman tucked in very close and tight on the right hand side. When the lead plane made a left turn the view from the wingman's eye changed slightly as he now saw more of the underside of his leader's aircraft. When Bob rolled into his first left turn I now had this different perspective and was looking at the bottom of his plane. Then I began to get vertigo and could not follow what was happening. I stayed under his aircraft and began to think that he was in a continuous left turn—I was tucked in so tight that I was unable to take my eyes off the leader to look at my instruments. Sweat was starting to roll down my face and into my eyes but no way could I use either hand to wipe my eyes! My right hand had a death grip on the control stick and my left hand was frozen on the throttle. The silence was deafening—since my radios were dead I had no idea where we were or how close we were to the carrier—and I began to think that we were surely in a deadly left spiral into the ocean. I could not break away as the visibility was so bad that I would never find the ship on my own—I thought that I was a goner! Suddenly the gear on the lead plane dropped—almost on top of my canopy—and I had to chop the throttle to avoid passing him by. I was able to drop my own gear and stay in position as the flaps now were being deployed—I shoved the flap lever full down and jammed on the power to keep in position. Now I remembered the tail hook and threw down that lever also—thank God all of these switches and levers were now so familiar that I found them without visual reference. Suddenly my leader disappeared—Oh Shit, I thought, what do I do now! I looked forward and the lights of the carrier deck were right under me. I instinctively closed the throttle and dove for the deck. I was not the least bit concerned with getting a "Greenie" this night. With great relief I felt the tail hook grab a wire and I was aboard!

After Hawaii our next port was Yokosuka, Japan where the carrier was able to berth at the pier and we were able to walk ashore for liberty. This was a great place to shop for electronics—tape decks, record players, cameras, etc. It was springtime and the country was green and beautiful and the people were friendly. There were also many "friendly" bars—some that catered to Officers and others that were frequented by the enlisted men. A huge bottle of the local beer cost less than ten cents and a really good meal was less than one dollar. We were paid aboard ship in MPCs (Military Payment Certificates) instead of greenbacks but the Japanese gladly accepted this type of scrip. This first visit to Japan lasted less than a week and then we were back out to sea. Over the next several months we were to return to Japan several times, not just to Yokosuka but to Sasebo and Atsugi. There was a Naval Air Station located at Atsugi so we would fly our planes ashore and continue flight operations while the ship was in port. I volunteered to take up a "test" hop while in Atsugi—again knowing that I would be flying all alone. I had my brand new 8 mm movie camera purchased in Yokosuka and I decided to take pictures of Mt. Fuji. Almost all the snow was now gone from the top of that majestic peak but it was as incredible sight as I took off from Atsugi's runway and headed directly for a sightseeing tour. I circled the top at least twice and looked down into the crater of that extinct volcano. I decided that there was enough room for me to actually fly down into that crater! I slowed the plane down, eased over the brim and dipped down into the pit that appeared to be about the same diameter as the length of the aircraft carrier. I began taking pictures with my movie camera until things became quite large and it was time to pull up quickly! Occasionally, to this day, I will look at those pictures just to remind me of how stupid I was then at the fearless age of 22!

Hong Kong was a very exciting, vibrant, bustling city that the ship visited only once during that first cruise. This was strictly a liberty call and the carrier anchored outside the entry to the bay—a distance of several miles from the city itself. We used tenders or liberty boats to shuttle the men to shore and back. As a Junior Officer I was assigned as the "Boat Officer" one night and was in charge of one of those liberty boats for several round trips. As the evening grew late the sailors returning to the carrier were becoming more and more drunk and rowdy. Each boat held over sixty men and it seemed that half were throwing up and the other half wanted to fight. Maintaining some semblance of order was next to impossible and several times I thought that I was going to get tossed overboard. Luckily there were always a few senior Petty Officers on each trip who were sober enough to back me up. I was very happy to be "brown shoe" Navy as opposed to "black shoe" Navy and only had this duty once. Aviators were called "brown shoes" because we wore khaki uniforms with brown shoes that the surface Officers did not have.

The Philippines would be the next port of call. The carrier operated around the many islands that make up this nation for several weeks before we entered port at Subic Bay. As the Navigation Officer in the squadron it was my duty to plan and develop long range, low-level routes (sand-blowers) for our pilots to fly while in this area. When planning these routes my main concern was to fly over uninhibited areas but yet see as much of the beautiful countryside as possible. And there was plenty to see in the Philippines! One particular route followed railroad tracks through the jungle until suddenly there appeared a huge volcano. There were no visible signs of life near this volcano such as villages or even roads—probably it had been active in the recent past. The crater in this perfectly formed inverted cone was over one mile in diameter and was filled almost to the brim with sparkling blue water. Then in the center of this beautiful lake was a small island that had its own tiny lake—an incredible bright green that glistened like an emerald! This remains one of the most breathtaking sights I have ever seen in aviation.

Before the ship arrived in Subic Bay we flew our planes ashore to Cubi Point, a Naval Air Station located near Subic Bay and not too far away from Manila. Cubi Pt. was a great place to be for a young Naval Aviator. There was a beautiful sandy beach near the runway where we could swim and water ski, the BOQ was clean and modern, the O'Club had great food, cheap drinks and a magnificent view over the bay—what more could one ask for? Oh, yes— there was Olongapo—sin city of the Far East, just outside the main gate to the Air Base. The only reason for the existence of this city was to entertain the Navy crews who ventured outside the base to sample the sights and sounds of this neon jungle. It was Bourbon Street in New Orleans, Times Square in New York, and the Strip in Las Vegas all rolled up into one long dirty street filled with every bar imaginable! Rock and Roll music blared from loud speakers, Jitneys (WW II jeeps that had been converted to taxis) roared up and down the dusty or muddy street—depending on the weather—and girls of the night were displaying their charms. One could buy carvings of Naval Aviator wings made from monkey-pod wood, cocktail tables made from solid brass, paintings of everything from airplanes to nudes, and San Miguel Beer for ten cents a bottle. The local delicacy sold on the street was called a "balut" which was a duck egg that had been buried in mud before hatching and allowed to ferment—basically it was a rotten embryo of an unborn duckling that smelled as bad as it looked. A few of my more adventuresome friends sampled these delicacies but I stuck to only bottled products! There were some exotic shows at some of the "night clubs" in Olongapo but most were just strip joints like Tijuana. One show that I could not pass up was one that I had heard a lot about from the "old hands" in the squadron—those who had been there before. This show was called the balloon shooting gallery and it was certainly interesting. Three or four young ladies would step onto the stage, completely nude of course, and line up in front of a wooden wall that held a dozen or so colored balloons that were stapled onto the wood. Each girl would lie on her back with legs apart, knees pointing up and insert a DART into her VAGINA (pointy end sticking out of course). Then the MC, speaking broken English, would instruct each girl to shoot at different colored balloons; i.e., the first girl was assigned blue, the second red, etc. These balloons were spaced randomly over the backboard which measured probably 8' X 8' and was located maybe fifteen feet from where the darts were launched. These girls had talent that I never knew was possible—they would fire a dart, reload, fire again and rarely miss their target. At first I thought that there had to be some trickery or use of mirrors but no—they had muscular control and dead aim that would be the envy of the best marksmen in our military! After the first round they fired at balloons from various positions—sitting in a chair, facing backwards while looking between their legs, and leaning against a railing. It was fascinating to watch—not in a sexual way—but I think that all who observed this show were amazed at such a remarkable performance.

After leaving the Philippines the ship operated in the South China Sea and then slowly headed northward to Taiwan and Korea. We flew exercises against the Chinese Nationals on Formosa (Taiwan) to test their air defenses and found them to be quite worthy adversaries. The only way that we were able to reach their island undetected was to come in very low—just what the Skyraider was designed to accomplish. By flying at fifty feet above the ocean's surface we were able to avoid their radar. On one particular exercise I was in sight of land when suddenly we were "shot down" by two ChiNat F-84 jets that flew **beneath** us! We did not think it possible that we could be detected at such a low altitude and were really surprised that they were bold enough to get behind us and fly under our two plane section. During the debrief after the exercise was over I asked the adversary pilots how they located us as I was sure that we were flying too low for radar detection. The Chinese pilot grinned and said, "You were flying so low that your propeller was actually leaving a wake on the water and we spotted it from twenty thousand feet above you!" A lesson learned—fly too low and you will get caught—the best altitude to avoid both radar and visual detection was about 80 feet above the surface. We next flew against the North Koreans to test their reaction times. On this exercise we flew high enough to be detected by the Communist radar to see how rapidly they could scramble their fighters to intercept our planes. We would head directly up the South Korean peninsula toward the 38th parallel as though we were going to penetrate North Korea's airspace—once we saw their interceptors heading toward us we would turn around, and then so did the Communist jets. It was a game we played called "international chicken".

At night the flight deck of an aircraft carrier was not only a very dangerous place during flight operations but it was also a very eerie place to be when flight operations were not being conducted. Often I would walk around the deck late at night when all the airplanes were tied down and little or no activity was going on. Maintenance was performed on planes in the hangar bay so the birds on the flight deck were ready for the next day's operations. All the aircraft except the A4's had their wings folded—the A4 was so small it did not require folding wings—and the wind blowing through the wing racks (where bombs and rockets could be mounted) created a cacophony of whistles and noises heard nowhere else on earth. With every wind shift or change in the ship's heading the noises would change—sometimes louder, sometimes softer, like an orchestra playing hundreds of musical instruments off key and in serious need of a tune up! The ship itself would moan and creak—noises that were not audible during the day with the hustle and bustle of flight operations. I would squat down at the forward end of the flight deck (sitting was out of the question because of all the grease and grime) and feel the wind in my face as the ship plowed through the seas, then walk to the aft end to watch the huge white wake churned up by the massive engines of that mighty ship. One could feel very small at times like those.

Our planes, the AD's, were always parked at the very rear end, usually with the tail hanging over the edge so it was not possible to walk completely around your aircraft while doing the pilot's preflight inspection. At night the plane captain, an enlisted man who was assigned to a particular aircraft, would place a device called a "rudder batten" to anchor the rudder and prevent it from being blown from side to side when hydraulic power was not available. This device was removed before flight as the rudder was a very important flight control for an airplane with such a powerful engine. One night one of our most junior pilots managed to get his airplane airborne with the rudder batten still attached! He was launched from the waist catapult which was located on the angled deck of the ship and therefore did not have far to taxi. The pilot, plane captain and catapult officer all failed to notice that the rudder batten was still attached when it was fired off the deck into the night sky. The rudder was locked in the neutral position and yaw could only be controlled by use of aileron. The pilot discovered this quickly and declared an emergency. I was the Squadron Duty Officer that night and the Skipper was in the ready room when we received the news that the aircraft was airborne with no rudder control. We were hundreds of miles away from land so it was not practical for the problem aircraft to divert to a conventional airport. The Skipper sent me to Pri-Fly (Primary Flight Control Center), where the Air Boss was located, to discuss the technical aspects of trying to land aboard the carrier without use of a rudder. We had only two options—

the plane must land on the carrier without a wave-off, or the plane would have to ditch into the ocean near the carrier and be picked up by the plane-guard Destroyer. If the plane missed the landing cables or had to add power to go-around, it would surely torque roll into the sea without rudder control. The bad news was that this particular pilot was the worst aviator in the squadron and his landing record at night was mostly filled with the color code RED! I explained this to the Air Boss, the Air Operations Officer who was responsible for everything that happened during flight operations, and he decided to let the pilot make one attempted landing on the carrier. The LSO was instructed to wave off the plane if it became unstable no closer than a half mile from the deck. This was so that the aircraft would crash into the sea instead of hitting the carrier if power was added for the missed approach. We all said a silent prayer and had our fingers crossed as the aircraft began its approach. The pilot knew that he had only one chance to get aboard and he flew an almost perfect pass—at the last second he started to go high and his tailhook passed over the number one wire, number two wire, number three wire and then just barely snagged the last wire which brought him to the deck with a terrible landing. It was another RED square on this pilot's chart but he was safely on deck! This was the final carrier landing that this aviator made— he turned in his wings that night and the Skipper gladly accepted his decision.

One night I returned from a routine training flight and had a routine night arrestment—if a night carrier landing can ever be considered routine—and was taxied all the way forward to park on the very edge of the bow with my nose actually over blue ocean. The taxi director, a very brave soul, would stand just to the left of the cockpit and forward of the wing stub to give hand signals for the pilot to follow. He knew exactly where he wanted the wheels to stop and once he gave the "hold brakes" signal he would insert chocks fore and aft of the tire to keep the aircraft in place once the engine was shut down and the brakes were no longer effective. I always had the feeling that I was going over the edge and it took a lot of power to move that plane the last inch or two as I had a lot of pressure on the brakes! After being chocked and getting the "cut" signal from the director I shut down the engine and completed the parking check list to ensure that all switches, knobs, radios and lights were secured. It was a warm evening and I removed my helmet before leaving the cockpit to allow the breeze to cool my sweaty brow. I tossed my flight gloves and kneeboard into my helmet and jumped from the wing to the flight deck, a distance of about three feet. It was pitch black and I lost my balance for a moment—the result was that I dropped my helmet and it started rolling down the flight deck. I scrambled after it and was down on my hands and knees when I finally retrieved the helmet and other items. Just as I started to stand up I felt (rather than heard) a rush of air above my head! I glanced upward and discovered that I had crawled directly under another aircraft that was taxiing forward and the turning propeller was right above my head! Time seemed to pause for an instant then I rolled away to my left as the plane made an emergency stop. This was one of my squadron planes, another AD, and when the pilot hit his brakes hard the nose tipped over and the prop almost hit the deck—right where my head had been a second or two earlier! I stood up and was brushing myself off when another pilot rushed up to me and said, "Are you OK? I saw how close that prop came to you! You better be a little more careful out here." I laughed and said, "Just another routine night carrier landing!" I did not mention that my knees were shaking so much that I could hardly walk!

We normally did not remove our flight helmets, especially at night, until clear of the flight deck. I believe that was the last time I removed mine. However, had I been wearing my helmet I would probably not have "felt" the propeller above me. On the other hand if I had not removed it, then I would not have been in such a predicament in the first place. Another lesson learned, perhaps? The next several months the carrier operated near Japan and we visited Okinawa, Sasebo, and Atsugi before our last stop which was to revisit Yokosuka. As dangerous as carrier operations were, we had experienced only one accident during five months at sea. The Skipper (Commanding Officer) of one of the A4 squadrons was lost one night—evidently he flew into the ocean for some unexplained reason. Maybe he lost his engine and was not able to make a distress call or maybe he had vertigo and lost control—since the plane was never recovered and there were no eye witnesses, I suppose no one will ever know the real reason for that fatal accident. It was easy to get vertigo at night and the worst time of all was on a perfectly clear night with no moon. Stars were everywhere—not only in their usual positions in the sky, but also reflecting on the water—and there was no visible horizon. No matter where you looked—up, down or sideways all you could see were millions of stars. Some of these stars, probably planets, blinked and appeared to move. Some blinked green and red! One of those beautiful clear nights I approached the rendezvous point to join on my leader's wing—we had briefed to meet at 10,000 feet at a certain distance and bearing from the carrier at a speed of 200 knots. I spotted what was surely my leader and could see the red light on the tip of his left wing and the green light on his right wing as I tried to get into position to rendezvous. I didn't seem to be getting any closer so I added power—soon I was almost full throttle—so I called, "Lead, give me a few inches." Manifold pressure was measured in inches and I wanted him to back off on his power a bit so that I would be able to catch him. My leader responded, "I'm indicating exactly 200 knots at the rendezvous point but I don't have you in sight." I replied, "I'm almost on your left wing but can't quite join up." Lead said, "Check your distance and bearing—I still don't have you in sight."

I had been looking out of the cockpit trying to visually join on my elusive "leader" and I now looked down at my instruments. I was indicating almost 250 knots, climbing through 14,000 feet and I was 10 miles from the rendezvous point—obviously I was trying to join up on a star! I now concentrated on flying instruments and disregarding visual cues until I approached the proper meeting place, found my leader and successfully joined up for our assigned training mission. In aviation sometimes you must disregard what your eyes and other senses are telling you and trust those instruments—they will save your life! **Blue water Navy truism: There are more planes in the ocean than there are submarines in the sky.**

One day I was positioned on the port side forward catapult awaiting launch and an A4 was on the starboard cat—his plane was fired first. It was a beautiful clear sunny day with a glassy sea that looked deceptively smooth—but there were deep swells. The Catapult Officer was in control of when the catapult fired. After the pilot went to full power, checked his instruments and gave a salute, the Cat Officer dropped his hand to the deck to signal the launch. In rough seas he timed it so that when he gave this signal the bow was down and the pilot was looking directly into the water ahead! When the plane was launched it left the deck just as the ship's bow was now pointing up! In this profession—Timing Was Everything! The A4 to my right was fired off and I watched as the aircraft left the deck—something did not look right. The plane seemed to decelerate as it left the carrier and the nose came up but the plane started to slowly sink instead of making a normal climb. I heard the Air Boss yell: "Power, power!" Then: "Eject, eject!" The aircraft was now dangerously low less than half a mile from the ship when it started a left turn—the left wingtip was almost touching the water when the pilot ejected. I watched in horror as the pilot in his ejection seat was fired from his disabled aircraft and skipped on the water two or three times before it was all over. The aircraft did a slow cartwheel and disappeared into the sea—suddenly all was smooth on the surface as though nothing had happened. The aircraft was not recovered and only parts of the pilot's body were found by the helicopter. Again we never learned the cause of this tragedy—was it a "cold cat shot," or did the aircraft experience engine failure on the launch? A cold cat shot was when the aircraft weight was miscalculated or the wrong setting was entered into the mechanism that controlled the force with which the aircraft was propelled down the catapult track. Most likely the engine lost power and could not sustain the speed necessary for flight. This was the second and last accident that resulted in a fatality on my first cruise.

This cruise was now nearing its end and we were about to enter port at Yokosuka for a week of liberty before heading back to the U.S. Two nights before this last port call my cruise ended suddenly and painfully. I completed a routine night training flight and made a "routine" night landing. I made my way down the flight deck after parking and securing my aircraft—wearing my helmet, of course—and was about to step through a hatch in the island that led to a ladder down to the hangar deck. An A4 landed on the angle deck and after retracting his hook the pilot started to taxi forward when his left brake locked and the aircraft swerved 90 degrees to the left. The pilot had a lot of power on when this happened and the jet blast of his engine hit me as I was entering the hatch. I felt a hot blast of air on my back and suddenly I was being propelled through that hatch and looking at the ladder going down to the hangar deck some thirty feet below. I stuck out my left arm (my right hand was holding my kneeboard) and caught the railing on the side of the ladder. This broke my headlong fall but also broke my arm! I heard a loud snap and knew immediately that my arm had broken. I was still dangling on that ladder when a sailor below came to my assistance. He grabbed me around my knees and said, "I've got you, sir, let go of the railing and I'll help you down!" My broken arm was bent over that railing at a very ugly angle and I was not able to "let go." With help from two other crew members I was finally taken to sick bay where the ship's surgeon gave me a shot of morphine (and a shot of brandy) and tried to set my arm. He was able to determine from an x-ray that my humerus had broken in two places about two inches apart and the wedge shaped piece of the broken bone was not lined up with the rest of that bone. The doctor told me that he was not equipped to perform the type of surgery that was necessary to align the bones properly. All he could do was put my arm in a "hanging" cast—a very heavy cast that would pull my arm down so that the broken parts would try to align properly. To make it work I had to sit upright so that gravity would do its part and hopefully my arm would straighten out. After a very uncomfortable night I was flown off the carrier the next day to Yokosuka Naval Hospital. That flight was quite an experience!

We had a very small detachment of VAW-11 (Early Warning Squadron Eleven) aboard the Midway and they flew a strange looking aircraft called the WF-2 Tracer. We all called it the "Willie Fudd." Basically, it was a twin-engine prop plane that had been specially configured for electronic warfare. It had a huge circular disk above the fuselage that contained a radar antenna and other "secret" equipment that was used for detecting enemy radar and intercepting enemy communications. We joked that it looked like an airplane that had been captured by a "flying saucer." One of those planes was scheduled to fly to Yokosuka the next day and I was placed on board—still sitting upright with my hanging cast. I was strapped into a crew member's seat facing **AFT!** I was used to a catapult shot facing forward with a back rest for my neck and head—but I never dreamed of launching off a carrier going backward! The "Willie Fudd" was a heavy aircraft so we were given a powerful shot off that steam catapult to get the plane safely airborne. I thought my eyeballs were going to pop out of their sockets and I believe that my tongue leaped out of my mouth as we blasted off that carrier! There was simply no way to prepare for such a rocket shot and my shoulders were bruised for days from the straps that held me in my seat. I forgot all about my broken arm—at least for a few minutes.

I was checked into the Naval Hospital at Yokosuka and soon examined by the orthopedic surgeon. After several x-rays and a thorough physical exam the Doctor gave me the bad news. He said that the humerus was badly broken, with several splinters, and that he would have to place a steel rod in the bone from the shoulder to the elbow. I said, "That's fine, do whatever is necessary, when will I get back to flying?" That's when he looked at me with sadness in his eyes and said, "Son, I'm afraid that this operation will end your flying career." I did not understand and asked him to explain. He told me that a steel rod in my arm would limit my movement both in the shoulder and elbow and added that the Navy did not allow their pilots to fly with metal holding their bones together! This made no sense to me but I asked if there was an alternative to such an operation. He shook his head and said that without the operation my arm would have an angle of approximately 17 degrees and would probably not heal correctly. I could end up with a withered arm! I was not ready to accept the fact that a simple fracture (actually a multiple fracture) of a single bone could end my flying career and asked the doctor if there was any other solution. He said that he would arrange for me to be flown to Oakland, California to the Oak Knoll Naval Hospital where there were specialists in bone grafts. It would take about a week before a flight was available to fly me to California.

I was a very sad patient and my spirits were at an all time low when three of my squadron pilot buddies came to visit about three days later. The carrier had arrived in Yokosuka and my pals came to visit me in the hospital to cheer me up. They had already stopped at the O'Club and were pretty much "cheered up" themselves. They smuggled a bottle of booze into the hospital and soon we were having a bit of a party. I think that I was the only Officer in the hospital and I enjoyed a private room. Suddenly the head nurse interrupted our party and told my friends to leave—she was a tough old broad and a Lieutenant Commander, much senior to me and two of my fiends. My third buddy was the Operations Officer of our squadron and a Lieutenant Commander also. He stood up and told the nurse, "I'm a LCDR too, and probably much senior to you, so I suggest that you leave our group alone and just butt out!" With a big huff the nurse departed and we decided that maybe it was time to move the party somewhere else—surely she would return with a more senior medical officer. My pals had rented three motor scooters and talked me into going with them to the O'Club to continue our party. They helped me get dressed in my white, short sleeved uniform (the only thing I could wear with that hanging cast) and I got onto the back of a motor scooter behind my roommate Rex and we zoomed off to the O'Club.

As we bounced along over the rough roads leading to the O'Club I could feel and HEAR the bones in my broken arm grinding together! The cast extended from my wrist to just below my armpit and the part of my arm visible above the cast was very colorful—blue, black, yellow and red! It was only a short trip to the club but I was in a lot of pain by the time we arrived. A few drinks took care of that problem and we proceeded to have a great time. I don't remember the trip back to the hospital but I woke up the next morning with a bad headache and a very sore arm. The nurse seemed to enjoy my misery and the doctor just shook his head. In a few days I was flown to the

U.S. and placed in the orthopedic unit of Oak Knoll Naval Hospital. The head orthopedic surgeon there was a career Naval Medical Officer and he seemed to take a personal interest in my case. He looked over my records, took several x-rays, and performed a personal physical exam. I was impressed with his thoroughness but his "bedside manner" left a bit to be desired. I asked him about my prognosis and when would I be able to return to flight status. His first statement was to the effect that it was unfortunate that my broken arm had not been properly set by the surgeon on the carrier. I thought that the ship's surgeon did the best he could under the circumstances but now I was only interested in the future. This doctor, a full Commander, confirmed what I had already been told. My humerus had been shattered and there was a wedge shaped part of the bone, three inches on one side and two inches on the other, that had been separated from the rest of the bone. The Commander reiterated that the normal (and best) procedure was to operate and insert a steel rod from the shoulder to the elbow. Then he confirmed the opinion that I probably would not be able to return to flight status after this operation. I asked if there was a plan "B"—something that could be done to fix the bone other than the steel rod. He thought for a moment or two, looked at me with a smile, and said, "I can rebreak the bone and start all over—maybe we can reset it properly—probably a low percentage procedure." I thought it over and said, "Will it hurt?" He laughed and said, "You won't feel a thing—I promise."

I did not feel a thing—I was completely sedated—and the procedure went well. However, I was now fitted with an even larger cast that extended from above my shoulder to my hand. Now I could not move any of those three joints, the shoulder, elbow or wrist, and the cast was **very heavy!** It was still a hanging cast so I had to continue to sleep sitting up. I spent over two weeks in this hospital and was starting to get very bored. Thankfully, my girlfriend visited often and we went to movies on the base and had dinner and drinks at the Officer's Club. I was not allowed to leave the Hospital complex and was starting to get "cabin fever." My spirits were lifted one day when some unexpected visitors paid me a call. The USS Midway had returned and my squadron was now back at Moffett Field—the Skipper and several of my pals stopped to see me at the Hospital. I was especially impressed that they had taken the time to stop and visit with me when their family obligations were so pressing. I was eager to get back to the action!

When the day finally arrived for me to be discharged (with the stipulation that I must return every two weeks for check-ups) my girlfriend picked me up in my little MGA. I insisted that I was going to drive and with a lot of help I was able to get into the left seat with my big cast and we were off! The manual four-speed transmission was a bit of a challenge but I thought I was doing great until I heard a siren and a police car pulled me over—just a few blocks from the hospital. The Officer came to my window and asked for me to step out of the car. I tried my best but finally had to ask for help to get out. The Officer looked me over and said, "How the hell did you ever get into that tiny seat with that huge cast in the first place?" He asked to see my driver's license and registration. I was not able to reach my billfold but the Officer was kind enough to give me a hand. My girlfriend produced the registration. The Officer perused the documents, looked at me and said, "You have a Virginia driver's license, your car is registered in Florida, and you live in California— is that correct?" I mumbled, "Yes sir." He said, "At least two of those three things should agree—let me guess, are you in the military?" It turned out that the police officer had served in the Marine Corps and we spent several minutes talking about the military. Then he helped me to get back into the driver's seat, told me to take it easy, and wished me good luck. As he was walking away I asked, "By the way, why did you pull me over, I wasn't speeding." He said, "Oh, I stopped you to tell you that your rear window needs to be replaced—there's no way that you can see through it." I had noticed that the sun had blackened the small plastic window in the convertible cover but obviously I had not had time to get it fixed. He pulled a pocket knife out of his uniform trousers and added, "Want me to give it a temporary fix so you won't be pulled over again?" I nodded and he proceeded to cut the opaque piece of plastic out, folded it up, gave me a sharp salute and said, "Semper Fi, Lieutenant!" and walked away.

I moved into the BOQ at Moffett Field and checked into my squadron— again it was early post-cruise and very little was going on as most of the Officers and men were on leave. The Executive Officer welcomed me back and informed me that I was now the permanent Squadron Duty Officer (SDO) until I could return to flying. I was not happy with this assignment but had to admit that it made good sense. The other J.O.'s in the squadron were very pleased as they were mostly relieved of this onerous duty. I had two days off each week—sometimes on weekends, sometimes during the week—and was not required to spend the night at the duty desk. However, I was on call through the night in case anything out of the ordinary occurred. As squadron operations began to get back to normal with day and night flying I became quite busy as the SDO. In a way it was rewarding as I was doing a service to my fellow pilots and after a while it became routine. It also made the time of my healing pass quickly. On my second biweekly visit to Oak Knoll Hospital I was able to convince the doctor to remove the big cast and replace it with a smaller one—I was about to go nuts trying to relieve the itching on my arm deep inside that cast! The Doc did me one better—he replaced the old cast with a bi-valve cast that was basically a cast that had been sawed into two pieces that were held in place with a tightly wound ace bandage. I was told that I could remove the cast once a day for a shower but must replace it promptly. I was appalled at the appearance of my arm when the cast was removed. My muscles had atrophied to the point that my arm was only half as large as the other arm and it was downright ugly! The doctor, however, seemed pleased with my progress and promised that we could start physical therapy in another month or two. Then in six months or so I could be evaluated for return to flight status. There was no way that I was going to remain the SDO for another six months!

The cast came off within hours of leaving the hospital and I started my own physical therapy. By the end of the first week I only wore the cast at night and on my next visit to the hospital I had trouble finding those two pieces of plaster! The doctor was impressed with my progress but insisted that I was not to start therapy for another month. A week later I had a meeting with the squadron flight surgeon. Each squadron was assigned one physician who was a qualified flight surgeon—meaning that he had received special training in aero medical studies and had actually flown a few flights in Navy aircraft, with an instructor of course. When the squadron was shore-based he was assigned to the base hospital or clinic and when we were aboard ship he was assigned to the ship's medical facility. Therefore, we rarely saw our flight surgeon except during routine physical exams, but he was available for any medical problem or question that any of the pilots had. Our flight surgeon, whose name was Bob, was really a great guy who was always invited to our parties and squadron social functions. He later became a flight surgeon for United Airlines and we continued our professional and personal relationship for many years. I told Bob that I was ready to return to flight duty and asked that he give me an "up chit" which was a written authorization for a pilot to return to flying after being medically grounded. He knew that I was still under treatment at the orthopedic department of Oak Knoll Naval Hospital and he also knew that he was outranked by the Commander that was my physician. What I was asking of him could get us both in a lot of trouble. I told Bob how badly I wanted to get back to flying and insisted that he, as the squadron flight surgeon, had not only the right but the duty to return qualified pilots to flight status. He looked at me and said, "You've been practicing that little speech, haven't you?"

I felt that I had been caught with my hand in the cookie jar but I challenged him to check me out and decide for himself if I was ready to go back to flying. He conducted a cursory physical exam—vision, blood pressure, lungs, etc.— then began a very thorough testing of my left arm. He checked my reflexes with the little rubber hammer to my elbow, had me stretch and reach in every direction, and then said to give him five push-ups! I had been working very hard on regaining my strength but I was aware that the arm was not yet back to one hundred percent—I had not attempted push-ups. Without hesitation I assumed the prone position and gave him five—hoping that my left arm would not snap under the pressure. I admit that my RIGHT ARM was doing most of the work but I hoped that the doctor would not notice. Bob had a suspicious look on his face then his features softened and he said, "I don't think that you can win many arm wrestling matches, but I'm going to go out on a limb and return you to flight status." I was ecstatic and thanked the doc profusely. He said, "Get out of my office, and let's hope that we both don't get court-martialed!"

It had now been almost three months since my last flight and I was "rarin' to go" but just a bit apprehensive after such a long lay off. I flew as wingman for the Operations Officer, a good friend, and everything went well. I had a little difficulty operating the flap control as it was on the left side and could only be moved with the left hand—but I was able to rapidly get back into the flying "mode." I flew on his wing for the first part of the flight, then we changed lead and he flew on my wing. I signaled for him to get into the "tail chase" position (the wingman would fly about two plane lengths behind and below the leader) and I started mild aerobatics. After a few wing-overs and barrel-rolls I did several aileron rolls, a loop or two, and ended up with a full Cuban-eight! Not a word from my wingman who was not visible to me in the tail chase position and I was not sure if he was still with me. I wagged my tail—a signal to join up on my starboard wing—and instantly he popped into position. By the big grin on his face I knew that he had enjoyed our little tail chase fun! We returned to base and I made several touch and go landings until I was comfortable with the landing pattern, then I made a full stop and taxied to our ramp. As I shut down the aircraft and stepped down from the cockpit I noticed about a dozen of my fellow pilots waiting for me by the hangar. They all greeted me with handshakes and back slaps as if I had been away for a year or two. It felt really good to be back! However, more than one of the junior aviators commented—"Guess we have to start being Duty Officers again, huh?" Shortly thereafter we all headed over to the O'Club for happy hour— it didn't take much to give us a reason to celebrate!

My next visit to Oak Knoll was something that I was not looking forward to—I had disobeyed the Commander's orders but felt that I had done the right thing. I believed that I was indeed ready to return to flight status and that the orthopedic surgeon was way too conservative. I was examined not by the Commander but by a nurse who implied that everything was on schedule and my progress was more than satisfactory. I asked to speak with the Commander and was taken to his office where he was busy with paper work—the scourge of Naval bureaucracy. He seemed happy to see me and apologized for not examining me himself, then commended me for my excellent progress to date. He ended with the comment, "You know, we might have you back to flying in less than six months!" I cleared my throat and confessed, "Sir, I have already returned to flight status and everything is just fine." His face started to turn red and the veins on his neck became prominent. He roared, "Who cleared you to go back to flying?" I stammered that it was my fault but I had talked my squadron flight surgeon into returning me to flight status and he had cleared me after a thorough examination. The Chief Orthopedic Surgeon looked at me and sighed, "Get out of here, Lieutenant, you are dismissed!" Before I left his office he added, "My life would be a lot easier if I didn't have to take care of Naval Aviators!"

Life as a Naval Aviator became much more pleasant now that I had returned to flight duty. The routine of our training cycle was comfortable, rewarding and FUN! We spent a lot of time with weapons deployments to Fallon, Nevada and Yuma, Arizona and we visited an aircraft carrier almost every month to maintain our proficiency with shipboard operations. We flew a lot of sandblower missions to interesting places throughout the western half of the United States—and we had fun flying what we called "non-productive hops." These were the hops that were spent doing things like "tail chase"— often in a flight of four. The leader would put all of us into that loose trail formation and proceed to do his best to lose his wingmen! The object of each of the wingmen was to hang in there and stay in formation. It was a daisy-chain type of thing as the last man was getting whip-sawed with every turn and maneuver. A good wingman focused on one spot—a relative position on his leader such as where the leader's wingtip lined up with the leader's canopy and controlled his throttle and stick to keep those two points in alignment. The tail chase changed everything—the wingmen were now trying to stay in position behind the leader with only one thing to look at—his tail! We often conducted these fun flights in the late afternoon when the clouds were starting to wane and the sun was beginning to go down. A good leader used all of these things to his advantage—flying into the setting sun or dipping in and out of a fluffy white cloud. The wingman tried not to be distracted by the glare of the sun or the loss of visibility in the clouds. When the lead entered the clouds the wingmen naturally tucked in closer to keep the aircraft in front in sight—however it was now a quandary as it was hard to maintain position on a fast moving leader while in the clouds. Drop back a bit and you were out—stay in tight and you were looking straight up at the bottom of the aircraft in front—neither situation was advantageous. I sincerely believe that this type of flying, not listed in the syllabus, was just as important as the structured training cycle, if not more so.

Three of us bachelor pilots decided to move out of the BOQ and into a "snake ranch" outside the base. We found a three bedroom ranch-style home for rent located in Los Altos, a suburban community only minutes from Moffett Field. This house was fully furnished down to sheets, towels, pots and pans, and even toilet paper! The owners were a young couple going through a divorce who seemed to trust their belongings to three Officers and Gentlemen! The house was located on a large lot with a beautifully landscaped yard and several citrus trees in the back. We always had a lime or orange slice for our drinks! This was a great place to hold parties and soon most of our squadron functions were held at our house. To prevent our neighbors from complaining about our noisy gatherings we decided to always invite them to our parties and most enjoyed the levity we brought to their neighborhood. There were only a few problems and they usually involved the female neighbor. Several of our lady neighbors began to spend too much time trying to either reform us and change our wicked ways or to fix us up with their single girlfriends. A few had other motives. One night as one of our parties was winding down I went out the back door to take out some trash (mostly beer cans and liquor bottles) to deposit in our outside garbage can. As I turned to go back inside I saw one of the neighbor ladies blocking my way— she was breathing hard and had a look about her that told me that I was in trouble. She grabbed me before I was able to get back inside and started to smother me with wet sloppy kisses while grinding her pelvis into mine. She was not unattractive but a bit over weight—plus, her husband was inside and he was at least twice my size! I tried to get out of her clutches and began trying to calm her down. She said, "Don't play with me—I'm serious, we can do it right here." I'm thinking—RIGHT HERE?—on top of the garbage can or up against the fence—which would be the most romantic? I wanted to laugh at the absurdity of it all but I was too frightened that someone (her really big husband) was going to come out and catch us in this embarrassing situation. I finally pushed her away and dashed for the door and the safety of a crowded room. In a few minutes she came in also and acted like nothing had transpired between us. Later when she and her husband were leaving she whispered into my ear, "I'll get you sooner or later and you will see what you missed out on tonight!" I smiled and replied, "Good night and good luck!"

My relationship with my girlfriend was becoming more serious and we were becoming a "couple" as she joined in with and was accepted by our little group of pilot's wives. I was not sure if this was what I wanted as I knew that I was not yet ready to settle down, even though the married life was something that I looked forward to eventually. I was obligated to fly as a Naval Aviator for several more years and was not sure that marriage was a good idea with the separations and dangers inherent in my job. I guess that I was just not ready to "commit!" As usual the Navy took care of the problem— it was time to move. Another Navy saying: **IF THE NAVY WANTED YOU TO HAVE A WIFE, THEY WOULD HAVE ISSUED YOU ONE!**

A new Naval Air Station had been commissioned in the San Joaquin Valley thirty miles south of Fresno, California and we received orders to relocate all light attack squadrons to this base in Lemoore, a rural community known mainly for cotton and grape fields, scorching summers and dismal foggy winters.

Chapter Nine

**"Airspeed, altitude, brains. Two are always needed to
successfully complete the flight."**

NAS Lemoore was a real cultural shock. I always wondered just why a
NAVAL station was built so far away from the ocean in the middle of the
desert—the obvious answer, politics! The squadron relocated to its new
shore base in January 1963—in the middle of the fog season. I thought I knew
something about fog but I was totally unprepared for what was known as **tule
fog**—a dense, heavy, pea soup type of fog that settled down to the ground and
stayed for weeks. The name of this type of fog was derived from a large
bulrush indigenous to lakes and marshes throughout the San Joaquin Valley.
The top of this thick muck was usually about 1500 feet above the surface and
it was crystal clear once above this altitude—the problem was trying to land
in such poor visibility. The type of crops grown in what was called "the big
valley" depended upon a specific number of days each year of such fog—too
much fog was bad for the grape and raisin harvest, too little fog was bad for
cotton and melons. The fog season was simply bad for aviation!

I moved into the BOQ at the Naval Air Station and was impressed with the
facilities and amenities on this gigantic base. It was about eight miles from
the Administrative end of the base to the Operations side and the speed limit
was 55 MPH—I was used to speed limits of 25-35 on every other base where
I had been stationed. On one of the first nights at NAS Lemoore I was driving
from Ops to the BOQ and unfortunately hit a jack rabbit with my sports car—
there were literally thousands of such hares on the base—and I stopped to put
the poor creature out of its misery as it was still alive. My only experience
with rabbits had been the small cottontails I hunted as a young lad in Virginia
and I was unprepared for such a huge animal as I lifted it from the roadway

and tried to mercifully end its suffering with a blow to its neck. I almost broke my hand—this rabbit was tough! I dropped the poor thing on the ground; it shook its head, looked at me and hopped away into the darkness. Maybe my little tap to its neck was just what it needed to shrug off this encounter with my automobile!

My buddy, Jim (nickname Snag) and I decided to look for an apartment in town. The town of Lemoore was quite small and apartments were in short supply with all the Navy personnel and their dependents starting to arrive. We decided to look in Hanford, a slightly larger town a few miles further away from the base than Lemoore. We looked at apartments one afternoon after work, then had dinner and took in a movie in Hanford. When we left the movie theatre it was now dark and the fog had settled in—we had trouble finding my car parked in front of the theatre. As we tried to drive back to the base the visibility went down to near zero. I was driving about 10 MPH with my head out the window on the driver's side and Snag was trying to help with his head outside on the passenger's side. I finally had to drive with the left wheels on the pavement and the right wheels on the shoulder to ensure that I stayed on the road. We were about to give up when another car passed us with a friendly toot of its horn. I immediately fell in behind this car and "flew formation" on its taillights—the driver was obviously more familiar with the highway and the fog conditions than me and he was traveling at almost 20 MPH. After several stops and turns the vehicle I had followed came to a complete stop and the driver got out. He walked up to my window and said, "Fellows, I'm in my driveway and this is as far as I'm going tonight!" I explained that I had followed him hoping that he was going to the base and I was basically hopelessly lost in this fog. He was very helpful and gave detailed instructions on how to find my way to NAS Lemoore. We thanked him and started off again—after a while Snag got out of the car and walked down the highway in front of the car. That was the only way that I could keep on the pavement. Eventually we found the air base and breathed a sigh of relief that we had survived our first episode of the dreaded TULE FOG!

There were very few cultural activities such as museums, live theatres, or social clubs to occupy the spare time of the Navy personnel. The Officers Club was the only place to go for socializing but it was not open to the local citizens—unlike the clubs at Pensacola, Corpus Christi, San Diego, and Moffett Field where single females were allowed to enter the base almost without question. Our country was not at war but NAS Lemoore was considered a strategic base and therefore the security was considerably stricter. Since the ladies could not come to us, we had to go outside the base and find them! Necessity being the mother of invention, a bright entrepreneur opened a bar/restaurant just a mile or so from the main gate to the base and named it "The Flying Spinnaker." This place catered to the pilots and it was just what we liked—lousy food, warm beer, watered down drinks but a great happy hour with a huge wheel of cheese, some grapes and crackers. You could whack off a large chunk of that cheese with the meat cleaver provided and make a meal of the hors d'oeuvres. On Friday afternoon the place was loaded with the local girls looking for exactly the same thing that we were there for. The first time I walked up to the bar there was not a single empty stool—each seat was occupied with a young lady who had the exact same appearance as the young lady to her left or right. Each had a bee-hive hairdo, lots of make up, a skimpy skirt and a mouth full of chewing gum! They were all talking to each other at a mile a minute and simply did not slow down to say hello to us eligible males. It was like a High School dance—girls on one side and the guys on the other. After several drinks the lines began to merge—our advances were no longer turned down flat by the ladies and the men began to find that these young ladies had many subtle charms that were accentuated by the amount of alcohol consumed. **AVIATION TRUISM: THE DIFFERENCE BETWEEN A FIGHTER PILOT AND A PIG? A PIG IS SMART ENOUGH NOT TO SIT AT A BAR UNTIL 0300 WAITING TO PICK UP A FIGHTER PILOT!**

Flying was fun and challenging at NAS Lemoore, especially during the foggy season. Often we had to delay operations until the fog lifted, usually around noon, and try to complete our hops before the fog arrived again after sunset. Several times we were not able to return to land at our home base and we had to divert to NAAS China Lake or another military airport out of the fog belt. We learned to carry a bit of cash and a change of underwear to prepare for these diversions. NAAS China Lake (Naval Auxiliary Air Station) was the location of the Naval Test Squadron that tried out new aircraft and weapons systems—the equivalent of Edwards Air Force Base for the Air Force. When we had to land at China Lake we usually ended up having "food and beverage" at the Officer's Club. The test pilots were eager to talk to us about fleet operations and we were eager to ask them about the new "stuff" that they were testing. These conversations usually lasted for several hours and often ended up at one of the local off-base saloons. We were usually grateful that the fog in Lemoore did not lift until after noon so we were able to sleep-in a bit the next morning. Some of the test pilots were starting to become involved in a new space program—something called astronaut training—and I was intrigued. I soon applied for the NASA space program—along with a few thousand others—and was subsequently turned down because I did not have a degree in Aeronautical Engineering, a prerequisite at the time.

The routine at NAS Lemoore became deadly. We would fly all week and drink all weekend—many of my friends would end their lives not in an airplane crash but at the wheel of their sports car trying to drive while intoxicated—often in the fog. It became a problem that the Navy could not ignore—twice as many aviators were being killed in auto accidents as in airplane crashes. The obvious solution was to open the gates so that the local ladies could gain entry to the base and the weekend trysts could be confined to the BOQ. This did not sit well with the Officers wives and only lasted a month or two. I decided that I needed a vehicle that was more sturdy and safer than my little peach colored MGA roadster. As soon as I made the final payment to the Navy Federal Credit Union it seemed logical to trade it in on a new vehicle so that my payments would continue forever. I found a 1962 Mercury Monterey Custom Convertible that I could not live without—black with a white top—just what I needed for my new lifestyle in the Central Valley. Shortly after getting this car I was assigned as the "movement officer" for the squadron's deployment to NAAS Fallon in Nevada for weapons training. The entire unit moved to Fallon for three weeks of intense training in conventional and nuclear weapons delivery and one of the Junior Officers was given the duty to arrange for men and equipment to make such a move—it was my turn for this assignment. It was necessary for me to go to Fallon in advance to lay the groundwork for the squadron's arrival and I decided to drive my new car there—it was springtime and the weather was forecast to be excellent. My previous weapons deployment to Fallon, just to the East of Reno, had been during the winter when it was bitter cold and I was looking forward to having my own vehicle to enjoy a few off-base excursions. I also became very popular with my fellow aviators as I was the only Officer with wheels!

Every fighter and attack squadron in the Pacific fleet was required to deploy for weapons training at least once and usually twice during each training cycle between cruises. Most of these deployments were to Fallon but occasionally we went to Yuma, Arizona. Fallon later became the base for Top Gun School, made famous by Tom Cruise's movie. We flew two hops each day six days a week with only Sunday being a down day. Our flights were scheduled early each morning and we were finished by noon—except during the third week when we practiced night bombing and strafing. Each flight lasted only about one hour but it was a very busy hour as we were pulling a lot of "G's" on each dive bomb run. We also practiced low level bomb runs where we flew at a target at "masthead" height of less than one hundred feet above the ground—simulating an attack on enemy ships. We often dropped napalm on these runs which were spectacular to watch from the cockpit as we pulled up and rolled over to see the results behind the aircraft. If you got too close to the conflagration on the ground you could feel the heat in the cockpit! Another maneuver we practiced was for nuclear weapons delivery, called the LABS (Low Altitude Bombing System) maneuver. We flew as low and fast as our aircraft were capable toward a target and then pulled up into what was called an "idiot loop" to perform a vertical u-turn and depart the target area on the same track we followed inbound. The pilot experienced six G's on this maneuver and the object was to not black out entirely. When the pilot began getting tunnel vision, leading to loss of consciousness, he would relax a bit on the stick and start the roll-out to end up on the reciprocal heading from his inbound track. This maneuver required unique piloting skills as it was performed partly on instruments but mostly by the "seat of one's pants." The purpose of such a maneuver was for the pilot to survive the fireball of the nuclear weapon that would be launched from the aircraft as it pulled up into the idiot loop. Many of us had serious doubts as to the soundness of such a procedure—luckily we were never required to drop those nukes to see if we could survive!

As pilots, we led a regimented life during our weapons training deployment. On the positive side, we left the paperwork at NAS Lemoore and concentrated solely on honing our flying skills. The bottom line was that weapons delivery was what we were all about—and we needed to train to put those weapons that we carried on target. We arose each morning before dawn, grabbed a quick bite at the Officer's Mess and were briefing our flights by 0500. We were in the air by 0600 to various bombing ranges scattered throughout the restricted areas surrounding NAAS Fallon. Back on the ground about an hour later to debrief, rearm, and brief again for the next flight which launched around 0900. By noon we were finished for the day—and our butts were dragging from the intensity of the flying and the constant pulling of "G's." Normally we would head to the Officers Club for lunch, each of us solemnly pledging that we were going to take a long rest in the afternoon to recover from the rigors of the night before and the stress of that morning's flying. Guess what—after a couple of beers with lunch we began to talk about the fun we had the day before and maybe we were not so tired after all! Instead of that long nap or restful afternoon we ended up taking a quick shower, changing into civvies and heading to town by two PM. Most of us headed to our favorite gambling joints—Fallon did not have Casinos like Reno and Las Vegas—and the dealers knew us by our first names. Beer was free while we gambled and food was available at a nominal charge. None of us ever admitted that we lost money and most bragged about how much money was won at the blackjack or crap tables. I was happy to break even and rarely did I lose more than I could afford. There were a few serious gamblers in our squadron—my old roommate "Bum" was probably the worst of that lot and he always said that he never lost. However, he was always borrowing from the rest of us—you figure!

After an afternoon and evening of drinking and gambling we returned to the Air Station, usually after midnight, and after a few short hours of sleep we started the process all over again—déjà vu! One Friday afternoon we stayed as a group at the Officers Club to enjoy "happy hour" instead of going to town to gamble. Our Skipper was a great guy who was known to us Junior Officers only as "Skipper" but was called Smitty by the LCDR's and above. As happy hour was winding down (about nine PM) the Skipper stood up and announced in a loud authoritative voice, "We're all going to the Mustang Ranch, and that's an order!" The notorious Mustang Ranch bordello was located halfway between Fallon and Reno and was less than 30 minutes away from the base. Not wanting to disobey a direct order we all stood at attention and shouted, "Yes Sir!" We piled into three or four vehicles—the Skipper came with me as I had the newest and most reliable car—and off we went to the little town of Fernley, Nevada, home of the Mustang Ranch.

Fernley was too small to need a traffic light but there was a flashing red light at the only intersection in town—a four way stop light. This being Friday night there was a traffic cop on duty at this intersection to control the stream of vehicles, some heading for the bright lights of Reno, others turning into the compound known as the Mustang Ranch. I stopped at the four-way stop light, rolled down the window to ask the officer for directions and before

I could open my mouth he said, "It's just to your left, have fun gentlemen!" and continued to direct traffic. I made the left turn and at the end of the block there was a well-lighted group of buildings surrounded by a twenty foot tall barbed wire fence that was illuminated as though it was a prison compound. The pavement ended at a large parking area that was also lit by bright lights on tall poles. We walked to the main gate as a group—about twelve Naval Officers, most of us still in uniform—and pressed a button on the heavily fortified gate. This place had state of the art security and we were all quite impressed. It was obvious that we were being observed by surveillance cameras, not common during the early sixties. Shortly a female voice came over a loudspeaker, "May I help you?" We assured the voice that we were not planning an invasion and that we were not the authorities on a raid. After a short delay the gate was opened electronically and we entered this fabled place.

As we walked toward the main building the door opened and the silhouette of a large woman appeared. She looked large because she was elevated from our position and she had her hands on her hips—we were not able to make out her features due to the light streaming behind her. As we took the few steps up to the porch she seemed to shrink and now appeared to be a normal sized female with ample proportions—especially as the light behind her was shining through her skimpy clothing and very little was left to the imagination. All in all it was a very sexy introduction to this palace of pleasure. The Skipper was in charge, as he should be, and he introduced himself to the Madam and requested permission to come aboard! The Madam snorted and said, "You Navy guys are always welcome, just don't try to wear out my girls!" We entered a large reception room that had a bar at the far end. I and several of my JO buddies headed for that bar to get a cold beer. The Skipper was negotiating with his new friend, the Madam, about prices and amenities for his men. A good Commanding Officer always took care of his men first, and Smitty was a great C.O. Soon the Madam produced the available ladies of the evening for his inspection. He lined them up—about ten in all—and walked by each one as though conducting a parade drill. He lifted a few skirts and peeked down a few necklines but it was done in a very Officer-like fashion and no one was offended—in reality the girls loved it and giggled a lot. I think that they were given more respect by our Skipper than they were used to in their chosen line of work. Several of our group picked out their favorite and departed to other rooms—I ended up playing poker with the

Skipper, the Madam and two other pilots until the wee hours. We laughed and joked and were provided with snacks and drinks—after a while there were no charges for either! Several of the girls joined our group and we all had a fun time. Strangely, the girls made no advances on us and we did not hit on them—they seemed to relax and have a bit of fun without the norm—paid for sex. When we left we all felt that a good time was had by all, the girls begged us to return, the Madam promised that we could always get a "freebie" and the Skipper received a sincere smooch from the boss. This was my one and only visit to the infamous Mustang Ranch and the conclusion I made: Really a nicely run establishment that provided a basic service for a decent price with employees who seemed happy and well-compensated. One of my pals, the most junior pilot in the squadron, a happy-go-lucky kid from New York City named Abe, fell in love with his paid partner that evening. He paid for her services three times that night (five bucks each orgasm) and thought she was the finest lady he had ever met. He wanted to take her out on dates and even talked about introducing her to his parents. He was sincerely infatuated and it was several months before he realized that it was probably best that he move on without this lady of the night. I often wondered what would have happened if they had ended up getting married—it might have been the best thing for both. I do believe that whores make excellent wives!

On weekends I would drive around the local desert area and do some hiking with several of my pals. We always took our .38 pistols to protect us against rattlesnakes and we spent our annual allotment of ammo trying to shoot the elusive jackrabbits that were so numerous in the high desert. I decided to climb a small peak with a flat sandy top that we flew over each time we departed the base en route to the bombing ranges. It turned out that this little hill was about an eight hundred foot climb over very rugged terrain. Several of us climbed to the top and decided that we should erect a monument to our squadron for all other pilots to look at each time they flew from the base to the target range. We spent a long Saturday afternoon arranging lava rocks on the white sand to spell out—VA-25—THE FIST OF THE FLEET. We later talked the base helicopter pilot into taking some photos of our artistic accomplishment and we proudly had those pictures posted in Approach—the Magazine of Naval Aviation. Perhaps that monument still exists—doubtful!

After finishing our project we stopped at a road house called the Wagon Wheel Saloon on the way back to the Naval Air Station. This was a local hangout that catered mostly to the Piute Indians and local ranchers in the area.

116

It was shortly after sunset when we stopped for a cold beer or two. We were tired, dirty and very thirsty after our work on the mountain top and only planned to have a short stop for beverages. The place was not crowded when we arrived but it was apparent that they were preparing for a big crowd that evening. A small band was setting up their equipment for entertainment and the bartender promised that there would be a lot going on shortly. The four of us were in need of showers and a change of clothes but all in all we were in better shape than most of the arriving clientele. We all had our .38's strapped around our waists and no one seemed to notice or be the least bit concerned— I began to realize that most of these cowboys were also packing hardware. The band started playing and the place was beginning to get crowded. Several of the Indian ladies were becoming aggressive and asking my friends and myself to dance—it was time to leave before things got out of hand! We were finishing our last drinks when a couple walked through the front door—a beautiful lady and an older man, unlike the other rough women and young men in attendance. We watched as the two found a small table near the bar and sat down to order a drink. We all thought that the old geezer was the sugar daddy and the siren was taking him to the cleaners—what a pity. The lady appeared to be in her late twenties and was very well dressed—but it was hard for her to hide her voluptuous body no matter what she wore. The old guy, on second glance, was not well dressed and seemed almost seedy—something did not add up. They did not show any affection toward each other and when drinks were ordered the lady paid—not the old guy. My pals were ready to leave and I decided that we should stay for one more beer. Since I was driving, I had the deciding vote.

In a few minutes the old guy ambled off to the rest room and I was tempted to go ask that gorgeous lady if she wanted to dance, kiss, fornicate? I snapped out of it and realized that I was as grungy and smelly as all the other men in this bar and she could have her choice of them all. Surely I would be in the back of the pack! I was finishing my beer when the old geezer returned from the latrine and tapped me on the shoulder. In a shaky voice he said, "I'm just a taxi driver and this lady asked me to take her somewhere she could dance— would you mind dancing with her?" I tried to stay calm and nodded in the affirmative. But before I had a chance to ask her to dance I saw a large raw-boned cowboy lean over her table and invite her out onto the dance floor. She smiled but shook her head no—I was elated and headed her way—with less confidence than I wished for. It seemed that the cowboy was not about to take no for an answer and I was not sure that I should continue. I thought—what the hell, let's see what happens, and barged right in. I took her hand and said, "I believe that this is our dance." She smiled and said, "Yes it is, thank you for remembering!" She stood up and we stepped out onto the dance floor where we came together and she whispered into my ear, "Thanks for rescuing me." She was wearing a very simple dress and when I placed my arm around her waist it was evident that there was nothing beneath this wisp of cotton. She pressed her body against mine and I suddenly wished that I had taken a shower and was wearing something other that a smelly old flight suit. We danced and I lost all thought except how good she felt against me—when the song stopped we clung together until the next one started—I was breathless and she was moaning. We had to get out of this place. She breathed in my ear, "I'm staying in a motel in Fallon, can we go there?" I said, "Let's go, I'll have my friends take your taxi back to the base." I returned to the bar, told my pals that they were on their own but that they should go with the cab driver, slipped the old geezer five bucks, and headed out the door with this beauty—pinching myself all the way!

We hardly talked during the drive to her motel. She held my hand and sat very close to me as we drove the twenty miles or so—she said her name was Debbie and that she was from Sacramento. When we arrived at her motel on the outskirts of Fallon, she asked that I please leave my gun in the car. I had forgotten that I still had the .38 around my waist so I quickly took off the gun belt and put it into the trunk of my car. Once inside the motel room we both decided that a shower was an urgent necessity for me. I peeled off my flight suit and my underclothes and jumped into the shower. "Debbie" said that she would mix drinks for us. As I stood under the shower washing off the dirt and grime from the hike and project, I suddenly had a very uncomfortable feeling. Here I was, in a motel shower with a person I did not know in the next room, and my billfold, money and car keys were there with her! My weapon was in my new car and she had the keys to that automobile—had I fallen into a fatal trap? I began to think that when I stepped out of that shower I would find "Debbie" and her boyfriend waiting for me with my gun pointed between my legs! I dried off with the skimpy motel towel and opened the door cautiously—expecting the worst. Debbie was sitting on the bed in a sexy, revealing negligee with two drinks waiting on the night stand. She looked at me and said, "Are you all right, you look a bit frightened—I promise I won't bite—at least not very hard!"

My fears were unwarranted, but I checked to see that the room door was securely bolted from the inside just in case. Debbie was delightful. She was submissive and aggressive, uninhibited and reserved, coy and bold, eager to please and eager to take her own pleasure. She was an artist in bringing me to the brink of climax, and then easing me down until she was ready herself. Her lips were incredibly sexy and she kissed me in places that I had never been kissed before. She taught me that a man's nipples were erogenous zones also and showed me how sensitive a woman's breasts were to the touch of a penis. She rubbed oil between her breasts, held them together while on her back and let me make love to those beautiful boobs! At the top of each stroke she would kiss, lick or suck the end of my penis until I could no longer hold back—then she took two of her fingers and applied pressure at just the right spot to bring me down off that mountain! I was beginning to think that this lady was probably a high priced hooker on a day off—she had love-making skills that I never knew existed. We continued various and sundry methods of lovemaking throughout the night, slept a few hours and resumed our fun and games the next morning. We ordered breakfast delivered to the room and as we began to eat it was really the first time we talked—at least other than sex talk! I asked her if she was going to stay in the local area long enough for us to get together again. She was noncommittal and changed the subject quickly. I decided that she wished to remain the mystery lady so I did not pry into her personal life. It was obvious that she was a well educated person and it certainly did seem strange that she was all alone in a small town such as Fallon, Nevada—not noted for tourist attractions.

It was early Sunday afternoon when I bid my farewell to "Debbie"—don't know if that was her name but I rather doubted it. At the door to her room, our little love nest during the past 18 hours or so, I asked one more time if we could get together again. Tears came to her eyes and she started speaking in a very soft voice. She told me that no, we could not see each other again, and blurted out the real reason for her being in Fallon. It seems that Fallon was the location of a noted abortion clinic with one of the best physicians available for that procedure in the entire country. She was scheduled to check into that clinic the next morning to terminate an unwanted pregnancy. She went on to relate that she was an attorney in Sacramento and she had met a man at a bar and had unprotected sex with him on a "one-night-stand" type of relationship. She was now over seven weeks pregnant and her decision was firm to end the pregnancy. I felt very sorry for this young lady and apologized for being inquisitive. She thanked me for the evening and added that it was her way of having a last fling and certainly the last time ever that she would have unprotected sex. We enjoyed a long hug and several goodbye kisses—then it was over.

The squadron returned to NAS Lemoore and we began a long hot summer of training—at least the fog season was over. We made several trips to the carrier, usually the Midway, but we also operated aboard other carriers such as the Coral Sea and the Hornet, whichever carrier happened to be off the coast of California at the time. We also enjoyed one more weapons deployment, this time to Yuma, Arizona, where it was incredibly hot. I remember one flight in particular during that training period. I was the number three aircraft in a flight of four returning from the gunnery range as we entered the break over the duty runway. We prided ourselves in executing a tight pattern with about two seconds between landings—we alternated our touch downs so that the leader landed on the side of the runway that was closest to our parking ramp, the next plane landed on the other side, etc. This particular day was warmer than usual (about 110 degrees) and it was only noon! There were several dust devils around the runway and the winds were variable in direction and gusting. The number one airplane landed on the left side of the runway and number two was still in a banked turn preparing to roll wings level just before touchdown on the right side. I saw the leaders wheels touch down and tire smoke puffed up and immediately drifted across the runway to the right. This indicated that there was a strong crosswind gust from left to right. I was about to key my mike to warn number two when his plane hit the prop wash from the leader's engine that had drifted directly into his flight path. Number two was less than 100 feet from the ground and still in a left turn when the wash caught his left wing and flipped him almost inverted. The pilot, a new squadron member named Andy, somehow managed to recover and rolled back upright just as his left wheel touched down in the dirt slightly off the left side of the runway. The plane bounced on the one tire and then roared ahead in a cloud of dirt blown up by the engine at full power directly toward the tower—then I saw a burst of 20mm cannon fire erupt from his guns! There was a lot of screaming from the tower and the plane pulled up and missed the top of the control tower by less than twenty feet! I watched it all while in the landing groove myself then added power and followed the number two plane streaking out over the desert. I called his number and asked if he was okay. A shaken voice came back, "I think so— can you check me over to see if the plane is okay?" I responded, "You bet, but if you don't come back on the throttle a bit I'll never catch you before we're in Mexico!" I joined on his wing, had him drop his gear and looked him over for damage—everything seemed okay. I told him that his plane did not appear to be damaged, then added, "Check your guns switch and the master arm switch in the off position." He keyed his mike and uttered those two most used words in aviation, **"OH SHIT!"**

Two rounds of 20mm cannon ammo had penetrated the control tower, happily below where the tower personnel were stationed—no one was hurt. Our safety officer conducted an investigation into the incident and the conclusion was simple. Andy had forgotten to safety his guns and during the maneuver to recover from the prop wash had squeezed the stick so hard that he pressed the trigger and fired several rounds. He was not even aware that the guns had fired—he remembered that he heard loud noises and thought that he had crashed for sure. No damage occurred to the aircraft and after Andy was chewed out by the Skipper for not properly following our safety procedures, he made the trip to the tower to personally apologize to the two men on duty there. I believe that there was an exchange of several fine bottles of spirits before everyone's feathers were soothed.

In the fall of that year, 1963, I attended my first Tailhook Reunion in Las Vegas at the Stardust Hotel and Casino. This was really a big party for Naval Aviators who were carrier qualified and quite a party it was! We flew all of our airplanes into McCarran Field and taxied one of them down the strip and parked it in front of the Stardust. With the wings folded, the Skyraider was not much wider than a large truck and it could be taxied in one lane of the roadway. The Tailhook Association of today is a fine institution that is involved with education and community service and once again has the blessings of the top brass—in the sixties it was more of a group of pilots who wanted to party. There were no female Navy Pilots in those days and the male pilots who attended did not bring their girl friends or wives—something about **"why would you take a peanut butter sandwich to a free banquet?"** The only females at these reunions (now called Conventions) were locals— hookers, strippers, groupies and young ladies looking for a good time. There was a lot of drinking and debauchery but little or no real damage was done and we all left with fond memories of camaraderie with our fellow pilots. It was really the only time that you could run into old buddies who were now located throughout the world—it was indeed just what it was designed for, a meeting place for aviators to exchange stories, tell tall tales and renew old friendships.

It was soon time to prepare for the next cruise, again aboard USS Midway, departing in November for Westpac. Snag and I gave up our apartment in Hanford and I arranged to have my automobile put in storage. At least I was now senior enough to fly aboard instead of walking aboard the carrier.

Chapter Ten

**"Mastering the prohibited maneuvers in the Flight Manual is one
of the best forms of life insurance for pilots!"**

We flew our airplanes aboard the carrier three days after the ship had
departed from Alameda and settled into the normal shipboard routine of
preparing for the ORI enroute to the Hawaiian Islands. As the Weapons
Training Officer, I was especially busy planning and briefing for the weapons
delivery part of the exercise. In addition to dropping bombs and napalm,
firing rockets, and strafing with our 20 mm cannons, we had just been
assigned a new mission—laying mines! I was assigned the task of developing
a "mine warfare doctrine" and developing a training program for our pilots to
prepare for the eventuality of being required to drop mines, if and when
necessary. I knew nothing about dropping mines from aircraft—usually
performed by multi-engine aircraft that were capable of carrying several tons
of mines internally. Our single-engine aircraft had a total of fifteen external
stations (bomb racks) but because of the size of the mines we were to carry;
only five or six mines could be attached to each plane. I developed delivery
tactics based on visual reference to landmarks such as a point of land or a rock
formation near the entrance to a harbor that was to be mined. Such delivery
was not going to be very accurate but I figured that random placing of mines
would be a bigger problem for the enemy than if the mines were precisely
positioned!

The ORI went well and we were cleared to continue the deployment to the
Western Pacific after the usual week of liberty in Hawaii. We flew our planes
to Barber's Point NAS and the ship docked at Ford Island, near Pearl Harbor.
Every American who was five years of age or older in November, 1963
remembers where he or she was when President Kennedy was assassinated.

I happened to be in a top secret briefing for nuclear weapons training officers being held in a large room on the base at Pearl Harbor. A senior officer was at the podium conducting the brief—giving us the latest intelligence about our cold war adversaries, the Soviet Union and Communist China—when an aide approached and handed him a small slip of paper. The briefing officer read the note, looked up and said, "Gentlemen, this meeting is now adjourned, President Kennedy has been shot and I have a lot of work to do right now!" We were all shocked to hear that sad news but were not sure if he was only wounded or was assassinated. We left the briefing room and were walking back toward our carrier when we noticed a sudden stream of official, black Navy vehicles streaming from an underground garage and driving at a high rate of speed to exit the base. Later we learned that these cars were heading for the Barber's Point Naval Air Station because the Secretary of State was being diverted from landing at Honolulu International Airport to the safer navy base. In the event that there was a conspiracy against the top leaders of our country, procedures were in place to protect those who may be in harm's way. We all realized the gravity of this development and suddenly knew that our "peace time" cruise was taking on a new meaning.

We departed the friendly waters of Hawaii and steamed westward. Our briefings were more serious and we spent quite a few extra hours planning our SIOP missions after it was confirmed that our Commander-in-Chief had indeed been assassinated. About a week out of Hawaii the ship encountered an unusually severe storm and we were tossed around like a small boat instead of a 90,000 ton aircraft carrier, the largest and sturdiest type of ship afloat. Many of us were a bit green around the gills. We were not conducting air operations at this time but the ship continued their routine drills—unfortunately one of these drills caused a major incident that changed the complexion of our cruise. I do not recall exactly how it happened, but the number two elevator (there were three large elevators on the flight deck to transport airplanes from the hangar deck and back) was washed away in heavy seas when it was accidentally lowered during a sharp turn. The ship had now lost one third of its capacity to move aircraft. Our readiness level was severely compromised. Under normal conditions we were not required to keep any of our planes loaded with "War Reserves"—the name given to real live nuclear weapons. These weapons were stored in special spaces located several decks below the hangar bay and would be brought to our airplanes if and when the "flag went up" (we were at war and it was time to launch our nuclear arsenal). After the loss of the aircraft elevator the decision was made by the top brass that we must keep a certain number of aircraft loaded with these War Reserve nukes at all times to be able to react in a timely fashion to the beginning of WW III. This became a real "pain in the ass" to keep two of our twelve aircraft unavailable for routine flights because they were loaded for the "big one!" Armed guards were required 24 hours each day to make sure no one accidentally pushed the wrong button or ran a cart into these nukes. We were stuck with this requirement for over two months until we were able to get a new elevator installed in Yokosuka, Japan in February, 1964. Perhaps this bad luck at the start of the cruise was an omen for the remainder of that deployment.

Our first port on this cruise was to the Philippines and then to Hong Kong for Christmas. There was a tradition among Navy pilots that they were supposed to throw a party each time they were promoted. Most of us waited until we were in the Philippines for our "wetting down party" because the booze was so cheap. I had been recently promoted to full Lieutenant (equivalent to Captain in the Marine Corps, Army or Air Force) and joined with several of my squadron mates to have a big bash at the Cubi Point NAS Officers Club. We put on quite a party! We invited pilots from other squadrons in our air group, ship's company officers, CAG (air group) staff, and basically anyone who wanted to come to a good party. We ended up with over one hundred officers that spilled out of the O'Club and into the pool area where we had flowing French Seventy-Fives from a fountain. There was plenty of food and more booze that we needed and it cost each of us sponsors about $50.00 each! There were many people tossed into the pool, in full uniform, before the party was over. A fine time was had by all!

The carrier operated in the South China Sea for a couple of weeks before we headed for Hong Kong. We conducted day and night flight operations under ideal weather. Our Operations Officer, a senior LCDR by the name of Scottie, was one officer who thought "outside the box" and he was always trying to invent new ways to utilize the capabilities of our aircraft. Normally we flew at low to **very low** altitudes, the A-4's flew somewhat higher, and the fighters (F-8 Crusaders and F-4 Phantoms) were way up there! Scottie figured out that we could do it differently, so one day he briefed a "special" mission and we launched off the carrier in a flight of four, he being the division leader and I the section leader. We climbed for over an hour until those poor airplanes were literally hanging on their props—we were on 100 percent oxygen and not used to being in such rarefied atmosphere above 30,000 feet. Scottie had it all figured out that the AD was able to get to 40,000—we never made it that high! The controls were like mush and the engine was gasping as we topped out just above 32,000 feet—well above the certified service ceiling of our aircraft. At full power we were barely able to keep above stall speed and I was concerned that a stall/spin could spoil our whole day! We were now in position to accomplish the real reason for this "mission." Scottie spotted a flight of two F-8's several thousand feet below us and signaled to roll-in! We cautiously rolled over and dove towards the "enemy" and as our airspeed built up the controls became more effective. As we roared past the fighters, Scottie keyed his mike on the guard channel and said, "YOU'VE BEEN HAD BY A SPAD!" We zoomed back up to the "perch" and waited to attack the next group of fighters. We repeated this maneuver on several flights of unsuspecting jets until it was time to return to normalcy and enter the landing pattern at the ship. The experience was exhilarating and the four of us wore wide grins around the ship for several days. Our jet pilot friends were amazed at our performance and they found new respect for the venerable and versatile Skyraider. I found new respect for my friend Scottie!

The carrier next headed for Hong Kong and my roommate (Snag) and I decided to take some leave and stay in a nice hotel while the ship was in port. We were able to make reservations for accommodations at the Hotel Merlin in Kowloon—a very nice place to stay in this fabled British Crown Colony. We were assigned to Suite 10, basically the entire tenth floor, where we had three bedrooms with baths, a large main room, a fully stocked bar and a servant who was at our beck and call around the clock—all this for $100 Hong Kong per day, the equivalent of about fifty dollars American. We were in HOG HEAVEN! The only down side was that all of our buddies came to visit a lot and there was rarely a time that the suite was not crowded—some even spent the night in the bathtubs! Nevertheless, it was an adventure to remember and everyone enjoyed this week in Hong Kong. I was focused on buying a new wardrobe of clothes from one of the tailors that catered to the pilots. Each day I stopped by my tailor for new measurements—no matter the time of day they always offered me a drink, and no matter the time of day I always accepted! I ordered three suits, four sports coats (two cashmere), six pairs of trousers, and a dozen dress shirts, each with my personal logo on the cuff of the sleeve. Each day as I came in for a new fitting my measurements were a bit smaller—maybe something to do with the fact that I was not eating Navy chow but drinking most of my nourishment! I left Hong Kong with a trunk full of clothes that were too small by the time I arrived back in the USA!

There was an old fashioned English pub on the ground floor of our hotel and I discovered that British food was not all bad if one ate only fish and chips and my favorite—French onion soup. Every day I partook of this delight—that great tasting onion soup, in a crock, that was so thick that one almost needed a knife to cut it—chased with a decent wine. The second or third day that I was there I met a nice young lady, Rita, who was referred to in chapter two as the school teacher from Clark Air Force Base in the Philippines. She was staying at the Hotel Merlin with a fellow teacher while on a bit of vacation herself. Rita was a real hoot—a fun-loving gal from Tennessee who graduated from Ole Miss and was adventurous enough to do something different. We began a relationship that would eventually change the course of my life. In the meantime, she became one of our "buddies" and we had one hell of a great time at this hotel. She could out drink the entire pilot group and never seemed to need rest or sleep—where do we find such women? Obviously she should have been a Naval Aviator! Eventually all good things come to an end and we sailed away from Hong Kong with many fond memories. During my stay I enjoyed several tours around this exciting city and found the sights and especially the smells to be something I would never forget.

The carrier was often on "water hours" and we were not allowed to use any more water than absolutely necessary. The term "Navy bath" meant that you barely got wet, soaped up and rinsed off with less than a pint of water—not a lot of fun after a long hot flight in the tropics. The ship made its own fresh water while we were at sea and it was interesting to me that while we were moored outside the harbor in Hong Kong, the ship provided more that **one and a half million gallons** of fresh water to the people of Hong Kong! That city was in the middle of a severe drought and the ship's contribution made a considerable contribution to their need for water. The U. S. Navy was not only providing a military presence to that region but was really a good neighbor on more occasions than I can recall. After leaving Hong Kong the carrier made its way north and the weather changed from the pleasant temperatures we enjoyed over Christmas to more winter like conditions. We operated at sea for almost a month before we headed toward our next port—Iwakuni, Japan, where a Marine Corps station was located. Several Marine fighter squadrons were stationed at Iwakuni as well as some "special ops" units. The Marine pilots were required to requalify each year in carrier landings, called carquals. It was time for one of the F-8 units to carqual, so their group flew out to the Midway to renew their proficiency in carrier landings—not something these guys looked forward to!

The Marine pilots had the same flight training as Naval Aviators and they were generally very good pilots. The problem was two-fold: First, the F-8 was inherently not a good aircraft for carrier operations; second, the Marine pilots only made carrier landings once a year and shipboard operations were so different that one really needed to do it frequently to maintain any acceptable level of proficiency. I later decided that these Marine fighter squadrons picked the biggest, meanest, and most foul-mouthed aviator in their unit and made him the LSO! The day that the Marines were to land was highly anticipated by us Navy types and tickets could have been sold for $100 each on "vulture's row" where we lined up two deep at the rail to watch the show! The Marine LSO was the first to arrive and he managed to complete his six landings without any significant problems. Then he took command of the LSO platform to "wave" the rest of his fellow pilots onboard. We were able to hear his every word as each of the Marine F-8's started their pattern to land. He yelled, screamed, cussed out and threatened each arriving airplane to the point that the pilot must have been so intimidated that it became a "do or die" situation. There were many wave-offs, several near-misses at the platform and some really ugly landings before it was completed. Only one accident— after what appeared to be a decent landing, the nose gear collapsed on one plane after it hit the deck. Turned out that the pilot was the C.O. and he was pissed! After shutting down the engine he opened the canopy, took off his hard hat and threw it as hard as he could down on the flight deck. I'm sure that he was able to get a new one!

We spent a few days in Iwakuni, but there was little to do other than go to the O'Club. There we met and talked to many of the pilots who had "carqualled." We began hearing rumors about where the carrier was going after leaving this port. We had been told that the ship would go immediately to Yokosuka for installation of a new elevator as we were still operating without that lost aircraft elevator. There were always many rumors aboard ship—each cruise departed with the rumor that we were going to AUSTRALIA! This never happened but the bad rumors always seemed to become factual. Several of the Marine aviators had friends in the "special ops" group and the rumor was that a rather large contingent of Marines would be on board when the carrier departed Iwakuni. The ship departed on schedule early one morning and we were several hours out to sea before the ship's Skipper made a special announcement to all hands. We were heading north of Japanese waters to the Kuril Islands, a group of a dozen or so islands belonging to the Soviet Union but claimed by the Japanese, for a special exercise. We were to prepare for severe winter weather operations. A group of Marines, at least fifty, had slipped onboard the carrier in the middle of the night before we sailed. We began seeing these "special ops" people in groups of never less than five throughout the ship. They wore no insignia or marks of ranking, although it was obvious that there were both officers and enlisted men in each group. They stuck to themselves, worked out every few hours it seemed, and could be seen running around the flight deck in shorts and t-shirts at all hours of the day and night, no matter what the weather. These guys looked tough, serious, and completely focused on whatever mission they were planning to accomplish.

The next day we started flight operations as usual and we were getting prepared to start wearing our anti-exposure flight suits, called "poopy suits"—never knew where that name came from but perhaps pilots on occasion had to "poop" in them? There was a simple formula we used to determine if a poopy suit was required. If the air temperature and water temperature added together was 100 or less we had to don those cumbersome, awkward, rubberized, and exceedingly uncomfortable suits that looked like something Jules Verne described for a deep sea diver. Just getting into one of those things took thirty minutes, and once you were all buttoned up you could forget about having to urinate—it was not worth the effort required! At the end of that first day of flight ops, just before dark, a "special" aircraft flew on board, obviously from Iwakuni Marine Corps Air Station. This was a Douglas A3D similar to the "whales" flown by Heavy Attack Squadron 8 but it had no markings and was configured not to carry bombs but to carry personnel. The A3 was affectionately called the whale because of its size— it was the largest carrier aircraft in the Navy at this time and was equipped with two jet engines and carried its weapons internally. Later the whales would be used for ECM (Electronic Counter Measures) and IFR (In-flight Refueling) missions during the Vietnam War. This unmarked aircraft dubbed by us the "queer whale" was parked all alone in the hangar bay and was guarded more closely than the planes with nuclear weapons.

As the ship proceeded northward the weather became significantly more severe with rain becoming freezing rain, sleet and snow. The flight deck was often covered with ice and the rough seas threw water over the bow that would freeze when it contacted any object, human flesh included. Most of our flying was cancelled as the conditions became too dangerous. First the fighters were cancelled, then the light attack jets were cancelled, next the heavy jets were cancelled—finally only the props were able to fly. We were not happy to fly in such weather, especially at night, while our sister squadron pilots watched movies in the comfort of their ready room. One really bad night we were sure that even the reliable AD's would be cancelled but we still had to go through the drill of briefing in our poopy suits, getting night vision adapted and standing by for the order: PILOTS, MAN YOUR AIRCRAFT! There were only four planes scheduled to launch and I was not the leader— the Skipper felt that he was the one with the most experience and he magnanimously assumed that responsibility. We still believed that the launch would be cancelled—our mission was certainly not very important (I don't even remember what we were assigned to do)—and we were a bit surprised when the order was issued for us to man our planes. Walking on that slippery flight deck was a challenge in itself as the wind was brutal and the ship was being tossed around like a tin can. I especially felt sorry for the poor guys working the flight deck; the fuelers, mechanics, taxi directors and catapult crews—it was not a night to be exposed to such bitter weather. It just so happened that my aircraft was the first one to reach the catapult and as I was being hooked up, I still believed that the operation would be cancelled. There was a long pause once I was positioned to go—I felt like the guy on death row waiting for a last second call from the Governor to grant him a reprieve— surely the powers to be were making a sane decision and shortly I would be in the ready room watching the movie! Suddenly the Catapult Officer was giving the signal to go to full power and I eased the throttle forward, knowing that at the last second I would be given the signal to cut power and it would be over. I reached full power and felt the aircraft straining to go forward—I looked over the instruments more carefully that I had ever done in my life, perhaps hoping that something would not look right and I could call for an abort. Everything looked perfectly normal. I braced my head against the headrest, locked my throttle hand fingers around the bar provided to prevent the throttle from being retarded during the explosive cat shot, flicked on the light switch to indicate that I was ready and said a silent prayer! I looked forward into the blackness and could not tell the difference between the sea and the sky. Out of the corner of my left eye I saw the Catapult Officer drop his lighted wand to the deck and then point it forward—I was going!

The catapult fired and I was blasted off into the black—I looked down at my instruments and they were all over the place, nothing looked right. It occurred to me later that I had really never looked at the instruments immediately after a cat shot and it was probably not unusual for the readings to be a "bit weird" for the first second or two. I held the control stick in my lap and knew that I was flying—nothing was visible out front, no horizon to help me keep the wings level—I had no choice but to glance again at the instruments. Everything was starting to settle down and the attitude gyro seemed to become more reliable—the altimeter was showing a definite climb but the airspeed was dropping—shit, I had forgotten to raise the landing gear! Once the gear was up I caught my breath and reported airborne to the ship's departure control, adding that I was going tactical (meaning that I was switching to our squadron discrete frequency for the rendezvous with my other three planes). I was told to "remain on this frequency." I was in solid clouds and I could see ice starting to build up on the edges of the canopy. I could not see my wings but knew that ice was surely starting to accumulate there too. I was navigating to our briefed rendezvous point but decided to level off when I reached an altitude between layers and clear of ice. It was very quiet on the radio and I wanted to talk to someone! My call sign was Canasta 503 and I transmitted, "Schoolboy departure, Canasta 503, request to go tactical for rendezvous, over." After a long pause I heard a new voice, "Canasta 503, what are your flight conditions?" I wanted to say, "Really shitty!" Instead I replied that I was "popeye" (meaning IFR conditions) and encountering heavy icing. The controller came back with just what I did not want to hear: "The launch has been cancelled and you are the only aircraft airborne." He added that it would take at least one hour to respot the deck and be ready to recover my aircraft—in the meantime I was pretty much on my own! I asked if there were any areas on the ship's radar that might indicate lighter precipitation—less ice. The response was negative. I tried every altitude between sea level and ten thousand feet and settled on two thousand—the icing seemed a bit less there. I could not avoid flying into the clouds as the few clear areas were starting to close in—I was picking up more ice on the wings and it was taking more power to hold my airspeed. I kept checking on the weather at the ship—the ceiling was 300 feet when I launched, now it was 200 feet and dropping. Even worse news was the fact that the visibility was now less than half a mile and the flight deck was covered with ice. There were no "bingo" fields (land airports used as alternates) so I was stuck with getting aboard the carrier that night or ditching in the ocean! I was also wishing that I had not consumed that last cup of coffee before leaving the ready room—my bladder was full and I needed to use the "relief tube" that was installed in the cockpit floor. It consisted of a funnel attached to a tube that could be extracted from its stowed position and used by the pilot for "physiological necessity."

The Skyraider was equipped with a rudimentary auto pilot but it was seldom used and therefore not maintained or even tested. I decided now was the time I needed that device to at least keep my wings level while I went through the contortions required to use the relief tube. I was all trimmed up so that the aircraft would almost fly straight and level without any help from the auto pilot, but I knew that it would take at least five minutes to accomplish what normally took 30 seconds, and I could not rely on the plane behaving for that long without my hands on the controls. I pushed in the red button on the right console that said AUTO PILOT and the aircraft immediately rolled inverted! I grabbed the stick to stop the roll but the autopilot was in control—then I pulled out that red button that I had used to engage the AP, and I was back in control and able to recover from what was now an "unusual attitude!" Suddenly I no longer needed to relieve myself and silently cussed myself out for even trying to use the AP. I remembered that the auto pilot in our planes received its information from a small standby gyro that was located between the rudder pedals—a location that was impossible to reach. I took my flashlight and shined it on that gyro and discovered that it had erected inverted—not unusual but something we rarely checked. That problem could be corrected by pulling out on the small knob beneath that tiny instrument—again an impossible task while flying the airplane. The Ops Officer, my friend Scottie, later came up with a simple solution. He designed a "standby gyro erection device" that consisted of half a washer on a string that the pilot inserted under that tiny knob before the aircraft was started. Later, after power was available and the gyro was up to speed, the pilot simply pulled the string to remove the half washer and the gyro was normal!

Meanwhile I continued to circle in the vicinity of the carrier awaiting a ready deck. I knew that my squadron pals were probably watching some corny movie but when the order was made to "STANDBY TO RECOVER

AIRCRAFT" they would all be locked in to the small TV receiver installed in the front of the ready room that displayed the flight deck. When an aircraft was approaching for landing the pilots could watch the plane through the lens of a camera installed in the landing area. We always critiqued each other's landings and either cheered or groaned when each plane hit the wires. The Skipper was always in attendance in his assigned seat when his "boys" were landing and he often helped us get aboard with body english and a few helpful hints shouted at the TV set. One of our Skippers, whose name was Press, was a real nervous type who would go through wild gyrations while watching these landings—so we presented him with a "plumber's helper," painted green of course, that we stuck onto the deck in front of his seat so he was able to "fly" his chicks on board! After what seemed an eternity, I was cleared to contact approach control for vectors that would put me in position for a CCA (carrier controlled approach). Since I was the only airplane to be recovered I received special attention and was given a long straight-in type of approach. This enabled me to get stabilized with gear, flaps, and hook down about three miles aft of the carrier. There were no instruments available in the cockpit to fly this approach—it was strictly flown by the pilot following instructions of the CCA controller. He would say things like, "You're slightly left of center line, turn right five degrees" or "On glide slope, starting to go low," etc. The whole purpose of this type of approach was to get the pilot in position to acquire the landing area visually, follow the "meatball" on the mirror landing system, and listen to the directions given by the LSO. The prop planes like the AD were given a "cut" signal, both verbally and by use of a green light atop the mirror system, when in position to land the aircraft. The jets, on the other hand, pushed the throttle to full power just as the plane touched down so that the engine would be spooled up in the event of a hook skip or bolter. A hook skip was when the landing hook bounced over the wires, not the pilot's fault, but a bolter was when the aircraft was too high for the hook to catch any of the wires.

As I started the approach I inquired about the weather and was told that the ceiling was "indefinite" with visibility ¼ mile—not good news at all. Normally our landing minimums were 200 ft ceiling with ½ mile visibility— tonight there were no minimums, either I landed on the carrier or landed in the water to, hopefully, be rescued by our plane guard destroyer. I really did not want to be in that cold water on such a miserable night! I flew the approach as precisely as my piloting skills allowed and concentrated on flying solely on instruments until my radar altimeter read 200 feet above the water, about 140 feet above the carrier, when I peeked out through the windshield—I could see nothing. I went back to the gauges and continued down to 100 feet—I could go no lower without visual reference to the landing area. I had not heard a word from the LSO, my friend Bob; obviously he did not have my aircraft in sight. I eased on the power and started a go-around. I really did not want to have to do this all over again but I had no choice. I keyed my mike and announced, "Canasta 503, waving off, no visual on the ship!" The LSO replied, "Bill, I heard your plane go over—you were right on centerline—but we never picked you up visually."

The approach controller began giving me instructions again for another approach. I took a moment to wipe the sweat out of my eyes and started to think about the very real possibility of going for a swim this night! I had plenty of fuel and asked if there were any emergency airports within my range—I already knew the answer. We were well north of Japan's northernmost island and if there were any airports they were not in "friendly hands." Normally I would be able to circle around for another hour or two in hopes that the weather would break—but that was no longer an option as it was taking way too much power to maintain flying speed and the controls were getting very stiff. It was obvious that my aircraft was picking up too much ice and I had no way to remove that extra weight. I told the controller that I wanted another approach right away and if I did not get on board I would most likely have to ditch. My chances of surviving, even with my poopy suit, in that icy water for more than a very few minutes were slim to none and we all knew that! I was quickly vectored into position for another approach. This time it required almost full power to fly the aircraft in the dirty configuration—with everything hanging out—and I was beginning to realize that a third approach was probably out of the question.

I started down the glide slope and focused completely on following the directions of the controller. This time I did not peek out until below 150 feet—nothing. Back on the gauges until 100 feet—again nothing. I only had 40 feet to play with and I did not want to endanger the ship by getting so low that I would hit the island that extended above the flight deck. I started to push the throttle forward to wave off when I saw two dim lights directly in front— I eased the nose over and suddenly spotted the landing area. I heard only one word from the LSO—"CUT"—and I closed the throttle and felt the hook grab a wire! What a great feeling to go from 105 knots to zero in about fifty feet!

There were lots of backslaps and handshakes when I arrived in the ready room—what I really wanted was to get rid of my "soggy" poopy suit—it needed to be thoroughly cleaned. Later the LSO and the CAG himself came to the ready room to debrief me after this eventful evening. Also the flight surgeon presented me with a special gift, a small miniature of "medicinal Brandy" which was truly appreciated. The LSO shook my hand and said, "Guess I'll give you a greenie on that landing—you actually caught the number three wire—you deserve an OK-3!"

We continued operating off the Kuril Islands for about two more weeks and resumed flight operations when the weather improved. Finally we were briefed about this special exercise which involved the group of Marines and their unique aircraft aboard our ship. Our ready room adjoined ready room 6 where the heavy attack squadron (VAH-8) was located. We met the pilot who flew the unmarked "whale" and it turned out that he was a Navy Pilot, not a Marine, and many of the special ops personnel were also Navy, both Officers and enlisted men. They were part of a newly organized force made up of "Frogmen" from the Navy's UDT (Underwater Demolition Team) and were called SEALS, a name we had never heard before. Their mission, top secret at that time, was something not even James Bond would attempt! We listened with complete disbelief turning to awe as we heard exactly what they were going to accomplish. It seemed that our intelligence had determined that the Soviets had built a new, top-secret base on one of the Kuril Islands and it was suspected that this base was being equipped to fly nuclear bombers that could easily reach the United States in less time than we could react. This could change our strategic war plans significantly. Keep in mind that this was long before satellite or even U-2 surveillance was available and the only way to confirm this intelligence was to place a team on shore there! We were to conduct routine flight operations to convince the Russians that our ship was in their vicinity simply to train for cold weather procedures. Then the carrier and support ships would turn south toward Japan. The hope was that the Soviets would relax their vigilance when the fleet returned to Japanese waters—thinking that our exercise was completed. Then the Midway would launch this single secret "queer whale" and it would fly below enemy radar until just off the shore of the new installation on that particular Kuril Island. Flying at wave top heights as slow as aerodynamically possible the team of four SEALS would be dropped into the water from an aft facing ramp that was to be extended from the bottom of the aircraft. I believe that there were two rubber rafts that contained two men each to be "ejected" onto the water, at night of course! These two rafts were now to make their way to the enemy shore less than a mile away, accomplish their "mission," return to their stashed rafts, and make their way back out to sea to be picked up later by a submarine! Exactly what they were to accomplish was never revealed to me—I was not cleared for that type of information—but we all felt that those SEALS were not going ashore to only take notes!

Normally I would not have been involved with this brief but it had been decided that this single whale should have support in the case that it was spotted by the Soviets and they launched their fighters to shoot it down. It could become an international incident if it was destroyed or forced down in Soviet territory. The decision was made that an ECM aircraft, a WF-2, a dome-covered, twin-engine prop plane that contained a combat information center, would be launched shortly after the "queer whale" to provide early warning if the Soviets scrambled their fighters. This "Willie Fudd" would require fighter escort and somehow I had been selected for that assignment. The AD had no real air to air capability but we were slow enough to escort the ECM aircraft so it was stretching the imagination a bit to call me fighter cover. The real fighters, F-4's and F-8's, would remain on the deck, hooked up to the catapult, to be launched in the event there was a threat to the mission aircraft. In theory the WF would spot (electronically) the enemy fighters in time for the ship to launch those fighters to come to the rescue. It was also felt that a single WF with an AD escort would not arouse any suspicions from the Soviet radars that generally tracked our movements. The plan was for the "queer whale" to launch off the ship, head toward Japan as though flying to Atsugi or Iwakuni, then drop down to extreme low altitude, turn around and head for its target. The WF and my plane would launch thirty minutes later and loiter in the vicinity of the carrier until the mission was completed. After the whale dropped its "cargo" it would reverse course and proceed at low altitude to the carrier where it would land. Everything went according to plan.

Flying escort on a "Willie Fudd" at night was not a lot of fun. His mission was to fly at 10,000 feet in an elliptical pattern at a constant airspeed of 140 knots. I could fly that slow but found that if I was on the inside of his turns it was a bit uncomfortable so I tried to stay above and behind him and weave back and forth to maintain a relative position. We were often in the clouds so then I had to join up on his wing and fly tight formation. We were airborne over two hours and it was with a real sigh of relief when we were given the

"Charlie" signal. That meant that the ship was now ready to recover its aircraft. After we were back aboard I asked about the "queer whale" and was told only that he landed in Iwakuni and the mission was complete.

The ship arrived in Yokosuka a few days later and we all were ready for some R & R. The remaining special ops team members (SEALS) departed the ship, again at night, were loaded aboard waiting unmarked busses and transported, I assumed, to their base in Iwakuni. We never heard another word about their mission. The elevator that we had lost was replaced and all repairs were made to make us a whole ship again—no more requirements to keep fully loaded nuclear weapons on our aircraft. It was interesting to me that all of our carriers had nuclear weapons on board but the Japanese would not allow nuclear weapons of any type to be in their territorial waters. They knew we had nukes on board, and we knew that they knew! Politics! After a week of liberty and repairs the ship began a slow journey south that would complete our Westpac cruise. The weather was rapidly improving and certainly much warmer than what we had been exposed to up north. We all thought that the rest of the deployment would be a piece of cake. It did not work out that way. The next two months would be one of the worst periods in peace-time Naval Aviation. The Air Group aboard Midway would lose six aircraft and seven pilots in a tragic series of unfortunate accidents. Most of these accidents happened at night during "routine" flight operations.

The ship's goal was to recover aircraft with less than one minute between landings. As soon as the aircraft came to a stop, the pilot raised his hook and cleared the landing area as rapidly as possible—at the same time raising flaps, folding wings and following the signals of the taxi director. The LSO on the platform waited for a "clear deck" signal from a spotter before letting the next plane land. One night there was a bit of confusion and the clear deck signal was given when a plane was still in the landing area—the next aircraft was cleared to land and slammed down on top of the plane that had not cleared. The pilot of the second aircraft ejected at the last second but did not survive— the pilot of the first aircraft was killed instantly. Even more tragic was what happened next—the ejection seat from the second aircraft came down directly onto the cockpit of another aircraft that was parked forward. The pilot of that aircraft was still in the cockpit and was also killed instantly— three pilots lost and two planes demolished—the third aircraft was able to be repaired. The Navy handled aircraft accidents aboard the carrier in a most logical and efficient way—if the airplane was damaged beyond repair it was simply pushed over the side, never to be examined again. If a pilot was killed, a simple but somber ceremony was held the next day—an at-sea burial, even if there were only parts of a body—and the ship continued on its way with minimal interruption to the normal routine.

One beautiful spring afternoon I returned to the ship and entered the break behind a flight of two A4's. I was leading a flight of two AD's and was close behind the number two A4. The lead A4 was almost ready to touch down and this number two was still flying downwind—this long interval was unacceptable so I simply cut him out and landed in front of him. This was generally okay if it did not cause the next plane to wave off. We were trying to complete a landing every 45 seconds or so and I did not delay that A4 who was so long in the groove. Not a word was said until I landed—as I taxied clear of the arresting gear I heard an announcement over the flight deck loud speaker, "That was the 115,000[th] arrested landing on the Midway—there will be a ceremony on the quarter deck!" I was surprised and pleased but the big shock was yet to come. I was taken to a small ceremony being held on the quarter deck where there was a large cake with icing that read "115,000[th] landing, 27 March 1964, CDR Streeper." Whoops! I had just cut out CAG who was all lined up to make that landing and have his name placed on a brass plaque along with each aviator who made a 1,000[th] landing during the ship's history! I was handed a sword to pose for a picture making the first cut into that cake when in walked the CAG. He walked up to me and said, "Either we change the number to 115,001 or we change the name to (he looked at my name tag) LT Eads!" He had a big grin and shook my hand firmly while stating that I did exactly the right thing as he was way too long in the groove. He added, "Son, I would have done the same thing if our roles were reversed." I felt badly about the situation but the CAG was a true gentleman and we shared the small celebration with a large slice of cake each! Later that same day I was asked to report to the wardroom where I found a new cake with MY NAME on it and had the ceremonial picture taken again—I still have that picture! I believe that the CAG was personally responsible for that new cake from the ship's bakery!

About this time I was designated a division leader—meaning that I could brief and lead a flight of four aircraft, a lot more responsibility on my young shoulders. On one of the very first occasions that I led a flight of four it turned into an experience I will never forget. The ship was operating about half way between Japan and the Philippines and again we were conducting night flight ops. My flight of four was the last group scheduled to land that night and we were to follow a flight of two A3 Whales. The first A3 landed normally but the second snagged a wire left of centerline and the wire snapped. The aircraft had been slowed by the cable and was not able to continue flying and went over the port side into the water upside down—the pilot and crew of three were lost. Another tragic consequence of this accident was the fact that the snapped cable whipped across the flight deck and cut the legs off of a sailor working on the starboard side. Considerable damage had been done to the carrier and the cable would have to be replaced before my group could land. We began a holding pattern as we had sufficient fuel to remain airborne for at least two more hours. The closest land was the Chinese island of Taiwan, formerly Formosa, and our holding position was gradually changed until we were holding 100 miles west of the carrier and about 200 miles east of Taiwan—the writing was on the wall. I finally determined that it was time to "bingo to the beach"—meaning that we only had enough fuel to go to a land airport with comfortable reserves. Neither I nor any of my wingmen had ever been to Taiwan and we had not briefed about such a remote possibility of having to make an unscheduled landing there. The weather was relatively good with only scattered clouds and haze but it was now very late at night when my flight arrived at a small military base with a single runway on the west side of the island. The only navigation aide to locate the field was a radio beacon about five miles south of the runway which was orientated parallel to the coast line or roughly north-south. I had been given a radio frequency by the ship to contact the airfield for landing and after several calls I was able to talk with someone on the ground there who spoke a little English. I was told that the airport was closed for the night—turned out that it was closed every night because it was not equipped for night operations! I asked the person to whom I was talking if he could turn on the runway lights as we were over the radio beacon and the runway was not in sight—only five miles away! I was then informed that there were no runway lights but "smudge pots" were available if I requested them. I made that request and the reply was, "Right away, sir!"

We held for at least thirty minutes before we began to see very dim lights outlining what we assumed to be the runway. This was an old Chinese Nationalist base that supported F-84 type aircraft that obviously flew only during daylight hours. After there were about six lights on each side of the runway I led my group into the break—the traditional Navy way to land a formation in VFR conditions. I was the first to land and I touched down between the first two lamps at the south end of the runway—wow, this runway was dirt! I was about to warn my wingmen when I hit a bump and was now on the asphalt—the runway actually started at the **second set of lights!** I had landed on the dirt overrun but it was compacted enough that it caused no problems. I quickly informed my buddies to land between the second set of lights and everyone landed safely. We parked our planes near a group of Quonset huts and all had a good laugh about my landing "short of the runway." There were several support personnel trying very hard to be helpful but it was obvious that they knew nothing about our kind of planes and we began to do our own fueling from an old truck that showed up with the proper type of aviation gasoline. I was standing on the wing of my plane doing my own fueling when one of my buddies walked up and said, "Hey, Bill, want a beer?" Seems that one of the Quonset huts was a makeshift pilot's lounge that had a huge cooler stocked with decent beer and we were told to help ourselves. We always carried some money in our flight suits just for these unexpected excursions and I had greenbacks, MPC's, Japanese Yen, Philippine Pesos but no Chinese currency. Not a problem—no one I have ever met in any foreign country has turned down old fashioned American currency! Most would also accept our MPC's (Military Payment Certificates) without question. We left more than enough to cover the beers we consumed.

By the time we finished fueling our planes and drinking several beers each, it was time to call it a night. Rooms were available in one of the barracks but I opted to take the blanket and pillow from that uncomfortable bunk and sleep outside under a palm tree near our airplanes. It was a warm balmy evening—now almost morning—with a light breeze blowing from the sea and I fell asleep gazing at the stars overhead. Suddenly someone was shaking me and it was daylight—I felt that I had just closed my eyes but in reality had about three hours of deep sleep and was refreshed and raring to go! The Chinese soldier took me in a jeep to the base operations building, another Quonset hut, near the small control tower that we had not seen during the darkness. The Officer on duty there handed me a typed message stamped SECRET and stood at attention while I read it. I almost laughed when I read the message from the carrier—all it said was that I was to return to the ship ASAP as repairs had been completed. The Chinese made a big deal of the fact that the message revealed the carrier's position. Since we were not at war I did not consider that information to be of importance to anyone but myself as I had to find the ship to land my flight. Then I realized that the Chinese Nationalists on the island of Taiwan were, at least in their own minds, in a perpetual state of war with their big brothers on the mainland of Communist China. I thanked the duty officer for all the assistance we had received and started to depart when I spotted a large bowl filled with beautiful fresh tomatoes on a table in a corner. My stomach was growling as I had not had any solid food for over twelve hours so I asked the Officer if I could take some of those tomatoes for my fellow pilots. He graciously offered me the entire bowl but I settled for what I could stuff into the pockets of my flight suit. I returned to our parked airplanes, rounded up the other three pilots, shared my tomatoes, did a quick brief and we jumped into our planes and launched into the rising sun. I had briefed a "special departure" so after we had joined up I led the four planes, in a tight diamond formation, over the airport at very low altitude, as fast as we were able to fly, and buzzed the tower! The ground crews loved it and my pilots all got a big charge out of our little "escape from the ordinary!"

The ship was over 300 miles away and I started to have a real problem after only thirty minutes of flying. I had consumed three of those lush tomatoes and suddenly I was having waves of nausea and had a most urgent need to take a crap! I began to realize that vegetables and fruit in this part of the world were not grown as controlled as those in the good old USA! I later found out that they used HUMAN MANURE to fertilize many of their crops in China—and we Americans were not as resistant to the microbes present in their crops as were the locals. Only one of the four of us had not eaten the "forbidden fruit" and he was the only one not having the same symptoms that I was experiencing. By the time we reached the carrier I was sweating profusely and finding it more and more difficult to control my bowels. I contacted the ship and requested an immediate "Charlie" and was told that our signal was "Delta"—we had to hold while the ship finished the respot of aircraft and turned into the wind. We started into the holding pattern when one of my wingman announced, "You don't have to worry about me anymore but you owe me a new flight suit!" I knew what had happened and it was just a matter of minutes before I would have the same "accident." Suddenly we were cleared to land and I had the division into the break in a matter of seconds. Due to the privilege of being the leader, I landed first. I thought that I had avoided the "accident" but the landing caused me to relax the "pucker" that was holding my sphincter muscle and I ruined my flight suit too! As I taxied clear of the landing area the Air Boss transmitted over the landing frequency to me, "Your flight is the only group airborne and we have some deck time available—would you like to get a few extra landings?" This was usually music to a carrier aviator's ears—to get unscheduled landings was a rare and most welcome occurrence. I really hated to pass up such an opportunity but I responded that I was "down." This normally meant that the aircraft had a mechanical malfunction and needed maintenance work before the next flight. It was important for the pilot to report this information to the ship as soon as possible so that a "down" aircraft could be positioned for transfer to the hangar bay for repairs; as opposed to being left on the flight deck where only "ready" birds were spotted. The Air Boss shot back, "Understand the aircraft is down, is that correct?" I weakly replied, "No sir, the aircraft is fine, the PILOT is down!"

I stepped down from the cockpit, handed my hardhat, MaeWest and kneeboard to the airplane captain and walked stiff-legged to the catwalk on the starboard side just aft of the island. There I took off my gun belt, removed everything from the pockets of my flight suit, laid these items down on the deck, removed my flight suit and hurled it over the side! My underwear soon followed and after picking up my possessions I entered a passageway to my stateroom. I later heard that the Air Boss watched the whole show and got quite a chuckle from my performance.

The carrier now headed south to the Philippine Sea and we began conducting those low-level navigation hops that we all loved—sandblowers. There were several bombing ranges that we used, usually uninhibited small islands with old automobile tires arranged in circles to simulate a target bull's-eye. After our sandblower mission we would deliver a practice bomb to one of those targets to simulate a successful conclusion to the navigation portion of the flight. A few of the targets were not so well marked and the target might consist of a partially sunken barge located in a small cove of one of the "uninhibited" islands. On occasion we carried live ammo and real weapons on these training flights. One particular flight we were authorized to carry two HVAR's on each plane. These were 5 inch High Velocity Aerial Rockets that we did not often get the chance to use—probably because they were very expensive. The Skipper himself led this flight of four and I was the second section leader or the number three man in the formation. Our target was that "partially sunken barge" that I had bombed on previous occasions.

After two hours of enjoying our sandblower we approached the "target"—unfortunately there were heavy clouds and thundershowers in the area. We all knew that the Skipper did not have very good eyesight and he had been spotted wearing "cheaters" at night—nevertheless he was an excellent aviator and a very intelligent person. We climbed to 5000 feet so that we could roll in on the target and fire our rockets at an altitude of 1500 feet. At 5000 feet we were above most of the clouds and we could only catch glimpses of the sea and occasional land below—but we knew we were in the right area. Suddenly the Skipper said that he had the target in sight and we shifted into a right echelon formation to start our attack. We all rolled in with a three second interval between aircraft through a small hole in the clouds. As I acquired the "target" something did not look right—there was something sticking out of the water in a protected cove but it was not the "partially sunken barge" that I had bombed before! I spotted a small dock to the right of the "target" and a small boat was tied to its end—on the hillside above that dock was a small house! Maybe we were in Smallsville—but we were certainly not where we were supposed to be. I keyed my mike to call for an abort just as the Skipper fired two rockets—his aim was slightly above that object protruding from the surface (whatever it was) and his rockets exploded into a rocky cliff just above the water line and the whole hillside seemed to collapse into the sea! Number two aborted and we all joined up above the clouds. The Skipper's only comment, "Guess that was not the right target." We soon found the real target—about three miles away on another small island—and successfully fired our remaining rockets at that "partially sunken barge!" We returned to the ship, debriefed and never heard another word about this incident. I often wondered if there was someone in that small house when the rockets hit—must have been an exciting time.

There were two accidents that happened in quick succession. The first was an F8 that was launched from the catapult just as the right wing went to the folded position—the airplane rolled into the sea before the pilot could eject. The next involved an A4 on a bomb run at one of the target areas with the automobile tires marking the bull's-eye. That plane flew into the target and we all figured that it was "target fixation" where the pilot lost situational awareness due to his concentration on the target. The last accident was after the ship was moored at Subic Bay and the ship's planes were at Cubi Point NAS. An A3 Whale was making an instrument approach to the runway at Cubi when it flew into a hillside—all aboard were lost.

We were all a bit numb from the tragic losses our air group had experienced and our liberty was more subdued that usual. Nevertheless, I was happy to be in the Philippines where I could renew my relationship with the school teacher from Clark AFB. When I contacted her after we were ashore at Cubi, she said that she would come to me for the weekend. I always knew that the Air Force people lived better than us Navy types—the Navy spent all their money on ships, the Air Force spent their money on bases and amenities for their personnel. Rita arrived on Friday afternoon in an official Air Force limousine driven by a Filipino driver—he was at our disposal for the weekend. We spent the first night at the Cubi Point Officers Club, one of those rare places in the world where you were treated like you always wanted to be treated. The club looked out over Manila Bay on a hilltop just above the runway and the views were spectacular over at least 270 degrees. The main room consisted of a large dance floor with dining tables around the perimeter—all enclosed with screens that were favorite spots for the colorful geckos that were always present at night. We enjoyed a wonderful dinner and then danced "the night away." The band played just the right romantic tunes and I was beginning to think that I was finally "falling in love." The two of us consumed at least SEVENTEEN stingers each after dinner before I lost count! It was foolish for me to try to keep up with this lady with the hollow leg. We closed the club and staggered across the parking lot to the BOQ where I had a room for the night. We were both roaring drunk when we entered my room—we fell across the bed AND—there was someone already in it! This poor guy jumped upright and said, "What the hell's going on?" or words to that effect. We were laughing so hard it was not possible to even reply—we backed out with a few mumbled apologies and found my real room. I think we both passed out before we were able to even attempt to make love.

I awoke the next morning with my tongue stuck to the roof of my mouth— I rarely ever drank stingers again! For you non-drinkers, stingers consisted of pure booze—mostly cognac with a splash of crème de menthe. We brushed our teeth, took showers, and headed for the O'Club for breakfast—we had a busy day planned. After several Bloody Marys and a hearty breakfast we summoned our driver (who evidently slept in the car in the parking lot) and departed to a place called Baggio—a resort in the mountains that catered to the Philippine elite and American Officers. Again we were treated like Royalty and enjoyed a most pleasant day and evening—this time without the "stingers." We returned to Cubi Point late Sunday afternoon and after a fond farewell Rita departed with her driver to return to Clark AFB. It had been, all in all, an incredibly enjoyable weekend and I was having serious thoughts about the direction my personal life should now take. Was this the "real deal" or was I infatuated because Rita was the first "round-eye" I had seen for several months? Food for thought!

The squadron flew regular training flights from the Cubi Point base for another week before it was time to depart for the carrier and head back to the US. It did not look like I would get to see Rita again as she was involved in her weekday job as a school teacher and I was busy with normal flying. However, one of my new duties in the squadron was that of being the Schedules Officer—I worked out all the assignments for the flight schedule each day—and I "scheduled" myself for a solo night proficiency flight one evening that would take me to the vicinity of Clark Air Force Base. We Navy types were normally not allowed to land at Clark because we had our own base at Cubi and the Air Force did not really like to handle us "squids." While in the proximity of Clark I suddenly developed a "rough engine" and requested to land there. The controller asked the pertinent question, "Is this an emergency?" I replied in the affirmative, adding that I was not sure my aircraft was able to get me to Cubi—less than fifty miles away but over a small hill! The controller gave me permission to land and I was amazed at the length and width of this Air Force runway—it appeared almost as wide as the carrier was long and extended for miles! I used less than one tenth of that runway before I taxied clear and was directed to follow the "follow-me" truck to park on the VIP apron just under the control tower. I was very impressed with such red carpet treatment and this was my first experience with a "follow-me" truck. I was led to the most beautiful white concrete ramp that I had ever seen! After shutting down my engine and stepping off the wing I noticed a few ugly drips of oil splattering on that immaculate concrete from my R-3350 engine—notorious for having oil leaks! I pretended not to notice this violation of such a pristine ramp and jumped onto the jeep awaiting my arrival. The Aerodrome Officer greeted me at the door of the Operations Building—it looked like the Taj Mahal compared to our Navy facilities—and inquired as to what assistance he could provide for me and my aircraft. I responded that he should contact my unit at Cubi Point NAS and request that a mechanic be sent to check my engine. I figured that this would take at least two days and then I would be able to fly my aircraft back to Cubi. Just enough time to enjoy a visit with Rita! I was taken to the Air Force version of a BOQ—this was called a VOQ (Visiting Officers Quarters)—and was treated to a suite equivalent to a four star hotel. There were no Navy showers to worry about here!

I contacted my new love—I had alerted her that I had planned this diversion—and she joined me by the time I stepped out of the shower. Rita brought two bottles of very fine wine and we enjoyed a wonderful evening together. We were rudely awakened early the next morning by a call from the base Operations Officer, a Lieutenant Colonel who was all business and requested my presence at once in his office—adding that a car was waiting for me outside my quarters. I donned my flight suit—the only clothing I had—kissed Rita goodbye (she was due for her usual school duties shortly) and jumped into the awaiting vehicle. We arrived in two or three minutes at the Ops Building, next to the tower, and the Lt Col was not a happy person. He extended the customary military courtesies to me, an Officer of lower rank, and then asked, "Have you seen the damage your aircraft did to our apron?" I admitted that I had not (thinking to myself—what the hell, it's just a few drops of oil) and he asked me to accompany him to the ramp. When we exited his office and walked toward where my beautiful Spad was parked, I noticed a large group of Air Force personnel standing, hands on hips, in a semi-circle in front of my plane. They were all looking at a humongous, ugly oil spill that extended for at least a twenty foot radius beneath my engine on that glistening white concrete!

The AD was limited in range and endurance not by fuel but by oil! That huge engine required massive amounts of oil to keep all those moving parts properly lubricated and our planes were equipped with a 32 GALLON oil tank! Evidently a main seal had ruptured and the plane dumped what was left in that tank—estimated at 20 gallons of oil—and it was now seeping into the concrete of that gorgeous ramp! The Lt Col was pissed but my decision to make an emergency landing was vindicated—bad luck for the Air Force but good luck for the Navy! The Operations Officer had made the decision not to move my aircraft after the spill was discovered—a wise decision as movement would have surely dripped more oil over a wider area—and he politely inquired if I knew of any way to clean up such a spill. I did not have a clue but said that I would contact my outfit for guidance—in the meantime I suggested that his personnel use towels to sop up the mess.

A maintenance crew from my squadron arrived that afternoon and repaired the aircraft in fifteen minutes! The clean-up would take several weeks and, I am sure, several thousand dollars! The only down side was that I was now obligated to fly my plane back to Cubi that afternoon and my little tryst with Rita came to a quicker ending than I had hoped. In a few days the ship departed for CONUS (Continental United States) and we flew our planes aboard two days later. The deck was "locked" and we were not to conduct flight operations again until our fly off when the ship was within several hundred miles of the good old USA. This was a very boring time for the pilots but we were supposed to stay busy with ground training and paper work. The Junior Officers spent that time gambling and consuming whatever booze had been smuggled aboard and stashed in their staterooms. We were all anxious to return home after this seven month deployment that had more than its share of tragedy.

Chapter Eleven

"Any flight over water in a single engine airplane will absolutely guarantee abnormal engine noises and vibrations"

The squadron returned to NAS Lemoore in May 1964 and would depart on the next cruise in less than nine months—these would be busy and eventful months. The social and cultural life in the Central Valley had not changed and it could easily become a bit depressing. Three of us bachelor pilots rented a nice house in town and tried our best to lead respectable lives and be good neighbors—good luck! The fine citizens in this part of the country were wonderful—they accepted the itinerant Navy personnel who had been placed in their small town and treated us with respect and kindness. One wealthy farmer by the name of "Jack" turned a part of his ranch into a party facility that was available at any time for Navy people to enjoy. He renovated an old barn and equipped it with a sound system, stage, dance floor, and all the modern conveniences available at the time. He donated it to any Navy group that requested to use it. We enjoyed many weekend barbeques and parties at what was called "Stone's Barn." The only thing the owner asked—clean it up when finished. This gentleman and his wife would continue for over forty years to provide those facilities to several generations of military personnel stationed at NAS Lemoore. People like those two are true American Patriots.

About this time a buddy and myself decided that it would be fun and a change of pace to try sky diving. I found a small airport near Fresno that advertised "we can have you making your first jump in one week." We were checked out in how to pack our chutes and given the necessary training for our first jump in one short afternoon. We made our plans to make that first jump the following week-end. However, we made the mistake of talking about our new adventure to some of the other pilots in the squadron and the

148

Skipper got word of our plans. The C.O., Smitty, who was about to be replaced by the Executive Officer, Harry, was fair and reasonable to all the pilots in the outfit. He called my buddy and me to his office and asked us just why would we what to do something as stupid as jump out of a perfectly good airplane? I stammered that it would be good training for us to learn the basics of sky diving as it would prepare us for the eventuality of bailing out of our military planes. Seemed to be a reasonable explanation to me but the Skipper did not buy it! He gave us a five minute lecture about how dangerous it was to sky dive, a fairly new type to recreation that had not gained the popularity that it has today. He stressed that the Navy had spent over a million dollars to train each of us to be Naval Aviators and he would not stand for us to jeopardize that training for such a lark! That was the end of my sky diving career!

Three things happened in quick succession that summer. I turned 25 years of age, I got married, and I finally decided to make the Navy my career. Smitty, the C.O., who I considered to be my friend and mentor, had been trying to convince me for the past year to augment into the regular Navy. I had been commissioned as an officer in the Naval Reserve and my required active duty period was due to be completed in November, 1964. By "augmenting" into the Regular Navy I would continue to serve until I chose to resign or retire (or was forced to retire). The only difference I noticed was that I now had USN after my rank, not USNR! I requested and was granted a six month extension of duty with Attack Squadron 25 so that I would be able to make at least part of the next cruise. Things were starting to heat up in Southeast Asia and we knew that soon our ship and air group would be involved in the action. I now had almost 300 carrier landings and had been in the squadron longer than any other pilot. It did not seem fair for me to miss out on "the action" after three long years of preparation. I enjoyed flying the AD, I enjoyed carrier operations, and I enjoyed the camaraderie of the pilot group in my squadron.

Attack Squadron 25 was still the only unit in the Navy flying the AD-7, the last version of the Douglas Skyraider. Other AD squadrons flew the earlier version, the AD-6. There was no visible difference between the two aircraft—they both had the same engine and airframe. There were only minor differences but we felt that our planes were the best in the fleet! Sadly, we received orders that we were to exchange our planes for older ones—planes that had been "mothballed" and out of service for several years. Twelve AD-

6 planes were taken from Litchfield Park in Arizona—the location of the Navy's retired aircraft—and shipped to Alameda Naval Air Station near Oakland for major overhaul to return them to flying status. As each plane was completed we would fly one of our AD-7's to Alameda and make the exchange. The AD-7's were then modified to meet special requirements of the South Vietnamese Air Force. Eventually all of our "good" airplanes were shipped to Danang and donated to the South Vietnamese. The airplanes we received were barely airworthy and would require extensive repairs by our squadron maintenance department before being suitable for our needs. I made several of those sad trips to exchange a "good" plane for a "bad" one in Alameda.

Usually I would fly to Alameda in the morning (about a one hour flight), make the exchange, and return to Lemoore in the afternoon. Rarely did this exchange go smoothly as the airplanes to be picked up were in very poor condition and had not been flown in several years. One afternoon I took off with one of those "bad" planes and only one of the landing gears would retract so I had to return to have that problem repaired. By the time it was fixed to my satisfaction it was after dark and no way was I going to fly this piece of junk at night—these planes were to be flown in daylight VFR conditions only until our maintenance people had them airworthy. The next morning the plane was ready to go but the weather was not good—it was foggy with conditions expected to improve by noon. Slowly the fog lifted but the ceiling remained very low, about 200 feet. I could see the lower portions of the Bay Bridge about two miles to the northwest and knew that the weather across the bay in San Francisco was mostly clear. I decided that I had all the visibility I needed and requested to take off with a "special VFR" clearance—this meant that I would remain clear of clouds and be responsible for my own navigation. I did not trust the instruments in this aircraft enough to attempt to fly IFR or in the clouds. I took off and stayed very low over the water, planning to climb as soon as I found a clear spot. There were no clear spots and the bridge was straight ahead—I could see the bottom structure and part of the road but the top part of the bridge was in the clouds. Well, why not just fly under that bridge and therefore remain clear of the clouds? That's exactly what I did and I never heard a word about it! My airplane had plenty of clearance as I dropped down to below 50 feet and looked upward as I slipped under the roadway—lots of room! I doubt that my airplane was visible from the tower at Alameda and I was too low to be spotted on radar—if anyone saw me from the bridge (highly unlikely in the fog) they probably did not believe their eyes! I spotted sunlight ahead and found that clear spot just about the time I saw Alcatraz Island to my right. I climbed to a comfortable altitude in clear sunny skies and continued an uneventful flight to Lemoore. I told only a few close friends about this stunt—in reality it was a very stupid thing to do—but it was also **a lot of fun!**

After several weapons training deployments to Fallon and several carrier periods it was time to deploy to the Far East again. This time we knew exactly where the ship was going—we did not even have the usual rumors about liberty in Australia! The Midway was to be the second carrier stationed off the coast of Vietnam. Our assignment was to be the northern carrier—Yankee Station. This meant that we would be conducting strikes against North Vietnam—the other carrier, on Delta Station, was responsible for air support in South Vietnam. Our roles would often be reversed, depending on where the action was needed. The ship departed March 6, 1965 from Alameda; we breezed through the ORI, and arrived at Yankee Station during the night of April 9th.

The USS Midway was commissioned in 1945, too late to see service in WW II, and was deployed to the Mediterranean during the Korean conflict so this great ship had not fired a shot or launched an aircraft into combat during her twenty year history. That all changed early in the morning on the 10th of April. We had been conducting detailed briefings for almost a month that covered everything we needed to know about Vietnam—and we were ready! Only one of the squadron pilots had ever flown in combat before and that was our Skipper, Harry, who had flown the AD from a carrier in the Korean War. He had been shot down, captured, held as a POW, escaped, been recaptured and was finally repatriated at the end of that conflict—Harry had some amazing stories that he could relate. He was (and still is) a real American hero. The rest of us were on our first flights into combat and the adrenalin was pumping! Like most of the other pilots, I had put together my own survival equipment and I had far too much "stuff" stashed in my survival vest and every pocket in my flight suit—I could hardly stand up when fully suited to go! I had every conceivable type of weapon; my regulation .38 with about one hundred rounds of ammo (tracer, ball, incendiary, armor piercing, etc.), a second hidden "surrender" gun with several clips, several knives, a flare gun with lots of flares, and even a fingernail clip! I carried two canteens of water, enough rations to last at least a week, maps, money (even gold coins), and everything from band aids to prophylactics (for waterproof containers, of course). Most of these items I had crammed into A4 relief bags—surely the very first Ziploc baggies—that were used by the A4 pilots whose planes were not equipped with relief tubes. With all this extra "stuff" on my person I was barely able to put on my life vest and G-suit—I'm sure I looked like a stuffed turkey!

On this first combat mission we were assigned the task of dropping bombs on the Ho Chi Minh Trail—that infamous supply line connecting the North Vietnamese to their counterparts, the Viet Cong in South Vietnam. Our planes were loaded to the max take-off gross weight of 25,000 pounds and we carried heavy bombs (500 and 1000 lb) that were equipped with exotic anti-withdrawal, time-delay fuses. The pilots did not even know when these bombs were set to go off once dropped into the jungle along that winding trail that stretched for over 500 miles. The bombs were designed to penetrate the jungle canopy, imbed themselves several feet into the ground and just sit there awaiting their signal to explode. If the enemy found these bombs, they were set to explode if tampered with! When they did explode they took down a large part of the mountain and disrupted that supply line for a few hours, days or even weeks. Very seldom did we actually see trucks or personnel on this trail—they traveled mostly at night in convoys without lights.

After that first launch from the carrier our eight aircraft joined up and we headed toward the "beach"—what we called the first landfall. We were assigned fighter escorts, both F-8 and F-4 types who would protect us in the event we encountered enemy MIGs. The AD's (now redesignated the A-1's) were much slower and when we finally arrived in the area to drop our bombs the fighters reported that they were now low on fuel and were returning to the carrier—we were on our own! This logistical problem was soon solved by launching the fighters later and by the use of in-flight refueling—but this first trip into harm's way was not well planned. The flight from the carrier to the bomb area was almost two hours in length and before the first hour had expired I needed to take a nervous pee—I had to use the relief tube. I extracted that funnel from its compartment on the deck and prepared myself to "be relieved" by pulling the small trigger on the devise that would allow my urine to pass through the tube and overboard. Within a very few seconds that tiny funnel was full and nothing was going overboard! Now I was stuck holding a funnel full of urine and nowhere to empty it—and I was not finished. Finally I figured out that the only solution was to dump some of my survival "stuff" out of the A-4 relief bags and use them for the purpose they were designed for! Within minutes my fellow pilots were reporting the same problem in their airplanes. Unfortunately, several did not have the Ziploc bags and were forced to relieve themselves on the cockpit floor. When I returned to the ship some six hours later I had four of these relief bags stashed in various spots in the cockpit and my survival gear was scattered all over. It turned out that the outlet for the relief tube, underneath the cockpit, was covered over when our maintenance personnel added armor plating to our aircraft. For years the squadron had carried around armor plates designed to protect the pilot but had never had the occasion to use them until this time. This plating added 800 pounds to the empty weight of each aircraft that was not necessary in peacetime. It had been decided to "strap" on this added protection for the pilot while we were operating in the combat area but no one thought of such a simple thing as the relief tube exit being covered by those plates!

Our "road work" on the Ho Chi Minh Trail often included dropping bombs on the part of the trail that was in Laos and Thailand. Those areas were under the control of the North Vietnamese. After our ordnance had been expended we would check out of the area by contacting a controller located at a small Air Force Base called Nakhon Phanom, which was in Thailand. We jokingly pronounced it "Naked Phantom" and the Air Force controller would usually ask if we had time for a "morale check" before leaving the area. This meant that the controller wanted us to buzz their tower—this was good for the pilots' morale as well as the ground crew located in the middle of the jungle. Usually the jets were low on fuel and were not able to do a flyby but the AD's always had enough gas and we certainly wanted to take the time for a little fun. We were not as fast as the jets but we flew at tree top level and made a hell of a lot of noise as we swooped down and rattled their little tower. The ground guys loved it and we could see several personnel waving and cheering as we roared by—usually followed by a victory roll or two!

While the carrier was on Yankee Station we conducted flight operations around the clock. Life became very simple for the pilots—we briefed for our missions, flew those missions, and debriefed with the air intelligence officer when we completed our missions. The rest of the time was spent on the basics—eating, sleeping and writing letters to our loved ones. We began to realize that some of us would not be going home—we were flying over enemy territory and the enemy was getting better at defending their land. At this time there were severe restrictions on what we could and could not do over North

Vietnam. We were allowed to only attack targets to disrupt the flow of supplies from the North to the South. We bombed bridges that were rebuilt overnight, we attacked elusive targets that moved on the Ho Chi Minh Trail, we fired rockets at SAM sites, we bombed and strafed military naval vessels, and we flew over military airports filled with MIGs that we were not allowed to touch! Only when the MIGs (mostly flown by Russian and Communist Chinese pilots) were in the air and actually attacking our aircraft were we allowed to take them on! It was a very frustrating way to conduct a war.

The young men who worked on the carrier—most were not yet twenty-one—loading bombs, fueling aircraft, moving airplanes, repairing damage and doing all those necessary duties to make it all work, were incredible. At all hours of the day and night they could be seen sleeping in corners or under planes on the hangar deck, too exhausted to return to their sleeping berths, catching whatever rest they could before working another twenty hour shift. They were truly amazing. Chow lines were open around the clock for the enlisted men and a special room was always open for the pilots to grab something to eat twenty four hours a day. Most of us got into the habit of only wearing our flight suits and we ended up eating almost all our meals in this "dirty shirt" part of the wardroom.

I realized one day that I now had completed 300 carrier landings on the USS Midway. When a pilot made 100 landings on a particular ship he became a "Centurion" and was issued a patch that he could wear on his flight jacket. After 200 landings a special Double Centurion patch was awarded. I told the squadron "coffee mess officer" that I had now reached the Triple Centurion status and needed a new patch. The junior officer in the unit was always assigned the dubious duty as "coffee mess officer" and one of his numerous and menial duties was to get new patches for the pilots. He reported to me later that there were no such patches available—probably because no pilot had ever made that many landings on the same carrier. This was not true as quite a few aviators achieved that goal—but maybe not enough to make it worthwhile to have a new patch made. Suffice to say—I never received that patch!

Many of our sorties over North Vietnam were flown at night and that certainly increased the level of stress among the pilots. During the day we could usually see the SAMs being launched from the ground and were able to successfully evade them but at night we might see a bright flash when the missile was fired but were not able to follow its flight path. We began to drop parachute flares over the target areas to not only help us in our bomb runs but to enable us to see the missiles in flight. It didn't work very well—these flares were rated at one million candle power each and when there were several in the area it completely wiped out our night vision. These parachute flares could also cause vertigo to the pilots and even be a hazard to aerial flight! I pulled up from a dive bomb run one night just as another aircraft dropped one of his flares and it illuminated in front of my plane so close that I could actually see the parachute! I thought that I was going to hit that small chute and had to make a drastic evasive maneuver to avoid being shot down by one of our own flares!

We often carried two rocket pods on each aircraft—one on each wing-stub rack. These rocket pods held as many as 32 individual 2.25 inch rockets each and could be fired singly, in pairs or all at once. We were not allowed to land on the carrier with unexpended rockets still attached to the aircraft—obviously an arrested landing might cause the rocket pod to detach and proceed down the flight deck! This happened on several occasions when the aircraft was unable to jettison an unfired rocket and it dislodged and continued off the angled deck of the carrier. Thank God for the British who were the first to come up with the concept of putting angled decks on aircraft carriers. One night after an unsuccessful road reconnaissance flight my wingman and I returned to the carrier with 64 unused rockets on each aircraft. It was a beautiful clear but moonless night over the ocean and we were positioned about 10 miles behind the carrier and cleared to drop our rocket pods into the sea before being allowed to land. I briefed my wingman, a relatively new pilot to the squadron, quite thoroughly about making certain that his armament panel was set up properly before I gave the signal to drop those rocket pods which would fall harmlessly into the water. The most important thing was to ensure that the "rocket/bomb" switch was in the **BOMB** position and not the **ROCKET** position. My wingman, Mickey, said that he was ready to drop his pods on my command. I was able to see the carrier ten miles away and several other support vessels, one only five miles in front of us. We were flying toward the fleet at 5,000 feet when I gave the command to "pickle now!" My two rocket pods fell harmlessly away but my wingman, flying in close formation on my right wing, seemed to explode as 64 high velocity rockets were fired from his pods all at once! When I saw the bright flash off my right wing I thought that my wingman had been blown apart by a missile—then I saw all those rockets heading for our ships! It was quite a sight to behold—I had never seen so many rockets fired at the same time. Thank goodness they all fell into the ocean at least two miles from the nearest ship—but this fireworks display did not go unnoticed as we immediately heard from the carrier. I do not remember the exact words but the first transmission from the carrier to my flight was something like: "What the hell's going on out there—looks like you are trying to sink the whole God damn fleet!" It was a spectacular display but those rockets were air to ground unguided missiles that fizzled out after less than one mile and I did not witness any explosions as they dropped into the ocean. There was a lot of explaining to do when we landed on board the carrier but the bottom line was that my wingman, Mickey, was forthcoming with the fact that he placed his switch in the wrong position and it was entirely his fault. Luckily, no harm was done and there were no repercussions about this incident.

Mickey was the worst bomber in our squadron—possibly in the entire Navy! One day we were assigned a very difficult mission to take out several SAM sites near Hanoi. The North Vietnamese had learned to build their Surface to Air Missile sites near schools, hospitals or religious buildings— knowing that by doing so it would make it much more difficult for our pilots to precisely hit the right target. If a bomb or rocket went astray the news media were quickly on the spot to take photos of the civilian casualties caused by our "WARMONGERING" pilots! Our targets this day were literally surrounding a rather large pagoda type structure which had special religious significance to the North Vietnamese. During the briefing by the Air Intelligence Officer we were repeatedly warned to avoid hitting this building if at all possible. It would require precise bombing by our pilots—we did not have "smart bombs" in those days and our bombsights were little better than putting an X on the cockpit forward glass to line up the target. All available aircraft were used for this mission and Mickey was included—in spite of his reputation for missing the target. We managed to successfully take out the SAM sites but Mickey dropped a 1000 pound bomb directly on the center of the religious structure—to no surprise to me! He was in serious trouble when we returned to the ship and reported what happened. Our Skipper and the CAG both chewed out poor Mickey—but Mickey came up with the best excuse I have ever heard for his errant bombing. He said, "Sir, I never hit what I'm aiming at—so I put the pipper exactly on the center of the building we were supposed to avoid, knowing that surely I would miss it by several hundred feet!" I suppose that was the first and only time that Mickey hit what he was aiming at. Shortly after this incident Mickey turned in his wings (with lots of pressure from the Skipper) and entered training to become a SEAL. I hope he had better luck under water than he had in the skies.

My favorite combat missions were what were referred to as "coastal reccies" or early morning reconnaissance flights that launched off just before dawn and patrolled the coast line of North Vietnam looking for targets of opportunity. Basically we were looking for enemy naval activity which included PT boats and supply ships from other Communist countries. Obviously we were not allowed to attack enemy shipping outside the three mile limit from the shore line, but once a military ship was inside that international boundary it was okay to attack. The enemy knew those rules and they tried to slip into the docks just before daylight. Once they were tied up to the shore, they were no longer legitimate targets—again, one of the rules of this political war. The object was to find them before they were "attached to the land" and dissuade them from further attempts to supply the North Vietnamese. It was really a game of cat and mouse—if those ships made it to the dock they were safe, if we caught them inside the three mile limit before they docked, they became fair game! Our rules of engagement became even more restrictive—if a military ship was flying a flag from the USSR or any of the other soviet bloc countries, we were not allowed to attack. It finally boiled down to one simple fact—we could not attack a surface vessel unless it was flying the North Vietnam flag! In order to ascertain that it was indeed a legitimate target we must fly over that vessel at a slow speed and warn them— if they were smart they hoisted a flag that indicated that their vessel was off limits. If they were not too smart they fired at our aircraft—that was our real signal that it was okay to attack! One morning my wingman and I followed a large military ship that was trying to slip into an estuary to the north of the coastal city of Vinh. We approached from astern to make one final identifying pass when the ship stopped dead in the water, uncovered two large anti-aircraft guns and commenced firing upon us! Several "orange balls" went between my aircraft and that of my wingman and suddenly my "buddy" broke off and turned away! I yelled for "Freddy" to get back into position but he was terrified and was heading back out to sea toward the carrier. I made it official: "This is an order, get back into position—now!"

Freddy recovered from his momentary lapse of military discipline and we rejoined—he was now okay and no longer in shock from his first taste of combat. We made several runs on that enemy ship before it was disabled. It was finally sunk after several sorties from the carrier came to our assistance. We lost one A-4 during that operation—shot down by anti-aircraft fire from the sinking ship—and it was finally sunk by a flight of A-1's dropping napalm! All in all it was a lesson well learned—we were fighting a tenacious enemy prepared to fight to the death!

After a while we began to get used to the intense anti-aircraft fire up north. We could evade the SAMs if we had enough warning and could see them launch from the ground. Often those SAMs were defective and either exploded prematurely or flew into the ground shortly after launch. I sincerely believe that a lot of the so-called collateral damage to non-military targets blamed on our pilots was actually caused by those missiles that went astray. We also got used to seeing those orange balls of flame from the 37 and 57 mm AA guns. What we did not usually see was the heavy small arms fire that was always present. Sometimes we saw muzzle flashes from the ground and knew that there was a lot of metal coming at us but we could only hope that they did not get a lucky hit. The only battle damage I ever received was from small arms fire and only found out about it after returning to the ship. The plane captain walked up to me as I was getting out of the cockpit and said, "Looks like you got at least one bad guy today!" I did not know what he was talking about until he showed me a small hole in the leading edge of the horizontal stabilizer on the tail of the aircraft. There was also an exit hole in the trailing edge of the stabilizer. Obviously, for a round of ammunition to follow such a trajectory, the aircraft had to be in a bombing or strafing run and flying directly toward the enemy who was firing from the ground. Maybe this was my only kill of the war?

It seemed that all too soon my combat tour was coming to an end. I had received orders to report to VA-127, based at NAS Lemoore, as an instructor. This RAG (Retraining Air Group) squadron was where fleet Naval Aviators and older pilots transitioning to new aircraft were trained. I was a bit surprised and quite pleased to have been given this assignment— I would be an instructor in single-engine jet aircraft checking out pilots in jets and teaching instrument flying in F-9F Cougars. It was bittersweet, however, as I really did not want to leave my A-1 squadron and my dear friends and fellow pilots of VA-25. I also knew that I would never again fly the AD, A-1, Skyraider, or Spad after leaving the Fist of the Fleet! My final flight, my 43rd combat mission over North Vietnam, occurred almost two months after the ship first sailed from Alameda. Fittingly, it was an early morning coastal reconnaissance flight that would be routine but also one to be remembered.

My wingman and I manned our planes before dawn and our aircraft were positioned at the very aft end of the flight deck. We were part of a large group of airplanes from our carrier to be launched just at first light to hit various targets throughout North Vietnam. I started my trusty R-3350 engine and went through the usual preflight checks—everything checked out. Since I was at "the back of the pack" on the flight deck it was almost 30 minutes from the time I entered the cockpit to the time I started taxiing to the catapult. I should not have had that second or third cup of coffee before leaving the ready room—I needed to relieve myself. I had never heard of anyone using the relief tube while still on the ground (or the flight deck in this case) but I figured that I would be more comfortable if I "did it" before launch. It was barely daylight and surely no one would notice—the propeller wash would dissipate my urine and very little would fall to the flight deck. I was almost finished when I noticed a flight deck crewman waving frantically to me from his position forward and to the right of my aircraft. He was pointing beneath my plane and was obviously concerned about something leaking under my belly. I waved him off as best I could with hand signals but he was determined to check out the source of this leak. He gave me a "hold your brakes" signal and ducked under my wing. I knew what he was doing—checking that suspicious puddle to determine if it was fuel, oil or hydraulic fluid! I cringed while he was under my aircraft and did not want him to see my grin when he reappeared. I lowered my sun visor in my hardhat so he had no eye contact as he looked at me with a very pissed-off look—perhaps he felt pissed-on as he wiped off his fingers on his cleaning rag. I'm sure that he wanted to give me the finger instead of signaling that everything was OK!

After launch, my wingman and I joined up and began our flight to the coastline to patrol for targets of opportunity. It was a beautiful, clear morning with just a touch of haze along the shore as we flew northward toward Hanoi. We avoided the city of Vinh as it was a hotbed of SAMs with very few military targets and continued our shoreline surveillance. We were ready to reverse our course when I decided to check out a river running northwest from the coast toward Hanoi. This was usually as far as we ventured without fighter escort and we were all alone that morning. About ten miles upstream I spotted a new bridge—actually in the process of being built at that very time. We flew over that "work in progress" to get a closer look and spotted bulldozers and heavy equipment putting the finishing touches to what was to be an "underwater bridge." Our airplanes had knocked out most of the traditional bridges connecting the North to the South and the enemy had begun cleverly building bridges that were just below the surface of the water where they were not visible from the air. At night the supply convoys could travel across the rivers without lights and not be spotted from the air and during the daylight the bridges were invisible. After our "look-see" pass, my wingman and I reversed course and came in for a strafing run. As we pulled away I noticed that we had certainly awakened the anti-aircraft batteries in the area as we began encountering heavy flak. We then made several runs firing rockets and finally finished with dive bomb runs until we had expended all our ordnance. On the last run we encountered no flak and noticed several secondary explosions on the ground. We returned to the ship with a feeling of a job "well done."

During the customary debrief with the Air Intelligence Officer, I was asked the all important question: "Was the bridge destroyed?" I could only answer truthfully that I really did not know—we dropped several bombs where we knew the underwater bridge to be but there was no evidence that it had been hit, much less destroyed. At least we knew of a new bridge that would be the subject of surveillance in the future. The next day I departed the USS Midway aboard the COD aircraft and was flown to Clark Air Force Base in the Philippines to await a MATS (Military Air Transport Service) flight back to the U.S. mainland. All of my belongings were shipped in a foot locker to my next duty assignment so I was able to travel very light with one small personal bag. When I arrived at Clark I was told that it would be two or three days before the next flight to Travis Air Force Base in California, so I checked into the Officers Quarters and enjoyed some much needed R and R (rest and relaxation). The next day I picked up a copy of "Stars and Stripes," the military newspaper that we did not receive aboard ship, and found a most interesting (and amusing) article on the front page. A small paragraph near the bottom of the page proclaimed that: **Midway Aircraft Attack Bridge Near Hanoi!** It must have been a very slow day for news in the war as this article described my last mission with a bit of military propaganda. I chuckled when I read the part that stated: The A-1 aircraft did *extensive damage to the approaches to the bridge!* What a tactful way of saying that we missed the damn bridge! To this day I am not sure just how you can inflict damage to the approaches to a bridge—but I'm sure that it made sense to someone in the military press corps.

While awaiting my flight to Travis I ran into an old fraternity brother of mine from Virginia. He was now an Air Force pilot who had just received an assignment to fly A-1 aircraft in South Vietnam in a "Sandy" squadron. I was not familiar with the Sandy mission until he explained—his group would be flying the A-1's in close air support missions down South and would be deeply involved with rescue operations for downed pilots. He was very excited about his assignment and we spent several hours in the O'Club bar discussing the versatility of the trusty Spad. He had been flying single-engine jet fighters for the Air Force and was thrilled that he was now going to take a step back in time and fly that old prop plane in combat. I was thrilled that I was now going to report to a jet squadron as an instructor! I hated to leave my fellow pilots while they were in harm's way but it was time to move on in my naval career. I knew that several of my friends would not be returning from that cruise—in fact, fifteen pilots were lost from the Air Group during that first Vietnam combat cruise on the Midway. The good news was that VA-25, the Fist of the Fleet, would shoot down a MIG-17 over North Vietnam! Four A-1's were attacked by two MIG aircraft whose pilots made the fatal mistake of trying to mix it up at low altitude with the much more maneuverable prop planes. I read about this fantastic feat shortly after returning to the U.S. and felt an enormous sense of pride that our pilots were so skilled that they were able to defeat the enemy who were flying aircraft a generation more advanced!

I boarded the MATS flight from Clark AFB to Travis AFB in my Tropical White Long Uniform (long pants, short sleeve shirt with epaulets) and was expecting to be picked up by my wife at Travis. After landing, I walked into the Air Force terminal and heard a page: "Lieutenant Eads, report to the information desk." After being directed to the info desk I headed that way, expecting to meet my wife for a joyous reunion. As I approached that destination I heard a familiar voice calling my name. It was my old friend, Rex, who was now an instructor in one of the Lemoore based RAG squadrons. We embraced and I asked what he was doing at Travis of all places—what a coincidence, I thought. He grinned and said, "Follow me; I'm giving you a quick ride home!" He was in his flight gear and as we stepped outside the terminal, he pointed to an F-9 Cougar parked on the ramp. I grinned but admitted that I had no flight gear, hard hat, oxygen mask, g-suit or any of the necessary equipment to get into that single-engine jet trainer. Rex assured me that everything was under control—just step on board! I

assumed that the required flight gear would be in the rear cockpit—wrong—
there was only one thing sitting on the ejection seat, a six pack of beer that was
almost cold! I strapped in, we took off, Rex leveled at ten thousand feet so that
I would not need oxygen, and we covered the 250 air miles to Lemoore in a
little more than 30 minutes—I could only finish two beers! What a great way
to be welcomed home from the war!

Chapter Twelve

**"An airplane may disappoint a good pilot,
but it won't surprise him."**

I checked into VA-127 a few days after returning from Vietnam and it seemed like a different world. The squadron was about the same size as VA-25 with an average of twenty pilot instructors and the normal complement of twelve aircraft—all F9F-8T Cougars, which were tandem cockpit single engine jet trainers. It was a very senior group of officers, three full Commanders, about a dozen Lieutenant Commanders and the rest being second tour types like myself—fairly senior Lieutenants. All had extensive experience in jets and I was the first pilot to report as an instructor with ZERO hours jet time! However, I was also the first pilot to check in with recent combat experience so I was treated by some as a hero and by others as an unqualified interloper. I believe that it all averaged out and I was soon accepted into the "brotherhood" as just another instructor. The mission of VA-127 was two-fold: Primarily; to train and check fleet pilots in instrument flying. Secondarily; to transition pilots from flying props to jets. Many senior Naval Aviators who were ready to report to fleet squadrons as Executive Officers or C.O.s had limited jet experience—many had spent their last tour in a non-flying job such as War College, the Pentagon, or staff assignments. They needed to be checked out in jets before reporting to the RAG that would finish their training in the type aircraft that they would be flying in the fleet. After being transitioned to jets in VA-127, most would then report to VA-125, the RAG for A-4s in the Pacific fleet. There they would receive training in formation flying, weapons tactics, and carrier operations. First, I had to be checked out in jets before I could be an instructor in this squadron.

I was amazed at how easy it was to fly a single-engine jet aircraft. There were no prop or mixture controls, not as many instruments to monitor your engine, and little or no rudder input was required! The jet was a clean (non-oil-dripping) aircraft that had only two speeds—fast or faster—and I really enjoyed the transition training that was provided by my new fellow pilots. The second hop was what I had been looking forward to for a long time—we were going to go supersonic! The F9 was considered a supersonic aircraft—the better definition was that it was a TRANS-SONIC plane—in other words it could break the speed of sound only if pushed to the max by the pilot. On that second flight I climbed out to the west over the ocean to an altitude of 40,000 feet—higher than I had ever been by far. The instructor pilot was in the rear cockpit and he had briefed how delicate the F9 was when it went faster than the speed of sound. It seemed to take forever to reach FL 400 and I was not comfortable with the forced oxygen system that we were equipped with—above a certain altitude the pilot was given 100% oxygen that was pushed into your lungs. Instead of the normal breathing pattern of inhaling and exhaling, it was now necessary to force that oxygen out of your lungs—a process that required a lot of grunting. Every time you opened your mouth to say something, you were given a lung full of O2 that took an effort to expel. Once at the required altitude, I rolled inverted and dove straight down with the throttle pushed full forward. I watched with great anticipation as the airspeed approached Mach One! Finally we were supersonic—and I had not felt anything that was remarkable—then I heard the pilot in the back calmly saying, "I think you should pull out now." I looked at the altimeter and saw it unwinding rapidly through 20,000 feet—seemed to be plenty of altitude to pull out to me! I started to pull back on the stick and it felt like it was imbedded in concrete—I pulled harder and the aircraft finally started to recover from that extreme nose down attitude. It required at least a four G maneuver to recover before we passed 10,000 feet and I could hear the instructor pilot laughing in the rear cockpit! Later he related that almost every pilot that broke the sound barrier the first time was so focused on airspeed that he did not pay enough attention to the most important instrument—the altimeter!

Towards the end of my training—shortly before I would be certified as an instructor—I was asked by the squadron C.O. to fly a "cross-country flight" to take a friend of his to Buffalo, New York. I'm sure that he had two goals in mind—it would be a good experience for me and his friend would get a free ride to the East Coast. I was eager to go (as though I had a choice) and planned this coast to coast flight with special care. My passenger, the Skipper's friend, was a Navy Captain and a really nice guy. He was not current in the F9 but wanted to "get some instrument time" during our flight to Buffalo. I planned a very conservative flight that consisted of three legs—we would stop twice for fuel. The first stop was at Hill Air Force Base in Utah, the second stop was Wright-Patterson AFB in Ohio, and then it was on to a small Air National Guard airfield at Niagara Falls, New York. Everything went as planned and the trip was mostly uneventful. I found out, however, that the Captain was more than rusty with his instrument flying from the rear cockpit so I ended up hand-flying most of the trip. We had a short delay at Wright-Pat due to a fueling problem (the Air Force personnel put the wrong fuel into our airplane) and arrived at Niagara Falls at around ten o'clock PM. I knew that the runway at this ANG Base was relatively short and the F9 did not have a drogue chute to shorten the landing roll like many Air Force jets. The F9 took a considerable amount of runway for landing and we used aerodynamic braking to shorten our roll-out. This meant that after the main gear was on the ground, the pilot would pull back on the stick to raise the nose into the air to increase drag as much as possible. The plane was equipped with a "tail-skid" or a large metal plate that would contact the runway before the tailpipe—thus causing no damage to the engine while slowing the aircraft. It was not policy to drag that tail skid on landing but it was there to accomplish what I needed that night in Niagara Falls. It was a "dark and stormy night" as I touched down as close to the end of the runway as possible and raised the nose for the maximum aerodynamic braking. I felt the tail skid touch the runway and sensed the deceleration. Then I heard the tower controller scream: "NAVY JET—YOU'RE ON FIRE!" Before I could respond he related that flames were engulfing the rear of my aircraft and maybe I should eject! I knew that the tail skid would create lots of sparks when it encountered the runway so I eased the nose over and slowed the aircraft down with normal braking until I was slow enough to depart the runway. The tower controller, the only one on duty that evening, then asked if he should call crash and rescue. I tried not to laugh as I replied, "Just a normal Navy landing, no assistance required."

The next day I returned to NAS Lemoore by retracing my steps. Due to the headwinds on this Westerly flight it was a bit more challenging. Forecast winds were not as accurate in the mid-sixties as today and I ended up with very little fuel remaining as I approached Hill AFB in Utah. I learned a very important lesson that day that I never forgot. When I was given a clearance to descend about 100 miles from the airport, I simply stated that I was a bit short on fuel and would like to remain as high as possible for as long as possible. The controller could not have been more helpful—he said, "Navy Jet, you are cleared to descend at your own discretion—report the field in sight and you will be given priority to land." The point was that the controllers were there to help in any way possible but if the pilot was not honest in admitting that there was "a problem" this help would not be forthcoming!

After completing the transition and instrument syllabus I became an instructor. Most of the pilots that I "instructed" had many more hours in jet aircraft than I did and I probably learned more from them than the other way around. Soon I settled into a routine—flying two hops a day and spending several hours handling paperwork required by my "collateral duties" such as the squadron Legal Officer and later the Personnel Officer. Each flight required a one hour brief, an average of two hours aloft, and at least a 30 minute debrief. Two flights each day with the normal other duties added up to usually a ten hour day! This was not a problem as long as I was having fun and enjoying the flying. After a while, less than one year, I was starting to get bored and asked to be assigned as the jet transition officer in the squadron. This was the perfect billet for me as I had undergone the transition from props to jets and understood just what the syllabus required. I continued flying instrument training hops but each time a new group was scheduled for transition, I was the instructor who gave the ground school training as well as the flight training. This was a much more satisfying arrangement than being strictly an instrument instructor.

It was tremendously rewarding to check out pilots in jet aircraft. After ground school the new pilot flew in the front cockpit on his first and every flight and I sat behind with my usual big grin as he felt the rush that we all felt the first time we flew a really fast airplane and knew that we were in control of that powerful beast! After three or four flights we introduced aerobatics and low level flying. I was probably the easiest instructor in Naval Aviation when the "student" performed aerobatics—I would get airsick in the back seat during loops, rolls and spins when I was not actually at the controls. Funny how that worked—I could demonstrate aerobatics without a problem but once the student took over I quickly turned green and told the guy in the front cockpit that he had performed the maneuver to my complete satisfaction. After this abbreviated introduction to aerobatic flying, I would tell the student that it was now time for a bit of low-level flying and we would head for Death Valley. It had always been a big thrill for me to fly through Death Valley in the AD and watch the altimeter read below ZERO! The lowest point was over 200 feet below sea level and the view was extraordinary as one flew over this barren wasteland at an altitude of 100 feet AGL (above ground level). In the F9 the view was not so good at 300 knots but the effect of speed was mind-boggling! Every pilot that I took on this trip was fascinated to observe the ground moving so rapidly while the altimeter was reading in the negative! After flying over the lowest place in the "lower forty-eight" we would zoom up to 14,500 feet and buzz the stone shelter at the top of Mt. Whitney, the highest place in the US outside of Alaska! I am happy to announce that our military pilots have continued this ritual to the present date. I climbed to the top of Mt. Whitney in June, 2004 (on my 65th birthday) and observed both Navy and Air Force airplanes doing the same thing we did forty years previously—basically burning up the tax-payers dollars in jet fuel while having the time of their lives! Thank God that we still have such aviators in our American Armed Forces.

The F9 Cougar was a very reliable jet trainer and I never encountered any serious engine problems. The ejection seat, however, was a primitive Martin-Baker model that did not inspire confidence if one had to eject. One day I thought for sure that I would find out if that seat worked or not! The summertime temperatures on the ramp at Lemoore were more than just hot—they were blistering! To keep the seats as cool as possible for as long as possible, the plane captain placed ejection seat covers over both cockpit seats which were removed by the pilots as they climbed aboard. After the covers were removed they were given to the plane captain who stowed them in the nose compartment. The nose compartment was the only place on the aircraft to stow anything—from the pilots' personal luggage to such things as ejection seat covers, pitot tube covers, engine covers, tie down gear, etc. This nose gear compartment opened from both sides and when both doors were open it looked like gull-wings extending from each side of the nose. On this particular day the plane captain, a relatively new enlisted man, did not properly secure those doors after stowing the seat covers—and this was not discovered by the taxi director, a rare case of "double errors." There was no indication in the cockpit to warn the pilot that the doors were not latched securely. The pilot in the back cockpit was on an instrument training hop and he would take control of the aircraft approaching 100 knots on the take-off roll when I announced, "You have it!"

I started the take-off roll with the pilot in the back "under the bag" and after everything looked normal I passed control to him while still on the runway and approaching 100 knots. As the aircraft lifted off I retracted the gear and felt a sharp flutter—then the nose pitched over and we were headed for the ground! I noticed those clam shell type doors moving to the full open position and bad things started to happen very quickly. I grabbed the stick and told the pilot in the rear that I "had it" and to pop his bag (lower his instrument hood) and stand by to eject. The control tower transmitted, "Parts of your aircraft are coming off!" What was happening was that those ejection seat covers, and other "stuff," were being blown out of the nose compartment into the slip stream. Unfortunately, one of those covers flew into one of the intakes for the engine and the EGT gauge went to the full hot position and the engine began to surge. I pulled back on the throttle to try to avoid an engine seizure and pulled back on the stick to avoid ground contact—not exactly what they teach in pilot training! The aircraft responded with a slight climb and the temp gauge came slightly off the full hot peg—then I began to stall! I eased forward on the stick and added enough power to keep the EGT right at the red line. I began to notice that I could control those nose compartment doors with throttle and attitude—if the doors opened too much the nose dropped, if the doors closed too much the airplane stalled! I had almost forgotten the pilot in the rear seat when he said, "Sir, is there anything you want me to do?" I responded as honestly as I could, "Be ready to eject on my command!" In this aircraft if the front seat pilot ejected, the rear seat pilot was also ejected, but he could eject on his own without me being punched out. He asked me a very important question: "What are you going to do?" I was nursing it over the ground at an altitude of less than 300 feet and we were alternately stalling and coming apart in the air. Before I could answer, the FIRE WARNING LIGHT came on and the tower reported flames from the tail pipe. The throttle was almost full forward—close to 100%—and I eased it back to about 90% and dropped the flaps, thinking that I would at least get a level attitude before ejecting or maybe just put it down straight ahead on the mostly level desert. We had taken off on the easternmost parallel runway that was oriented NW/SE and the aircraft was now located only about three miles from the upwind end of the departing runway. The tower was asking, "What are your intentions?"—just like they are supposed to do in these situations;

the guy in the back seat was bugging me about my "intentions" and I was staring at a red fire warning light that I could not extinguish! I was thinking that it would be better to put the aircraft down than to eject—perhaps because of my prop plane background where the pilot had a better chance to "ride it in" than to try to get out. I also knew that the closer we crashed to the airfield the better our chances of survival would be. I decided to try a shallow turn to the left to see if I could nurse the crippled bird a bit closer to the rescue equipment. I was very aware of the many fatalities caused by a pilot trying to return to the airport in an aircraft that was doomed—instead of ejecting or landing straight ahead!

I found that I could hold altitude (about 300 feet) and airspeed (about 120 knots) with 15 degrees of bank angle. If the gull wing doors remained at a certain angle, slightly higher than 90 degrees, the aircraft remained out of a stall. If I kept less than 90% of thrust on the throttle the engine did not surge. Out of the corner of my left eye I could see the parallel runway coming into view and was tempted to increase the bank angle to line up for a landing. I could feel the airframe starting to shudder and the engine temperature was again on the red line—not a good idea to increase the bank angle. I told the pilot in the rear that he could eject if he wanted but that I was going to try to get the aircraft on the runway. After a second or two he replied that he was going to remain on board! I told the tower that I intended to land downwind on the westernmost parallel runway and please roll the crash equipment. I was overshooting a proper line up for the runway and was now aimed at the end of the runway off heading by at least 30 degrees. The tower cleared me to land, reported that I had a lot of black smoke coming from the engine, and gently reminded me that my landing gear was not down. I was trying to wait until wings level before extending the gear as I was not sure how that change in configuration would affect the flying characteristics of my disabled craft. Thank God that NAS Lemoore had the longest runways of any Navy Base— over 14,000 feet—as I was still in a turn as I passed the end of the runway. After another overshoot from the other side I was now almost halfway down the runway before the wings were level and the gear indicated down and locked. I closed the throttle, pulled back on the stick and let it fall to the ground! After one small bounce we were on the runway for good and I shut down the engine and used maximum braking. We came to a quick stop with about 1000 feet of runway remaining and the crash vehicles had us surrounded. There was no damage to the aircraft other than the ruined engine which was replaced in a day or two and the plane was returned to service. The plane captain was chewed out by his Chief as was the taxi director and everyone else went on about their business—another routine day in Naval Aviation!

The squadron call sign was "Royal Blue" and a small group of us formed an aerobatic unit that we called "The Royal Blues". We were certainly not trying to compete with the real Naval Flight Demonstration Team, the Blue Angels, but we had a lot of fun and did several air shows at NAS Lemoore and some surrounding airfields. The F-9 Cougar was a great airplane for formation flying with one exception. The large "flying tail" had the horizontal stabilizer quite high which presented a small problem when flying in the slot position (number four in a flight of four). If you tucked in too close when in the diamond formation, that flying tail would be in the jet wash of the leader above and ahead, not where you wanted to be! Naturally, I was the slot man in our group and learned quickly to stay below the leader's jet blast. Later the squadron transitioned to the A-4 trainer and that particular problem ceased to exist. The A-4 was a much better aircraft for aerobatics as it was much smaller and the turning radius was such that we were able to remain very near the crowd as we did our maneuvers. During my three years as an instructor in VA-127, the "Royal Blues" flew in two air shows with the Blue Angels—both at NAS Lemoore. The first show we were flying the F-9 and the second we had the TA4F, the latest of the A-4 series at that time. The Blue Angels were flying the F-4 Phantom aircraft at this time, a great airplane but we always joked that it was proof that if "you put big enough engines on a barn door, it will fly!" The F-4 had a terrible turning radius and although they were fast and very impressive with their formation flying, there were times when they were out of sight of the crowd for several minutes as they regrouped after certain maneuvers. The F-9 that we flew was hardly any better and our performance as compared to the Blue Angels was rather poor. When we flew in the next air show against the Blues, it was a different story. They still had the F-4's but we now had the agile "Scooter" as the A-4 was sometimes called. We spent many hours practicing for this air show and felt that we were able to perform a very entertaining demonstration that was only about fifteen minutes long but would be concentrated directly over the crowd. Our final maneuver was to fly down the runway in a tight diamond formation at 450 knots only one hundred feet above the ground—we then pulled up into a loop, dropped gear, flaps, and hook while inverted and arrived back over the runway in the same tight diamond—this time at an airspeed of only 100 knots! The crowd loved it as we were always in sight during the entire show and because of the smaller size of the A-4 as compared to the F-4; it seemed that we were flying faster! Many persons who watched this air show thought that we, the Royal Blues, did a better job of entertaining the crowd than the famous Blue Angels—obviously these were our friends and loved ones, but it made us feel good! Within a very few years, the Blue Angels changed aircraft to the versatile A-4 and remained with that demonstration aircraft longer than any other in the Blue's history. The Blue Angels also began to use the 'clean to dirty' loop that we invented as part of their air show!

VA-127 had three different C.O.'s or Skippers during my tour—each was completely different. It seemed that the position was a bit of a transition point in a Naval Officer's career. The first C.O. was known as "Brownie" to all of the other pilots and he was as laid-back as one could get. He was obviously planning to retire after this last assignment and his only agenda was to have as much fun as possible and not cause any ripples. He and his wife had lots of parties and he was indeed a pleasure to work with. The third C.O. was so bland that I cannot recall his name. The second Skipper was a different story altogether! He did not have a first name, only a series of initials, and was never on a friendly basis with any of the other Officers. His agenda was to set new records in number of flight hours flown and do things differently than his predecessors. He had aspirations of Flag Rank for sure! He decided that all of the squadron pilots should be carrier qualified—although our mission was only jet transition and instrument refreshment training. Fine with me as I finally got to get carrier landings in a jet—in reality not an overwhelming event as by now I was very comfortable flying the F-9 and the A-4. The squadron began to receive the new A-4's in October 1966 and we would retire our F-9's in March of the next year. For a period of six months we flew both types and you never knew which one you would strap into until checking the daily flight schedule. Our carrier qualifications were in the A-4, in my estimation a much better aircraft due to its stability on approach. After we were all current in carrier operations the "problem Skipper" decided that since we were teaching instruments we should all be proficient in actual night instrument flying. Almost all of our training flights were flown in daytime, VFR conditions, and only during the winter tule fog periods did we log "actual IFR" time. This Skipper discovered that Monterey, CA, where a small Auxiliary Navy Field was located, had the lousiest weather on the entire West

Coast during the summer months at night. By midnight the weather would be **WOXOF**, which meant that the ceiling was obscured and the visibility was zero in fog. In other words the airport was below landing minimums and was basically closed. Our intrepid Skipper began to schedule a flight of four aircraft to depart Lemoore each night at 0200 hours (yes, 2 AM!) to fly to Monterey and conduct approaches for at least one hour before departing for the return trip back to our base. These "night-fright" schedules continued for almost two weeks before the squadron received a scathing letter from the C.O. of the Monterey base (a senior Captain, I might add) who basically asked our Skipper (only a Commander) just what the hell did he think he was doing! The citizens of the fair city of Monterey were irate and bitterly complaining about the incredible noise of our aircraft making repeated approaches and missed approaches to their sleepy coastal resort town in the middle of the night. As the Legal Officer at the time I had to reply to this letter—it was hard to resist stating that we were all—with the exception of our C.O.—very unhappy to be doing such a senseless thing. After letters of apology to the Mayor, Chamber of Commerce, and the Base Commander, we discontinued those flights of stupidity! Don't know whatever happened to that C.O. but hopefully he was not put in a place where he had to make decisions of any importance.

Most of our flying was of a more fun nature. The pilots that we trained were highly skilled aviators who only needed a refresher course in instrument flying and most breezed through our syllabus with little difficulty. Occasionally, I encountered a pilot of rare ability who had a natural talent for flying that was a pleasure to observe. One such pilot could do aerobatics "under the bag" better than I ever hoped to, either on the gauges or flying visually. He was incredibly smooth and each maneuver was perfect—I did not even get airsick when he did loops, spins, rolls, etc. He later shot down a North Vietnamese MIG with an Air-to-Ground rocket while flying an A-4 in combat—did not surprise me the least bit when I heard of this feat as he was truly an exceptional aviator. Often, after completing the required training on a particular hop, there was a little time remaining to have a bit of fun. In the winter over the Sierra Mountains we flew over several ski areas and frequently checked out the runs up close and personal! One of my favorite spots was a small ski area called China Peak (now known as Sierra Summit) which was located south of Yosemite and near Huntington Lake, a small body of water known for its trout fishing. I would drop down to fly over the lake, usually frozen during the winter months, from the southwest and then fly UP the lift line to watch the skiers coming down the hill toward my aircraft. It was quite a view for me and I'm sure a bit of a surprise for the downhill skier to see a low flying jet going up the hill from the lake. One day I met another airplane (Navy, of course) coming down the hill the opposite direction and we almost had the dreaded mid-air collision. After discussing this problem with several of my fellow pilots we decided to publish an "unofficial traffic pattern" for the China Peak ski area! Planes were to be flown in a clockwise pattern only and one must enter the pattern from over the lake and fly up the hill, not down! This pattern was posted on the pilot bulletin boards for all the squadrons at Lemoore—and the safety officers pretended that it did not exist. Legal or not, pilots would continue to do such stunts and we all accepted the fact that it was best to be safe not sorry.

The final flight in our instrument training syllabus consisted of a cross-country trip to another airport and return. Usually this was accomplished in one day with a flight in the morning to an Air Force or Navy base and return after lunch to Lemoore. This was always interesting and fun to go to a different place for a change and the instructor usually picked out the destination. One trip worth remembering was to New Orleans—a bit longer than the usual cross-country—and we remained over night. It just so happened that Mardi Gras was going on in the Crescent City at the time! Actually, I visited with my sister and her husband who lived in Baton Rouge and did not participate in the debauchery in the French Quarter. My student pilot was not as reserved, however, and he was in pretty bad shape when we departed the next morning to fly to the West coast. He had some interesting tales to tell about his evening experiences and I began to feel like the "old guy" who was becoming a bit staid at the ripe old age of 28! At least I felt better than my buddy in the back who threw up twice (in his gloves) before we got back home. Usually I preferred to take the student to El Paso, Texas for his final flight. My ulterior motive was to make a booze run across the border to buy cheap tequila and rum in Mexico. Each American was allowed one gallon of booze duty free and it was helpful if the student was a non-drinker so I could get a double ration. One such trip to El Paso turned into quite a "colorful" event. We did not carry external fuel tanks on our F-9 Cougars and therefore had a fairly short range, normally around 1200 nautical miles or a duration of 2.5 hours. The internal fuel tanks were always filled to capacity without exception. I taxied my aircraft to the departure end of the runway one hot summer afternoon and after checking my charts and tables, found that the temperature and altitude combinations were not conducive to taking off for a while. The airport at El Paso was a joint use field—the civilian part was El Paso International Airport and the military side was called Biggs AAF (Auxiliary Air Field). The elevation of the airport was approximately 4000 feet and with a temperature of 105 degrees, the density altitude was off my chart at my calculated take-off weight. The solution was simple—wait until the temperature dropped a few degrees or burn off some fuel to reduce the take-off weight. I figured that I must wait at least ten minutes before a safe departure could be made on the longest runway. As I sat patiently waiting for the right combination of weight, wind and temperature another F-9 taxied out for take-off. This F-9 was from the advanced training command located in Kingsville, Texas and I had met the instructor pilot while filing my flight plan at Operations. Although he had a shorter distance to fly to his home base, I knew that we were at the same weight as we both had full internal tanks. I was sitting in the run-up area at the end of the runway as he taxied by and announced to the tower that he was ready for take-off. I began to do a quick recalculation—maybe I had made a mistake—surely if my aircraft was too heavy for take-off in these conditions, so was his! The tower cleared his aircraft for take-off on runway 8 just as I completed my new computations—I was still about 1000 pounds too heavy! Maybe he knew something that I did not know or maybe he just had more balls than me! The runways at Biggs had a rather unusual configuration— runway 4 and runway 8 started at the same point but #4 was considerably shorter than #8—it was important to check your compass heading before roaring down the runway! The pilot of the other F-9 waved to me as he passed by and lined up at the very end of the runway. At least he was smart enough to use every foot of available runway—and he held his brakes as he went to full power, another smart move, I thought. He released his brakes and started his take-off roll—something did not look right—about half way down the runway I thought, **HOLY SHIT, HE'S TAKING OFF ON THE WRONG RUNWAY!**

I was about to key my mike to warn the pilot when the tower beat me to it with a frantic call that he was departing on runway 4, not runway 8! It was now too late for him to abort and we all watched helplessly as he tried to get the aircraft into the air. The nose lifted off but there was not enough lift to get his heavy bird airborne—the nose was lowered to regain some airspeed then the nose came up again just as the runway ended. The airplane was literally trying to walk on its tail as it left the pavement and the jet exhaust began blowing sand everywhere. The airplane disappeared in the cloud of sand and I thought that he surely had crashed—then the nose reappeared and the plane seemed to stagger for a few seconds. I began to think that he might be able to make it fly—we (the tower personnel, my student and myself—the only witnesses)—were all silently rooting for his success when slowly the nose lowered again and a huge cloud of dust erupted. The pilots did not eject, again the F-9 was equipped with the old Martin-Baker seat that was not reliable at low altitudes and airspeeds and I am sure that they made the right decision to pancake it into the desert. There was no fire and I found out later that the pilot secured the engine before ground contact and was able to "ride it out." Both pilots survived with minor cuts and scrapes but the instructor pilot probably ended his career with that almost fatal error in judgment.

During the transition from the F-9 to the A-4 trainer, I had the opportunity to pick up several new airplanes at the Douglas plant located at Palmdale. What a thrill it was to me to fly a brand new aircraft just off the assembly line—the cockpit smelled new, like a new car at the dealership, and it was so clean and responsive that I really felt that I should be paying for this opportunity to fly such a neat plane! Most A-4 pilots have always felt that the "Scooter" was an airplane that the pilot strapped on—not the other way around. It was like an extension of the pilot's arm as it responded to the slightest input from the aviator. This version, the TA4-F, had all the latest improvements that made it the hottest and most pilot friendly trainer ever built for the Navy, at least to that date. It was equipped with nose wheel steering which made it very easy to taxi, it had a radar that really worked, an auto-pilot that would allow the pilot to fly hands off (at least while straight and level) and automatic spoilers that shortened the landing roll considerably. The engine was the most advanced in the A-4 series and the thrust to weight ratio was almost 1:1—which meant that it could basically climb straight up (at least for a short while).

One day while at Palmdale Plant No. 42 (where Skunkworks was located) to pick up a new aircraft, I walked by a hangar that was in a restricted area and spotted an incredible aircraft that was visible through a partially open door. I was with a tech-rep from Douglas who gave me the usual bit about—if you look in there you will have to be killed! I promised to never tell a soul what

I was observing (with my fingers crossed of course) and took a long hard look at something that seemed to be out of a science fiction movie. It was known as the YF-12A, a proto-type of the SR-71 or Blackbird that would be used for high altitude surveillance for the next thirty years and was like no other aircraft that I had ever seen. It was completely black—because it was flown only at night—and looked like it was going supersonic just sitting on the ground! A few months later I happened to be flying an instrument approach into Edwards Air Force Base as one of those Blackbirds took off. I listened as the pilot became airborne and requested to climb "above flight level 400" which was 40,000 feet. The controller cleared him to FL 230 (23,000 feet) and told him to stand by for higher. Within a few seconds the pilot reported, "I'm out of FL 230, request above 400." Now the controller cleared him to 35,000 feet and again stated for him to stand by for higher! The pilot now calmly stated, "I'm out of FL 400, will be above FL 600 shortly—leaving your frequency, good evening!" That aircraft was more of a rocket than a conventional airplane—I believe that it still holds most of the climb records to this day.

After two years as an instructor it was time for me to make a serious decision. I had one year remaining with VA-127 and would then be assigned to a non-flying job in the surface Navy. Maybe on an aircraft carrier as the Catapult Officer or Flight Deck Officer or more likely on a Destroyer or other vessel as ship's company to qualify as a real sailor! This was necessary for a career Naval Officer and it was not very appealing to me—the worst part was that I would not be flying except to maintain "proficiency" which really meant trying to wrangle four hours of flight time each month in whatever aircraft were available, usually multi-engine older planes. Many of my friends were leaving the Navy for jobs with the airlines. Flying big passenger airplanes had never really appealed to me as it seemed to be more of a "truck driver in the sky" type of job, but I was beginning to realize that I would not be able to fly Navy fighter/bomber aircraft for many more years. It was really a young man's job and in two years I would reach that significant old milestone of **THIRTY YEARS** of age. If I stayed in the Navy I would be over forty when I retired and the airlines, at that time, would not hire a pilot over the age of 35. I enjoyed flying too much to try to pursue a new non-flying career after my Navy career was over and flying for one of the major airlines was becoming a more popular option. My buddies who had left the service to fly commercial seemed to be quite happy with their new career and they all gave glowing recommendations for that lifestyle. Many of them remained in the Naval Reserves to fly single-engine jets and therefore satisfy their desire to continue to fly high performance military airplanes.

I submitted the necessary papers to resign my commission in May 1967 and was immediately "involuntarily extended" for one year—I would not be able to leave the Navy for another year. This was not unexpected as we were still very involved with the war in Viet Nam and pilots were in short supply. Most of the pilots in my squadron would submit their resignations within the next year—almost all of the Lieutenants, at least half of the Lieutenant Commanders, and one full Commander (who had already been screened for command—meaning that he would be assigned as the Skipper of an A-4 squadron soon) would be leaving the service. All of those resigning pilots were given the one year "involuntary extension" and most were assigned as replacement pilots for war casualties and were sent to combat duty aboard carriers off Viet Nam. Since I had already "done my combat tour" I was allowed to remain as an instructor in my present squadron. That last year was not the best for me—the flying became more of a job instead of a pleasure and I spent a lot of time preparing for life after the military.

Our local newspaper, The Fresno Bee, began to run ads from major airlines for pilots to apply for Flight Officer positions. One ad in particular caught my eye with the line: **TIRED OF FLYING THE UNFRIENDLY SKIES? COME FLY THE FRIENDLY SKIES OF UNITED!** I submitted an application for employment to every major airline and ended up with a very short list of companies that were hiring during the time that I would be available. At the top of the list was United Airlines, and I was accepted for an interview, a physical exam and something called the Stanine Test. I was flown to San Francisco for this hiring process which took two days. The interview was basically a chat with a senior Flight Manager which ended up with us trading jokes and discussing the fun we both had with military flying. The physical exam was quite thorough and I was impressed with the Medical Department at United. The Stanine Test was administered by a think-tank group in Palo Alto and consisted of NINE hours of written tests—nine different tests that had a duration of one hour each. It was probably the most intense test that I ever experienced. A few weeks later I was notified that I had been accepted for a position as a Flight Officer and assigned a class date in early May 1968. There was, however, a condition to this offer of employment. It seems that United was not satisfied with my chest x-ray as it revealed a lesion or scar tissue in the upper part of my left lung. I was aware of this problem and had explained to the examining physician during the physical that this lesion was the result of my being exposed to coccidioidomycosis, a respiratory infection caused by a fungus found in the soil in the San Joaquin Valley of California—exactly where NAS Lemoore was located! The common name for this disease was "Valley Fever" because it was prevalent in the area where I had been stationed for the past four years. It was estimated that fifty percent of the people living in this valley had contracted Valley Fever, some with little or no symptoms. Other people had severe reactions to this disease and were hospitalized for treatment. To the best of my knowledge it was never fatal or life threatening. My episode was very mild—more like a bad cold that lingered for about two weeks. Later, during a routine flight physical by the Navy, my chest x-ray showed a dime sized granuloma that was diagnosed as scar tissue from Valley Fever. It was considered insignificant by the Navy Medical Department and I had no adverse symptoms from that exposure to the fungus, which was airborne in the dust and sand that blew almost constantly in the desert areas of NAS Lemoore. It seemed that United Airlines wanted a clinical diagnosis of this lung spot and would not hire me as a pilot without a conclusive medical determination.

I discussed this problem with the squadron flight surgeon, a fine physician and all around good guy who would later join United Airlines and retire a year or two before me. He told me what I already knew—the only way to really solve this problem was to have surgery and a laboratory biopsy to determine once and for all that there would be no future medical problems from this small souvenir left over from Valley Fever. It would also give me peace of mind as I did not want to spend the rest of my life worrying about routine x-rays that would raise questions. I was scheduled for surgery at Oak Knoll Naval Hospital (where I had spent some time with my broken arm some five years previous) in March 1968, about two months before I would be leaving the military. I wanted to make sure that I would be able to return to flight status after the surgery and leave the Navy without any restrictions.

I checked into the hospital the afternoon before the scheduled surgery and went through the routine pre-surgery tests and exams. Later that evening the surgeon who would be performing the operation stopped by my room, introduced himself, and asked if I had any questions about the procedure that would take place the next morning. I asked him to explain in layman terms just what would take place in the O.R. He said, "I'm going to crack you open and remove part of your lung." I was sorry I asked! His bedside manner was atrocious and I began to wish that there was another option—unfortunately there was not. I awoke after the surgery in a strange place with a lot of pain. I had been placed in an enlisted men's ward where there were about twenty beds, all occupied by patients who had respiratory problems such as a collapsed lung, tuberculosis, emphysema, or other disorders of the chest. I was sitting upright in my hospital bed and was strapped in where I could not move. I asked the nurse if my operation went okay. She said, "Of course it went well, can I get you anything for pain?" I tried to be the macho man but admitted that I was in quite a bit of discomfort. I was given morphine for pain relief and the restraining straps were removed. I noticed two tubes extending from the left side of my chest and disappearing under my bed—the Doctor had not told me about this part of the surgery.

Later that day two orderlies approached me and announced that it was time for me to go for a walk. I needed to use the bathroom so I agreed to "take a little walk." The orderlies reached under my bed and removed two large bottles partially filled with fluid—this was where the two tubes from my chest terminated. It was not a lot of fun to try to walk with the assistance of one orderly while the other carried those huge drainage bottles, and I was exhausted after that short trip to the head. That evening the surgeon paid me a visit and immediately chewed out the nurse for putting me in the enlisted ward instead of the officer's section where I would have a private room. The nurse stated that she was merely following orders that all open chest patients were to be placed in what was called the "infectious diseases ward" after surgery. The doctor asked me if I wanted to be moved and I replied that I was perfectly happy to stay right where I was. I had already met several patients near my bed and we were having a fine time telling jokes and stories about **MEDICAL TREATMENT IN THE NAVY!** I asked the doctor when would the drainage tubes be removed and he said that the first tube would be removed in two days. I could hardly wait as it was not only awkward but very painful to move with those hoses still attached. When the time arrived for the first tube to be removed the doctor asked if I wanted something for pain before he removed it. I did not want to appear to be a wimp in front of my new friends so I replied, "No, but I really wish that you would remove both tubes today." The doctor rolled his eyes and replied, "I think one tube will be enough for today." Then he placed one foot on the bed near my chest, took

179

one of the tubes in both hands and gave a mighty yank! I had assumed that the tubes were only an inch or two inside my chest and almost passed out as this eighteen inch perforated hose was jerked out of my chest cavity—the pain was incredible! As I came down from the ceiling the doctor calmly asked, "Would you like some pain medication now?"

When I was able to speak I weakly responded, "I had no idea that the tube was so long—thank God you didn't take out the other one—I hope it's a bit shorter than the one you just removed." The doc replied with a wicked grin, "I removed the short one first—I'll be back tomorrow to take out the really long tube." Then he sadistically asked me if I wanted to keep the tube that he had just removed for a souvenir. No thanks! The next day I took all the pain killers that the nursing staff would give me before that second tube was removed. This had been quite an experience to go through such a painful, unnecessary procedure to remove something that was not really a problem just to satisfy my new employer.

Before I left the hospital, a group of my buddies came to visit. I was now able to walk on my own and we went to the Officer's Club for lunch. My friends had flown several of the squadron planes into Alameda NAS just to spend an hour or two with me and I was really grateful for their concern. One of my buddies, Tony, handed me a piece of paper and said with a grin, "I think you will get a chuckle out of this." The piece of paper was an official Navy letter announcing the latest list of promotions. My name was on this list of those to be promoted to Lieutenant Commander, effective April 15th, 1968. I would be a LCDR for two whole weeks as I was being released from active duty on the first of May! I would be the youngest LCDR in the US Navy; at least until the next promotion list was issued! I would not be 29 years old until June.

I did not return to flight duty until the middle of April and was not very enthusiastic when finally cleared to resume flying—it was time to begin a new career. The scheduling officer, a close friend, was very helpful and I flew mostly test hops until time to leave. My last flight in the US Navy would be one to remember, however. Our squadron flight demonstration group, the Royal Blues, was invited to participate in an airshow at the south shore Lake Tahoe airport on the last weekend in April. Unfortunately, there was no fuel at that field that was suitable for our aircraft—we needed JP-5 and only JP-4, used by Air Force jets, was available at that small airport. The Skipper decided that instead of sending our aerobatic team, we would send only one aircraft to be used for a static display. I volunteered to fly the plane there and be available to answer questions from the general public who would be attending the airshow. Since I would not be able to refuel at the Tahoe airport, I did some serious flight planning so that I would be able to fly there and back with enough fuel left for a little fun! Usually the A-4 flew with two 300 gallon drop tanks which gave it an endurance of about three hours—I needed less than two hours so requested that only one drop tank be on the plane that I would fly for the show—this would be fitted on the centerline station, giving the aircraft a cleaner look while enhancing its performance. I departed NAS Lemoore early Saturday morning and arrived at Lake Tahoe in thirty minutes. Although the runway was short compared to our home base, it was sufficient for my plane which was equipped with automatic spoilers that deployed on landing and shortened the landing roll considerably. I spent most of that day standing beside the aircraft and explaining to inquisitive children and adults just what type of airplane it was and how fast it flew. This was really a small airshow as there were no military demo teams such as the Blue Angels or the Air Force Thunderbirds in attendance. There were several military aircraft on display, like mine, but the airshow performers were all small airplanes—and they gave quite a show. Those small aerobatic planes were so maneuverable that they stayed over the runway and thrilled the crowd with their amazing flying skills. They needed a lot less airspace that the faster jets and were in many ways more entertaining to watch.

At the end of the day I strapped into my beautiful A-4 (or strapped it on!) and departed for the return flight to NAS Lemoore, knowing that this would be my final flight in the military. As I taxied out, many of the people who had attended the airshow were starting to leave, but many others were waiting to see the one Navy jet depart. I asked the tower for a HPTO, and they admitted to not knowing what I was requesting but were agreeable to anything I wanted to do. HPTO stands for High Performance Take Off (some called it the **HOT PILOT TAKE OFF**) and was usually used for aircraft with afterburners. I was not equipped with an afterburner but I planned to stay low after take off, build up airspeed as rapidly as possible, and then pull up into a vertical climb. I requested two flybys down the runway—one in each direction—before departing for my destination. The tower gave their enthusiastic approval and off I went. The aircraft was light enough now to have a thrust to weight ratio of almost 1:1 and the acceleration was, as usual, like a huge shot of adrenalin. As soon as I was airborne, I raised the gear and leveled at ten feet above the runway, letting the airspeed build as rapidly as possible. The runway ended just before the lake and I'm sure that a bit of spray went up as I pulled back into a vertical climb over the water and climbed straight up! Before I reached 2000 feet above the surface I rolled the plane over and pointed it down toward the middle of the runway that I had just departed from, then pulled up to repeat the maneuver in the other direction, each time descending to less than 100 feet at the bottom of the dive over the runway. What I had performed was called a Cuban Eight maneuver, but it was not normally done immediately after take off. I had just the right airplane and the right conditions to pull off such a feat on this day. At the end of the second pull-up I executed a couple of victory rolls and reported that I was departing for my base. The tower controller answered, "Quite a show, Navy, hope to see you back next year!" I felt a twinge of regret that I would not be able to do such fun flying again— at least not in this airplane.

Chapter Thirteen

"A check ride ought to be like a skirt, short enough to be interesting, but still long enough to cover the important stuff!"

I drove to Denver, Colorado in time to start flight training with United Airlines on May 13, 1968. I did not know just how important this employment date would be for the rest of my career. I had heard the expression: **YOU DON'T GO TO WORK FOR AN AIRLINE, YOU MARRY IT!** It seemed that I had entered a relationship that revolved around that all important "date of hire." Seniority was everything to an airline pilot—it determined not only your pay but how you would advance throughout your career. Seniority controlled your vacations, whether you would get on an airplane for pleasure travel, your monthly bidding for flying, and determined when you would advance in status. The "new-hire" pilot was given a seniority number on that first day of employment and it changed each year when a new seniority list was released. A pilot with a lower seniority number would be senior to you forever (or until he died or retired!) and there was nothing that could change that simply fact. There were five pilots in my new-hire class, all from the military. Seniority among our group was determined by age—the oldest was the most senior and had a lower number than the next oldest, etc. My age, 28 for another month, placed me in the middle with two more senior and two junior to me. The five of us had a total of 49 years flying experience! Quite a senior group with lots of flight time in our logbooks.

The classmate who was one number senior to me (and he never let me forget it) was a Marine pilot who had flown the USMC version of the A-4 in Vietnam. Tom and I rented an apartment together for the duration of our training and it was the beginning of a lifelong friendship. We were both married at the time but our wives would not join us until our training was completed. We were assigned training for the Boeing 727 as flight engineers and both would be stationed, or domiciled in airline lingo, to Chicago's O'Hare Field—again this was determined by seniority. The senior man in our class, Jim, would go through training on the DC-8 and be domiciled in New York. The DC-8, being a larger aircraft, paid more than the smaller 727, so the senior guy obviously picked it for his initial training. I was happy to get the 727 as I had heard that it flew a lot like a fighter as it had severely swept-back wings and the three aft mounted engines gave it center-line thrust— much like a single engine military jet. Our initial training would last almost two months, four weeks of ground school then simulator training leading up to actually flying the aircraft for our "check ride." This would be the first of countless check rides that an airline pilot encountered throughout his career. I use the "male" pronoun when writing about pilots because at this time there were no female pilots, military or airline. The pilot profession was still white male dominated and would remain so for almost another decade. On the other hand, flight attendants at this time were called stewardesses and they were all single females. More about this later.

The starting pay as a pilot in training was $550 per month and it would increase to $600 after successful completion of that training. After the first year the pay doubled to $1200, and it would take several years before I would reach the pay level that I was receiving as a Naval Aviator. Loss of military fringe benefits such as free medical and dental care, commissary shopping, the Officer's Club for dining, and base housing added up to a very significant reduction in income for me and my family—I now had two small children. The good news was that I had no debts or financial obligations and had managed to put a bit aside in anticipation of this not unexpected change in income. The next several years were going to be rough but we had planned accordingly, or so we thought! First I had to successfully complete training in Denver.

I had not previously spent any time in Denver but found the weather to be just what I enjoyed—the air was clean and fresh, visibility at the airport was usually reported as 100 miles or more, there was very little humidity, and the views of the mountains could be spectacular. There was a saying about the weather, however: If you don't like the weather in Denver, wait a couple of hours and it will change. How true—I recall one morning in late May when it snowed in the morning as I was going to class; later that afternoon I was enjoying the swimming pool with the temperature in the 70's. I was impressed with the thoroughness and quality of the training I received from United as the instructors were mostly ex-military retired pilots who were too old to be hired as airline pilots. This would later change as "age discrimination" became an issue. At the time, however, the instructors were happy to have a decent job to supplement their retirement pension and the trainees benefited greatly from that arrangement. We spent a lot of time those first few weeks learning about the culture of United Airlines—a carrier with the reputation for quality service. I had wanted to go to work for United, Delta, or American Airlines and had picked UAL because they were the only airline hiring pilots at the time I left the Navy. Interestingly enough, I received a letter from both American and Delta while in Denver stating that they were ready to hire me for their training! I was too impressed with UAL at this time to even consider another airline.

Our ground school consisted of the usual subjects; meteorology, aerodynamics, specific training on the Boeing 727, and a totally new subject—the Flight Operations Manual, the FOM. This three inch-thick loose leaf binder contained all that the airline pilot ever needed to know—we called it the PILOT'S BIBLE! Pertinent FAR (Federal Air Regulation) rules were included along with specific instructions in how to find one's minimums (how low can you go), and how to handle almost any problem, even the unruly passenger. We spent a lot of time going through this manual and I was beginning to feel that the airline pilot with United was expected to conform to these rules and regulations at all costs! Thank God that there was usually a disclaimer that said: Common sense and the Captain's authority shall always prevail—obviously, a real pilot had some input in the writing of this manual. This FOM, along with its weekly revisions, would be a significant part of my life for the next thirty years. It was carried in the pilot's flight bag at all times, along with flight manuals, approach charts and enroute maps. We were issued this flight bag and a matching suitcase and were fitted for our new uniforms—the uniforms, however, were paid for by the pilot. Fifty dollars each month was deducted from our pay until those uniforms were paid off—a lot of money at the time.

United Airlines was in the process of building a new flight training center at the time I went through my training at Stapleton Airport but it would not be officially open for business until after my training was completed. The simulators were in place and functional, however, and the last few weeks were spent in the new facility—it was very impressive. The simulators were state of the art and quite advanced from the rudimentary trainers that I had been exposed to in the Navy. Most of the time that we spent in the simulators was at the engineer's panel but we did have at least two periods of training at the pilot's station. After the check ride in the simulator I was scheduled for my check ride in the real airplane—the first time that I had ever been in the cockpit of the Boeing 727. Two of us were scheduled for check rides at the same time—I was paired with another new hire pilot from another class that I did not know. By a flip of the coin, we decided that he would go first and I would follow. It was a four hour flight so I had to sit in the cabin for the first two hours while the other pilot was checked—then it was my turn. I had met the FAA Examiner earlier when he had followed me around during my "walk around" or pre-flight check of the airplane. He was a fat slob with a very disagreeable personality who seemed more concerned with stuffing sandwiches in his mouth than conducting a professional check. He asked several questions during the walk around that I answered easily. Then he asked me if I knew how many static discharge wicks were installed on the 727. I knew that there were several on each wing tip and several on the tail but I had never really counted how many there were total. I honestly replied that no, I did not know exactly how many there were. He snorted and came back with, "How in the hell do you know if one is missing if you don't know how many there are?" I thought the question was absurd and replied, "Well, I don't know how many windows are on my house but I would certainly know if one was missing!" Seemed like a logical answer to me but it did not please the examiner, who had a terrible reputation with the instructors and was nicknamed "mumbles." He mumbled something to me about me being a smart-ass and I knew that I was in trouble.

After the other pilot completed his two hour check at the panel in the airplane, it was my turn. I thought that my check ride went reasonably well but the examiner only grumbled and "mumbled." After it was all over and we were back on the ground the examiner told me and the other pilot, who had been riding in the cabin during my check ride, to follow him. Not a word was said as the other pilot and I trailed the FAA examiner to the training center. We looked at each other and both rolled our eyes—did we pass or not? As we entered the training center for the debriefing, my instructor who had been with me throughout my training was anxiously standing by the door. He asked the examiner if the check ride went well—"mumbles" replied, "One up, one down." That meant that one of us passed and one failed the check. The three of us reached a small room for the debriefing and "mumbles" turned to me and grunted, "You wait out here."

I sat outside that room for over an hour and I don't think that I had ever spent a more nervous time in my life. I was beginning to think that this airline job was a big mistake—maybe I could get back in the Navy and start having fun flying again. If this was the way check rides were conducted, I did not want to spend the rest of my working life in this environment. I was about ready to walk away and tell my instructor that I was quitting when the door to the room opened and "mumbles" walked out. He glanced at me with a surprised look, and said, "You still here? You're finished—good check ride." Then he walked away. The other pilot came out of the room with a very dejected look—I knew then that he was the one who had failed. I felt so sorry for that pilot and told him so. I found out later that this was his second bust and he would be washed out of the program. As I was leaving the building my instructor was waiting for me and shook my hand with the usual congratulations. I was not happy with the conduct of that check ride and told my instructor that I really did not want to go through that type of stress for the rest of my career. He assured me that "mumbles" was probably the worst examiner in the FAA and I could rest assured that most check rides were not like that at all. Thank God that my instructor was right!

The next day I got to fly the airplane as a real pilot. My training was over and this was basically a fun flight to let the new pilot get the feel of flying from the "front seat." A flight manager was in the Captain's seat and he performed the take off and climb out. Then he turned the aircraft over to me and I flew for about an hour, doing various maneuvers and changing configurations—this was a beautiful airplane to fly and I quickly forgot all about yesterday's thoughts of going back into the Navy. I could hardly wait until the day I would become a co-pilot and get to fly every other leg. We had a fun day as the flight manager was a really nice guy who gave me lots of tips and friendly advice on how to fly the 727. All too soon it was time to return to Denver and land. The Captain said, "I don't usually let the new hire make the landing but if you want to give it a try, I'll talk you through it." Of course I was eager to give it a whirl but really did not know the correct speeds and thrust settings. With LOTS OF HELP, I was able to get the plane on the ground but I could feel the Captain's hands on the controls during the landing and without his help it would not have been very pretty! It was a lot of work for me but the feeling was one that every pilot remembers—the first time in control in a new airplane is always a real rush! Maybe this airline flying was going to be fun after all.

I had never been to Chicago before and knew very little about the city or the surrounding area. All I knew was that Chicago was the location of the corporate headquarters for UAL, and O'Hare Field was the largest domicile for pilots. It was common knowledge that every United pilot would spend several tours in Chicago during the course of his career. I arrived in the middle of July with my family and we rented a small apartment near the airport until we found exactly where we wanted to be located. The weather was completely different from that in Denver—it was hot and humid with severe thunderstorms almost every afternoon. The apartment was not very nice and it was very expensive compared to what I was used to in the Navy— obviously we needed to move into nicer, more permanent quarters as soon as possible. I was on reserve as soon as I reported for duty with the crew desk at O'Hare. Being on reserve would become a way of life for me throughout most of my career. The reserve pilot did not hold a scheduled line of flying and was "on call" 24 hours a day, with only eight days off each month. When on call, the reserve pilot had to remain near his telephone and be available for a three hour call out—in other words be at the airport ready to fly no later than three hours from receiving a call from the crew desk. Reserve pilots were the most junior pilots and being on reserve was not a choice duty—at the time I had no other option. I was very surprised at how busy I became as I was used almost every day that I was on call. I soon learned to always have my bag packed for a three or four day trip on a moments notice. The trips that I was assigned were quite a variety, everything from a quick-turn flight to New York and back on the same day to a four day trip that would involve flights literally to all four corners of the United States.

After meeting and flying with several crews I started to learn that many pilots seemed to live in the northwestern suburbs, so I began looking for a house in that direction. Finally I bought a nice three bedroom house that was being built in the little town of Crystal Lake, located about 35 miles NW of the airport. It was finished and ready to be occupied in about a month—it was quite a relief to get out of that small apartment and begin a new life in the suburbs. The cost of the move and the down payment had used all of our savings, however, and things would be very tight for the foreseeable future. I found that I could sign up with the local school district to be a substitute teacher on my days off—the pay was $25 per day. I found out that I could only make about $100 a month doing substitute teaching so I looked for other ways to earn some extra money. When I resigned from the Navy I had planned to remain in the Reserves, although I had no obligation to do so as my service commitment had been satisfied. There was a reserve outfit located at Glenview Naval Air Station, located only about thirty miles northeast of O'Hare Field—and they were flying A-4s! I contacted the unit at Glenview and made an appointment to meet with the Operations Officer of the squadron. When I arrived, he took me on a tour of the facilities and said that a position was available for me—I could be flying in a week or two. This seemed to be just what I was looking for! Then we went out on the flight line to look at the airplanes that I would be flying. These A-4s were the sorriest looking group of airplanes that I had ever seen in the Navy—they were the A-4B model, one of the earliest of the series built by Douglas and really in the dark ages as far as avionics and flight control systems were concerned. They were obviously not being well maintained and on closer inspection I could see signs of corrosion and neglect. I was going to have to give some serious thought about becoming involved in this outfit and I told the Ops Officer that I would let him know my decision within a week. He seemed eager to have me join the outfit and seemed very sincere when he talked about all the good guys that were involved with the squadron. I left his office and started walking back to my car, mulling over the decision that I needed to reach. I stopped to talk with an enlisted man who was working on an aircraft in the hanger and asked him how he liked the outfit. He was very unkempt with long scraggly hair and did not look like any of the maintenance personnel I had known in my years on active duty. He bluntly told me that he was here only because he needed extra money and hated his job. I had the feeling that the "extra money" was being spent on drugs or booze—maybe both. I did not have a good feeling about flying poorly maintained airplanes that were outdated and in bad condition to start with. Especially in this environment where the winters were harsh and miserable for flying and the summers were not much better due to the thunderstorms. I never returned to Glenview and made the decision that I would not join the reserves just for money—I knew, however, that I would sorely miss the flying.

During the initial training with United, I was told that the company was still expanding and would be hiring new pilots for the foreseeable future—I would probably be checked out as a co-pilot before my first year was completed. That first year was considered as a probational year during which a pilot could be discharged without cause. The pilots union, ALPA, (Airline Pilots Association) did not consider probationary pilots as members and would not accept membership application until the first year was completed. My first year ended with very little fanfare—I was still on reserve as a 727 Second Officer, a co-pilot bid was well out of my reach, and I seemed to be stuck in a rut in the Chicago area. ALPA accepted my application for membership (as if I had any choice) and began to collect dues from my pay every month—a process that would continue for the rest of my career. I had never been involved in a labor union but I knew that ALPA was a "necessary evil" in my chosen profession and I had no qualms about the membership dues. The airline pilot pay and working conditions were the result of union bargaining with company management. What I did not expect was the adversarial relationship that existed between the company and the union. It was a strange arrangement in many ways—I worked for UAL and they paid my salary, yet the union was the entity that controlled my life style. Where did one's loyalty really lie?

The flying during those early years was interesting and diverse. Being on reserve meant that I seldom flew with the same crew so I met many different pilots—without exception they were all unique! Pilots are the most regimented labor group in the work force but pilots are all very much individuals. We all conform to a certain standard but yet are able to express our own persona both in and out of the cockpit. I was not used to flying in a large cockpit with two other individuals—and they were both senior to me. The Captain was in command at all times and set the tone for the conduct of the flight. Some Captains were very strict, some liked to tell jokes, some were friendly, and some never knew your name. It was a real learning experience in personalities. That first winter in the Chicago area was not pleasant—the weather was terribly cold with frequent severe snow storms that dumped snow that turned to ice and stayed on the ground until spring finally arrived. Then it turned into brown mush that was as even bigger mess. It seemed that I worked every day that I was "legal"—after returning to one's home domicile following a trip, the reserve pilot was not legal to fly for the next twelve hours, after that he was "legal" to be assigned another trip. Quite often I would contact the crew desk when I returned from a trip and was assigned another sequence that would depart after the twelve hours off. It was sometimes difficult to get eight hours of real rest between trips. With only eight days off each month and working almost every day that I was on call, there was very little time for recreation or other activities—I was beginning to wonder about all those stories that airline pilots seldom worked and had too much time off!

Being on reserve was a 24 hour a day job. We did not have cell phones or pagers and were expected to answer the phone when the crew desk called. If there was no answer or the pilot was not immediately available to speak to the scheduler, the crew man went to the next name on the list and the pilot was listed as unavailable—resulting in a call from a flight manager and a deduction in pay for what was called "WOP." Withdrawal Of Pay meant that your paycheck was reduced by one day's pay. If the pilot was not available a second time he was taken off pay status until he was counseled by a flight manager. This could be very expensive but most importantly it could jeopardize the pilot's job. Bottom line—the pilot on reserve had to be by the phone at all times. Chicago was the largest base for United Airlines and there were departures from O'Hare and Midway around the clock. The Boeing 727 was perhaps the most versatile aircraft in the fleet, not only because it was efficient in both long and short range flights but because it also had a cargo capability. United had quite a fleet of 727-QC (quick change) aircraft that could fly passengers during the day and be converted to cargo configuration for nighttime. The pilot on reserve seemed to get more than his share of cargo trips—the least desirable of all. Maybe this was because the pilots who held the line of flying for these "all-nighters" were more prone to call in sick!

I recall one time that I flew one of those cargo trips and arrived back at O'Hare just after sunrise—it seemed that eastbound trips were scheduled to land at dawn and the approach was always to the east. Looking into the rising sun while trying to land after being up all night was not a lot of fun! By the time I arrived home it was probably ten o'clock AM—and I had a lot of things to do that day around the house. I was scheduled for two days off starting the next day and knew that I would not be legal for another assignment until around six PM. Then I was off at midnight—what was the chance of getting a trip that late in the day that would get me back to O'Hare before midnight? Slim to none, I figured! Instead of getting some sleep that day, I did those chores that needed to be done and planned to have a normal dinner and an early bedtime. I was tempted to enjoy a glass of wine at dinner but since I was technically legal for several more hours I refrained from such an indulgence. I was headed for the bedroom at seven PM when the phone rang—I could not believe that it was the crew desk! They needed me to fly a trip to Saginaw,

Michigan, departing at ten PM that would return to O'Hare at 11:59 PM! The regularly scheduled crew was stuck in a weather delay back east and a reserve crew was needed. I was "legal" to fly such a trip but in my mind I was not sure that it was a wise thing to do—the weather was crappy, the roads to the airport were slick and I was dead tired from being up for more than 24 hours. On the other hand, I was still young and stupid—I agreed to fly the trip. I quickly changed into my uniform, took a small overnight bag (just in case), and headed to the airport. When I checked in with the crew desk at the airport I was informed that the flight was delayed for at least one hour. There was no way that I could fly to Saginaw and back before midnight. The crew scheduler knew the rules better than I and he informed me, "The legality for flying the trip lies with the SCHEDULED TIMES not the ACTUAL TIMES!" I met the co-pilot, also a reserve who was a very new co-pilot, and he seemed to be quite anxious. He asked me if I knew the Captain. I replied that I did not and he informed me that the reserve Captain had a very bad reputation, not only for airmanship but for being a real ASSHOLE! This was going to be a trip to remember.

The Captain arrived over an hour late but the trip was having what was called a "creeping delay" and we were now scheduled to depart just before midnight. The crew would now lay over in Saginaw and deadhead back to O'Hare the next morning. I met the Captain when I entered the cockpit after doing the walk-around or pre-flight inspection. The first thing out of his mouth was, "Forget what you've heard about me and remember that I am the Captain and in command!" I could only reply, "Yes Sir!" It was after midnight before we departed the runway at O'Hare with less than fifty passengers—most of the scheduled passengers had gone to motels or had made alternate arrangements. The weather was improving as we departed and after the short flight to upper Michigan, we found clear skies and calm winds with a full moon overhead. I was starting to feel a lot better about this ill-fated trip. The Captain was the pilot doing the flying, the co-pilot handled the radios, and I took care of the aircraft systems and other duties such as coordination with the stewardesses and handling the PA (Passenger Address) system. Flying time was little more than 30 minutes and we arrived with clear moonlit skies at what was called the Tri-Cities Airport that served not only Saginaw but Midland and Bay City. The control tower had already shut down—government workers, you know—so we had no control for our approach. Not a problem as we were in VFR conditions and had the runway in sight at least 30 miles away for a long straight-in approach. The Captain had informed us that he had been on vacation for the last three weeks and was also a new Captain—however, he seemed to be doing at least an average job of flying the airplane to this time. The co-pilot was also new and one of those types who "would not say shit, even if he had a mouthful" so I was trying to be extra vigilant during the approach. Everything seemed to be normal until we were about one mile from touch-down when we started to go a bit low. I was hoping that the co-pilot would say something but he did not utter a single word as we continued down a visual flight path. The runway was surrounded by snow but the runway itself was plowed clear and was reported dry with normal braking. I held my tongue as long as I could before I said, "You're low" in a soft voice, but loud enough for the Captain to hear. There was no correction and we continued to descend even lower from a normal three degree flight path. At about ¼ mile I repeated, a bit louder, "You're low!" We continued descending and I began to think that maybe I was dreaming all this—I should have gotten some sleep! Just as we were about to touch down the Captain crammed on a fistful of power and pulled back on the controls but the aircraft touched down lightly with a strange sound—like WOOSH—not a hard landing but a sound like we barely grazed the surface before we started back up again. The Captain then chopped the power and after about two hundred feet we hit the runway with a mighty blow! It was the hardest landing that I had ever experienced and I thought that we had crashed for sure. We continued the roll-out, turned off the runway, and taxied to the gate without a word being spoken. I could hear some shouting and harsh words coming from the cabin as we arrived at the terminal. As the Captain shut down the engines, he said, "Parking check list." These were the first words from his mouth since we had departed from O'Hare field! After the check list was completed, he added, "Keep the cockpit door closed." No shit! I sure didn't want to feel the wrath of the passengers as they were deplaning! I could hear the remarks that they were making as they left the aircraft—most were businessmen who were frequent travelers who knew just how bad that landing was. After the passengers were deplaned I went into the cabin and tried to calm the flight attendants who were all scared to death—they were never going to fly with Captain X ever again! Then I went out on the ramp with my flashlight to check the landing gear—I felt that there was surely some damage during that horrendous landing. I was startled to find that the main landing gear and the gear wells were covered with hard-packed snow—

obviously we had touched down in the snow bank that was just short of the paved surface. The Captain joined me as I was looking at all that snow stuffed in the gear wells and said, "Looks like no damage was done, let's go to the hotel."

I did not have a chance to talk to the co-pilot until I ran into him in the hotel restaurant the next morning. I asked him if he had noticed that we were low on the approach and he said yes—then I asked him why he didn't say anything. He replied that he was afraid to because he did not want to get chewed out by the Captain! I responded to that statement with: "I'd sure prefer to get my ass chewed out rather than go up in a ball of flames!" I was beginning to learn that this airline flying was not at all going to be dull and boring. I would continue to speak up whenever I was uncomfortable and always asked my crew to do the same when I became a Captain.

The crew desk seemed to have an uncanny knack for finding a trip that would just barely be legal for the poor reserve pilot. One evening I received a call just before midnight for me to report to the airport for a 0500 departure to Detroit and deadhead back to O'Hare before noon. After very little sleep I checked in at 0400 and was handed a ticket to deadhead to Detroit on a small airline called Lake Central. I told the crewman that I was told that I would be flying the trip to DTW and deadhead home. He assured me that it was just the opposite and the only way for me to get to Detroit to fly a trip back was to go "off-line" and deadhead on Lake Central Airlines. I found the one and only gate that LCA maintained in that large airport and checked in to find that the aircraft would be stopping FOUR TIMES before arriving in Detroit! Now I knew why they were called "puddle jumpers." We took off with a full load of passengers in a beat up old Convair prop plane with two sleepy stewardesses almost on the scheduled time. We landed in Muskegon, Grand Rapids, Battle Creek, and Lansing before finally arriving in Detroit. By this time I was exhausted! I had talked to the flight crew and they were scheduled to turn around and fly back to O'Hare with those same stops—they would not finish their day until dark! I was certainly glad that I was flying for UAL and not LCA! I checked in with United operations at Detroit and was handed a ticket to deadhead back to ORD! What the hell was going on? I was told that the trip I was scheduled to fly had been cancelled and I was not needed. At least I was on a non-stop United flight back to Chicago. When I finally arrived at my home late that afternoon, I had been away over fourteen hours, I was worn out, and I had not turned a productive wheel all day! I have always felt that "deadheading" is harder on the pilot than actually flying the airplane. The cockpit is comfortable, there are two other people of similar interests to talk with, and time flies when busy with the routine duties of the airline pilot. Deadheading sucks!

At this particular time, the late 1960's, I would guess that 95% of all airline pilots, at least with United, were ex-military pilots who learned how to fly courtesy of Uncle Sam. Those who chose to go to work for a commercial carrier did so because of a sincere love for flying airplanes, not because of pilot's salaries or lifestyles. Many of those pilots were happy to just be in the cockpit of an aircraft—any other perks were gravy. Most of the Captains that I flew with in those early years had combat experience in WW II, and they had some amazing stories to tell. Many of the co-pilots, called First Officers by United, were from the Korean War era and they too had some incredible tales to tell about their experiences. The flight engineers, Second Officers to United, were largely from the Viet Nam conflict and we tried to add our war stories to the mixture. Comparing stories among the cockpit crew became one of the most enjoyable parts of the job. I hesitate to use the word "job" as I have always felt that flying was never work—it was always a pleasure and never a "job!" Some would disagree with that statement as there were times that one felt that no amount of compensation was sufficient to pay for the level of risk and exposure to accidents that we often faced in the aviation industry. However, I feel that the satisfaction that a pilot feels after making a good approach and a smooth landing in lousy weather with bad winds and slippery runways is enough to make him forget the bad parts. The pay was not that great during those years; Second Officers were paid about $15,000 per year, First Officers received around $25,000 and the top Captain pay was only about $40,000. Those salaries would double and quadruple over the next ten and twenty years, mainly due to the influence of the union, and the culture of the airline pilot profession would be forever changed. Suddenly, young men and women in America began to look to aviation as a profession that paid good wages with lots of free time and some considerable degree of prestige. Instead of planning to attend law school or medical college, many young college undergraduates began to seriously consider a career in aviation. These prospective pilots pursued their career in aviation not because of a love for flying airplanes, but because it seemed to be a rewarding and well paid way to make a living. And it sure as hell beat the nine to five type of "job" at the office!

I knew that the airlines were considered "cyclical industries" in that there were ups and downs depending on the economy, but the extreme gyrations that prevailed during my career were completely unexpected. United Airlines had started a rather long period of expansion in 1964 that would continue for about five years. New pilots would be hired, trained, and placed on "the line" almost every week during this thriving period. The Flight Training Center in Denver was growing every year with new simulators that represented the new types of aircraft that were being introduced into the fleet. New instructors were being hired and an entire separate cottage industry was being quietly created that would begin to train pilots for other airlines, foreign as well as domestic. Later, training would be conducted at this center for the U.S. Air Force and several other foreign military groups. These were the boom times that slowly ended in 1969—new pilot hiring was terminated and there would be no new pilots hired for almost TEN YEARS! This was an extremely long period of stagnation. There were very few retirements even though all airline pilots were required to retire at the ripe old age of 60. Most of the Captains were WW II vets who were born in the 1920's and would not retire until the 80's. The only way to advance, because of the seniority system, was through retirements or expansion. Instead of expanding, the airline began to shrink! The aircraft that were in the UAL fleet in 1968 consisted of the following types: DC-6, Viscount, Caravelle, B-727, B-720, and the queen of the fleet, the DC-8. Only the 727 and DC-8 would be around three years later—the other types would be replaced by the B-737 and the new queen, the gargantuan whale, otherwise known as the B-747. These new aircraft were faster and more efficient than the ones they replaced and since pilots were paid by the hour it only made sense that fewer pilots were needed to fly the faster airplanes to destinations that once took twice as long to reach. The pilots union reacted to these cutbacks by demanding more pay for bigger planes—more seats meant more productivity and the pilots should be rewarded with more pay, at least that was the union's line of thought. As with most unions, the senior members prevailed—the Captains flying the largest equipment received more pay and the junior guys took the shaft (at least that was our way of thinking). Most of us junior types felt that the pilots flying through the Michigan cities in the middle of winter in a 727 type aircraft with four or five stops in each duty period were working a hell of a lot harder than the crew flying non-stop from LAX to HNL whose only worry was getting to the beach on Waikiki in time to enhance their tans. The carrot at the end of the stick was always that we (the junior pilots) would eventually reach that exalted position of flying the "big ones" with enough seniority to fly the most senior routes—those routes at the time were to Honolulu.

Down-sizing at an airline was an extremely painful, expensive, and lengthy process. Painful to the pilots, expensive to the company and lengthy to everyone concerned. The process was started at the top of the seniority list and it slowly filtered down. The company would begin by declaring that there were too many Captains in various fleets; those that were not needed were declared "surplus." These junior Captains were sent a letter from the company that stated that their services were no longer needed in the position that they held. They were faced with several options, all part of the union bargaining process. For instance, if a junior Captain flying the DC-8 at the San Francisco domicile received such a letter, he could do one of several things. He could opt to transfer to a more junior domicile, say Chicago, and "bump" a pilot junior to him there who was also flying the DC-8. Perhaps he did not want to move from the Bay Area, then he could choose to bump a Captain in San Francisco flying the B-727 who was junior to him. Every "bump" generated a surplus somewhere down the line that created a need for a new round of "surplus letters." Perhaps a pilot who was declared surplus in Chicago really wanted to live on the West coast—then he could bump a pilot junior to him in LAX or SFO. The company now was obligated to pay for the move for the pilot and his family. If that pilot could not sell his house when he was transferred, then the company was obligated to buy it from him! Many pilots took advantage of this option—dump that undesirable piece of property in Podunk and move to where they really wanted to be—all at UAL expense. Other pilots who did not want to move or did not want to take a pay cut to a lower paying piece of equipment chose to commute to their new domicile. The company was obligated to give them positive space tickets for travel between their old and new domiciles for at least one year—another expensive option. Still other pilots bumped down to a lesser paying aircraft, say from DC-8 Captain to B-727 Captain in SFO. This generated training for that Captain on his new equipment, the 727, and all the expense and loss of productivity that was involved. Needless to say, when the Company decided to downsize, it became a real can of worms for all concerned!

Eventually, this process would create a pool of junior pilots at the very bottom of the seniority list who had nowhere to bump. As this evolved, those pilots were FURLOUGHED! The down-sizing began in 1969 and it took about a year before the first list of pilots to be furloughed was released. At first the list was small but each month it became larger. Those on the TERMINATION LIST were told to report to their flight manager with their flight bags, manuals, IDs and WINGS! These items were to be turned in before the furloughed pilot was released with the promise that he would be on the list to be recalled as soon as circumstances permitted. For many, this was a sad conclusion to their career as an airline pilot with United Airlines. Some went to work for other carriers, some sought other career paths, some went back into the military, and others took interim jobs until they were called back by UAL. For me, it was like waiting for the other shoe to drop—I did not like being junior and on reserve and I especially did not enjoy being a non-flying pilot (flight engineer). This was not the reason I signed on with the airline to start with! I decided that if and when I was furloughed, I would try to go back to active service in the Navy, knowing that it would be Viet Nam again for sure.

After two years with UAL, my marriage of six years came to an end. I moved into an apartment in the Chicago suburb of Des Plaines, very near O'Hare Field. Interestingly enough, this was the very first time that I had ever had a place to live all alone (without a roommate or wife) and after I got over the loneliness I began to enjoy the freedom. The apartment complex where I found an apartment was called North Shore Trace and the manager was a furloughed American Airline pilot whose name was Vince. He was about my age and had gone through Naval Flight training a couple of years after me in the Nav Cad program. Vince had not completed his college education when he entered the Marine Corps and was selected for flight training—this meant that he was not commissioned until earning his wings. He excelled in flight training and after a tour in a Marine fighter squadron flying the F-4 Phantom he was chosen to fly with the Blue Angels aerobatic team. After his two year stint with the "Blues," Vince chose to go to work for American Airlines—about the same time that I started with United. All of the airlines were effected by the economic slow down and he had been declared "surplus" and then furloughed by American. Vince had chosen to stay in the Chicago area awaiting his recall from AAL and was making his living as the manager of this apartment complex. My new pal took me to a very nice furnished one bedroom apartment in the same building where he lived. I was impressed with the lay-out (it even had a bar!) but admitted that I simply could not afford such a nice place. With a twinkle in his eye, Vince stated that he needed an "athletic director" for the complex—the pay would be the same as the rent! This was an offer that I could not refuse. My new position as AD required very little time or effort. In the winter the only athletic activities were confined to the gymnasium; in the summer it meant managing sports such as volleyball, tennis and water polo. This part time job was just what I needed to lift my spirits and occupy my time now that I was single again.

Vince had converted two apartments into his place of residence, one above the other that was joined by a spiral staircase and a FIREMAN'S POLE! The upstairs consisted of two bedrooms, kitchen and two baths. The downstairs, however, was nothing but a party room with a very large bar, several pinball and slot machines, and room for several dozen people to congregate and socialize. There was a well organized and well attended party held there every Wednesday night. I was curious why Wednesday was the designated day for a party until I attended that first event. It seemed that United Stewardess School was still going full strength with weekly classes that graduated every Friday. By Wednesday, the new Stews knew where they were to be based and those who were assigned to Chicago needed to find apartments! Vince had connections with the Stew School and invited these prospective renters to his party to convince them to rent at his complex. The strategy worked as the complex was conveniently located near O'Hare and the apartments were large enough for several young ladies to share as they started out on their new ventures as hostesses in the sky! I began to enjoy my new lifestyle, being surrounded by lovely young stewardesses who had chosen to fly "the Friendly Skies" to seek travel, adventure and fun. At that time the typical stewardess was a single young lady in her early twenties who signed an agreement with UAL that she would terminate her employment if she became pregnant, got married, or reached the ripe old age of 32! The average flight attendant lasted only NINETEEN MONTHS before quitting or getting fired—therefore the training center was constantly turning out replacements.

This was a very uncertain time in the aviation industry and morale was quite low among the junior pilots. None of us knew where the bottom would be after the dust settled. Every month there was a new surplus list and these lists were getting longer. I felt that I would be furloughed for sure within another year. About this time the B-737 was introduced to the fleet at UAL. This aircraft was Boeing's answer to the highly popular DC-9 series of aircraft built by the Douglas Company. The DC-9 was probably the first commercial jet that was designed to be flown by only two pilots—all others had a cockpit crew of at least three. Aircraft that had been designed to be flown by a Captain, Co-pilot, Flight Engineer and Navigator were being rapidly phased out—most navigators had already been replaced. Flight engineers were next on the list! The B-737 was built to be flown by a two-man crew (now called a two-person crew because of gender sensitivity concerns). The union had other designs. The gauntlet had been tossed by airline management—future commercial aircraft were to be flown by a crew of only TWO PILOTS. ALPA insisted that all commercial aircraft that carried over 50 passengers must be flown by three pilots. A compromise was finally reached that provided that the B-737 would be flown by a Captain, First Officer, and a THIRD CREW MEMBER, called, appropriately, the TCM. Because of this arrangement I was never furloughed—although I came to within 100 numbers from the bottom of the pilot seniority list at one time.

This down-sizing process would continue for several years before the pilot list began to stabilize. During this time there were some rather strange opportunities created by all of the movements and training created by the surplus and furlough procedure. When a new surplus letter was circulated, the company had to guess just where those pilots would bump. Pilots generally did not follow the laws of probability and many submitted their "letter of intention" to bump somewhere that was totally unexpected. This would create a shortage of pilots, sometime only briefly, on a particular aircraft type at a certain domicile. The company was obligated, by union agreement, that such shortages must be filled by any pilot on the seniority list through the normal bidding system. Any vacancy, anywhere throughout the system, at any of the nine domiciles, on any type of equipment must be advertised for any and all pilots to submit bids. Every time there were vacancies posted, I would fill out a "bid sheet" for that particular position— regardless of how absurd my chances of success were. Most pilots did not bother to submit bids for these vacancies, called "paper bids," because they knew that they would never be filled before the next round of surplus lists. I once received a successful bid to a First Officer position on the B-720. It was being phased out of the fleet and obviously I was never trained for a position that would not exist by the time my training was completed. I also received a successful bid as a First Officer on the Caravelle aircraft—I always wanted to fly that unique French-built first generation commercial jet— unfortunately that too was never to result in actual training. It became a game to submit a bid for every opening throughout the system—hoping that maybe somewhere the down-sizing would stop and I might actually fulfill that spot.

In late 1971 the downsizing took a short hiccup and stopped for a period of about two years. There would be no new pilots hired nor would any of those on furlough be recalled. However, it now seemed that I would be stuck indefinitely in Chicago as a Second Officer. Just as I was beginning to wish that I would get furloughed so that I could go back into the Navy, I finally had a stroke of good luck. United suddenly decided to expand the Denver pilot domicile, at the time one of the most senior bases in the United system. The most junior pilot based in Denver was senior to me by over 1,000 numbers and I had not even dreamed that I would be able to successfully receive a bid there. Nevertheless, I submitted my request for several openings that were posted to be effective in March, 1972. When the Denver bid results were announced I was pleasantly surprised to see my name at the bottom of the list—probably only because many pilots senior to me thought it was only a "paper bid" or else they were finally positioned where they wanted to be and did not want another move. Also on the list was my friend, Tom, the Marine who had been my roommate in new-hire training. I contacted him and found that he was also single again and we agreed to find an apartment to share in Denver.

I was very happy to leave Chicago for Denver that early spring—not knowing that this would be the first of eleven moves that I would endure during my career with United. All of my meager possessions, including my uniforms and flight bag, easily fit into my automobile, a 1967 Pontiac with bad tires and an unreliable engine. After almost four years since departing the Navy, my means had been reduced considerably. I needed something positive to occur in my life at this time. Upon reaching Denver, I met with Tom and another pal, Don, and we began looking for an apartment suitable for three junior, poorly paid, recently divorced or separated airline pilots. Knowing that we would be on reserve (probably forever) I insisted that we find a "nice place" with three bedrooms located near the airport. We found the ideal spot, Heather Ridge Country Club, a newly developed complex located in Aurora, a suburb of Denver that had all the amenities we were looking for. There were condos and apartments located around a nine hole golf course (soon to become eighteen holes) and there was a very nice tennis club, several swimming pools and a fine clubhouse—everything we needed! We rented a three bedroom apartment located on the ground floor with a patio that opened onto a swimming pool. Things were definitely looking up!

We soon found that the building we resided in, the only one with three bedroom apartments, was considered the "family building" as most of the people who required a three bedroom unit had several children. Most singles or young couples lived in other buildings that consisted of one and two bedroom units. Had we committed a tactical error by moving into the family building? Turned out that more than half of the units there were occupied by divorced ladies with one or two children and they were starved for adult male conversation and companionship! In other words, it was the ideal spot for three single aviators to reside. Being at the very bottom of the seniority list we were still B-727 Second Officers and still on reserve. The flying, however, was much more enjoyable—perhaps because the pilots in Denver were there because THAT'S WHERE THEY WANTED TO BE as opposed to many of the pilots at the more junior domiciles. Also, Denver was a much smaller pilot group that socialized more than those in Chicago. In a very short time I became acquainted with most of the 727 crews and enjoyed their friendship. The flight office consisted of a very friendly group of people—from the Chief Pilot down to the office clerks—who were always available to answer any questions and help us "new kids on the block" get settled. The crew desk consisted of only three or four schedulers and I soon knew them all by their first name—unlike the large staff at Chicago. Although I was still a flight engineer and still very junior, I began to really enjoy the lifestyle in the Denver area.

The three of us who shared the apartment, Tom, Don and I, were quite compatible even though we had very different types of personalities. Tom was the quiet, stable sort, Don was the jock, and I suppose I was the one who just wanted to "have fun!" We did not work as often in Denver on reserve and therefore had more time off. We still had to remain available by phone but the crew desk was much more lenient and understanding than what I had experienced in Chicago. The crew desk quickly discovered that at least one of the three of us was available on a moments notice and they often took advantage of that fact. On the other hand they treated us very fairly and even did big favors for us if we needed to change our schedules or wanted a special day off. In other words, the crew desk worked with us and we formed a mutual working arrangement that was beneficial to all concerned—the company had reliable, dependable pilots and we were able to enjoy some new freedoms. It was springtime in Denver and Don, the jock, was itching to play tennis and golf. I had started playing golf in the Navy but was still pretty much a beginner. Tom was about the same as me and we both struggled to stay up with Don, whose game was much superior. Don was also an excellent tennis player—a game that I had not pursued to this time. I credit my friend with introducing me to the wonderful game of tennis that I continue to enjoy to this day. On a typical clear sunny day we would call the crew desk early in the morning and check if there were any trips open for us—if not we would head for the tennis courts or the golf course. If we were told that we needed to stay by the phone, one of us would remain in the apartment and the other two would go play. We did not have cordless phones in those days but we bought a LONG extension phone cord that would reach all the way to the swimming pool, so the designated phone-man could at least enjoy fresh air and sunshine. When the weather was bad and we were confined to the indoors, Tom and I would spend countless hours playing chess.

I discovered that the B-727 flying from the Denver domicile was much nicer than that in Chicago. The versatile 727 was just the right aircraft for Denver—it could easily reach both the East and West coasts and every place in between. A typical trip would depart Denver; fly to LAX, return to DEN, then fly to somewhere else, such as Des Moines, Iowa to lay over. The next day the crew might fly to Chicago early in the morning, then to Minneapolis and then back to Denver. Other trips would last three days and were generally more senior. The schedules for three day trips usually meant that you had four days off between trips, those schedules made up of two day trips usually meant that you flew two trips back to back followed by only three days off. On reserve, the pilot flew whatever was open—a one, two or three day trip. Trips were "open" for reserves because of many factors—not only to replace pilots who called in sick, but to replace pilots on vacation, pilots who were in training or those who were scheduled for their semi-annual proficiency checks. Reserve pilots were also needed when the weather turned bad and crews were delayed and out of position. Pilots on reserve were a very necessary part of the work force and we usually flew at least once a week. Flying one or maybe two trips each week meant that we had a lot of time off— if you could call it real time off. The only days that the reserve pilot could count on as off time were those eight days each month that were "scheduled days off"—a day on reserve that was not utilized was not a quality day off! Nevertheless, I began to enjoy both the trips I flew and the time in between— I had the best of both worlds!

There were only a few trips in the Denver domicile that were undesirable, and these were the cargo flights that flew to each coast during the night. We made up names for these ugly trips: Boston Strangler, Baltimore Ball-buster, Kennedy Killer and the San Francisco Suicide Run. Most of these trips departed the cargo area in Denver around midnight and returned before noon the next day—without a layover. Perhaps the worst of these cargo trips was the one to San Francisco and back. It departed Denver at two AM—assuring that it was almost impossible to get some sleep before departure—arrived in SFO two hours later and then was converted from the cargo configuration to a people carrier. The crew then "ferried" (no passengers) the aircraft across the bay to Oakland, picked up a full load of early morning passengers and flew back to Denver, arriving around ten o'clock local time. I often wondered what those passengers were thinking as they boarded that United jet for a seven AM departure from Oakland and observed three bleary eyed pilots who needed shaves greeting then as they entered the cabin. They had no way of knowing that we had been up all night flying from DEN to SFO, had waited on the ground for three hours while the plane was reconfigured, had flown the empty aircraft across the bay and were now heading home for some much needed rest! Even the stewardesses looked at us a bit strangely—then brought more coffee to the cockpit. To make matters worse, the last leg to Denver meant looking into the sun all the way to the landing!

If there was a silver lining to the SFO Suicide Run it was that we had breakfast in the employee's cafeteria in the terminal at SFO and could ogle the stewardesses from PSA who had begun to wear "hot pants" as their flight uniforms. Surely it was a case of "the grass is greener on the other side of the street" syndrome but those gals sure looked a lot better than our stews who wore such drab, conservative uniforms. Most of the stews in Denver at that time were very senior, had been flying for almost ten years and were pushing the age 32 ceiling. Suddenly it all changed. For many reasons—the EEOC (Equal Employment Opportunity Commission), pressure from minority and women's lib groups, and a general change in the American work force—those onerous age rules were lifted and stewardesses were now permitted to fly until rigor mortis set in and could even be married! What could happen next? Yep, stewardesses could even be males! A new name had to be coined to describe this new profession—some of us proposed to call them stews and ball-bearing stews, but this was quickly voted down. The new name for the cabin crew became FLIGHT ATTENDANTS.

Because the Captain set the tone for the cockpit crew, a junior pilot always remembered those pilots who were fun to fly with, those that were a pain in the ass to fly with, and those who were regarded as "real characters." Denver had its share of all three types. Most of the Captains were quite senior and had been in the left seat for many years and were used to "doing it my way." Most of the co-pilots were also a bit long of tooth as they had been flying in the right seat for many years—at the time it was averaging almost twenty years seniority before getting a Captain bid in Denver, and nearly that long at other domiciles. The three of us new guys, Tom, Don and myself, were the first really junior pilots to report to Denver in quite a few years and were looked upon with more that just curiosity by the older pilots (and the senior stews). I often flew with a Captain and Co-pilot who had been flying the same schedule for months together and were like an old married couple—they were very comfortable in the cockpit and I was amazed at the aviation skills they displayed. They were true veterans and they made the job of flying from A to B look like child's play. I learned a lot about airline flying from these professionals. During the busy portions of a flight everything happened like magic; very few words were spoken and procedures were accomplished by a simple nod or gesture of the hand. I was beginning to realize the importance that EXPERIENCE played in this type of flying.

One of the more notorious "characters" was a short, grouchy, ill-tempered Captain by the name of Pinky. I don't know how he earned that nickname— maybe because his complexion was always on the pink side? The first time I flew with this curmudgeon I was warned by the copilot that Pinky was very superstitious and I should never put a number on the take off card that had THIRTEEN in it. The take off card listed the V speeds (V-1 was the decision speed, V-R was rotation speed and V-2 was the speed to be flown with an engine failure) and it just so happened that the speed of 113 knots was quite common for the V-1 speed. In reality the V-1 speed for the Boeing 727 was a moot point—it was always (except in very unusual configurations) higher than the speed for rotation, so the speeds were combined as V-1/V-R. I was careful to not put anything on the card to agitate the Captain on that trip and I thought that his behavior was acceptable. He was just not a very friendly type as he would not shake my hand when we met and he never called me by my name during the two day sequence that we flew—probably six or eight legs. The copilot was a great guy named Keith who was at least six foot five inches tall—Pinky was at most five foot five and the two looked like Mutt and Jeff as they walked down the concourse to the airplane. Since I had been called out as a reserve, I asked Keith, "What happened to your regular Second

Officer?" I figured that he was on vacation or maybe sick—but Keith grinned and said, "He flew one trip with Pinky and decided to use his sick leave for the rest of the month!" I felt lucky that all went okay on that first trip.

At the end of that two day trip with Pinky I was still on reserve for one more day before scheduled days off and it was seldom that a pilot was used in Denver for a one day trip unless it was one of the ugly cargo trips. I would not be "legal" for one of those so I figured that I probably would not work on that last day of reserve. The crew desk had other plans for me. I received a call that evening begging me to fly a two day trip the next day—that meant that I would work on my scheduled day off. I had no personal plans so agreed to fly that trip—then the crew scheduler, Red was his name, confessed that he was not able to get any other reserve to fly this trip because it was with PINKY! Since I had just finished that same sequence with Pinky and had experienced no really major problems, I agreed to the arrangement, knowing that I was building up some big markers with the crew desk for future negotiations. It was déjà vu as Pinky, Keith and I flew the exact same sequence the next two days. Keith and I talked about military flying, told jokes and pretty much ignored Pinky, who seemed to be trapped in his own narrow little world. We also enjoyed dinner and breakfast together in the hotel while Pinky stayed in his room and showed up just in time for the limo pickup to the airport after our layover. Everything was normal until the very last leg of the sequence—that final flight home to Denver. As fate would have it, the V-1/V-R speed that I calculated for the takeoff was exactly 113 knots! I was sorely tempted to put that number on the plastic takeoff card that I passed forward to the copilot before each takeoff—but decided not to tempt the wrath of the Captain and instead put the number as 112.5! Keith did not notice my attempt at levity as he placed that card in its usual spot over the radar screen on the center console. Pinky looked at the card and roared, "What the hell is that number?" I replied, "It's one hundred twelve and one half knots, slightly below one thirteen." Pinky picked up that card, made of heavy duty plastic, turned and threw it as hard as he could to the rear of the cockpit. It missed my head by several inches and bounced off the cockpit door and ended up on the deck behind my seat. I was more than startled, I was pissed that he had thrown that card with such force that it could have done serious damage if it had hit me. Pinky's face was now more than pink—it was deep red, almost MAGENTA! We were still at the gate at whatever airport we were departing and the jetway was still attached to the aircraft. I took off my headset, bent over and started closing my flight bag when Pinky said in a calmer voice, "Where do you think you're going?" I replied, "You will have to find another Second Officer to fly this leg—I won't tolerate that type of behavior!" Suddenly, Keith, the senior copilot who should rightly have been a Captain by this time in his career, spoke up in a voice of authority and tactfully took command of the situation. He told Pinky to apologize to me, admonished me for my less than professional behavior with the takeoff speeds and basically told us both to calm down! Pinky did apologize to me then ordered me to give him a proper takeoff card. I refused to pick up that card that was still on the deck, and Pinky was certainly not going to pick it up—we seemed to be at an impasse! Keith, the arbitrator, solved the problem by unstrapping, getting out of his seat, picking up the card and handing it to me. We completed the flight to Denver with very few words spoken in the cockpit. Pinky retired a few months later. Less than one year after his retirement he put a gun to his head and ended his unhappy life.

A few short miles from our apartment at Heather Ridge CC was a neighborhood bar that many of the Denver pilots frequented—called Casey's Castle & Annie's Palace—and it was the typical hangout with lousy food, bad music and watered down drinks. I never met the owner, Casey (maybe he never really existed), but Annie was always there to handle the cash register. It was the type of place where dollar bills were stapled to the walls and ceiling with names and notes scrawled illegibly over them—did people really expect someone to see and recognize their names? Due to the irregular hours and schedules that pilots routinely worked, this place was as busy on a Tuesday night as most places that catered to the normal populace were on Saturday. On one occasion my old friend, Temple, now a TWA pilot, called me to let me know that he would be in Denver for a layover and wanted to know if we could connect. I picked him up at the airport and we later ended up at Annie's Palace. "A good time was had by all" and when I was ready to call it a night, my buddy was nowhere to be found. The last time I noticed, he was enthralled with a very cute brunette and they seemed to be destined to spend the night together. Shortly before closing I checked around one more time for my pal (he was nowhere to be found) and finally departed for my apartment. Two hours later, when I was sound asleep, I received a frantic call from Temple— he was in the parking lot of that bar and needed a ride to my place. I was not in very good shape but after throwing some cold water on my face I went to pick him up. At the first stop sign I encountered, I misjudged the distance and not only skidded **through** the intersection but did a complete 360 degree turn. After a quick **recovery I** proceeded toward my destination—suddenly there was a flashing **light behind** me! I was busted! I pulled over—stepped out of my vehicle **and fell down!** The police officer looked at me and only shook his head. I quickly **explained that** I had just awoken and was on the way to pick up my friend **when he** interjected with, "That was quite a maneuver at the intersection—you ended up exactly where you started at the stop sign." Again I apologized and eventually that nice cop decided to follow me to my destination—warning me that the slightest waver would result in a sobriety test. I picked up my friend, thanked the cop, and concluded the evening with a very slow ride home!

One night, Annie called our apartment with a problem. She stated that there was a United Pilot by the name of Scottie who had passed out and was in need of some help to get him home. Tom and I went to the friendly neighborhood bar and found Scottie, a 727 Captain that we both knew, sound asleep behind the bar. We checked his billfold, found his address (not very far away) and carried him to our car for the ride home. We arrived at our destination, dragged him to the front door, rang the bell—and then departed! We were both laughing hysterically as the front door was opened by his sleepy wife and he fell into their entryway! Tom and I both flew with Scottie several more times during our tour in Denver and found that he was really a very competent pilot who just had a "drinking problem."

Those rules about drinking were very inconsistent. The FAA rule was "eight hours from bottle to throttle." Most airlines had a rule of twelve hours before flying, but United insisted that their pilots refrain from any use of alcohol for at least 24 HOURS before duty! This also meant that the reserve pilot must not use any form of alcohol for 24 hours before going on call. I believe that ALL of the pilots that I flew with honored the 8 hour rule, MOST obeyed the twelve hour rule, and FEW paid any attention to the 24 hour rule! I never flew with a pilot that I suspected had been drinking and I never knew of any pilot using any illegal drugs. As much as pilots enjoyed having a good party, they generally behaved themselves while on duty—I am not so sure about the flight attendants, however! I recall one very early morning departure from Denver when I stopped in the galley to introduce myself to the senior stew during my cabin inspection before the passengers were boarded. She was doing her routine duties to set up the supplies for the service and was sipping on what looked like tomato juice. I jokingly asked her if she was having a Bloody Mary to get her juices flowing. She looked me in the eye and retorted, "Hell yes—that's the only way I can face these assholes first thing in the morning!" I thought that surely she was kidding and was just pulling my leg until I noticed two opened and empty vodka miniatures in the corner of her work area. Then she held the drink up to my face and asked if I wanted a sip! I could smell the booze then and knew that she was serious. When I went into the cockpit I mentioned to the Captain that the "A" Stew seemed to be a bit of a character. He laughed and said, "Guess you just met Marge—we call her Sarge—she is one of the finest stews with United. She will have the passengers eating out of her hand in ten minutes—and she'll take real good care of us in the cockpit." The Captain is always right! Marge had the type of personality that was essential for her type of job. She could tell a passenger to shut the hell up and sit down and he did just that. She told ribald jokes and off-color stories and had everyone laughing till tears were streaming down their faces. The Captain would turn on the cockpit speaker for the PA system when she was making announcements so that I could listen—and she was fabulous with her comedy routine. I began hearing stories about some of her antics over the years—she should write a book about what goes on in the cabin of a passenger jet after the doors are closed. One time after a rather hard landing she entered the cockpit with her panties down around her ankles and demanded to know if the plane had landed or been shot down! She once made an announcement over the PA after a rough landing to the effect that: "It wasn't the Captain's fault, and it wasn't the copilots fault, it was the ASPHALT!"

Not all of the "characters" in Denver were Captains and Stews—some of the copilots were rather notorious in their behavior also. Doug lived some fifty miles east of Denver in an old farmhouse that he and his wife had restored. He was always telling funny stories and pulling practical jokes on everyone. He carried a plastic chicken, naked of course, in his flight bag and set it on the glare shield above his instrument panel before every departure. In those days, many passengers, especially those with children, stopped by the cockpit while boarding to look at all "those knobs, switches and dials" that the pilots played with. Only the most innocent of those small children had the nerve to ask about Doug's chicken. He made up a different story each time—it was his good luck charm, it was what the pilots ate if there no meals left over, etc. His very best practical joke was one that he pulled on his wife and her friends one day at their home. His closest neighbor lived more than five miles from their farm but Doug's wife liked to invite her lady friends over occasionally for tea. One day while she was entertaining a large group of ladies, Doug slipped a garden hose through an outside window into the guest bathroom which was adjacent to the living room. Then he ran into the house, excused himself to the ladies by saying that he was about to bust his bladder, entered the bathroom and left the door slightly ajar. He quietly pulled the garden hose to the toilet and opened the nozzle to full flow into the bowl until it was to the very top—then he shut it off, slipped the hose back out the window and flushed the john! Then he left the bathroom with a flourish while zipping up his fly. Some of the women gasped, some almost fainted, some laughed and quite a few looked at Doug with what could only be described as true admiration!

Doug had a small plane with his own airstrip on his property and he engaged in a running aerial battle with a neighbor, another United pilot, who lived about ten miles away. He would take off at dawn, sneak in from the east with the sun at his back, and drop flour sacks on his friend's barn and home. His adversary would reciprocate by flying his own small plane from the west at sunset to drop his own "bombs." Of interest is the fact that I first flew with Doug when I was a Second Officer and he was a copilot, later I flew with him when I was a copilot and he was the Captain, then in my last few years I flew with Doug when I was the Captain and he was the Second Officer! His personality never changed—he was always cutting up and full of mischief. He was also an excellent pilot and a real pleasure to work with.

My social life at this time was interesting to say the least. It was easy to meet attractive ladies at work (flight attendants) and our neighbors at Heather Ridge Country Club were really a party oriented group. I was not looking for any sort of permanent arrangement and most of the ladies I met were of a like mind—the seventies seemed to be the decade of casual and brief encounters. Often one did not have to even seek such affairs—they came to your door! One morning Tom and I were both enjoying a day off from being on call and Don was away on a long trip when the doorbell rang. I opened the door to find a lovely young lady with a salesman's sample case standing in the hallway. With a perky smile she said, "I'm the Avon lady, is your wife in?" I was probably drooling a bit as I replied that unfortunately there were no ladies at this residence, just Tom and myself. Without missing a beat she replied that she also had products for men and could she show us her wares. I ushered her into our apartment and she proceeded to show us her assortment of men's after shave and cologne products. Tom and I both had trouble keeping our eyes away from her personal attributes as she was wearing a very short mini skirt and her blouse was pretty much a see-through thing that revealed that she was not wearing a bra and certainly had no need for one. She was in her early twenties and had a perfect figure—she was also full of spunk and personality. After listening to her sales pitch for about thirty minutes, I asked her if she would care for a drink. She replied, "What type of drink do you have in mind?" As it was only around ten o'clock in the morning I offered her a Bloody Mary and she readily accepted. I quickly whipped up a large pitcher of my finest blend of BM's and we all started to relax a bit. We engaged in small talk for a while and when we mentioned that we were pilots she related that she was married to an airman who was going through ground training at Lowery Air Force Base in Denver and they would be in the area for several months. She was trying to supplement their meager income as her husband was just starting as an enlisted man and the pay was quite low. I was starting to feel guilty about my lustful feelings for this young lady when she asked, "Do you all ever play cards—I love to play cards!"

Tom found a deck of cards and playfully suggested that we play STRIP POKER! She giggled and said that she only had a very few pieces of clothing and was at a distinct disadvantage. We were all starting to giggle a bit as we began the game. She was a lousy poker player and soon she had removed both shoes—next came her blouse! She was rightfully very proud of her breasts and they were truly a sight to behold. Before long she was down to just her panties and Tom and I were still mostly clothed. She announced that she needed to "go potty" and as she left the room, Tom and I looked at each other and mutually agreed that one of us should leave. We flipped a coin and Tom lost—he left with his usual good-natured attitude and I eagerly waited for the Avon lady to return from the bathroom. Tom was just leaving as she reentered the living room and she gave him a quick kiss goodbye. Then she turned to me and said, "What do we do now?" I was grinning from ear to ear as she started to remove her only remaining piece of clothing. She helped me reach her state of nakedness and soon we were standing completely nude in the middle of the room. I suggested that we head to the bedroom when she asked, "What time is it?" I looked at my watch and replied, "Almost noon, why—do you have to leave now?" She giggled and stated that her "very favorite soap opera" started at noon and would it be okay if we stayed in the living room where the only TV set was located. Obviously I agreed and she asked me to bring some pillows from the bedroom to put on the floor. After placing a sheet and several pillows in front of the TV, things started to get serious. Just as I started to enter her, the music from her soap opera started—she jumped up and said, "We'll have to do it doggy style so I can watch my program." After rearranging the pillows, that is exactly what we did—watched the most boring soap I have ever seen while screwing our brains out!

The Avon lady and I repeated this strange way of mating several times over the next few months—I don't believe that I ever knew her name and I never looked her in the face during sex. She would call me to find out my schedule to arrange a meeting and only introduced herself as the "Avon Lady." I bought a lot of Avon products for men during this time—and eventually threw them all away, unopened.

I tried not to get involved with female neighbors but the lady upstairs, Marilyn, was just too tempting to resist. She was a bombshell blonde divorcee with two small children and she was definitely starved for affection. We spent a few evenings together to our mutual satisfaction until one weekend there was a miscommunication. I thought that we were going out together on Saturday night but on Friday she informed me that she had a date with a lawyer friend that particular Saturday and they were going to the clubhouse for a dance party. I was disappointed but called up an old girl friend named Annie and we showed up for that particular party and had a "chance encounter" with Marilyn and her date on the dance floor. The four of us sat together and began to have a "real fine time!" After many drinks we decided to continue the party at Marilyn's apartment—her children were with their father for the weekend and it seemed to be the thing to do. As we drove together (just across the street) to our apartment building, we encountered my roommate, Tom, who had just picked up his parents at the airport who had arrived from New York for a visit. My date, Annie, a very outspoken lady from North Carolina, spotted Tom and rolled down her window—we were in the back seat of the lawyer's car—and shouted, "Tom, come join us, we're going to have a group fuck!" I was mortified and to this day sincerely apologize if Tom's parents overheard this foul utterance. I had never engaged in group sex and was not sure just what was going to happen once we reached Marilyn's apartment. We decided to turn out all the lights, remove our clothes, and walk around the living room until we encountered someone interesting—I sure hoped that I did not run into the attorney first! It was pitch black as I groped around until I felt a female willing partner—happily it turned out to be my date, Annie. We were familiar lovers and soon completed our coupling—I could tell from the sounds coming from the other couple that they were still in the exploratory stages and were not yet "fully engaged." By sound and touch I found them on a couch nearby, gently tapped the lawyer on the shoulder and said, "Time's up, time to change partners!" I could not believe that he readily disengaged and I took over where he had left off—the "pump was primed!" I never saw that lawyer again but I bet he had some interesting stories to tell about our group event at Heather Ridge C.C.

One beautiful summer morning I returned from one of those ugly all night cargo liner flights around ten o'clock and found that both of my roommates were away on longer trips. I was tired and sleepy but hated to waste such a gorgeous day by sleeping so decided to put on my swim trunks and go to the main club swimming pool which was just across the street and within easy walking distance. Clad only in my swim suit and t-shirt and wearing flip-flops, I took a towel and paperback novel to the pool to get a bit of sun, read a bit and perhaps take a little nap. Things were going as planned until about an hour later when a cocktail waitress appeared and handed me a large drink. I told the waitress that I had not ordered a drink—she replied that it was compliments of a gentleman at the upstairs bar which overlooked the pool. I accepted the drink, told the waitress to thank my benefactor and enjoyed a very stiff drink that I assumed was from one of my pals who happened to be at the bar having an "early lunch." I was dozing off after that drink when the waitress appeared with another very strong drink—again from the "gent at the bar." I managed to drink that concoction and was starting back to the apartment for some much needed rest when the waitress appeared again with a third drink. This was too much—so I headed to the bar to see just who was being so generous. I was not dressed appropriately for our bar but it was still before noon on a week day and there was no one in the club but a female bartender, the cocktail waitress and one stranger sitting at the bar. I approached the man at the bar and asked him why he was buying me drinks. He replied, "Sit down; we have something to talk about."

He was about my age, well dressed, and a bit inebriated. With a lot of emotion in his voice, he related that he knew that I was having a "relation" with his fiancée, Marilyn, the upstairs divorcee. She had never mentioned that she was in a serious relationship with another man, much less engaged, and I was a bit surprised, especially in light of our "group grope." He was a career fireman with the local fire department and moonlighted as a model—specializing in doing hand commercials. I looked at his hands and believed he was telling the truth as his nails were immaculately manicured. He insisted on buying another round of drinks and we spent an hour or two talking about what we had in common—Marilyn. I assured him that I was not interested in a serious relationship and as far as I was concerned he had nothing to worry about as I was happy to step out of the picture. Before I could leave he began to become quite obnoxious and was very rude to the bar maid. He insisted that we arm wrestle before I left and I finally gave in—thinking that after this macho move we would shake hands and go our separate ways. He was surprisingly strong but I was a bit more sober and won that little contest. He wanted a rematch but I got up, thanked him for the drinks and departed. Before I left the club I stopped off at the men's room for a very necessary visit. When I exited the rest room I saw two police officers dragging my "buddy" out the front door. The bar maid, who was trailing the cops, pointed to me and said, "There's the other one!" Before I had a chance to say a single word, one of the cops threw me against the wall and slapped handcuffs on my wrists. I was placed in the back seat of one police car as the "fireman" was taken to jail in another vehicle. I asked the officer what was going on and he responded that the bartender had made a call to the police when we started arm wrestling—thinking that we were getting out of hand. When the police arrived and approached the fireman, he became belligerent and took a swing at one of the cops. He was being charged with assaulting an officer and I was being charged with "drunk and disorderly behavior."

I was taken to the local lock-up and ended up in the same cell with the jerk that got me into this mess. I was not happy about the whole situation and we began a real fight—not just arm wrestling! Quickly I was taken to another cell and I requested that I be permitted to make my "one phone call." Since there was no one home at my apartment, I called a neighbor and asked her to go into the apartment through the sliding screen door, which I had left open, find my billfold that was on the table, and please bring it to me at the County jailhouse! She did just that and after making bail of $35.00 I was released but told to appear in court in two weeks. What a fun day I was having and it was still early in the afternoon! I contacted an attorney, told him my story and he agreed to handle my case. A few days later, I met with that lawyer and he informed me that I had been arrested illegally, all charges had been dropped and if I wished to pursue the legal process, I had a very good chance of winning a law suit against the Sheriff's department for improper behavior. I decided to just forget the whole matter, paid a small fee to the attorney, and moved on with my life. A few weeks later I received a refund of the $35.00 that I had paid "for bail" from the Sheriff's Office, without any explanation.

After one year at Heather Ridge, my friend and roommate, Tom, decided to buy a three bedroom townhouse at another development just a few miles south of our current address. We worked out an arrangement where I would pay him rent for one of those bedrooms and we moved into a place called The Timbers in the spring of 1973. This was definitely a quieter environment and a welcome change of pace from the hectic social swirl of the Country Club life. We were still playing tennis and golf in the warm months and I had found a new sport to occupy the winter months—skiing. My first attempts at downhill skiing were disastrous, but slowly I began to learn why so many people loved the sport. In a few years I would be spending an average of 30 days each season on the slopes—I once skied at least one time each month for an entire year with the exception of August.

After a lull of almost two years, the downsizing at United started anew in late 1973. The surplus letters became a monthly reality and the furlough notices were soon to follow. It looked like I would surely get bumped out of Denver and there were no pilots junior to me west of the Mississippi! I decided that the time had come to attend a union meeting and find out just what my union was doing to help me keep my job. The Air Line Pilots Association (ALPA) was considered one of the strongest unions in the labor movement and my dues were withheld from my paycheck each month to help pay for the HUGE SALARY and SUPERB WORKING CONDITIONS that I enjoyed! After five years of pitiful pay, eight days off each month, no advancement and the likely prospect of being laid off in the near future—I needed to know what the union was doing for ME! The first ALPA meeting I attended was held at a Holiday Inn near the Denver airport and it was quite a revelation. As I entered a very large meeting room I noticed that the Captains sat in the front rows—by seniority probably—First Officers were in the back rows and the lowly Second Officers like me were left standing in the rear of the room. The main topic of concern at this meeting was to discuss a new company procedure that required the Captain to add his domicile when he signed the release for a flight. It was an FAA requirement that the Captain sign a piece of paper before each series of trips—now the company (United management) was insisting that he include his domicile! The bitching and complaining would go on for over two hours about how onerous it was for the Captain to have to write (or print) those three letters after his signature— DEN! There was absolutely no way that I could get my two cents in at this meeting so I quietly left and did not attend another union meeting until twelve years later!

The union and the pilots in general were not happy with the way things were going at United during those years of downsizing—but there was little that could be done to change the economic realities of the times. The union leadership felt that there was not suitable cause for a strike but the pilots needed to get the attention of management about the pilots concerns. The union decided to have a W.O.E. program (Withdrawal Of Enthusiasm) which would hurt the company where it counted—in the bottom line! Seemed to me to be a case of "biting the hand that feeds you" but I was in no position to challenge the senior Captains who set the policies. Some of the Captains followed the WOE program with pure glee—they taxied so slowly that it caused massive delays at busy airports such as O'Hare, flew lower than usual to burn more fuel, took long delays at the gate to have some petty gripe fixed, and generally pissed off the passengers and air traffic controllers. One Captain I flew with had the speed brakes partially extended during cruise from Chicago to Denver! This required much more thrust on the engines to maintain speed and wasted massive amounts of fuel. It also gave the passengers a very rough ride. At the end of this particular trip one of the passengers stopped by the cockpit on his way out and asked the Captain why he had flown with the speed brakes extended—obviously this passenger knew a little about aerodynamics. The Captain replied, "We're trying to teach the company a lesson!" The passenger, a well dressed business man who was traveling in the first class cabin, shook his head and said, "You guys are real assholes!" and walked away. The Captain was incensed that a passenger had talked to him that way—I was more than embarrassed to be involved in such antics that really hurt our cause and put the pilots in such a poor light. We needed a better way to get our concerns recognized by management and not cause the innocent passengers to suffer. Over the years I came to realize that the antagonistic relationship between employees (not just pilots) and management was part of the airline culture that had no reasonable explanation or solution—it just existed! Management made some incredibly poor decisions that I was personally aware of and I often felt that the airline survived only because the other airlines were equally inept. This was before the "upstart airlines" such as Southwest and Jet Blue emerged on the playing field.

One month I was assigned to fly a real schedule for two weeks—the regular second officer was on vacation and I "moved into his line" to fly the trips that he would miss. These were two day trips that were flown back to back—four days of flying followed by three days off—and they were not what were considered very senior type trips. Nevertheless I was happy to know what my schedule would be for the next two weeks and therefore able to make plans on my days off. I was a bit surprised to find that the Captain flying this line was one of the very senior pilots in the Denver domicile and was also an officer in the pilots union. He obviously had the seniority to fly much better trips—why was he flying what was considered a junior line? I don't recall exactly the sequence but each trip laid over in Boise, Idaho—one of my favorite places to stay, normally. This particular trip arrived late at night and departed early the next morning—what was called a "minimum layover" of less than eleven hours. We stayed at the Holiday Inn near the airport and it was a very boring place to spend the night. It was also during the winter and the weather could be cold and miserable at times. The Captain had the reputation of being a real pain in the ass and the first trip proved this to be true. He was rude and demanding to the flight attendants, cussed out the van driver who picked us up three minutes late at the Boise airport, and chewed out the desk clerk when we checked into the motel because his room was located where he had to walk outside for a few steps. When he stormed out of the lobby, the desk clerk looked at the copilot and me and said, "I only have to put up with him five minutes a week—I feel sorry for you guys who have to spend hours in the cockpit together."

The Captain was certainly not a pleasure to fly with and the copilot was an older type who disappeared into his room when we arrived at the motel and only showed up in time for the ride to the airport the next morning. This was a trip that was less than fun as I was the "third wheel" in the cockpit—the Captain never knew my name and only addressed me as "CARD"—which meant that he wanted a takeoff card or a landing card! I decided that this would be my new name—CARD! After the third trip of the month I began to notice that the Captain, who was always in a bad mood, was in an even fouler mood after the layover in Boise. I figured that he did not sleep well or perhaps was a closet boozer who hit the bottle each night—even on the short layover in Boise. Each night that I spent in the motel I dined alone at the motel restaurant and eventually struck up a relationship with one of the waitresses. By the time of the final layover she and I made plans to go out together after she finished work—at midnight! I managed to get a couple of hours sleep before she picked me up and we headed to a place that was an "after hours club" somewhere across the river. I was beginning to think that this was not a really good idea when we arrived after a long ride to what appeared to be an upstairs unit behind a run down motel complex. Just like the movies, we knocked on the door and a small hole was opened at eye level and a voice asked for the "password." I was beginning to think that this was all a big joke when my lady friend uttered the special word and we were admitted into a large room that was filled with people who were dancing, drinking and having a really fine time! We were seated at a small table and soon began to enjoy the party atmosphere that I had never expected to find in a town such as Boise, Idaho. The music was quite good, the lights were very low and we danced—and we danced! Just as I decided that it was time to call it a night as our departure was merely a very few hours away, we had one last dance. In the middle of this final dance, just as things were starting to get interesting, suddenly someone slapped me on the back! Obviously I did not know anyone in Boise, much less someone who would be at this speak-easy at this ungodly hour! I looked around to see who had interrupted my dance and there was my CAPTAIN—the asshole who had not given me the time of day for two weeks—standing in the middle of the dance floor with a huge grin! He gave me a big bear hug as though I was his best friend and even called me by my real name! He invited me to join him and his "date" for a drink. My friend and I were led to a secluded corner table where there were several other couples and discovered that my irascible Captain was the major domo of the group—he was certainly a completely different person than I knew. He was laughing, telling stories and generally having one hell of a time! He was definitely the life of the party.

The next morning he showed up as his usual grumpy self and was—as usual—a pain in the ass to fly with. He still only spoke to me when he wanted a "CARD" and acted like nothing had happened the night before. At the end of the trip, the last I would fly with him, he came up to me, shook my hand, and with a big smile, said, "It was really a pleasure flying with you, uh—well you know I'm not very good with names!" He still acted like he did not know my name. However, for years after this episode, every time I encountered

Captain "Boil" (as the junior pilots named him), he lit up, grasped my hand and said that it was great to see me again!

Eventually the inevitable happened—my name was on a new surplus letter (along with most of my buddies) and I had to submit a "bump letter." My choices were limited, I could go back to Chicago—been there, done that—or to the East coast. I had no interest in New York, so decided to try Washington, D.C. After almost exactly two very interesting years in Denver, I packed my belongings into my old car and headed to the East coast to start a NEW ADVENTURE!

Chapter Fourteen

"Physicians bury their mistakes, Lawyers appeal theirs, but the Pilot is the first to arrive at the scene of the accident!"

Because of the contract between the pilots and the company, a surplussed pilot was given a liberal travel time to his new domicile, he was entitled to a company paid move to that new domicile, and was reimbursed for expenses incurred for the first thirty days while "looking for new housing." I decided to take full advantage of those benefits!

I departed Denver for Washington, D.C. with all my belongings once again in my vehicle with plenty of room left over for several cases of Coors Beer, a beverage that I had taken a liking to but unfortunately was not available east of the Mississippi River. I realized the true value of my cargo when I had a tire blow out near Lexington, Kentucky a couple of days later. I changed the blown tire with the spare and then stopped at a service station to see if the old tire could be repaired. The mechanic on duty opened the trunk of my car, looked at the old tire, shook his head, and then looked at the cases of Coors. He said, "I can't fix your old tire but I will give you a new one for a case of that beer!" I drove away with a brand new tire and one less case of beer!

I decided to spend a night in Charlottesville, Virginia and check out the old fraternity house—it had been almost fifteen years since my graduation from The University and I was feeling a bit nostalgic. I drove into the parking lot of the ATO house at dusk and walked into the same run down, beat up old living room that I remembered so well. The brothers were gathering for dinner (having a few beers and playing bridge—some things never change) and they treated me with the respect that was always extended to an "old" alumnus—such as myself! The president of the fraternity—called the grand master—looked to be about fifteen years old and spoke to me as if I were his grandfather. When he offered me a beer, I asked if he had any Coors. He sadly shook his head and I asked him if he would accompany me to my car to help carry in some "real beer." When we arrived with two cases of that "beer with a mystique" I suddenly became the most popular alum in years! After consuming several of those beers that I provided, I left the rest to the "young guys" and retired to my motel—I was starting to feel old—at the age of thirty five! The old adage was true—YOU CAN NEVER GO BACK!

When I checked in with the flight office at DCA airport I was informed that a new surplus letter was now effective and I had been surplussed from (kicked out of) the Washington domicile. I would spend one month flying as S/O on the 727 in DCA before I would have to bump somewhere else. Each bump required a written letter that specified exactly where the surplussed pilot wished to go—any base that had at least one pilot junior to the pilot being surplussed was fair game! I checked the roster and discovered that there was one pilot in Miami that was junior to me. I submitted my bump letter for Miami and was told, "You are just wasting your time—the only pilot junior to you in Miami is surely going to be surplussed soon—and will probably be furloughed." I did not really care at this time and was looking forward to going to southern Florida for a bit of vacation—at company expense.

The one month that I spent flying out of DCA was very interesting. I checked into the Old Colony Motel, just south of Washington National Airport in Alexandria, and waited for the crew desk to call me for a trip. After two weeks without receiving a call, I was becoming concerned. I finally contacted the crew desk and they acted like they had no idea just who I might be! Seems like they had lost my name/file number from their rolodex. I often wondered what would have happened if I had never contacted them—maybe I would still be receiving flight pay to this date without ever working a single trip! Once I was back "in the loop" I began to be assigned reserve trips—the first one was a call from the crew desk late at night for a 7 AM departure. I said, "No problem," as I was just a few minutes south of DCA. Then the crew desk advised me that I would be departing from Baltimore (BAL)—not DCA! I now discovered that reserve pilots at the Washington domicile were responsible for trips from THREE airports, DCA, BAL and IAD! I would have to leave my motel at 4 AM in order to arrive in time for my 6 AM check-in at the Baltimore airport. No one had bothered to tell me that I needed an employee parking sticker on my car in order to park in the employee lot at

Baltimore—I ended up having to park in the regular passenger high priced lot! I was beginning to love this job—I could turn in an expense report and was paid cash for what I had to pay out of pocket. I would continue to submit a weekly expense report for the next several months. I flew with some very interesting crews in Washington—most of the Captains were ex-Capital Airlines pilots and they were certainly an esoteric group. Capital Airlines had been merged into United Airlines some years previously and most of the "old Capital pilots" felt that the merger should have been the other way around—the surviving airline should have been CAPITAL!

Many of the trips that I flew while in the DCA domicile were "cross-town" operations—meaning that the trip started from one airport and ended up at another—for instance the first leg departed from DCA and three days later the last leg arrived at BAL. The company was responsible for providing transportation for the pilot to get to the departing airport or from the arriving airport back to where his automobile was parked! It was a very convoluted arrangement and involved many vans to transport crews between the three airports. The company contracted with a limo company to provide this transportation—and the vans were all painted PINK! Lots of jokes were made by the pilots about those pink limos! In reality it was very easy for the pilots—just find the pink van and we were on our way. On several occasions the United crew was transported from one airport to another on a small commuter airline that flew STOL (short takeoff and landing) aircraft. The first time that I encountered this type of cross-town operation was from Baltimore to Washington's Dulles—a long way by vehicle but just a short hop via the airways. As the three of us United pilots walked out onto the ramp to board the small plane, we were greeted by the pilot—the same person who had taken our tickets at the boarding area! He welcomed us aboard again, mentioned that he was available if United was hiring, and asked us to leave our flight bags and overnight suitcases on the ramp as he would load them himself. This was definitely a "one-man operation." The small airplane had a full load of six passengers and we roared off the runway in about the same distance as an aircraft carrier launch! After less than twenty minutes in the air we dove for the ground at Dulles and stopped on the proverbial dime! I was very impressed with that type of performance—it was almost like a helicopter ride but without the wild gyrations that rotorcraft were famous for. We thanked the pilot for the interesting ride; each took a business card that he extended with several methods of reaching him in the event that United needed a new, highly qualified pilot, and were told that our bags would be delivered to us inside the terminal in less than five minutes. Right on time the pilot—now a baggage handler—arrived with four bags! Two bags were missing, the Captain's flight bag and my personal suitcase! When we asked the ticket agent/pilot/flight attendant/baggage handler about the missing bags, he nonchalantly responded that the flight had been overloaded and those two bags would arrive on the next flight from BAL. Just when might that be, the Captain inquired. The STOL pilot responded that it would be as soon as he flew a load of passengers back to BAL, and returned to IAD on his next trip! Our scheduled United flight was to depart in less than one hour and it appeared that we were going to be a bit late.

The Captain informed United Dispatch of the problem and the potential lengthy delay and then we proceeded to the aircraft that we were to fly—I believe that the destination was Denver. The passengers were boarded and the Captain was reaching for the P.A. to give the bad news that we would be delayed when we saw that same STOL aircraft taxi up beside our much bigger B-727. The STOL pilot was gesturing to us that he needed someone to get our bags from his aircraft. My Captain directed me to proceed down the ladder from the jetway and render assistance (he was a former Naval Aviator). I ran down to the STOL airplane, managed to open the passenger door and found the two missing bags within easy reach. After closing the door I saluted the pilot, he returned my salute and taxied away! I returned to the cockpit with the stray bags, we finished our check lists, and we departed on time—another routine trip with the airlines!

All too soon it was time for me to move again—this time to Miami. The pilot domicile there was the smallest in the system—usually about fifty crews, all flying the 727. The pilots based there left only when they retired or died! Most of the Captains were ex-Capital pilots who refused to ever be integrated into the "United Mainline" type of operation. The co-pilots were really old and senior and just waiting for the day that they could move over into the left seat. The engineers, in turn, were waiting to move up to what was called "a window seat." The Miami operation was like a completely different airline—with its own rules and procedures. As a pilot "bumping" into the domicile I was entitled to a paid move, temporary housing expenses, etc. and I took full advantage of these contractual privileges. I also was provided with a "travel advance" before leaving Washington so I was flush with free money! I checked into the Miami Marriott Hotel, a layover facility for out of town crews, and a beautiful place to reside. I assumed that I would be in Miami for only one month before being surplussed again so I wanted to be comfortable and enjoy my short visit to southern Florida. The weather was gorgeous but starting to get hot as summer was rapidly approaching. As a reserve Second Officer, I worked very seldom and had lots of free time to spend at the Hotel pool. I soon learned that the crew desk personnel in Miami were the most easy-going in the system and they closed down at 4:00 every afternoon! The last trip from Miami or Ft. Lauderdale departed at 3:50 and everything shut down until the next morning. If I did not hear from the crew desk by one o'clock in the afternoon I was off the hook until the next day.

Every week I received a "care package" from a girl friend in Denver— a case of Coors Beer that was checked in by her as luggage and addressed to me at the Ft. Lauderdale airport. I would bring out a six pack of that "special" beer, ice it down in a cooler at the pool, and watch people drool as they observed me popping those cans! It was a great way to meet people as most of those at poolside were seasoned travelers who knew that Coors was not available on the east coast. I was offered five dollars a can on several occasions—one gent even offered me $100 for a case! Perhaps I should have gone into the beer smuggling business while in Miami. It became a bit of a routine for me to go to the airport each week to pick up my "package" and I soon got to know the ground workers at the airport quite well. One day when I picked up my package, I noticed that it had been opened and several beers were missing. I noticed several employees standing around with silly grins on their faces and knew that I was being "had." Finally the guilty party walked over and I recognized a familiar face—it was a fellow pilot that I knew from my early days in Chicago, named Jim. He had been furloughed from the pilot ranks and was now working on the ramp as a baggage handler in Ft. Lauderdale. His father was the most senior Captain in the Miami domicile and I would have occasion to fly with "Moose" in the near future. Jim said that he figured that he was entitled to at least a couple of beers from my package each week as a handling charge—I agreed and we continued the arrangement while I remained in the area. He usually took two beers, and never more than three—I felt that it was a fair deal!

The trips that were flown from the Miami domicile were really quite ugly. In those days United was not permitted to fly non-stop to Chicago or New York from southern Florida. In the days of regulation, those lucrative flights were flown by Eastern Airlines. United flew non-stop to Cleveland, Buffalo, Rochester, Pittsburgh, Atlanta and Washington, D.C. Most of the layovers ended up in either Buffalo or Rochester, N.Y. Those places could be downright miserable during the winter but now that it was summer, I really enjoyed those cities. The very first trip that I flew from the Miami domicile I remember quite well. I reported to the airport early and was reading the bulletin board when the Captain and Copilot entered flight operations. They did not see me right away and I could not avoid overhearing their conversation. The Captain said, "Looks like we have a new guy as our engineer today—someone I've never heard of." The Copilot responded, "Let's hope he's an okay guy—we'll see." I walked over, introduced myself and added, "I'm an okay guy!" These two had flown the same trip for months, maybe years, and with the same stews, who were just as senior as the pilots. They all called me "Sonny." It was a very professional but laid-back group to work with and I quickly began to enjoy this type of atmosphere. The final leg of the day was flown into Buffalo and the senior stew entered the cockpit about thirty minutes before landing. She had her own cockpit key and came and went as she wanted—I had never flown with a stew who had a cockpit key before and each time she entered the cockpit I was surprised. She asked the Captain, "What do you want to drink tonight, the usual?" He grunted in the affirmative, and she next asked the copilot, "Gin okay for you?" Again an affirmative grunt. Then she looked at me and said, "How about you, Sonny, what do you want to drink?" I thought for a few seconds and answered, "Is a cold beer out of the question?" She rolled her eyes and said, "Too heavy to carry—bourbon, gin or vodka, that's the choice!" I mumbled, "Bourbon is fine."

After landing at the Buffalo airport I politely asked the senior flight attendant if I could carry her overnight suitcase from the airplane down the steep stairs to the ramp—there was no jetway at that time and we deplaned from the rear via the airstair that was lowered by the ground crew once we were properly parked. She had her purse in one hand and her suitcase in the other and it was a bit awkward to egress via the aft airstair with both hands occupied. She thanked me and with a smile said, "Carry my purse, please." As she handed me her purse I almost dropped it as it was very HEAVY! When I handed her that purse once we were on the tarmac, I commented about how heavy it was. She just smiled. Once at the hotel, the Captain said to me, "Be at my room in ten minutes." I quickly changed out of my uniform and reported as ordered. The Captain and Copilot were there, still in uniform but with their ties removed, and the three stews soon joined the little group. The Captain was setting up what appeared to be quite an elaborate bar—he had several buckets of ice and an unopened bottle of Scotch. The senior stew opened her purse and dumped the contents on the bed—there were seventeen miniatures there! No wonder that purse was so heavy! The other stews provided various types of munchies and everyone proceeded to have a big party that lasted for several hours. Everyone had a very relaxing time, no one had too much to drink, and we all had a most enjoyable time before we adjourned to our individual rooms for a good night's sleep. Our departure was after noon the next day and we all met for a late breakfast before heading to the airport. This was the way to fly!

When we departed Buffalo the next day for Chicago, the Captain asked departure control for the "Niagara Falls" tour. I had never heard of this type departure but the passengers (and I) were in for a real treat. After taking off toward the west, the Captain kept the aircraft down low and we headed up the river to those world famous water falls that were not often observed from above. After a complete 360 degree turn over the falls we climbed on a westerly heading and continued our flight to Chicago, and arrived ten minutes early! I learned an important lesson—if the pilot deviated from the flight plan to give the passengers a scenic tour, he better make sure that the flight was not late at its destination! The vast majority of the passengers thoroughly enjoyed those excursions, but there were always a few "business types" who were only concerned about their on-time arrival and would quickly write a letter of complaint if the flight was delayed—and put the blame on the pilots.

The Miami based flight crews, both pilots and stews, were a close-knit group. Most had been in south Florida for the major part of their careers and intended to stay there until the "end." There were quite a few "characters" in the pilot ranks—and I had the opportunity to fly with most of those colorful, legendary types that made aviation the exciting adventure it has always been. I flew with "Moose"—the most senior pilot—and found that he was not a lot of fun to work with. He was from the old school, flew as a copilot for a few months then moved into the left seat—had never been an engineer, whatever that was, and thought that all copilots were there simply to kill him! My favorite pilot was "Smiling Jack" who lived at the Jockey Club in Miami, hated stews (secretly having a relationship with "Rachel"—more on her later) and was one of the best pilots I had ever had the pleasure to fly with. Jack was the type of pilot that you either loved or hated—whether you were a pilot or stew—and most found him to be a real pain in the ass! His uniforms were tailor made by an exclusive haberdashery from London and were just a "bit different" from the usual uniforms that were provided by the contracted tailors for United. I thought that he always looked quite dashing with his French cuffed shirts with monograms and his uniform that actually fit his frame! He was truly a free spirit. My most notable memory of flying with Jack was a trip that was assigned to me after about a month in Miami. The crew desk called me and asked if I would fly the first day of a two day trip—a strange request but reasonable as I was scheduled for days off after the first day. The crew desk was desperate—they needed a body—and I wanted to go to Denver on my days off to see my lady friend. We struck a deal. I would fly the first day of the sequence that ended in Buffalo in time to connect to the last flight of the day to Chicago, which connected to the last flight to Denver. The crew desk booked me on those flights (positive space, first class) and I was a happy camper. We departed Miami, flew to Atlanta, and had a massive delay because of thunderstorms in the area. When we departed Atlanta our ETA for BUF was 15 minutes after the flight to ORD was scheduled to depart. There was no way in hell that I would connect to get to Denver that night! Jack knew of my predicament and simply asked if it was important for me to make that connection. When I responded in the affirmative he said, "Hold on to your hat!" He requested from air traffic control to fly at 24,000 feet, much lower than the planned altitude of FL 370 and called for max continuous thrust. We flew the entire trip on the "barber pole"—meaning that we were flying at the maximum speed for that altitude and the airspeed indicator was up against the diagonal striped bar that looked like a barber pole! Captain Jack was in his element—his teeth were exposed as he smiled and kept asking for more thrust until we heard the overspeed warning (clicker-clacker) going off intermittently. At the cost of several thousand pounds of extra fuel burned (fuel in those days was relatively cheap) we arrived in Buffalo 30 minutes early—plenty of time for me to make my connection. Captain Jack insisted that I change into my civilian clothes before we landed and made an announcement to the passengers that a very important person would be departing the aircraft before any regular passenger would be allowed to deplane. I was a bit embarrassed to bolt from the cockpit and be the first one off at the gate—but I was forever grateful to Captain Jack for his effort!

Rachel was famous throughout the airline because of her raunchy humor, colorful antics with the cockpit crews and her "treatment" of the passengers. She could handle the most unruly passenger and have him eating from her hand in a matter of minutes. She had no patience with demanding divas or ego driven businessmen and would cuss them out at the least provocation. One of the funniest incidents involving Rachel happened on a flight into Washington National Airport. We often had politicians of various levels of prominence traveling in and out of the nation's capital—usually in the first class cabin—and many were rude and demanding to the flight attendants. One particular self-important junior congressman made the near fatal mistake of being nasty to Rachel! Usually she did not complain to the pilots about problem passengers—she handled those situations quite well by herself. In this case, however, she entered the cockpit with her usual obscenities and stated, "You boys won't believe what a Goddamn slob this jerk in first class is—he has thrown his newspapers in the floor and now is trashing the entire cabin with his food and litter!" He had arrived on the airplane with a large brown paper shopping bag filled with newspapers from around the country and had proceeded to throw them all on the floor around his seat as he finished with his perusal. The Captain asked me to go to the cabin and check it out. I was appalled to see this elected official in the middle of his own pigpen—with his litter a foot high around his feet. He was also quite drunk. I really did not know how to handle this type of situation—thank goodness Rachel joined me as I stood looking at the mess he had created. The self-important slob looked at the two of us standing in the aisle and said, "Hey chief, tell this bitch to get me another drink!" I was about to show this pompous ass that I was not a chief when Rachel stepped in front of me and said, "Listen up, asshole, you're getting nothing from me until you clean up your mess!" This was said loud enough that surrounding passengers could not help overhearing. Suddenly they began applauding—they too were fed up with such low class behavior. The congressman turned beet red and looked like he was ready to have a heart attack as he shouted, "Do you know who I am?"

Rachel turned to pick up the Passenger Address phone and calmly made the following announcement for all the passengers to hear: "Ladies and gentlemen, we have a passenger sitting in seat 1-C who does not know who he is! Does anyone know just who this person might be? If so please report this information to a flight attendant so that we can return him to his Mommy!" The cabin burst into laughter as most of the passengers were now aware of the problem in the front row. The congressman looked at Rachel with pure hatred then looked at me and started to shake. Slowly he calmed down and started to pick up the trash around his seat and again the passengers in the first class cabin began to cheer. I returned to the cockpit and reported to the Captain that once again Rachel had performed her magic and the situation was well in hand!

Another unique routine with the Miami flight crews were PARKING LOT PARTIES! At every other domicile, when the trip was completed the pilots and flight attendants departed the airport in their individual automobiles and went their separate ways. Many of the trips in Miami and Ft. Lauderdale ended with a party in the parking lot. We would gather around the Captain's vehicle and enjoy a few beverages, compliments of the flight attendants, of course, and tell jokes and reminisce about the flights we had just completed. The flight attendants told their stories about weird passengers and the pilots related their tales about various funny or difficult events from the "front office." It was a great way to debrief the trip and decompress from the stresses of our jobs. Often spouses and others joined us for those parking lot parties—always held in the evening under balmy conditions. Miami was a fun place to be in those years.

I had anticipated that my stay in the Miami domicile would probably last only one month. It turned out that I was able to remain there for three months before being surplussed once again. Unfortunately my expenses were paid by the company only for thirty days and I was forced to move from the Miami Marriott. During that first month I submitted expense reports weekly to the Administrative Flight Manager who handled such matters. His name was Hank and he acted like every dime that he had to pay me was taken from his own pocket. After my very first expense report he placed a check in my mail box in flight operations with a note to see him about these "unusually high" hotel costs. Since I only went to the airport when I flew a trip, I did not spend much time hanging around the Flight Office where those management types worked, and seldom was I there during their 8AM to 4PM hours. Most of the trips that I flew departed early in the morning and arrived a day or two later in the evening. After the second expense report, Hank wrote another note to "see him at my very earliest convenience." The third report had a less friendly note with it: "See me at once or there will be no further expenses paid!" Of course I ignored this note as well.

One early Sunday morning I reported for a trip departing Ft. Lauderdale and found Hank waiting for me! He introduced himself with a sweaty-palm handshake and started telling me that I needed to move into a less expensive motel—he would be happy to find me a more "reasonable" place to stay. When I had checked into the Marriott, the clerk asked if I wanted the "airline rate" (about $35 daily) and I replied that no, the regular rate of $48 was just fine! I also charged my meals and laundry expenses to the hotel, being careful to pay any bar tabs personally, and my weekly expense report was quite large by the standards of the early seventies. I knew that I was within the guidelines of the contract between the company and the pilots union and had no sympathy with Hank's attempt to nickel/dime me! Several pilots had gathered around us and they rooted me on with remarks like, "You should move into the penthouse suite, Bill!" Hank finally gave up and left with his tail between his legs. I did not receive any more notes and all of my expense reports were paid promptly.

After living in luxury for thirty days, I had to come down to reality—there would be no more expenses paid. I moved from the Marriott into a tiny apartment (really just one room) in Ft. Lauderdale that rented for $30 per week. I got used to the cockroaches, called palmetto bugs in southern Florida, and started living the life of a beach bum. My new digs were located only one block from the beach and each day I took my new K-mart lounge chair and a good book and headed for the beach. I picked a spot on the beach near the public phone booth and checked in with the crew desk on occasion. That was the only phone that I had. I was working only an average of one trip each week and was beginning to wonder why I was still in the Miami domicile. As usual, United management was out of sync with reality and it would take another two months before they kicked me out of my summer resort. In the meantime, I continued to enjoy the great weather and worked hard on my tan!

The company was continuing to downsize and my morale was starting to sink. I was no longer living the life of luxury at the Marriott and it seemed only a matter of time before I would lose my job. Maybe I should have stayed in the Navy! Suddenly I met someone who would turn my spirits around—her name was Janice. She was a sweet southern lady from Georgia who was a United flight attendant in Miami. We began a relationship that lifted my spirits and made me forget the ominous specter of my future with the airline. Not only was she a gracious, considerate, thoughtful person—she was also a knockout! She actually won a contest for the "Farrah Fawcett look-alike" but I always thought that she was much better looking than the movie/TV star. She had been based in the Miami area for several years and knew her way

230

around. We flew to the Bahamas for five dollars each (and drank twenty dollars worth of booze) on an airline that I had never heard of—Mackey International, I believe it was called. No wonder it went out of business! We enjoyed perks and discounts that were available only to airline employees— things that I never knew existed—and managed to enjoy the good life on a shoestring budget. She had friends who lived in very nice developments in the area and we were invited to elegant parties that were attended by some of the rich and famous in southern Florida. I never wanted to leave this good life!

After one of those ritzy parties, Janice and I ended up at the home of two of her friends who lived at Miami Lakes, a very nice area built around several man-made lakes. These friends were a pilot with Eastern Airlines and his live-in girl friend, another flight attendant with United. We ended up skinny-dipping in the lake behind his home and then Janice and I thought it would be fun to "streak" through the community—streaking was the national fad at this time and we gleefully ran through the neighborhood in our birthday suits! Suddenly we were in the headlights of an on-coming car and we ducked into some bushes beside the road. The car pulled over to where we were trying to hide and I thought that we were surely busted by the security patrol. The driver rolled down his window, looked at me peeking out of the bushes, and said, "Is that you, Bill?" I was mortified to see that the driver was my flight manager from the domicile, a senior Captain who I had only met once or twice and had never flown with. Evidently, he and his wife were returning to their home at this complex when they spotted the two of us running naked down the street. How in the hell did he recognize me out of uniform? Janice and I were laughing so hard that it was not easy for me to be respectful to my boss— thank the Lord that he was a really good guy who chuckled and merely recommended that in the future I wear a mask!

My summer vacation ended, as I knew it would, when I received notification that I was no longer needed as a pilot in the Miami domicile. Where would I like to bump now? There were only two locations where pilots junior to me were flying the B-727, Chicago and New York. The only other option was to swallow my pride and become a Second Officer, called "Third Crew Member" or TCM, on the B-737 aircraft. I chose to return to Washington, D.C. as a TCM. Before reporting to DCA in my new assignment, I was required to go through training in Denver on the 737 aircraft—only a two week course for the "third crew member" on an aircraft designed to be flown by only two pilots. I departed Miami early one morning for Denver, with a stop in Pittsburgh. Naturally my new lady friend, Janice, was with me, and we met another pilot from Miami who was to be my "stick buddy" for this training. I had met Steve briefly before but we obviously never worked together as S/O's never flew together, F/O's never flew together, etc. The three of us were together in the first class cabin and were treated as royalty by the Miami based flight crews who knew Janice quite well. When we arrived in Pittsburgh, we were already half blitzed on the Bloody Marys and other refreshments we had consumed. We spent about two hours in the terminal at the Pittsburgh airport—in the bar of course—before our next leg to Denver. Again we were seated in the first class cabin and were treated like VIP's all the way to our destination. Needless to say, we were in "fine shape" when we arrived. After a cab ride to the downtown hotel where pilots stayed during these types of training, we checked into the Gotham Hotel, home of the world famous "Scotch and Sirloin" bistro. Most of the clientele there were my fellow pilots and a few locals who actually enjoyed the food and piano player—the pilots only came there to drink and talk about flying. My new friend, Steve, met a young lady there who chose to join our rowdy group and we decided to do the town that evening as it was still early and we did not have to report for training until 8:00 the next morning! We hit quite a few of the local saloons before calling it an evening in the wee hours of the morning.

When Steve and I departed the hotel the next morning for the United Training Center, we were not in very good shape for any type of training! By this time, I had been with United for six years and was being demoted to a status that was lower than when I had started this illustrious career! I had reached the point that I was looking forward to being furloughed—then I could seek another career path—perhaps go back to the Navy or go to Law School, maybe even seek employment with another carrier that was expanding, not contracting. I was not highly motivated—and neither was Steve. We checked in with our instructor and were taken to a CPT (cockpit procedures trainer) where we would learn the fundamentals of our new job as TCM's. The CPT was a poor mans version of a simulator—it did not move and none of the knobs and switches worked. The trainee would merely sit there and develop a flow pattern for cockpit procedures. After about five minutes in this enclosed trainer, the instructor announced, "Gentlemen, I'm getting drunk just inhaling the fumes coming from you two—why don't we take a break and you go have some breakfast?" Steve and I agreed and headed for the terminal to grab something to eat. We arrived in the Stapleton International terminal, just steps away from the training center, and started for a restaurant. Along the way I spotted a bar that was just opening and suggested that we might go there for a bit of an "eye-opener." After several Bloody Marys we purchased a large package of chewing gum and headed back to the training center. We resumed our training and both did an excellent job—according to the instructor, who patted himself on the back for making the suggestion that we "get something to eat" before finishing our training for that day! Instead of getting fired for our behavior, we successfully completed our required training and were soon certified as "Third Crew Members."

Once again I received a "paid move" from Miami to my new domicile in Washington, D.C.—another thirty days in a decent hotel! After that I shared an apartment and later a house with my old buddy, Tom, who was now also a TCM on the B-737. The B-737 was called FLUF by many of the pilots who flew this "speed bump in the skies." FLUF stood for Funny Little Ugly Fucker and it became the butt of many aviation jokes. In reality it was an efficient airplane that was designed for short haul, quick-turn flights from hub to spoke and back. The main problem with the design was its relatively slow cruise speed. It was designed to cruise at .72 mach, with a top speed of .75 or so—much slower than the 727, DC-8, DC-10, 747, etc. which all flew at .82 mach or greater. Therefore the 737 was a nightmare for air traffic controllers as well as pilots of faster aircraft.

The duties of the Third Crew Member were basically the same as those Second Officers of other equipment—with the exception that there was no flight engineer's panel. The TCM checked in at flight operations with the Captain and First Officer an hour before departure, then went to set up and inspect the aircraft while the other two pilots completed the flight planning. The goal was to arrive at the airplane 45 minutes before departure or else meet the plane when it arrived from its previous downline station. After checking and testing instruments and systems in the cockpit, the TCM made a cursory inspection of the cabin—checking emergency equipment, etc.—then proceeded to conduct a walk-around, or pre-flight inspection of the aircraft. By the time this was completed, the other two pilots had arrived and began their own cockpit set up. Since the B-737 was designed and built for two pilots, there was no seat designated for the TCM. There was an observer seat directly behind the Captains seat but United had cleverly removed the cushion from that seat to make it unavailable for occupancy! Every commercial airliner cockpit was required to have at least one seat available for a check pilot or FAA ACI (Air Carrier Inspector) so there was a small, very uncomfortable jump seat that was "pulled down" from its stowed position in the bulkhead and was positioned between and aft of the two pilot seats, just barely inside the cockpit door. Since this seat could not be placed into position until both pilots were seated and the cockpit door was closed, the TCM spent a great deal of time "swinging on the door" trying to keep out of the way of the flight attendant setting up her galley, staying clear of the "blue room" door (the forward bathroom for use by the first class passengers) and generally trying to be invisible until time to start engines. It was, in many ways, a very demeaning job!

Most of the 737 Captains were fairly young although it was still taking twenty years seniority to get to the left seat and were enjoying their first Captain bid after many years spent as flight engineers and copilots. Most treated the TCMs with respect and recognized that we were not there by choice. The First Officers loved us! They had the best job in the airline industry—they were relieved from walk-arounds, paper work, handling the company radio communications and all the menial jobs that were delegated to the Captains underlings. The TCM was unnecessary, according to the company and the FAA, but the operation went very smoothly with that extra person on board. The TCM was expendable and was used to handle problems in the cabin of a mechanical nature as well as dealing with unruly passengers. I tried to be the best TCM in the airline—otherwise I would have been bored to death. On one or two occasions I believe that I earned my pay!

One night during a flight between New York's JFK airport and Cleveland, I received a frantic call on the interphone from the first flight attendant. She reported that a passenger had "gone berserk" and was trying to open a cabin door to get off the plane—then she stated that he was now heading for the cockpit. About that time I heard a loud crash at the cockpit door just behind me. The passenger had run head first into the cockpit door and knocked out the upper panel—his bloody head was now extending into the cockpit less that a foot above my own head! I pushed his head back out through the door and rushed into the cabin to see just what the hell was going on! This pitiful deranged person jumped up from the deck and attacked me with a head–first lunge! It was all I could do just to hold on to this guy. I yelled for the flight attendant to throw me a blanket, which she did very quickly. I threw it over the poor man's head and wrestled him to the floor. He was a wiry, incredibly strong older gentleman who had snapped for some unknown reason. He continued to throw punches and kicks until I managed to toss him into the blue room and closed the door. As I could not lock the door from the outside I had to hold the door closed as he repeatedly tried to force it open—then the flight attendant calmly walked up, took a beer opener from her apron pocket, and locked the door by moving the outer sign from VACANT to OCCUPIED! At least temporarily he was locked up. I reported the situation to the Captain and he ordered me to remain at the blue room door until we landed in Cleveland—we were now on approach. The pounding on the blue room door from within continued until we landed then suddenly stopped. When we arrived at the gate the authorities (airport police) entered the cabin before any passengers deplaned. I was still holding the blue room door closed as the man inside had somehow figured out how to unlock the door and the thumping was now even more forceful. The police told me to step away, which I did happily, and the poor creature burst through—completely naked and covered with his own feces! We all gasped and gagged as the police threw another blanket on the poor lunatic and hauled him away. The smell and mess was incredible as the passengers all held their breaths as they rapidly filed out of the "airplane trip from hell!" I later found out that the poor man had boarded a flight some twenty four hours earlier in Turkey with his grandson and after many flights and plane changes had gotten on our flight for his final destination to CLE. The grandson slept through the entire incident and had to be awakened to deplane!

The B-737 trips from the DCA domicile were exclusively flown east of the Rocky Mountains—I believe that we occasionally went as far west as Omaha, Nebraska but no further. The majority of the layovers were in the small towns of America, places like Grand Rapids, Des Moines, Mobile, etc. I loved those places that were in the real heartland of America and tried to avoid the big cities such as New York, Chicago, and Atlanta. Unfortunately, sometimes I could not avoid the trips that terminated in the large cities for an over-nighter. One month I ended up with a downtown layover in Atlanta— actually one of my favorite large cities. The hotel where we stayed was located in the middle of Atlanta, good news and bad news! It was within easy walking distance to nice restaurants and shopping but also near the downtown bus terminal and some areas that were a bit undesirable. One day when we arrived, via cab, at the hotel, we noticed on the marquee in front a large sign that said, "Welcome, LPA." I asked the driver what LPA stood for and he just laughed and said, "You'll find out when you get inside." When we entered the lobby we did find out! The place was literally crawling with MIDGETS—LPA stood for Little People of America and they were holding their convention in Atlanta with over 1200 "little people" in attendance. And they were in a party mood! When I arrived at the elevators to access my room, there were several "little people" waiting. After I entered the elevator they followed. As soon as the door had closed they began calling out their floors— I was the only one tall enough to reach the buttons for the higher floors! I was amazed at how they had adapted to their smaller stature—they had a system for everything. A normal sized person takes for granted those things that are insurmountable for someone only three feet tall! The next morning for breakfast I entered the hotel café to find that the only place available to sit was at the counter—not a problem for me but quite a challenge for little people. They were up to such a challenge as one had a small step stool that he placed before each counter stool until his friend was seated, then he took it to the next stool—he was the last to be seated and necessarily had to be the first to finish in order to reverse the process.

The last lay over that I spent in that particular hotel in Atlanta was, I believe, the last time that any UAL crew stayed there—and for good reason. I was awakened in the middle of the night by the unmistakable sound of gunshot fire—lots of it—coming from the lobby area. I was on the third floor and it sounded like war had been declared below. Soon there were lots of police sirens and more shooting. I tried to call the front desk but obviously there was no one there to answer my call. I quickly got dressed and started out into the hallway. I met a uniformed police officer standing by the elevator with his gun drawn. He advised me that everything was under control but I must return to my room—I could not go to the ground floor. It was several sleepless hours later that a loud speaker announced that the lobby was now open and hotel guests were allowed to leave their rooms. When I arrived in the lobby, just after dawn, it still looked like a war zone. A heavily armed group of four robbers had entered the lobby and attempted to stick up the night clerk behind the registration desk. There was a night watchman on duty that happened onto the scene and a fierce firefight ensued. Two of the robbers were killed, the night watchman was critically wounded and the clerk had been shot before the police arrived. After another gunfight, the remaining robbers had surrendered and it was all over. The front glass doors had been blasted away—it was not clear if that was from the robbers or the police—and there were bullet holes, broken glass and lots of blood throughout the lobby area. I was happy to say goodbye to this hotel forever! United crews moved to the Atlanta Marriott, a nicer hotel by far and in a much safer part of town.

I could write an entire book about some of the characters that I flew with while spending THREE LONG YEARS as a TCM in DCA—suffice to say that it was hours of boredom with a few moments of humor and excitement. A few of those characters, usually ex-Capital pilots, were a bit unkind to the TCMs as they thought they were able to do it all themselves—even copilots were largely unnecessary. One Captain that I flew with told me to just sit there and keep out of his way. When we had a mechanical problem that I could fix, I offered my opinion and he responded, "If I want any fucking advice from you, I'll ask for it!" This statement gave me a whole new job description. When a flight attendant or passenger asked me just what were the duties of a TCM—I responded that I was officially the "Captain's sex advisor!"

Thankfully, most of the Captains were quite competent, fun to fly with, and sympathetic to the predicaments that the TCMs were going through. Many would allow the TCM to fly a leg on occasion—with the concurrence of the copilot, of course. Normally, it would be on a clear day (with no weather or crosswinds to be concerned with) when the Captain would offer to let the TCM fly a short segment. Whenever it was offered, I always accepted and enjoyed the privilege that was not approved by management. One Captain was very popular with the TCMs because of his lax cockpit attitude which gave the TCM an opportunity to fly almost every third leg. Unfortunately, Whitey carried his generosity too far and it cost the supreme penalty. He crashed on landing at Midway airport in Chicago on a stormy winter day and almost all on board were killed, including the cockpit crew. It was never released in the accident report but the rumor was that the TCM was in the copilot seat at the time of the accident. After this terrible accident, United Airlines made it official policy that Second Officers, Flight Engineers, or Third Crew Members were henceforth not allowed to fly the aircraft under any circumstance.

The first time that I was involved with shutting down an engine in flight occurred while I was the TCM flying into DCA National airport one fine summer day. The Captain was a character by the name of Clyde. His older brother was the Vice President of Flight Operations but Clyde was certainly not management material—he enjoyed life to the fullest and was a pleasure to work with. The copilot on this flight was a good old boy named Joe who was surely a narcoleptic as he had a tendency to fall asleep as soon as we reached cruise altitude. When Joe nodded off, Clyde quietly turned off his radios and I handled all communications while he took his nap! We were descending for landing when I noticed that the engine overheat light suddenly came on for the number two engine. I pointed it out to Clyde and he called for the checklist. We quickly went through the procedure called for but the next step required that the engine be shut down if the light did not go out. Clyde had me shut down the engine and asked me to inform the company on our discrete frequency that we would be landing in 15 minutes with one engine out. Then Clyde said to Joe, "Joe, tell the controller that we've lost an engine and request a straight in approach to National." No response as Joe was sound asleep! Clyde now yelled: "Joe, wake up, Goddamnit!" Joe woke with a startle and said, "What's going on, guys?" Clyde and I both started laughing as Joe had no idea that we had secured the no. 2 engine and were declaring an emergency! Joe quickly got back in the loop and the approach and landing were pretty much routine. We were still laughing when we arrived at the gate—five minutes early!

In 1976 the pilots union signed a new contract with United management. The Captains got a huge pay raise but very little trickled down to my lowly status. I remember hearing that with this new agreement even the most junior Captains would be making over $40,000 per year—a very large amount to me. However, it was beginning to look like it would be eons before I ever moved to the left seat—the furloughs had stopped but there would be no recall or new pilot hiring for at least another year. One perk that the pilots did receive with the new agreement was unlimited use of the OMC privilege. OMC stood for Observer Member of the Crew—a name given to a non-working pilot who wanted a free ride from point A to point B without having to use a non-revenue ticket. As long as there was an unoccupied seat in the cockpit, a pilot desiring to go somewhere for personal reasons could hitch a ride. Once the aircraft was closed up for the flight, the OMC could leave the cockpit for an unoccupied seat in the cabin, with the Captain's permission, of course. Often the flight attendants were not happy with this arrangement as they did not enjoy this privilege—later they too would get jump-seat authority that allowed them to occupy unattended stew seats in the cabin. This new ability for pilots to travel almost at will would lead to a significant cultural change within the airline. Now pilots could live wherever they wished and "commute" to their domicile to fly their trips. Many pilots had been forced to change domiciles due to the down-sizing and did not wish to move their families. The new OMC policy helped the pilots and saved the company lots of money in moving expenses. For me, it was now easier to travel to the West coast to visit with my children, now living with their mother in Bakersfield, Calif. My wife and I had separated six years earlier, in 1970, but we had never gotten divorced. That arrangement seemed to work for both of us—I continued to support the family and my wife received the benefits such as air travel, medical, and dental plans from United. We also both had our freedoms. I began to spend more time visiting with my two growing children, Tom, now ten, and Elizabeth, almost two years younger. Eventually these visits to Bakersfield led to the decision that my wife and I try once again to make our marriage work. We had both matured and neither had found anyone else that we wanted to share our lives with—it would take lots of work but we both felt that it was worth the effort. I bought a nice four bedroom house in suburban Bakersfield in late 1976 and we moved in as a happy family once again.

It would be another year before I could transfer to the West coast and I was getting increasingly anxious to move forward in my career—I never dreamed that I would be a Second Officer on an airplane built for just a Captain and Copilot after almost nine years with United! That last year seemed to last forever—I was spending all of my free time with the family in California and still flying a full schedule in the Washington domicile. I was senior enough to hold a regular schedule, no reserve, but not senior enough to have holidays such as Christmas off. I finished up a three day trip on Christmas Eve, 1976, at DCA airport and would travel the next day to California. As I left the airport that evening to drive to an apartment that I was sharing with an old buddy in Alexandria, it was starting to snow. I noticed a hitch-hiker standing alongside the highway at the entrance to the airport and started to pass him by—then I remembered how I had depended on catching a ride with strangers during my youth and decided to stop. I checked him over carefully before unlocking the door on the passenger side. The young man, in his early twenties, was well dressed but not prepared for the snow that was starting to fall harder. He wore only a sport coat and was hatless. As he jumped into my car he was very grateful for my generosity—it was Christmas Eve—and I was doing my good deed for the year! I asked him his destination and he replied that he lived just down Highway 1 in Alexandria—exactly where I was headed. We started driving that direction and he told me a very detailed story of how his car had broken down while visiting his girl friend in Baltimore and he had left it alongside the highway and hitched a ride to the airport where I picked him up. I was in my uniform with a heavy raincoat because of the cold and my hat and suitcase were on the back seat of my old '67 Pontiac. My passenger spotted my hat and asked if I was an airline pilot. When I replied in the affirmative, he said, "You guys make a lot of money, I hear." A small alarm started to go off in my head! There was something about this guy that was highly suspicious.

As we continued south on Highway 1, I asked my rider for more specific instructions as to where he lived and just where should I drop him off. He became very evasive and only repeated that he lived just a bit further down the road. I was approaching where I was staying and told the man that I would have to drop him off soon. He spotted a dark turnoff on the right—the visibility was lowering in the darkness and snow fall—and said that was his exit. As I turned down that road he suddenly turned and stuck something hard and sharp into my right side! He said, "Just give me your money and no one will get hurt!" I did not know if the object in his hand was a gun or a knife but I was in no position to argue with my assailant. I said, "Let me get my wallet out of my back pocket." Instead of reaching for my wallet, I reached down with my left hand and opened the driver's door and simply slid out. We were only traveling about two or three miles per hour and I was not wearing a seat belt—lucky for me this time. As I left the vehicle I spotted the object in his hand—it was a knife, not a gun! The car slowly continued moving forward but it was on an uphill incline and the vehicle slowed further. The assailant, instead of sliding across on the bench seat and driving away with my car, jumped out on the right side. We came face to face as I was running for the car which had now reached the crest of the small hill and was picking up speed. I yelled at my ungrateful rider, "You son of a bitch, I'm going to kick your sorry ass!" I was talking much braver than I felt but I was definitely pissed. He started running in the opposite direction and I was able to jump back into the car and bring it to a stop. I got the car turned around and spotted the bad guy running down the road. I tried my best to run him down but he leaped into some bushes and I eventually lost him. That would be the very last time that I picked up a hitch-hiker!

In the spring of 1977, I successfully received a bid to Los Angeles as a DC-8 Second Officer—not a copilot yet but at least a raise in pay and a more meaningful job. I left my old car in the employee's parking at Dulles International Airport, got a first class seat to LAX and crossed my fingers that perhaps my career was taking a step in the right direction. It would be almost a year later when I returned to Washington, called the Salvation Army to donate that car to charity, and signed the pink slip on the hood as I said goodbye to the East coast!

Chapter Fifteen

"In Aviation, Good Judgment Comes from Experience and Experience Comes from Bad Judgment"

The DC-8 was a real flight engineer's airplane. It was designed and built for that third person in the cockpit—and many Second Officers loved it just for that reason. I personally never really enjoyed being a flight engineer—I was hired by United Airlines as a pilot and that was what I was trained to do. Unfortunately the route to the copilot seat and eventually the Captain's seat started with duty as a flight engineer. The flight engineer became an expert in aircraft systems and one could build an "empire" doing what was considered as "flying sideways!" An old airline joke went as follows: How do you know which ones are flight engineers at a cocktail party full of airline crews? Yell out, "Traffic at twelve o'clock!" and see which ones look over their left shoulder!

After transition training on the DC-8 in Denver, I reported to the Los Angeles domicile as a reserve Second Officer—no longer was I able to hold a schedule. I found that the DC-8 fleet with United consisted of four different types of aircraft—all unique with different engines and systems. There were the old DC-8s with underpowered engines that were used for cross-country passenger flights, cargo liners that flew almost exclusively at night, the stretched version that carried over 230 passengers and was used mostly for charter flying, and a strange hybrid called the DC-8-62 that had the longest range of any commercial aircraft in the world at that time. Being on reserve, I had the opportunity and the challenge to fly any and all versions of this aircraft. After three years as a TCM, I really enjoyed these new challenges—especially the charter flights. At this time, United Airlines had a very large fleet of aircraft that were dedicated to charter operations. Almost all professional sports teams from the NFL, NBA and MLB were flown on United charters. It was an airline within itself and was larger than many major airlines! In addition to flying professional and collegiate sports teams, we flew many charters to popular destinations such as Hawaii and the Caribbean. Often these trips were flown to destinations that were not served by United and the crews were tasked with problems not normally encountered on "the main line."

One of the first charters that I flew seemed to be a pilot's dream—we flew a group from LAX to New Orleans (MSY) and spent 38 hours on the ground during Mardi Gras in the Crescent City. It turns out that this was the very longest layover that I ever enjoyed with United. The down side was that no rooms were available in the city during this most busy period so we were put up in a motel just across the street from the airport. The Captain was a good sort so he negotiated with the crew desk and we were allowed unlimited transportation from the airport to the scene of the festivities down in the French Quarter. We took full advantage of this perk! Generally, the pilots did not stay at the same lay over hotel/motel as the flight attendants. This was because of the different union contracts and the fact that pilots were part of **Flight Operations** and flight attendants were part of **Cabin Service**—two very different departments within the same airline. Charter operations were treated differently—the flight crews stayed together! We all enjoyed the long layover in New Orleans and there was no "hanky-panky"—perhaps pilots and stews could actually get along without being placed in separate hotels across town! After this fun layover, we checked in at the airport to find that the airplane that we flew into New Orleans was the same one that we were to fly out. Since United had no personnel at MSY, we were handled by Eastern Airlines, and they had parked our airplane away from the terminal—out in the sun and humidity—and when we arrived at the plane it was quite a mess! Eastern had simply parked the plane without cleaning the galleys or dumping the lavatories and the heat and smells were incredible! When I opened the door to this DC-8, the odor was overwhelming—the garbage had turned quite rancid and the smell from the unserviced blue rooms was worse than any thing we had ever smelled before! Our schedule was to ferry the plane from New Orleans to Houston, pick up a load of passengers, and then fly to Los Angeles. Since there were no passengers on the leg to Houston, we agreed to take the plane "as is" and fly it to where it could be properly serviced before "real people" boarded for LAX. The DC-8 was not the best airplane for charters because it was not self-contained. It did not have an APU (Auxiliary Power Unit) like the B-727 and needed ground power and air conditioning to keep the aircraft comfortable on the ground. Only electrical power was available from Eastern Airlines for our use in New Orleans and we were faced with no way to cool off the cockpit or cabin until we started the engines. When the three of us pilots sat down in the cockpit, it was unbearably hot—all of the temperature gauges were showing full hot and the humidity was close to 100%. Our uniforms were starting to get very wet so we took off all of our clothes except our underwear—wish I had a picture of this group! Sweat was dripping from every pore as we started the engines. The flight attendants came to the cockpit protesting that they were getting sick from the heat and smells and wanted to leave. When they saw us sitting at our stations in our shorts, they started laughing and soon stripped down to their own panties and bras—a most logical decision! An Eastern Airlines ground worker stuck his head into the cabin from the portable access stairs to ask if it was okay to close the cabin door, looked around at the stews in their underwear, spotted the pilots in their shorts, and said, "I think I should have gone to work for United!"

When I was not assigned a charter flight I often had to fly the cargo liner version of the DC-8. Cargo crews were treated like the bastard children of the airline. The cargo facilities were far away from the passenger terminals and the crews often had to wait for very long periods for transportation—unheated vans in the winter and the same vans without air conditioning in the summer. Most of the cargo flights from LAX were non-stops to New York's Kennedy Airport, JFK, and meals were boarded for the pilots due to the length of the flights. These "meals" were frozen and had to be cooked in a small oven that was placed in the rear of the cockpit—not a microwave oven but a conventional electric oven that was large enough to heat up one meal at a time. I soon learned that one of the unofficial duties of the Second Officer was to prepare, cook and serve these delightful meals. Most of the meals that I prepared were underdone, overdone or inedible! The cargo flights that I had flown on the B-727 were usually two to three hours long and there was always a welcome break between legs—not so on the DC-8 flights. It was always a real challenge to stay awake on those all-nighters.

The very first flight I flew on a DC-8 Freighter from LAX was a funny one. I reported to operations early and took a van out to the cargo area before the Captain and First Officer had reported in. Since I had never seen a DC-8 freighter airplane before, I wanted to spend some extra time looking over the plane and getting familiar with the whole cargo operation in Los Angeles. After a thorough pre-flight inspection of the aircraft, I entered the cockpit to find the Captain and Copilot in their seats doing their normal set up procedures. Before I could introduce myself, the Captain said, "Hit those lights for me, son." He pointed to the overhead bank of florescent lights that were illuminating the cockpit. Thinking that there was something wrong with those lights, I did just what the Captain ordered: I banged on those lights with my fist several times, hoping that this would solve the problem! I had learned that the best way to fix a faulty electrical discrepancy in the cockpit was often just knowing where and how hard to whack the suspected instrument. The Captain and Copilot turned in their seats to give me a strange look before they both started laughing! After a good laugh the Captain said, "Is this your first flight on a DC-8 freighter?" I was now thoroughly embarrassed and admitted that yes, it was. The Captain then patiently explained that the switch that controlled those overhead lights was on my panel and he simply wanted me to turn them off! After we all had a few chuckles, at my expense, we proceeded to deliver the cargo to its destination safely and on time! I would find that the DC-8 had so many different cockpit configurations that it was easy to lose track of one or two particular switches!

One month I was awarded a LINE—a real schedule, not reserve—and I was elated. Even though it was a very ugly schedule, cargo liners and working every weekend, it was still better than sitting by the phone waiting for a reserve assignment. The flight departed every Friday night around midnight from LAX and arrived at JFK at eight AM east coast time on Saturday—we were staring into the rising sun for the last three hours of the flight! By the time we arrived at a downtown Manhattan hotel, the Saint Moritz, for our layover, it was usually 10:00 and we departed that hotel Sunday morning at three AM. Seventeen hours at a hotel sounds like plenty of time to rest but by the end of the month I was a real basket case. Not only were the rooms terribly small—you had to step on the bed to get to the bathroom if the door to the room was open—but I had a very difficult time trying to get a normal amount of sleep. I tried going to bed as soon as I checked into my room and I was able to get maybe three or four hours of sleep. I tried staying up most of the day, going to bed late in the afternoon and leaving a wake-up call at midnight. Nothing seemed to work—I felt lousy after each layover and had a very difficult time staying awake on the trip back to the west coast. The Captain recognized that I was not sleeping well and took me under his arm on the third trip of the month. When we arrived at the hotel, he said, "Get out of your uniform and meet me in the lobby in fifteen minutes." I did as ordered and met the Captain in the hotel lobby. We walked across the street to the worst looking hole-in-the-wall bar that I had ever seen. When we entered this dark, gloomy, filthy rat-hole place that was called a bar—it was only 10:30 AM— the place was jumping with the regular winos, and they all knew my Captain! He was greeted with toothless smiles and greasy handshakes as we made our way to the bar—obviously he was a celebrity here! The bartender called him by his first name and inquired if he was having his usual. The Captain ordered his "usual" and one for his friend—me. The barkeep slid two dirty shot glasses filled with bourbon toward us and my Captain looked me in the eye and said, "After two or three of these you won't have any problem sleeping today!" I followed his lead and drank two of those double shots of really bad bourbon—then with my head reeling, I staggered back to the hotel and slept for ten solid hours!

This Captain, Chuck was his name, had a few idiosyncrasies—like most airline Captains—but was really a very likeable fellow. He had one ritual that was a bit unique. When we departed the hotel at three o'clock on Sunday morning, he always bought a copy of the New York Times. On the way to the airport he tore out the page that had the Sunday crossword puzzle and placed it in his flight bag. The rest of the paper he threw away without reading. Once we were airborne and at cruise altitude, he would push back his seat, take out the crossword puzzle, tell the copilot and myself to take "care of things" and proceed to spend the next four hours working his weekly puzzle. Most of the time he would complete that difficult puzzle before we landed in LAX. Sometimes he would finish only 80%—but he worked very hard at it while we were at cruise. The copilot would fly the aircraft and I handled the radios so as to not disturb our Captain. I decided to play a small trick on our Captain for the final trip of the month. I bought an early copy of the New York Times on the street around eleven o'clock, rushed to my room, and with the aid of a crossword puzzle dictionary and a regular dictionary/thesaurus, I was able to complete the puzzle before we departed for the airport at three AM. I kept the completed puzzle in my pocket—just in case that I could not memorize all of the difficult clues, such as: who was the Poet Laureate from France in 1949, or what was the name of a famous Italian Opera singer in the sixties! When we arrived at the airport I purchased a copy of the New York Times—

in full view of the Captain—and ripped out the page with the Sunday crossword puzzle.

As usual, when we reached cruise altitude, the Captain did his thing with the crossword puzzle. After thirty minutes or so, I quietly inquired if it would be okay if I worked the same puzzle, assuring the Captain that I would continue to handle the communications and the other duties that were expected of me. He agreed with a bit of a sneer as he was quite confident that he was the only one who could really finish such a complex task within the allotted time. I placed my blank puzzle on my flight engineer's desk and immediately commented, "This looks like a really easy puzzle this week." I started filling in the blanks as fast as I could write, making such comments as, "This is not even a challenge—there must be some mistake in this week's puzzle!" The Captain kept looking over his shoulder at me and observed that I was going to complete the puzzle before he had finished the first few lines. After five minutes or so I tossed my finished puzzle into the trash container, which sat by the center console on the copilot's side. The Captain continued to work on his project for another half hour before he gave up and reached for my answers in the trash. Without a word, he glanced over my completed puzzle, looked at me with a sense of awe, and said, "You are either a genius or a real asshole—which is it?" I was starting to laugh so hard that tears were rolling down my face as I admitted to being the latter. We all had a good laugh and the Captain and I remained good friends until he retired.

One of the very few benefits for the Second Officers on those cargo liner trips was the fact that many of the Captains would still allow us to fly the aircraft on occasion. Since there were no passengers or flight attendants to complain about the really bad landings, we were sometimes given the opportunity to try our flying skills—this in spite of United's strict policy that no Second Officers were allowed to fly the airplane! Thanks to several of those generous Captains, I enjoyed sitting in the Copilots seat and flying the aircraft on many occasions. Unfortunately, there was another major accident that ended this perk, probably forever. One of our DC-8 freighters took off from Detroit one night enroute to LAX—I knew both the Captain and Copilot—and the Second Officer was flying the plane from the Copilot's seat. Evidently, the Second Officer did not properly set the elevator trim before takeoff and once airborne the aircraft assumed a nose high attitude that was impossible to recover from—resulting in a stall-spin that destroyed the aircraft and killed the three crew members.

After two years as a DC-8 engineer, I became senior enough to bid the RESERVE schedules that would give me trips to Hawaii. It was interesting to find that the reserve crews who had weekends off were usually in line to fly those charter trips to Honolulu that departed every Tuesday. Those trips were considered some of the best flights in the airline. Charters to Hawaii usually departed around noon from LAX, arrived in HNL in the early afternoon and departed the next evening for a dawn arrival back in Los Angeles. There was plenty of time for the beach and the usual tourist activities while in HNL and many of the pilots that flew these trips had a condo in Waikiki and kept a sailboat there for crew use. The crew returned to the mainland on Thursday and were then in position for the same trip the following Tuesday—a nice pattern. Most of those flights across the ocean were routine—one sticks out as the exception. We were on the takeoff roll down the runway at LAX when the flight attendant call light/chime was activated. Normally the flight attendants did not try to contact the cockpit during this critical part of the flight and the Captain made the proper decision to ignore the call until we were safely airborne. Then he instructed me to find out what was happening in the cabin. I contacted the First Flight Attendant and she advised me that a passenger was having an apparent heart attack. As soon as I was able to leave the cockpit, I went to the cabin and found that the passenger had indeed had a heart attack and was quite dead. There was no chance to resuscitate and a physician on board confirmed that the person was deceased. Now it became a game of politics and legal regulations—did the person die before we left the continental United States or was the death over international waters? Of more immediate concern to the crew was the decision to return to LAX or continue to HNL. I was still in the cabin and talked to several passengers who knew the victim. They all confirmed that the deceased was not supposed to travel and did so against her doctor's orders. They all wanted to throw a blanket over the victim and continue to their vacation spot! Other passengers did not want to travel with a dead body for the next five hours! I looked to the flight attendants for their opinion and they agreed that it would not be a very fun trip with a cadaver onboard. I returned to the cockpit and advised the Captain that most of the passengers wanted to continue, but the crew, myself included, thought the best decision was to return to LAX. The Captain, whose name was Red, snorted, "No way in hell am I flying this plane to Honolulu with a dead body on board—start dumping fuel!" I dumped over forty thousand pounds of fuel from the tanks and we returned to LAX. After a five hour delay we resumed our flight to the islands—short one passenger!

That last year as a DC-8 Second Officer consisted of non-stop flights to the East coast or charters to Hawaii. Both had their elements of humor. Almost all of the flights to the East coast involved a pre-dawn departure back to the West coast. I was usually the first crew member to be standing in front of the hotel awaiting the "limo" to the airport at three or four AM. It was a very special time for me during these early hour departures as I could study humanity at its basest level. In front of the Saint Moritz at 3:00 AM I got to know some of the regular prostitutes who walked around the block every fifteen minutes. They would stop to speak to me, knowing that I was not a prospective client, but just passing the time—I, on the other hand, recognized that when they did not make their regular rounds, they had found a "John" and would miss a circuit or two. Then they would show up again, with a smile, and resume their nightly patrols. The interesting part was that the whores thought that I had it rough, they felt sorry for me as I had to fly all night to get back to the West coast—I thought that they had it rough—depending on a few tricks each night to pay for their rent, habit, or pimp! Neither would be willing to change positions.

For the most part, the long-haul flying on the DC-8 was not to my liking. I had what was called a three hour butt—I was ready to land after no more than three hours. Generally, the flights from coast to coast or to the islands were five to six hours in length and could become quite boring. Occasionally, however, there were events that kept up one's interest. The oldest version of the DC-8 that United flew was fairly small, with a large first class cabin of 24 seats and a coach configuration of around 150. In addition, there was a small first class lounge between the cockpit and the first class section. These six seats were not sold to passengers but were available for those in first class to relax, play cards or just socialize. One night I was flying the "red-eye" special from Los Angeles to New York on one of these aircraft—we departed LAX about 11:00 PM local time and arrived at JFK the next morning at around 7 AM. Halfway through the flight almost all of the passengers were asleep and the stews were usually huddled together in the aft galley where they had room to sit and talk. The pilots stayed awake by drinking coffee, telling jokes, and taking a walk through the cabin for exercise. The copilot announced that he was going to take a stroll through the cabin. There was a legal requirement for the other flying pilot, the Captain in this case, to don his oxygen mask while alone at the controls. Most crews ignored this antiquated rule and simply placed their oxygen mask in their laps while the other pilot was absent. As customary, the copilot looked out through the peephole in the cockpit door before exiting—this was not just for security but to make sure that the blue room was vacant before stepping outside the cockpit. After taking a look through that fisheye peephole the copilot said, "Holy shit, you won't believe what's going on in the lounge! There's a gal giving a guy a blow job right now!" The Captain jumped up from his seat, rushed to the cockpit door to brush away the copilot, and took a look himself. I also wanted to see what was going on but decided that perhaps it would be best if I moved to the copilot's seat just in case a pilot was needed at the controls. For several minutes the Captain and copilot took turns peering out the peephole and watching the conclusion to this event—then the Captain turned to me and said, "Report this behavior to the first flight attendant!" I almost asked if he wanted me to report his behavior or that of the passengers. After I returned to my seat as the flight engineer, I called the first stew and asked her to come to the cockpit. When she did, the Captain explained what had just transpired in the lounge and told her to file a report. The stew seemed reluctant to make such a report and finally announced that the parties involved were a United stewardess and her boyfriend, traveling together on space available passes. The Captain insisted that an official report be filed and stated that she should be fired for such behavior. I thought that the Captain was a real jerk.

I found out several months later that the "guilty" stewardess had indeed been brought up on charges that could lead to her dismissal. Her defense was brilliant: She insisted that her boyfriend suffered from terrible migraine headaches (and had medical confirmation of this fact) and the only way to relieve him from this severe suffering was to perform oral sex on the poor man! The flight attendant union backed the accused one hundred percent and the charges were eventually dropped! There's probably a moral to such a story but I can only say that everyone was happy with the conclusion—with the possible exception of the Captain! For several years after this event, whenever a really attractive stewardess entered the cockpit, at least one of the pilots immediately complained about a terrible headache!

During the mid 1970's there seemed to be a new fad among airline passengers—it became quite the thing to belong to "the mile high club." Perhaps it gave one bragging rights to announce to one's friends that he/she had gotten laid while flying through space near the speed of sound at several miles above the surface. I personally witnessed two of these events that are worthy of repeating. The first involved a flight from Washington's Dulles Airport to Los Angeles aboard a DC-10. I was not a member of the flight crew but was traveling alone on a pass in the first class section of the aircraft. The passenger load was extremely light with only four people in the front cabin, including myself. There was an elderly lady traveling alone across the aisle from me and in front of her sat a couple that were obviously intoxicated and having a "fine time." I found out from the first flight attendant that the gentleman, a well dressed businessman in his mid forties, had evidently met the young lady in the bar at Dulles Airport before departure. She appeared to be in her mid twenties and was traveling to Los Angeles on a coach ticket. Her new "friend" had paid the extra charge to upgrade her ticket to first class so that they could sit together. They enjoyed several drinks after departure and began to get more than just friendly as they reclined their seats to the limit and covered themselves with a blanket. The lady sitting behind them got up in a bit of a huff, went to the flight attendant and complained about their behavior. She was re-seated far away and soon fell asleep. I was trying to read a book but could not help noticing that the couple across the aisle was trying valiantly to find a position conducive to the sport that they were trying to complete. Shortly, the lady left her seat and went to the forward blue room on the left side. Then the gent left his seat and went into the blue room on the right side. After perhaps five minutes, the lady left her blue room, tapped softly on the door to the other blue room, and entered when the door was opened. We had been airborne about two hours and were at least three hours away from landing at LAX. The in-flight movie started and finished and those two remained in the confining space of that small rest room! The first stew pointed out that the gentleman's belt was sticking out under the door— I laughed and suggested that she give it a tug! The "fasten seat belt" sign was turned on several times due to turbulence—this illuminated a sign in the blue room that said, "return to seat"—but nothing could bring those two out of their little love nest. Finally we were starting our descent into LA and the first stew was becoming more than just a bit concerned. The Captain had told her that the two must return to their seats before he could land and she had to do whatever was necessary to get them out. She banged on the door several times and shouted, "You must return to your seats immediately!" Suddenly the door opened and the man stepped out, closed the door (which was quickly locked from inside) and returned to his seat. He appeared a bit pale and drained but otherwise seemed okay. Another five minutes passed before the door opened again and the lady stepped out. She looked like she had been pulled through a keyhole—she was ashen colored, very shaky and her hair was wet and plastered to her head. She took a seat two rows behind her friend and remained there until the plane landed. I have often wondered just what that couple did in that tiny space for almost three hours! I'm sure that there were drugs and sex—but how could they possibly be comfortable in such a small space for such a long time?

When the passengers deplaned in Los Angeles, I happened to be directly behind "the couple" as we walked through the jetway. They hardly spoke to one another but I believe that the man mumbled something to her like, "If you ever come to LA again, give me a call." When we reached the terminal area the two went their separate ways. The person who met the gentleman was a famous actor whose first name was Peter. I'm sure that his friend had a very interesting story to relate!

The other incident of "airborne sex" surely must have set a record that still stands today. I boarded a B-737 late one evening at LAX for the short flight to Bakersfield—23 minutes in the air. I was returning home after a trip and was still in my uniform. I took a seat in the first class cabin after the doors were closed—I was traveling OMC. There was only one passenger up front, a businessman who appeared to be in his thirties. Half way through the flight the first stew, who I knew personally, stopped by my seat and said, "You won't believe it, but there's a lady in coach who wants someone to meet her in the blue room so that she can join the Mile High Club!" The businessman, who was across the aisle, overheard her comment, and said, "What does this gal look like?" The stew replied, "She is somewhat attractive—probably in her early twenties." The businessman said, "What seat is she in, I'll just take a quick look." The stew replied that she was in row 23 and he couldn't miss her. The man left his seat and walked through the back cabin. Evidently he liked what he saw as he agreed to meet her in the blue room. The two rushed into the aft blue room and locked the door. Five minutes later the plane was on final approach and the gear was extended. The stew notified the Captain that there were two persons in the blue room and he made an announcement that "everyone must return to their seats immediately." The man came running forward, strapped in just before touchdown, and a loud cheer was heard from the back cabin—evidently the lady had returned to her seat at the same time and loudly announced that she had just become a new member of the "Mile High Club!" The gent that had returned to his seat was a bit out of breath and a little sweaty. I asked him if things went well—he replied with a sheepish grin, "We just played around a bit—nothing really happened!" When the plane arrived at the gate and the door was opened, this fellow was the first one out and he was in a big hurry to get out of the airport. The "lady" was a different story. I waited in my seat until she had deplaned—basically because I wanted to get a look at her. She was young and had a very nice figure, but she was also more that a bit trashy, with a big mouth and gamey attitude. I figured that the gent she had sex with was in a hurry because he wanted to take a shower right away!

By 1978 all of the furloughed pilots had been recalled by United and new pilots were being trained for the first time in nine years. Finally the cycle had swung the other way and the airline began moving forward again. I began hoping that I would be able to get a copilot bid soon. I had decided that I would take the very first copilot bid that I could get, regardless of the location—but I prayed that it would not be in Chicago or New York, still the two most junior domiciles. By the middle of 1979, I received a successful bid as a DC-10 Second Officer—flight engineer—and although it was not a copilot bid, it would mean a nice raise in pay. Also there was no freeze involved—a pilot could always bid UP in status—and I would not have to remain on the DC-10 when and if I received a copilot bid. I reported to Denver for training on the DC-10 in September and started class on a Monday morning. As I took my seat in the classroom at 8 AM, one of my buddies in the class came up to me and said, "Have you seen the new copilot bids that were announced this morning?" I admitted that no I had not and he said with a grin, "You better go take a look at the bulletin board right now!" I ran out to where the new bids were posted and found my name at the very bottom of the list for B-727 First Officer assignments in LOS ANGELES! It had taken eleven years with United to get to the right seat and I was on cloud nine. I returned to the classroom and found that two others in my group had also gotten copilot bids—the three of us were elated to say the least. The instructor finally calmed us down and started the training for the DC-10. I paid no attention to this instruction, knowing that for sure I would be removed from this school so that I could start copilot training that was programmed in just three weeks. At the first break I went to the Fleet Manager for the DC-10 program and asked, "Since I now have a copilot bid that starts training next month, why don't I just go home now?" The manager looked at me and replied, "Once you start the school, you have to finish it—there are no exceptions." My chin dropped to the floor—how asinine was this—to waste my time and the company's money to train me for a position that I would never fulfill! I was told to return to the DC-10 class.

This decision did not dampen the spirits of the three of us who now held copilot bids. We basically goofed off in class and celebrated each night, thinking that surely the company would come to its collective sense and excuse us from this training. By the end of the week I was very far behind the learning curve and suddenly was faced with the prospect that I might have to finish this training after all. I spent the weekend trying to catch up with what I had missed in the classroom and showed up the next Monday morning pretty much up to speed. As we settled into our seats, the VP of Flight Training walked into the room. He said, "I have an announcement to make. It seems that three members of this class are about to wash out, so to prevent any embarrassment to them and their loved ones, we have decided to send them home—hopefully to properly prepare for their next training that will commence in three weeks. Congratulations to those three new copilots!" Thank God that common sense prevailed—at least in this instance.

I returned to my old position as a DC-8 S/O and flew several trips before reporting once again to Denver for IFO (Initial First Officer) training, a one week ground school that covered basic procedures that new copilots needed to know—flight planning, weather analysis, and a review of landing minimums. When I walked into the classroom on that first morning I immediately thought that I had gone to the wrong room—this one was filled with a bunch of old guys! They must be senior Captains, not initial First Officers! Wrong, all of us had spent many, many years as Flight Engineers and it showed. We were all experienced and we were all eager for our new assignment—we also were more than a bit rusty in the basic flying skills that we had not practiced for those dormant years as Second Officers. One or two in the class of about twelve had been flying in the military reserve and were well ahead of the rest of us—we had some catching up to do. Since I had been through the B-727 school several times before, the ground school was a piece of cake. I was eagerly awaiting the simulator and actual aircraft training which commenced after the two week ground school was completed. Slowly my instrument scan returned and by the time the training was complete I was feeling somewhat comfortable with flying my favorite airliner from the right seat. After the check ride in the simulator, I flew the real aircraft from Denver to Pueblo, Colorado, and made several approaches and about a dozen landings before the check Captain said, "That's enough, let's go back to Denver." It was snowing at Stapleton Airport when we arrived and I had to fly an instrument approach to a slippery runway. The check Captain stated, "You just can't buy training any better than that!"

In those days the procedure for new copilots at a domicile was for them to fly their first trip with a flight manager. This trip could be a one, two or three day pairing, depending on the whims of the flight manager. The Captain that I was scheduled to fly with called me at home and told me to show up at LAX early the next morning for a flight to Seattle and back. This would give me over five hours flying time and two landings—sufficient to complete the "initial operating experience" or IOE. I spent several hours studying the two airports, the routes, approaches, departures and airport diagrams and was well prepared when I showed up the next morning. When I checked in with the crew desk I was informed that Seattle was closed because of an ice storm and I was now going to fly to Portland, Oregon and back. I had about one hour to quickly review the new route and look over the approaches to PDX. Just as I finished this new preparation, the check Captain, Dick was his name, arrived and informed me that Portland was now closed due to weather and we would fly to Reno and back. Since that was a shorter route, we would do it twice: LAX to RNO to LAX to RNO and back to LAX! I had no time to study the peculiarities of the Reno airport, and there were quite a few as it was a "special airport" due to the terrain and weather conditions at this high elevation field. The weather in Reno was rotten at this time with snow storms, slick runways and moderate turbulence in the area. I flew the first leg and landed without incident at the Reno airport. As we took off for the next leg back to LAX, other aircraft were reporting moderate "chop" in the area. As we were climbing out to the south we hit an area of what I would call heavy turbulence and then it subsided. I released my shoulder harness, thinking that we were out of the worst of it when we hit clear air turbulence that bounced me out of my seat enough so that I hit my head on the overhead panel! I heard someone reporting "extreme turbulence"—the highest level reportable, generally meaning that the aircraft is uncontrollable—and wondered just where that might be. Then I realized that the pilot reporting was the guy just to my left—my Captain! He was literally screaming to the controllers that it was too dangerous for aircraft to be flying in this area when just as suddenly as we had encountered the turbulence, it stopped and became perfectly still. As we continued toward LAX, I began to notice that we were moving across the ground much faster that normal. I did a couple of quick ground speed checks and discovered that we had over 100 knots of wind on our tail—we were right in the middle of a jet stream core. I decided that we needed to begin our descent much earlier than usual and asked the Captain to request lower from the controller. He looked at me and said, "You are starting down way too early, but I'll do as you asked just to prove my point." By the time we were cleared to descent, I figured that I was going to be hard pressed to make the crossing restrictions on the approach. I reached for the speed brake to help get down and the Captain put his hand on the speed brake handle and stated, "You don't need to use the brakes, and you're going to use too much fuel by getting low too soon." Before I could protest, the center controller saved my day by saying, "United, I show your ground speed at over 600 knots, do you need a 360 (complete circle) to help get down?" Before the Captain could respond, I told Dick that I could make it if I could use the speed brake. He chuckled and told the controller that we were okay, then folded his arms and leaned back to see just what I was going to do next. I used the speed brakes and barely made the first crossing restriction, then called for flaps (after slowing to the flap speeds) and made the next restriction. Then I called for landing gear and the final checklist. We turned final and passed 1000 feet before I ever touched the throttle, and the rest of the approach was stable and routine—with a decent landing I might add! The flight engineer gave me a "well done" and stated that he was very impressed. The Captain merely grunted. I knew that it was mostly luck that it all worked out as it did.

After changing airplanes in LAX, we repeated the round trip to Reno and back. The weather had not improved much but the visibility was better and the turbulence had abated somewhat in the Reno area. The last leg back to LAX was at night and the Captain wanted me to make a night landing. He had not touched the controls all day, but offered to fly the plane while we were at altitude enroute from RNO. I needed to eat something so I gladly let him take over for thirty minutes or so. When I took control again I noticed that Dick was starting to nod off—he continued to rest his chin on his chest until we started the approach into LA. After landing we went to his office in the operations area for "debriefing." I was exhausted after a very long day that had started almost eighteen hours earlier when I left Bakersfield to drive to LAX—I still had to drive back home that night. Dick sat at his desk, finished the paperwork, handed me a copy, shook my hand, and said, "Nice job, welcome to the right seat." That was the entire debrief!

As the junior copilot in Los Angeles, at least for a couple of months, I had absolutely no control over my schedule. I was generally awarded what was called "floater reserve" which meant that after all the bids were awarded for lines and reserve schedules, the crew desk looked over all the assignments, decided just where the coverage might be a bit short, and made up a schedule for those who had no choice! I could have cared less—I was so happy to be flying once again that I really did not care when or where I had to report for work. I looked forward to each trip and never complained about how early it departed or how bad the layover was. As usual, the flying was quite a variety of regular trips, charter assignments and fill-ins for crews that were out of position. Often I was required to deadhead to another domicile to fly a trip that was open due to a lack of reserves. Once I had to deadhead to Chicago to fly a trip to Phoenix—looked like a very easy assignment. The Captain and Second Officer were both very junior and we were to fly to PHX, layover for the night and return to ORD the next day. We departed Chicago in beautiful weather with the forecast in Phoenix to be "severe clear!" The Captain and I both agreed that there was no need to add additional fuel and an alternate was not required. We departed ORD and enjoyed a routine and scenic flight until we began to notice that we were arriving over each succeeding checkpoint a bit late with less fuel than planned. It seemed that dispatch had blown the wind forecast and we were encountering stiffer headwinds than expected. When we reached the point where it was time to descend, we had only enough fuel to make a normal approach. Then the Second Officer announced that the weather in PHX had suddenly gone down and the visibility was ¾ of a mile in blowing sand! The wind had shifted around and the only approach available was a back course ILS—bottom line, it was going to take a lot longer to land and fuel was going to become a serious concern. I looked at the Captain, whom I had never met before and never flew with again, and noticed that a small amount of perspiration was starting to form on his brow. He asked the Flight Engineer to check the weather in Tucson and we learned that the conditions there were just as bad as PHX. We were committed to flying a difficult approach into an airport that was VFR 99% of the time and it would be iffy if we were not able to land after the first attempt! We were to follow a Mexicana DC-9 that was arriving from the south and it was obvious that they were as surprised as we were with the unusual weather. The Mexicana pilot requested a long vector to get lined up for the approach—this in turn meant that we would be delayed even further—and we were now getting into serious fuel problems. As usual, pilots do not want to "declare an emergency" until it is usually too late because they hate to "write a report" as to why they declared an emergency—a real catch 22! We were as close behind the Mexicana aircraft as permitted and I began to worry myself that we might have to "go around" if his aircraft did not taxi clear of the runway quickly after landing. I started to warn the Captain about this but after taking a quick look at him I decided not to bother—the perspiration was now more than a mere trickle as sweat was starting to pour down his face! The engineer did not help the situation by calmly announcing, "We are now below the minimum recommended fuel for landing!" We were only about two miles from the runway and I could see nothing, not even the ground. Then we heard the Mexicana flight ahead of us saying that they were executing a missed approach at minimums—they could not see the runway to make a landing! We continued our approach until the Second Officer reported (as was his duty) "Approaching minimums!" The next call would be, "Minimums!" At that time a go around (missed approach) was mandatory if the runway was not in sight and the aircraft was not in position for a safe landing. At the last possible second I spotted the runway and shouted, "Runway in sight, slightly to your left!" The Captain looked up from his instruments, took over visually and made a decent landing. We were all very happy to be on the ground. The passengers and flight attendants never knew how close we came to an unhappy ending. Several passengers stopped by the cockpit on their way to deplane and remarked that it was a nice flight but the visibility on approach was not what they were expecting in Phoenix, the land of the sun!

After spending six months flying the 727 as a copilot, I was becoming very comfortable with the aircraft and its responsiveness to the aviators inputs. Most of us hand flew the plane from takeoff to cruise altitude before engaging the autopilot, then again hand flew from altitude to the landing. Probably ninety percent of our approaches were in VFR conditions and many of the smaller airports simply gave us clearance to land whenever we reported the airport in sight. This meant that the pilot could control his pattern for the most efficient type of approach. The flexibility of the 727 gave the pilot the ability to remain high and fast until quite close to the landing runway. A goal that we all tried to achieve was to close the throttles at altitude and control the descent and airspeed so as to arrive on final approach with gear and flaps extended before advancing the throttles from the idle position. I had spent many years watching the experienced pilots fly this aircraft when I was a flight engineer and the really good ones made it look so very easy. No matter how experienced the pilot might be, the thrill is still there when everything works out just as planned and the flight arrives on time (or early) with more fuel remaining than planned, the landing is smooth, and all the passengers walk off with smiles on their faces. Most of the pilots who flew the B-727 loved it as much as I did—it was the fighter plane of commercial aviation with its aft mounted engines and severely swept wings. The roll rate was not as eye-popping as a fighter, but still impressive for a large airplane. Landings were a different story. Most of us felt that with every ten landings you made in the 727, eight were average, one was exceptionally smooth, and the last one was a real cruncher! That bad landing seemed to catch you off guard, usually after several really nice landings, and just when you thought that you were going to get another "greaser." I think it was just the plane's way of letting the pilot know that he or she could be humbled at any moment.

Suddenly, after less than a year as a copilot, the airline entered another down cycle and the hiring stopped, surplus notices started appearing and furlough letters were being sent to the most junior pilots. Before the end of 1980 I received my letter that I was no longer needed as a 727 First Officer in Los Angeles. I chose to bump to San Francisco as a B-737 First Officer so that I could continue as a copilot and remain on the West Coast. Once again I reported to Denver for what I called "down-grading school"—I was moving down, not up, in my aviation career once again! I had spent several years on the 737 as a Second Officer or TCM, so the school was not difficult and the checkout went very smoothly. I had to commute to SFO from Bakersfield for my assignments and once again I was on reserve—not very convenient! However, the flying was the really fun part as the aircraft was still flown with the TCM and the copilot had the best job in the industry—no preflight inspections, no paperwork, no duties involving cabin problems, etc. The schedules from SFO were perhaps the best in the airline. There was no night flying to speak of and all the trips remained on the West Coast—one never had to change his watch! We flew to fun cities like Monterey, Santa Barbara and San Diego in California, and great spots throughout the northwest such as Eugene, Medford, and Portland in Oregon. I knew, however, that my stay in SFO as a copilot was going to be a short one—pilots were continuing to be laid off and the airline was shrinking again. After five months on the 737, that loveable speed bump in the sky, I was surplussed and once again had to make a decision about my career. I could go to Cleveland and continue as a First Officer or I could swallow my pride and step down to the Second Officer position once again. Cleveland, Ohio was not a very desirable domicile at this time and the standard joke among the pilots went thus: What did the pilot do when he learned that he had only one year to live? He remarried his first wife and transferred to Cleveland, so that that last year would seem to last forever! I opted to remain on the West Coast and went back to LAX as a 727 Second Officer—the same position that I started with some 12 years earlier.

Once again, things were not going as planned in my aviation career and my personal life had also reached a critical point. My wife and I had arrived at the decision that the marriage was simply not meant to be and we agreed in principle that we should dissolve our relationship. We had spent the last four years trying valiantly to keep our relationship together, but our conclusion was that our differences were irreconcilable. I transferred to Denver (as a Second Officer), packed my few personal possessions into a 1978 Toyota, said goodbye to my family, drove to Denver, and filed for divorce.

Chapter Sixteen

"Aviation is not so much a profession as it is a compulsion!"

Denver in 1981 was a far cry from the Denver that I had known in 1972. The city had grown—it was no longer a big "cow town" where the major event each year was the National Western Stock Show. It was now a major hub for United, second only to Chicago, and the schedules were quite good. I was at least senior enough to hold a decent line of flying as a Second Officer and, thank God, there were no more cargo liners in the 727 fleet! I bought a small (780 square feet) condo in Aurora, a suburb southeast of Denver, with a VA loan (one dollar down) and settled into the life of a middle aged bachelor—I was now 42 years old.

Once again I felt that Denver was my kind of town—I loved the weather, the folks were friendly and not too pretentious, the pilot group was a really fun bunch, and the United flight office was the best in the company. I did not enjoy being a flight engineer but decided once again that I would strive to be the best S/O in the company while waiting once again to move up to the copilot position. My time off was spent skiing in the winter, playing tennis in the summer, jogging year round, and my new activity, climbing those fourteen thousand foot high mountains in Colorado. I was introduced to mountain climbing (hiking really) by a Captain by the name of Jimmy, who lived in Colorado Springs. The first time that we flew together we departed to the south from Stapleton Airport and he pointed to Pikes Peak with the comment that he had just climbed to the top a few days previously. I was thoroughly impressed and we discussed hiking for the remainder of the trip. Soon I was hooked and began to climb what were called the fourteeners (there are a total of 52 peaks in Colorado over 14,000 feet high) and it almost became an obsession to reach the top of each one.

While I was still a Second Officer, I had the occasion to shut down the second engine in my career with United—there would be a total of FIVE! One day while flying from the west coast to Denver, we were enjoying a beautiful view of the Rocky Mountains and pointing out the different ski areas to the passengers when I noticed that the oil quantity for the number three engine was starting to slowly decrease. The minimum oil quantity for departure was 2.5 gallons in each engine and often that amount decreased after we were airborne. I had been keeping my eye on that particular gauge as the quantity was only three gallons when we departed from the west coast. It was not unusual for the quantity to drop below two gallons but I was now watching the needle slipping below one gallon—not normal. I alerted the Captain and he wisely advocated that we keep an eye on the pressure gauge—that would be the real indication that something was wrong. Slowly the needle on the quantity gauge went to zero and nothing happened—we all assumed that it was a faulty gauge. We were now about 45 minutes from Denver and we relaxed a bit—then I noticed the "low oil pressure" light flicker on the forward instrument panel. I focused on the pressure gauge on my panel and watched as it too started to drop. The Captain called for the engine shut-down list and we did the prescribed procedure. The copilot reported the engine loss to the air traffic control center and we were cleared for a gradual descent to Stapleton International Airport. It was classic text book procedure as we descended to a very simple straight-in approach and landed without incident. We actually saved ten minutes and over two thousand pounds of fuel with that engine shut down—perhaps this was the ultimate way to save money for the airline!

In the early 1980's, United Airlines was the largest airline in the country, with American running a distant second. United's new CEO, Dick Ferris, wanted the company to become not just an airline but a conglomerate that would be the quintessential solution for the sophisticated traveler. He bought Hertz Rental Cars and Western International Hotels (later Westin) in the belief that the businessman would jump at the chance to make just one call for his airline ticket, car rental and hotel stay. The pilots had signed a very concessionary contract in 1981 that reduced pay and increased productivity—it was not extremely popular with the rank and file members of the union, ALPA. Nevertheless, the airline expanded as Ferris had promised and the company reaped record profits in 1983 and 84. By then I was again flying as a First Officer on the B-727 in Denver and everything looked rosy to me! I was enjoying the flying better than ever and LIFE WAS GOOD!

United was probably the first airline to really go all out for the so-called "hub and spoke" type of flying. Chicago and Denver were the major hubs and banks of flights would arrive at these airports at the same time and then depart to other destinations after about two hours on the ground. This plan seemed to work for the passengers but it was not efficient for the flight crews. A typical three day trip for the pilots would consist of every other landing being in Denver with a layover perhaps on the West Coast the first night and the second night being spent on the East Coast. The flying therefore was quite varied and always interesting but it meant that there were the inevitable two and three hour "mini layovers" spent on the ground in Denver during each trip. Pilots don't like hanging around terminals with the passengers or eating that unappetizing and overpriced selection of food available to the traveling public. We had our own pilots lounge in the Flight Operations area where we did our flight planning—and there were TV sets and recliners for those who wanted to take a short nap or watch their favorite news show. Since there were a great many pilots on the ground at the same time due to the hub and spoke schedule, it was often a bit crowded in our lounge. Several of us complained and were able to get the spaces expanded eventually, but most importantly, we now had our very own popcorn machine! It became my mission in life to pop as many batches of popcorn as possible each time I passed through Denver. Of course, pilots from other domiciles were also enjoying the free "lunch" and as the news spread almost all domiciles were eventually equipped with their very own pop corn machines. As I mentioned earlier in this book, San Francisco was the only hold out—I still wonder why!

One of my favorite cities to visit has always been New Orleans, so I tried to bid those layovers whenever they were available. One month I was able to hold a very nice trip that included a decent layover in downtown New Orleans. My Captain was a good guy by the name of Gary who unfortunately always wore a very heavy men's cologne that announced his arrival long before he came into view. Even the flight attendants commented about his "fragrance"—generally they only complained if one of us smelled too ripe! The passenger loads in and out of MSY (airport code for New Orleans) were always very heavy and we were sometimes weight restricted on both ends— meaning that we had to limit our fuel and cargo to accommodate a full load of passengers. Often we were pushing the envelope with full loads on a hot day, both in Denver and New Orleans. One day we departed from MSY with the usual full load and one additional passenger in the cockpit, an FAA air traffic controller. These guys—and gals—were our partners in making the air traffic system work and we had a lot of mutual respect for one another. The controllers, whether they were local tower personnel or "scope guys" at one of the centers, were always welcome in our cockpits. I believe that they were allowed one "fam" trip each year—meaning that they could ride in the cockpit of a commercial airliner for a round trip of their choice to "familiarize" themselves with the pilot's perspective of the operation. Obviously, these controllers usually flew on trips that were of a personal nature—family visits, vacations, etc. and that was considered okay. This particular controller worked in the tower at MSY and was going on a fishing trip to Colorado. As we taxied out I asked him if we were entitled to some special treatment from the tower since we had such a VIP on board. He laughed and said, "Tell them that their boss is in the cockpit and see what happens." I told the ground controller that his boss was on board and asked if we could get priority for takeoff. He quickly replied, "Yes sir, you are now number three for takeoff!" I had to bite and asked, "What number would we be if your boss was not in our cockpit?" The controller replied, "Well now, I believe that you would be just behind the number two aircraft waiting for takeoff!" We all laughed as we awaited our turn for departure.

We were departing on the south runway and were right at the maximum weight for the conditions that existed, hot and humid with very little headwind. It was my turn to fly and we taxied onto the runway with a square turn to avail ourselves of every last inch of concrete before we started our takeoff roll. Normally we made what was called "a rolling takeoff" which meant that we made a gentle turn onto the runway and slowly applied takeoff thrust—making it as comfortable as possible for the passengers. In this instance, the Captain set the parking brake once we were lined up and then passed the control of the aircraft to me, the flying pilot, with the usual words, "You've got it." I pushed the throttles forward to set the maximum takeoff thrust and after checking that everything looked good, released the brakes. We roared down the runway and I awaited the call from the non-flying pilot, the Captain in this case, of V1, VR—meaning that we now had sufficient speed to rotate and get airborne. My main attention was looking forward and controlling the aircraft on the centerline of the runway—but I usually peeked at the airspeed just to be sure that we were accelerating normally. It seemed that it took a rather long time before that rotation speed was attained and the remaining runway was very short when I pulled back and began to rotate. I remember looking directly into the service bay of a Shell gas station as the nose began to leave the runway—this station was across the highway barely off the end of the runway! As the nose lifted into the air and we began to climb, all hell broke loose! A very loud bell began to ring, red lights started to flash and the Second Officer shouted, "Engine fire!"

We had drilled repeatedly for such an occurrence and everything happened exactly like the practice sessions that we had trained for so many times. The Captain said, "I'm shutting down the number one engine and pulling the fire handle!" He then announced to the tower controller that we had an engine failure and were going to continue straight ahead—meaning that we were no longer complying with the prescribed departure procedures. I had called for gear up but since the Captain was rather busy I pulled the handle up myself and again looked into the service bay of that Shell station! We passed over that roof top with less than 100 feet to spare and I bet that those workers who were there that day are still talking about the time that a United pilot tried to kill them all! With only two engines providing thrust, the performance of my beloved B-727 was rather anemic. We staggered along until we finally reached 1000 feet and were able to level off, accelerate and retract the flaps. The tower controller asked the usual question, "What are your intentions?" The Captain responded that we needed to dump fuel before returning to the airport for landing. We were vectored to fly over Lake Pontchartrain where the Second Officer dumped about twenty thousand pounds of fuel and then we were cleared to land back on the runway from which we had just departed. After I landed the airplane and the Captain had taken over to taxi to the gate, I looked back to the controller who sat in the jump seat behind the Captain. I had forgotten all about him being in the cockpit and of course he had not uttered a word since we started the take off roll. His face was white as a sheet and his eyes seemed as large as saucers! I asked him if he was all right and he finally stammered, "I have never seen three people work so hard and do so much in such a short time!" We had been airborne exactly seventeen minutes.

It turned out that there was another United 727 on the ground there in New Orleans that was scheduled to fly to Chicago several hours later and we were able to use that plane to complete our trip to Denver—less than two hours late. In the meantime, an Eastern Airlines mechanic checked out the engine that failed on takeoff—United did not have any maintenance personnel at MSY. He opened the engine cowling while I watched and a huge piece of metal fell out—the mechanic commented that it was a good thing that we shut it down when we did as he felt that it would have blown apart if fuel had been continued to that engine. I was happy that things worked out as well as they did. When we departed the second time, all of the passengers from the aborted flight were in their seats, with one exception—the air traffic controller decided that he had had enough fun for one day and stayed in New Orleans! As the Captain lined up the aircraft for takeoff once again on runway 19, he looked at me and stated, "Your plane—try to get us to Denver this time!"

Most of the Captains that I flew with during those years in Denver were a real pleasure to work with, with a few notable exceptions. One of those latter mentioned Captains was a very straight-laced, up-tight, no nonsense chap whose name was Howard. He was nervous about flying, never smiled and certainly never told a joke of any kind! He flew by the numbers and when things went according to plan, he was a competent aviator. When things did not go as planned—look out! He had a daughter, named Mary Ann, who was a flight attendant with United, also based in Denver, and she was probably the most promiscuous stew in the company—if not in the entire world! She readily admitted that she had slept with over two hundred pilots and her goal seemed to be to work her way through the entire seniority list. Despite her tendency toward nymphomania, she was an excellent flight attendant who was very popular with the passengers—she brought flowers from her garden to place in the blue rooms, greeted the first class passengers by name, and generally treated everyone with the respect that they wanted. She also treated the pilots like REAL PEOPLE as she attended to our every wish. One day as we sat in the cockpit at the gate getting ready for takeoff we were told that the flight attendants were running a few minutes late due to a delay from their inbound trip. The Captain was Howard and the Second Officer was a relatively new guy named Bob. When the flight attendants came on board, the senior stew stuck her head into the cockpit and said, "Hi fellows, I'm Mary Ann and I'll get your orders in just a few seconds—as soon as I take care of business in the cabin." As soon as she left, the Second Officer turned to Howard and myself and blurted out, "You know who that is? That's the Mary Ann who has screwed half of the pilots in the company!" I was holding up my hand, trying desperately to get his attention, hoping that he would shut the hell up—when it dawned on Bob that the stew he was talking about was the daughter of the Captain in the left seat! Howard never said a single word and continued to look straight ahead—we were surrounded by a silence that was deafening! Bob was trying to sink into the floorboards, I was looking out the right window, and finally Howard uttered a single word: "CHECKLIST."

Obviously there was a lot of tension in the cockpit for the remainder of our sequence and even Mary Ann noticed that we all seemed a bit up-tight when she came back to the cockpit. She had no idea what the problem was but she solved it a bit by asking, "What's the matter with you guys today, my old man being a wet blanket as usual?" Even old Howard almost chuckled and we all loosened up and started to relax.

About a year later, Mary Ann "discovered" a fire in the trash bin in a blue room on an aircraft in flight. She successfully put out the fire and was considered a true heroine by all. She was named United's "Flight Attendant of the Year" and was given a nice plaque and a small reward. After another year passed and her fame was starting to fade, she "discovered" another fire on an airplane in the same area. Fortunately this aircraft was on the ground and after a thorough investigation it was determined that this fire had been intentionally set! Mary Ann finally confessed to setting the second fire but insisted that the first one was real. Instead of firing this nymphomaniac turned pyromaniac, the company gave her some time off and paid for therapy—she later returned to work. As far as I know she may still be up there flying the Friendly Skies!

The first year back flying as copilot in Denver I was mostly on reserve—again! I was happy just to be back in the right seat and found that reserve flying with all of its uncertainties was really a lot of fun—and sometimes downright funny. United was still flying lots of charters and those trips were pretty much exclusively flown by reserves. Some of the really desirable charters, such as a trip to Bermuda with a 33 hour layover, mysteriously were picked up by "management pilots" but since quite a few were flown on the weekends, the regular reserve crews were called up. I flew only one trip to Bermuda and it did not involve a layover. It was a charter for a group attending a NAACP convention and it was a real hoot. We departed from Atlanta and flew along the coast as long as possible before heading out to sea—the 727 was not considered a long range over water aircraft as we did not have INS or inertial navigation systems on board. Once we were over water enroute to Bermuda we were out of the normal air traffic control system and communications became minimal. We started to relax when one of the flight attendants came into the cockpit and announced, "We have a real party group on board—mind if I stay up here for the rest of the flight?" Eventually the other two stews also came into the cockpit—they had basically abandoned the passengers, who had taken over the liquor supplies and were having one hell of a party. After a short while we were having trouble talking to one another in the cockpit—the noise from the cabin was that loud. The Captain made a few announcements over the PA system but I doubt if anyone in the cabin heard or heeded what he said. When we started our descent for landing it was necessary for the flight attendants to return to their stations in the cabin. When the cockpit door was opened for them to exit, it seemed that all of the passengers were standing in the aisles and gathered around the cockpit door. The noise was incredible as it seemed that everyone was talking—no, shouting—at the same time. The stews fought their way through the crowd and tried to get the folks to return to their seats—I doubt that they were successful. Nevertheless we landed in Bermuda and the passengers said that they all had the best trip of their lives! The Captain made the landing and due to the short runway he probably used more braking than normal. As we taxied to the parking area, the tower reported that we had smoke coming from the left gear area. We were not alarmed but as a precaution the Captain requested that the fire department be notified to send a truck to our aircraft after we were parked. After the passengers had all deplaned the Captain and I walked down the airstair and went over to check out the "smoking" brake, which by this time had cooled off and was no longer of concern. The Captain mentioned, "Wonder what happened to the fire truck we requested?" About this time we heard quite a commotion with squealing tires and spotted what appeared to be a fire truck of 1930 vintage roaring around a hanger and heading for our plane. It was like a scene from a Mel Brooks movie—this antique fire truck with a bunch of guys hanging onto the sides was bearing down on us and it did not appear that they were going to be able to stop before hitting our airplane! The two of us pilots started to run for cover when the truck screeched to a halt and several people literally fell off! Slowly the driver opened his door, got out of his seat, and *staggered* over to where we were standing. The rest of his crew was trying to look somewhat professional as he walked up to the Captain, saluted, and in a crisp English accent said, "At your service, governor!" He reeked of cheap rum and was trying valiantly to stand erect—we were trying to keep from laughing too loud! The Captain thanked him for his "prompt response" and said that everything was now under control. The fire chief saluted again and after climbing into his truck he roared off into the night.

Another interesting charter that I flew during this time was to transport a group of female bowlers from a tournament in Portland, Oregon to their home in Milwaukee, Wisconsin. The Captain was a gentleman by the name of Allan who was the epitome of the poster airline pilot—tall, athletic, tanned and with an incredible head of silver hair that was perfectly coiffed. His uniform was always immaculate and his habit was to stand at the cabin door when the passengers deplaned to shake hands and bid them good day. He was also an excellent pilot and a pleasure to fly with. The passengers on this trip were a bit unusual—these ladies were professional bowlers who averaged about 150 pounds each (I'm being generous) and had just successfully completed a tournament and were ready to celebrate. There was always plenty of booze boarded for those charters and the drinks were free—a bad combination. Even the flight attendants, all female, complained about that rowdy group as we headed toward MKE. My two hour butt required that I go for a walk about half way through the trip. When I stepped out of the cockpit, there was quite a line waiting for the forward blue room so I headed to the rear to use one of the two facilities there. Walking through the cabin in my uniform was quite an experience—I was propositioned at least a half dozen times, pulled into the laps of several women, and groped in the crotch several times. These gals would have made good Marines at Tailhook Reunions! When I returned to the cockpit, I recommended to the Captain and Second Officer that they think twice before going into the cabin! Neither one left the cockpit for the remainder of the trip. After landing in Milwaukee, the Captain did his usual thing—he straightened his uniform, donned his hat, and stepped out of the cockpit to bid the passengers adieu. I stood in the doorway, just far enough inside the cockpit to be out of reach, to watch what I knew was going to happen. Several of the departing women shook the Captain's hand and tried to give him a hug but he successfully evaded their advances. Then a very large, very inebriated woman stepped up, spotted the immaculate Captain, screamed, "My God, you're fucking beautiful!" and charged! She threw her arms around him before he had a chance to defend himself, planted a big wet smooch on his face, knocked off his hat, and almost brought the poor man to his knees! He reeled back into the cockpit with his hair mussed up, lipstick all over his face, and missing his hat. He looked at me and said, "That's the very last time that I will ever stand at the door when women bowlers are on board!"

United Airlines now changed its name to Allegis Corporation—a faux pas that gave Wall Street and Johnny Carson plenty of ammunition for cartoons and one-liners. Even the employees were known to say "Gesundheit" when the new corporate name was mentioned. In reality it was part of Dick Ferris's grand scheme to transform the airline into his version of a global travel conglomerate. We began to realize, however, that the airline profits were being siphoned off to cover other parts of the financial puzzle and the results were leading into one fatal direction. Ferris began to demand that the pilots give massive wage concessions and threatened once again to "shrink the airline" if the pilots did not capitulate. American Airlines had just signed a contract with their pilots, who were not part of ALPA, that provided for a "B-Scale"—meaning that future pilots would be paid only fifty percent of what the incumbent pilots were receiving. The pilots at United were unified in their opposition to such a pay scale—not wanting to see the airline pilot profession relegated to that of being truck drivers in the sky. Not only was it against the capitalistic theory of more pay for more education and training, but it was also against the fundamental concept of equal pay for equal work. This impasse slowly led to the pilot's strike of 1985—perhaps the only truly altruistic strike in the history of labor relations. The pilots at United were offered pay raises and improvements in working conditions if they would accept the onerous B-Scale. We turned down those enticements and insisted that future pilots be paid the same as those of us already on the property. Although the pay for initial pilots had improved somewhat since I had started in 1968, it was still little more than poverty wages for the first few years. Every new pilot recognized that it would take several years before he or she would make a decent salary—but that was part of the program and was generally accepted as the price for admission into the airline pilot profession. If the prospective pilot knew that he/she would never make the same as the senior aviators, then perhaps that candidate would choose a different line of work! Ultimately, the profession would be degraded and would not be considered as a career choice for the more gifted and intelligent candidates who might now decide to go to dental school instead!

The strike of 1985 lasted for 29 days—it seemed more like 29 years! No one wins in a strike and this one was no exception. Ferris was determined to crush the union and the pilots were resolved to "save the profession." For me, never a big union supporter, it was a matter of "who is lying to me the least?" Pilots, for the most part, are not devious individuals—we simply want to fly our planes and enjoy a decent life style. The pilots and the union were not trying to build an empire—simply keep the status quo—and we were dedicated to what we felt was a worthy cause. After seventeen years with the airline, who would have thought that I would be a junior copilot on a picket line? After about a week into the strike I received a letter from my employer stating that I had been fired because I did not cross the picket line and all pay and benefits were now terminated.

At least we picked a nice time of year to strike—the weather was beautiful in Denver that May and we all worked on our tans while carrying our picket signs. The flight attendants joined our strike and the relations between our two groups improved tremendously—it was almost fun to walk the line with some of those ladies, many of whom wore very attractive attire (read short shorts and halter tops). I was totally impressed with both the pilots and flight attendants who supported our effort—the pilot group was very well organized and the stews contributed in many, many ways. Many long term relationships were started "on the picket line" between pilots and flight attendants. In many ways those days spent in direct opposition to the company that paid your salary were like being on an emotional roller coaster. It was also a study in character—who had it and who did not! Some of the pilots and stews that I "walked" with during the strike were the least likely persons that you would ever imagine to meet on a picket line. A pilot who had a severely handicapped child whose medical expenses would be unbearable without the insurance from United and a single mother who would lose everything if she did not have a steady income from her employer—just two of those I met who impressed me so much with their personal sacrifices. Only 4% of the line pilots with United crossed the picket line and most of those were management want-to-be types or very weak pilots who were afraid that if they did not continue with UAL, they would never find another job. Howard and his nympho daughter, Mary Ann, both crossed the line on the very first day.

At the time of the strike, my son was living with me in Denver and my daughter was graduating from high school in California. Since I no longer had pass privileges I was faced with the dilemma of how to get to that graduation that I had committed to attend. Three weeks into the strike I got into my car and drove to Bakersfield in order to keep my promise. It was worth the long drive to see my daughter at her graduation ceremony but the trip back was filled with uncertainty over my future. I stopped to spend the night in a tourist trap of a town called Durango in the southwest corner of Colorado. I checked into a Motel Six type of place and planned to go out for cheap beer and pizza for my dinner. When I entered the room that I had just rented, I turned on the TV and caught the news that the United Airlines strike was over! I had purposely not watched any news nor read any newspapers for the past few days and immediately called a friend in Denver to get the details. My friend gave me the good news—the strike was indeed over and we would all be going back to work very soon! I was so happy that I quickly checked out of the dump I was in and got a room down the street at a decent hotel. Instead of beer and pizza it was steak and fine wine that night!

I somehow assumed that after the strike was settled we would all shake hands, slap each other on the backs and get back to flying the friendly skies—I was very wrong. The company had made many promises to those pilots who crossed the picket lines and they were given special treatment—they even had their separate pilots lounge in Denver accessible only via a special key given to the chosen few. The company had also hired what were called "fleet qualified" pilots to replace those of us who banded together to oppose the "B-Scale." Almost 400 pilots were hired in this group—mostly the scum of aviation—pilots who were not able to attain jobs with reputable carriers, many with criminal and shady backgrounds. If they had experience flying air carrier airplanes as pilot in command, they were hired as Captains making $75,000, copilots were given $50,000. Fortunately, the courts rightfully placed these misfits at the bottom of the seniority list but the airline was stuck with this group until they retired or were fired. Many were fired for cause within the next several years for various reasons; drug charges, criminal behavior such as child molestation, or because of deficiencies in flying skills. These Fleet Quals, as they were called, were now flying as Second Officers but getting the pay that they were promised—much more than new pilots were supposed to be paid according to the union pay scales in the pilot's contract. Obviously this did not sit well with the pilot group—it was in reality a reversal of the B-Scale that we successfully fought against. Now we had new pilots, the Fleet Quals, making either 75 or 50 thousand in their first year, about six times what a new hire pilot would normally earn!

Nevertheless, the pilot group felt that our strike had been a worthwhile endeavor as we prepared to get the airline back on track. The first order of business was to throw a big formal party for those flight attendants who helped our cause. The pilots pitched in to cover the expenses—complete with limos and corsages for our new allies—and the party was quite a blast. We entered a new era of closeness between the flight crews on both sides of the cockpit door. Unfortunately, the relations between the pilots and management were not so easily improved. The culture at United Airlines had been changed forever. There was a definite lack of trust between the line pilots and those in management. The company placed unqualified personnel into management positions in the flight department and many of these pitiful creatures became known as "hall monitors." My first trip after the strike was a true revelation of things to come. I was assigned to fly a three day trip with a Captain whom I knew well, a good old boy who looked and talked like Gary Cooper. The Second Officer was one of the Fleet Quals who had been hired as a Captain. When we checked into flight operations to plan our trip we were told that we were required to have a special briefing by a "management person." As we looked over the flight plan, we were approached by a young lady who introduced herself by saying, "Hi, I'm your flight manager and I need to conduct a special orientation briefing before you depart on your first trip." The Captain and I had never seen this person before and we looked at each other with complete shock. The Captain, a tall slender type who looked like he would be more comfortable riding a horse than flying an airliner, slowly took a cigarette out of his pocket, lit it with a strike-anywhere match, looked this lady in the eye, and said, "What type of equipment do you fly?" She stammered, "Well, I don't fly anything, but I have been appointed as a flight manager to conduct these special briefings." The Captain looked down at this poor creature and said, "You're no flight manager of mine—get me a real flight manager or you can find yourself another Captain to fly this trip!" There was a small round of applause as she quickly turned and departed the briefing area. After a short delay, a real flight manager came out of his office, reluctantly, I might add, gave a short, curt brief about safety being of paramount importance and we departed on our trip.

This first trip was not a comfortable one. The Fleet Qual was an ex-Braniff pilot who was in his late fifties and was not competent as a Second Officer. He complained that he had been hired by United to fly as Captain and his training for the Second Officer position was short and inadequate. Compared to the usual Second Officers that I flew with, he was severely behind the power curve. Every leg of our three day trip was delayed because of this incompetent crew member—he was really quite pitiful and I almost started to feel sorry for him until I reminded myself that he took the job with United as a scab to replace the real United pilots. The Captain and I maintained a professional atmosphere while in the cockpit but basically ignored the Fleet Qual when not on duty. On the third day of the trip, I was having breakfast by myself at the hotel before departure when the Fleet Qual walked up and asked if he could join me. I wanted to say no, but since it is just not my nature to be nasty to people (even scabs), I said, "Sure, sit down, but I'm about finished and ready to leave—I still have to check out of my room." He was almost in tears as he sat down at my table and started rambling on about how bad he felt about his decision to take a job with United as a scab. He told me how tough it was for him when Braniff went out of business and he was not able to find a job as a pilot due to his age. Then he told me that his wife had recently left him after 35 years of marriage. Then he came up with the *coup de grace* as he related a very sad story of how he was now taking care of his son who was living with him in a small one bedroom apartment in Houston. I was starting to feel very sorry for this poor man and I hesitated to ask for details about the son, thinking that perhaps he was severely handicapped. Nevertheless, I inquired, "Is your son able to work at all?" The Fleet Qual answered, "Oh yeah, he's a dentist—but he has a lot of big expenses right now as he's building a bigger office to expand his practice." I almost choked on my last bite of breakfast—never again would I feel the least bit sorry for those scabs who came to take my job!

For several years following the strike of '85, the flying was either really great or, on occasion, NOT MUCH FUN! We, the striking pilots, were treated better than we had ever been treated by the flight attendants—and the trips without a scab in the cockpit were the fun trips that they all should be! Due to the fact that many of the scabs and Fleet Quals were now hiding out in the Denver Training Center, the Denver domicile was exposed to more of the "non-striking" types than other bases. One month I was assigned to fly a schedule with a Captain who had scabbed—he had been a flight manager in Miami when I was based there—and I was not looking forward to the first trip. Fortunately, he did not show up for that first trip of the month—he called in sick. The trip was assigned to a reserve Captain who was a "good guy" and we had a fun, routine sequence. The Second Officer was a pilot who had flown for People's Express and several other carriers before finding a home with United. His name was Bob and he was a talented pilot with a great personality—he also had a girl friend who was a flight attendant who was flying the portion of the trip that involved a long layover in Spokane,

Washington, one of my favorite places to spend the night. We decided that on the next trip we flew together that month, I would bring my lady friend who was also a flight attendant. We planned to give the scab Captain a layover that he would always remember!

The night before our next trip I received a phone call from a Fleet Qual who was now working as an instructor in the training center. I recognized his name when he spoke to me on the phone and advised me that he was going to "displace" me on tomorrow's trip. Normally, when a training center pilot called to displace, it was a welcome event as the displaced pilot was paid as if he had flown the trip but got to stay home. I informed "Skip" (the Fleet Qual's name—later to be fired for drugs) that I did not wish to be displaced. He argued that I had no choice and I shortly hung up on him. I showed up for the trip the next day and found the Fleet Qual huddled with the scab Captain. Generally the "bad guys" who were hiding out in the training center only came out to fly when all three or at least two of the pilots were scabs. I walked up the Captain and introduced myself as the REAL COPILOT. The Captain looked very confused and muttered that I had been displaced by the Fleet Qual who was there to fly the trip. I stated that I did not wish to be displaced and therefore I was there to fly the assigned trip that was in my schedule. The Captain decided to call the crew desk in Chicago to settle the conflict— meanwhile "Skip" was standing beside the Captain with a big smirk on his face.

After the Captain talked to the crew desk he handed the phone to me. The senior crew scheduler, one of my old buddies from my days in DCA, asked me, "What are you up to, Bill?" I responded that I did not agree to be displaced and I was there to fly my assigned trip. The scheduler said, "I've never heard of a pilot refusing to be displaced—you can go home and get paid for the trip, you know." I held my ground by saying, "Red, it's my trip and I have the right to conform to the schedule that was awarded me." After a short pause, Red said, "Let me talk to the Fleet Qual." I handed the phone to "Skip" who listened for a few seconds, slammed down the phone, and stormed out of the operations area. I was never called again by one of those Fleet Quals to be displaced.

We departed for our trip and eventually arrived for our scheduled 33 hour layover in Spokane. Bob was with his girlfriend, Sheryl, who was working the flight, and I was accompanied by my lady friend, Trisha, who was traveling as a passenger—plus the poor Captain! There were two other working flight attendants, both nice ladies, who were informed as to our plan. I had previously arranged for my room to be next to the Captain's—this was our designated party room. Since Bob and Sheryl were sharing a room and Trisha and I were sharing a room, we had one more room than we needed. We brought beer, wine and champagne into the party room, made as much noise as we could, turned the TV set volume up extremely loud, and finally left that room in the wee hours of the morning—with the music still going strong! I checked on the room the next day and following night to be sure that the music was still loud enough to be heard by the Captain next door. When we departed the hotel early on the second morning, I arranged for a taxi to take the four of us to the airport, leaving the Captain to use the normal limo service. When the Captain arrived I had already initialed the flight plan, Bob had completed the preflight inspection, the flight attendants were on board and we were patiently waiting for his arrival. Needless to say, he looked like he needed a good nights sleep and was not in a very good frame of mind. I have to give him some credit, though, as he knew that he had "been had" and reluctantly expressed his feelings of respect for what we had accomplished. I doubt that he ever again flew with a striking pilot—he took early retirement less than a year later.

United was expanding rapidly at this time and the training center was filled to capacity with new pilots being trained. There was a large group of pilots that United had "pre-trained" before the strike—management thinking that these pilots would come to work and cross the picket line when the strike started—that became known as the "570." To management's dismay, only four of those 570 pilots actually crossed the picket line! The rest honored our cause and refused to go to work. These honorable gentlemen and ladies helped to shorten the strike considerably by their noble actions. After the strike this group was placed at the very end of the seniority list, behind the 400 Fleet Quals, as a form of punishment from Dick Ferris, who was livid that they did not go to work during the strike. Eventually the courts ruled that the 570 were entitled to seniority ahead of the Fleet Quals—in this case justice prevailed. For several months almost every flight that I flew involved a Second Officer who was in one of the two groups, the 570 (good guys) or the 400 (bad guys). The "good guys" were obviously treated much better by the other pilots and flight attendants than the "bad guys." Since the Fleet Quals were not members of ALPA they were not allowed to wear the union pin— the 570 were ALPA members. Therefore any pilot who was not wearing his/

her ALPA pin was considered a scab. The customary place for the ALPA pin was on the lapel of the pilot's uniform jacket. Suddenly, those pins began to disappear from jackets left hanging in pilot lounges or draped over a chair in an unattended area. At the same time the Fleet Quals began to wear unauthorized ALPA pins! We decided that from now on, the pin would be worn on the pilot's TIE—not on the jacket—making it a bit more difficult to steal. After about four months post-strike, the union published an unofficial but accurate list of all the pilots that crossed the picket line and identified each one by category—such as Fleet Qual, management, or line pilot scab. Prior to this list it was not always easy to identify the scabs—BECAUSE THEY LIED!

Before this scab list was published, called the "little yellow book," I had a very interesting encounter with one of the "bad guys." I was flying a schedule with a good friend, Wayne, who was perhaps the best "stick" I had ever met. Wayne had flown all three seats on the 727 and had probably over 10,000 hours on that type aircraft. He was also the Commanding Officer of a Phantom F-4 reserve squadron based in St. Louis. He was a very senior Captain but was flying a week-end trip that departed Denver each Sunday morning. The trip laid over in St. Louis that night and we did not depart until late Monday afternoon—giving Wayne time to report to his squadron and do some paperwork. Of course this also gave him credit as a "duty day" in the reserves. He was getting a day's pay from Uncle Sam while working a trip with United Airlines! The Second Officer that would be flying with us all month was a very large, overweight guy who seemed very nervous and uptight—he also sweated a lot. He wore an ALPA pin and introduced himself as one of the 570 group. Wayne and I were a bit suspicious, especially in light of his poor performance as a flight engineer, but gave him the benefit of the doubt. His story was that he had worked for a small feeder outfit in the Southeast—even showing us pictures of the planes that he flew—and he said that he had never flown jets nor had he ever been a flight engineer. Since both Wayne and I had such extensive experience on the 727, we were able to catch his mistakes before they became serious and we helped him as much as possible for the first two trips. On the third trip of the month I checked in to flight operations early and the crew scheduler motioned for me to lean over his counter so that he could speak to me confidentially. In a whispered voice he said, "Bill, I'm giving you a head's up—you and Wayne are getting a check ride this morning." Wayne had not yet checked in and when I glanced around the room I spotted the "check pilot"—a scab from the training center—who was examining the wallpaper in the corner of the flight planning area. In a minute or two our Second Officer entered the room and made a beeline for the check pilot. They huddled together for a few seconds and then departed the area. Wayne now reported in and I related what I knew to him. We both realized that we had been set up by the S/O—obviously he had not told us the truth. Wayne, in his usual cool manner, stated, "Looks like we have been really bad boys to get one of those TCA's (Training Check Airman) out on a Sunday morning." The crew scheduler, who had been listening in on our conversation, added, "Or maybe you two have been really good guys—wish that I could be in the cockpit during this check ride!"

The first leg was to San Francisco, then after a two hour sit we would return to Denver. After another two hours on the ground we would fly the last leg of the day to St. Louis, arriving after dark, a typical 12 hour duty day to get six hours of flying. Wayne briefed me that I would fly the first leg. Then he pulled a small voice recorder out of his flight bag, placed it in his shirt pocket and stated, "I think that I will record the conversation with the check pilot—let's both be very professional." When we entered the cockpit, the Second Officer was at his desk, sweating profusely, and the check pilot was standing at the door. He introduced himself and stated that he was there to give us a check ride. Wayne responded, "I just had a check ride last month— I'm not due for another check for almost six months." The check pilot, who was wearing his Captain's uniform—although I do not believe that he had Captain seniority—became a bit flustered and stammered, "I'm conducting a special check—requested by the flight office." We all took our seats, did the usual preflight checks, completed briefings and checklists and departed for SFO. I tried my best to fly the perfect trip and felt that it was indeed close to perfection—we departed on time, landed several minutes early with more fuel than planned and the landing itself was a real "greaser." After the parking checklist was completed and the passengers had deplaned, the S/O disappeared and the Check Pilot started to debrief me in the jetway. I told him that I preferred to be "debriefed" in the pilot lounge with my Captain present. I wanted to put him in the awkward position of debriefing me in the presence of my peers—the real pilots who would be in the lounge. When we entered the pilot's lounge there were probably twenty other pilots there—they all took notice when Wayne and I sat down and left the check pilot standing up to debrief. He was the only pilot in the room without an ALPA pin. He nitpicked several minor items about my flying—I climbed out 5 knots faster than normal (I explained that with a headwind that was what you were supposed to do), he claimed that I started my descent some five miles early (I explained that I did not have to touch the throttles until the gear was extended), etc. Wayne chimed in with the fact that we were early, we saved fuel, and the passengers were delighted with the landing. The check pilot stood his ground and insisted that he had to find something to critique! Wayne had heard enough. He took the recorder from his pocket and laid it on the table. He made the following statement: "The S/O is not only incompetent but a liar—he is not dependable or reliable and I refuse to fly with him again until he has been given a special evaluation. I want to know what he reported that resulted in the special check that you are conducting." The check pilot pulled a piece of paper from his pocket and read from it, "On several occasions you flew at higher speeds than standard, once you flew at an altitude that was not recommended by the S/O, and (the most damaging report) you allowed a flight attendant to sit in the cockpit during landing!" Wayne and I both laughed and thought that our reported mistakes were so petty that they needed no explanation. Wayne did explain the case of the "stew in the cockpit." A new flight attendant had taken ill during one of our trips and was brought to the cockpit by the senior stew to get oxygen. She was very "green around the gills" and the O2 seemed to help—we all agreed that it was better to keep her in the cockpit on oxygen than let her return to the cabin and throw up on the passengers!

The check pilot then informed us that the check ride was not yet over—he would continue the "check" on the return flight to DEN. Then he stated that there was not enough time to replace the S/O before our departure but that he would have a replacement waiting for us in DEN for the leg to STL. Wayne and I agreed on one condition—the check pilot would conduct a check of the S/O on the next leg. The check pilot was not qualified to conduct a formal check of the S/O but reluctantly agreed to observe him and schedule him for a CKE (check engineer) trip if warranted. We departed SFO with the same cockpit crew but different stews—they were from Denver and a bunch of really savvy gals. When we told them that we were getting a "special check ride" they chimed in that they would give the check pilot and S/O special treatment. The Captain lined up the aircraft on the departing runway, set the brakes, looked at me and said, "You have the airplane." I acknowledged, released the brakes, added throttle and began the takeoff roll. The check pilot began shouting, "No, no, the Captain has to fly the airplane on this leg!" Wayne and I ignored the check pilot until he said, "If the Captain doesn't fly this leg, then I will have to continue the check on the next leg!" Wayne and I looked at each other, nodded, and I passed command of the machine back to the Captain—just before lift off! Wayne flew his usual perfect flight to DEN and the debrief consisted of only two words, "Nice flight." During the flight the stews treated Wayne and I like royalty—we were given the best food on the airplane, served with fine china and linen napkins. The check pilot and S/O were ignored and offered nothing—not even a cup of coffee. The final treat was a special hot fudge sundae for me and the Captain after our great meal. The check pilot and the S/O fled the cockpit after arriving at the gate in DEN and we never heard another word from the flight office or the training center about our performance. Unfortunately the S/O was not fired and is quite possibly flying the Friendly Skies to this day!

Chapter Seventeen

"Passengers prefer old Pilots and young Flight Attendants!"

Thankfully, the bitter memories of the strike and its aftermath began to fade after about a year and the airline began to return to some semblance of normalcy. For me, those next few years were great—I was flying my favorite airplane to interesting cities throughout the country and began to enjoy some seniority. Although I was now senior enough to have weekends and holidays off, I chose to do just the opposite. As a bachelor, I gladly worked on the weekends and holidays so that my fellow pilots could spend that time with their families. I was not being magnanimous, however, as I really preferred to have time off during the week—the ski slopes were less crowded, it was easier to get a reservation at a nice restaurant, and people in general seemed less stressed than on weekends. I do not recall having more than a handful (five) Christmas or New Year holidays off during all my years as an airline pilot. Often I had no choice but even when senior I chose to work on the holidays. Pilots were not paid extra to work on holidays—flight attendants were. This resulted in junior cockpit crews and very senior cabin crews working on those holiday trips—an interesting combination.

One December my schedule included what was called a "holiday exception" at the end of the month. Often United cancelled trips that had very light loads around certain holidays and our flight schedules were changed accordingly. Our normal trip arrived into Lincoln, Nebraska late at night and departed the next day at noon. On New Year's Eve our trip into LNK was cancelled so we were scheduled to deadhead from DEN earlier in the day for a long layover and fly our regular flight out the next day. Both the Captain and S/O were fun troops and we decided that we would deadhead in civilian clothes so that we could celebrate an early New Years. The drinking rule had been changed to twelve hours during the strike because a scab Captain had a few too many on an international trip and was forced to cancel when he found out that the cabin attendants were going to report him for violating what was then the 24 hour rule. With the new 12 hour rule, we would be able to drink until midnight—we could have a toast a few minutes early and be completely legal. When we arrived in Lincoln we found that the station manager had arranged for us to stay downtown instead of at the usual airport motel. Since it was now almost a 24 hour layover, we were entitled to a "downtown" layover according to the pilot contract and the station manager had booked us at the Cornhusker Hotel. We chuckled a bit at the name of the hotel but were really impressed when a large limousine arrived and transported us downtown. We walked into the lobby and were greeted by the hotel owner, not the manager—the owner! He related to us that he had hopes of getting a contract with United for layover crews and was providing us with the red carpet treatment during our stay. He invited us to join him for lunch in his executive suite—of course we accepted. We were treated with fine cuisine and the bar was open for anything we desired. I asked the hotel owner if there was anything planned for New Year's Eve that evening in the state capital of Lincoln. He shrugged and admitted that it was basically a University town and since the students were away for the holidays there was not much going on for New Years Eve. Then he added, "There's the usual party at the VFW tonight—I understand that it can be a lot of fun." The three of us decided that we were not interested in attending a party of old fogies at the VFW that evening. After our great lunch we wisely decided to take a short nap and meet again at 5:00 to decide what to do for dinner and what would probably be an early turn-in that night.

We met at five and decided to walk around the town a bit—looking for a place to have a decent dinner. Instead we found a nice bar with lots of friendly people. Three of the friendliest were striking blondes who asked us to join their table—of course we jumped at the chance. During the course of the ensuing conversation these ladies stated that they were attending the VFW dance that evening and invited us to join them. We were wearing sport coats but not ties, which were required at the dance. One of the ladies said that she would pick us up at our hotel in half an hour if we could find neckties to wear. We rushed back to our hotel—convinced that the only action in town was definitely the VFW affair. The owner was still at the front desk and he gladly provided the three of us with ties. Shortly we were standing in front of the hotel when a huge white Cadillac pulled up. It was the gregarious blonde who had offered us a ride. We piled in and our next stop was what I can only describe as a mansion. We were greeted at the door by a butler who took us to a large bar/ recreation room in the basement. The blonde excused herself by saying that she had to finish getting ready for the party. The three of us amused ourselves with the games and machines at the well stocked party room and were having a really good time when suddenly the three blondes appeared—they were now decked out in long formal dresses, all in white, to go with their hair of course. The three of us pilots were in a bit of a shock—what had we gotten into? After about one hour it was time to proceed to the VFW dance and we started out in three separate cars—all three were white Cadillacs driven by the three ladies.

The lady I was with drove like a demon and we were the first to arrive at the VFW hall. It was already full of people who were having a great party. Since I did not have a ticket I was charged $8.95 at the door to cover my food and beverages. My "date" ushered me to a large table of her friends and after a few introductions we all fell into the prevailing party mood. The table was provided with at least one bottle of every type of liquor imaginable—quality Scotch, Bourbon, Gin, Vodka, etc—and the champagne and wine were free flowing. My two buddies arrived and were seated at different tables. The band was playing and we all started to dance—it was one of the best parties that I had ever attended. Before the evening was over I had met the mayor of Lincoln, danced with his wife (who propositioned me on the dance floor) and met some really fine folks. As we had agreed, the three of us pilots stopped drinking precisely at midnight to honor the twelve hour rule, but the party continued until the wee hours. Several people asked us just what were three strangers doing in Lincoln on New Years Eve and our story was that we were Continental Airline pilots on a charter trip—better than telling the truth! The next day when we boarded our aircraft we quickly closed the cockpit door and hoped that no one who was at the VFW party the night before was on board for our trip back to Denver!

All airline pilots are subject to spot checks by the FAA Air Carrier Inspectors (ACIs) and these government check pilots would show up, unannounced, at very strange places and at times that were completely unexpected. Most of these inspectors were nice people who were doing a job that was necessary but not well received by those being checked.

Occasionally, these inspectors were disgruntled ex-pilots who had not been hired by the airlines for one reason or another—these were the few that made our job more than just a bit risky—"Mumbles" fell into this category. Sometimes the ACI would introduce himself to the crew in dispatch—but most of the time he would just show up in the cockpit as we were getting ready for departure. The usual procedure was for him to check each pilot for their license and current medical certificate and then occupy the jump seat behind the Captain. He was not allowed to interfere with the crew during flight unless something was terribly wrong and his debrief was usually a handshake and comment about what a fine job we all did. I recall one very interesting encounter with one of the inspectors early one morning in Oklahoma City. Perhaps we should have expected an unannounced check ride in OKC as that was where the FAA headquarters was located. I was flying a trip that laid over in OKC with what was considered a "minimum lay over." This meant that the rest period between duty assignments was less than legally required. The company got around this less than legal rest by shortening the report time after the lay over to only thirty minutes—meaning that the crew did not have to check in for flight planning until 30 minutes before departure. Reporting to the airport only thirty minutes before departure was really pushing the time required for preflight inspections, flight planning, etc. and most of the crews actually reported earlier to make the operation run more smoothly.

On this particular occasion, we had flown the plane in the night before that we would be flying out the next morning so we left our flight bags in the cockpit with everything ready to go with minimum preparation. We were staying at a motel located within five minutes of the airport and always had breakfast in the restaurant before catching the limo to the field. The limo operated every thirty minutes and we always caught the one that left sixty minutes before our scheduled departure. On this occasion, the service was very slow in the restaurant and we missed our usual van. Not to worry, says the Captain, as we will catch the next ride and still arrive about 25 minutes before brake release. We were waiting for that next van when we were told that it had broken down on the way back from the airport and we had to wait until the motel was able to arrange for alternate transportation. The Captain asked that the front desk call immediately for a taxi and we waited for the first ride to show—either the van or the cab. When the taxi arrived it was 15 minutes before our departure! Enroute to the airport the Captain—a very sharp pilot—briefed the flight; told the S/O to proceed directly to the aircraft to conduct the walk around; told me to go to the cockpit, brief the flight attendants, do the cockpit setup, get the clearance and be ready to depart on time. The Captain would go to flight operations and complete the flight planning and sign the release—the most important step of all! When I stepped aboard the airplane the passengers were seated and the flight attendants were ready to go. I gave a very quick brief about the flight time, weather, etc (mostly making it up as I went) and stepped into the cockpit. Standing just inside the door was a gentleman dressed in a business suit—looking at his watch! Before I had a chance to challenge him, he flashed his credentials and announced that he was conducting an enroute check of our crew. Then he inquired, "Why is this flight departing late?" I responded, "If you will just step aside and let me get into my seat, we will get out on time." He laughed at my remark and pointed to his watch—it was now four minutes to departure time. As I took my seat, the S/O arrived and reported the exterior inspection complete and began working on the takeoff data for the pilots. I called clearance delivery for our clearance and turned on the Captains speaker as the clearance was transmitted—at the same time the Captain entered the cockpit to listen to our clearance. Both pilots were required to listen to the departure clearance to ensure that we were in total agreement as to just what our procedures were. The Captain strapped in, did a quick check of his instruments and oxygen system and called for the "checklist." As the last item was completed on the checklist, the mechanic below called for brake release. As the Captain released the brakes I watched the second hand on the cockpit clock pass twelve—we departed exactly on time! I took a quick glance at the ACI as we were pushing back and he uttered one word, AMAZING! While enroute we explained what had happened at the hotel that caused us to report late. The inspector was very complimentary about our proficiency—but his last comment was, "I certainly hope that all of your departures are not quite so close!"

Most of our layovers were a bit more relaxed with sufficient time for rest and recreation. During this time, the middle eighties, fitness was the "in thing" and our layover hotels for long layovers (more than twelve hours) were required to provide workout facilities. Many of the nicer hotels had published jogging routes for the pilots so that those of us who wanted to go for a run would be provided with a safe and healthy place to jog. Very few cities in the United States are without adequate places to workout or run, but the places I seemed to enjoy the most seemed to be located in the Northwest—cities and towns like Portland, Spokane, Eugene, Boise, etc. One summer I had a very nice schedule with a long layover in Boise and I usually went for a long run along the river on the afternoon when we arrived. At the time I was jogging an average of thirty miles a week and considered myself to be in pretty good shape. The Captain that I was flying with that month was short, fat and seemingly out of shape but he kept saying that he was going to start jogging that summer. On the last trip of the month he announced that his wife had packed an old pair of tennis shoes in his overnight bag and he was now ready to go for a run when we reached Boise. He asked if it would be okay if he went with me on my run as he did not know where to go to jog. I really did not want to run with him but since he was really a very nice "older man" I agreed to meet him in the hotel lobby 15 minutes after we checked in. He showed up on time but, as expected, he was wearing his white undershirt, a pair of shorts that looked like they were from the thirties, and a really cheap pair of old tennis shoes. I reluctantly led him to my usual jogging trail and we started a slow gentle run. It was a very warm afternoon in Idaho with the temperature in the nineties—I surely did not want my Captain to overdo it—so I maintained a slow pace. After about one mile I noticed that he seemed to be doing okay so I picked up the pace. After two miles I was starting to sweat a bit in the heat but my Captain seemed to be quite cool—and not even breathing hard. I started running all out and after four miles this little guy was matching me stride for stride and had a bit of a grin on his face. I was gasping for breath as I asked him, "About how far did you want to run today?" He nonchalantly replied, "Oh, maybe eight miles or so." With some relief I said, "Guess it's time to turn around as we've gone four miles so far." He replied, "I meant running for eight miles before we turn around!" I started laughing as I came to a walk—I knew that I had been had! He laughed also and admitted that he was a marathon runner—he had finished in the top hundred for his age group in the Boston Marathon a few years earlier! I was thoroughly impressed with his achievements and mild manner—I learned once again not to jump to a conclusion merely by appearance. He finished his 16 mile run and I barely completed my 8 miles.

Some layovers required athletics of another kind. Our crew arrived in Seattle early one afternoon for a nice long stay at one of the finest downtown hotels, the Olympic, a very classy traditional hotel with a beautiful lobby. When the three of us entered that lobby to check in we were confronted with a large group of women who were in a definite party mood. There was a convention of hairdressers from the Northwest region and they came to have a good time. By the time we entered the elevator for our rooms we had been invited to several parties, some of a very private nature. Some 700 conventioneers were in attendance and all but six were female—those six were not interested in women. The three of us pilots agreed to meet in the lobby at five PM to have dinner at a place we liked a few blocks from the hotel. At the appointed hour the group of ladies was even more boisterous and they insisted that we attend their banquet—all expenses were paid! Airline pilots are notoriously cheap so the decision was not difficult—we attended the dinner/dance and had quite a time. After the dinner the band began to play dance music—it was interesting to watch all those ladies dancing with each other—and the three of us became very popular. As I was sitting one dance out, a young lady crawled under my table and took one of my shoes off—then she ran away with it as though it was a trophy! As I only had one pair of shoes with me, I needed both shoes to fly the next day. I chased down the thief and she gave me the shoe back—with one condition—that I go to her room after the dance was over. She was quite a looker, with a funky hat made out of beer cans, and I "reluctantly" agreed. Actually we headed to her room before the event was over but I discovered that she had a roommate—we went to my room instead. It was definitely a night to remember as she performed every pleasurable act known to mankind before we called it a night! I'm convinced that women hairdressers are a very rowdy bunch when they get together as a group.

Another interesting layover during those years was at the Hotel Benson in Portland. This was one of the most elegant hotels in the country—the lobby was classic in the best sense of the word, down to the harpist that played for those who sat around the bar in overstuffed chairs. Normally the pilots avoided eating and drinking at our layover hotels—not only was it expensive but it was not a good idea to have a passenger see his/her pilot hurling down a beer or two the night before a trip. One month I had one of those holiday exceptions that entailed a 33 hour layover at the Benson—two nights at the hotel instead of one. On the first night I eagerly changed clothes and went to the beautiful lobby bar for a beverage before bedtime. It was almost ten PM as I stood at the bar and ordered a cold beer. The place was almost empty, just a few couples having a nightcap before retiring for the evening. Nevertheless, I was enjoying the atmosphere that the lobby permeated—everyone there was dressed up. The gentlemen had jackets and ties and the ladies were dressed as though they were attending a semi-formal party. My eyes focused on one young lady who was sitting alone at a small settee in front of a coffee type table. She was dressed in a white business suit, complete with white gloves, and seemed to be awaiting her companion. I wondered why on earth would any man keep her waiting—she was the one that was worth waiting for! She glanced at her watch several times and I seized the opportunity—I had consumed two beers and now felt quite glib! When I approached I felt sure that I would be rebuffed in short order. I politely asked her if I might join her for a drink. She demurely nodded and I sat down—feeling that I had at least passed through the first barrier. Her wine glass was almost empty so I motioned for the cocktail waitress and ordered a drink for the two of us—wine for her and another beer for me. I introduced myself, first name only, and asked if she was waiting for her date. She replied that it seemed that she had been stood up—I expressed my sorrow! We began a guarded conversation of small talk—I was trying to feel out the situation—and she continued to check her watch. Finally I asked her if there was a pressing engagement that was forthcoming—she looked me in the eye and asked, "Do you want to party?" I almost fell out of my chair as my jaw dropped to the floor—she was a hooker! She explained that at eleven o'clock the hotel staff would ask her to leave—before that time she was free to ply her trade. She again asked me if I wanted to "party"—evidently this was a term that she could use that would not get her in trouble with the law. I shook my head and my disappointment was surely quite evident. She stood up and said, "It's time for me to leave, there's another hotel down the street that allows me to work until midnight." I watched her leave and felt a true sense of sorrow for the way that she had to work for a living!

One of the best hotels in the system was the Ben Franklin in San Mateo—the place where crews, both cockpit and cabin, were berthed in San Francisco. Some crews complained about the small rooms, lack of air conditioning, and the fact that the hotel was located away from the action of downtown San Francisco. I loved the place as it was comfortable, perhaps a bit homey, but the rooms were always clean and ready when we arrived. The hotel was owned by United Airlines but was managed by the real "owner," a gentleman known by all of the pilots as "Mr. Best." He was always there to greet the arriving pilots—no matter what time of day or night—and he treated us with real respect. We knew that when we reached our room there would be a fresh apple and a piece of chocolate on the bed. He maintained an automobile at the hotel that was at the disposal of the pilots—the only requirement was that it be returned with a full tank of gas. Every time that I used that vehicle it was full of gas when I started it and it was returned that way! Adjoining the hotel was a nice coffee shop where we had breakfast each morning—it was not open for dinner. Whenever a pilot entered the restaurant for breakfast, no matter how he/she was attired—uniform, running shorts or casual dress—he/she was presented with a glass of freshly squeezed orange juice. Many of the locals also ate at the restaurant so one day I inquired as to just how the waitresses knew which patrons were entitled to the free juice. Most of the waitresses at that coffee shop had been there at least thirty years and they would respond, "You guys all look alike, we spot you before you get inside the door." I would enjoy a very leisurely breakfast while reading the paper and soon noticed that my coffee cup was always filled just before I took the last swallow. I asked my waitress how she knew and she rolled her eyes and stated, "I watch the angle of your head when you take a drink—when it reaches just the right angle I know that it's time for a refill."

The walls at the Ben Franklin Hotel were very thin and I have always felt that if those walls could talk they would be able to tell some incredible stories. Since it was one of the very few places in the entire world that both pilots and stews for United laid over together, it was conducive to some interesting liaisons. The most interesting story about the Ben Franklin did not involve a flight attendant, however. As the story goes, never proven—simply one of those fabled tales—one of United's Captains, from Chicago I believe, picked up a lady at a local bar and invited her to his room. After mutually enjoyable intercourse, they both fell asleep. A few hours later the Captain awoke for the usual middle of the night trip to the bathroom and decided that it was best to awaken his lady friend and send her on her way. He was not able to wake her up—she was dead! The Captain, trying not to panic, ran down to the front desk where he found Mr. Best. He explained the situation and after some serious thought they both decided that it would be best if they could place her body in her automobile, which was parked outside the bar where the two met. The Captain was married and did not want the scandal to ruin his marriage. Mr. Best did not want the adverse publicity to affect his contract with United. The two cohorts dressed the poor corpse—not an easy task—and "walked" her down to the front of the hotel where they loaded her into the crew car. Evidently, her car keys were in her purse, and the two were able to locate her automobile in the bar parking lot and place her body inside! They returned to the hotel and that is the end of the story—no one ever knew what happened and supposedly the poor lady was found the next morning and it was presumed a natural death!

I began to realize that I had reached the stage in my life that one only dreams about—I loved going to work and I loved not going to work! I had the best of both worlds and admitted to anyone who wanted to listen that I felt that I really had never worked a day in my life—FLYING WAS NOT WORK, IT WAS FUN! When I was not flying I was doing those things that I wanted to do. One of those enjoyable things was playing tennis. I had a tennis court in front of my townhouse and it seemed to be my private court—rarely did I have to wait for use of that court. I played regularly with a neighbor by the name of Jim—everyone called him Jimbo—who was a big tough looking guy who hit the ball very hard. Jimbo sported a Fu Manchu mustache and a heavy black beard and looked quite menacing when he strode onto the tennis court. We usually played fairly evenly—but he somehow managed to win about eighty percent of the time. One day he came over to play and I almost did not recognize him—he had shaved off his beard and mustache. Instead of his domineering demeanor he now looked almost meek, with a receding chin that matched his receding hairline. I don't believe that I lost a tennis match to Jimbo ever again.

One day while we were playing, I noticed a very attractive lady walk by the court—someone that I had not seen before in our little community. Evidently she was out for some exercise as she walked by several times and usually stopped to watch a point or two. Jimbo noticed her too and we agreed that she was certainly a welcome addition to the neighborhood. After our match we sat out on my front patio to enjoy a cold beer or two—as was our custom. The young lady—probably in her mid thirties—walked by again and we started a friendly conversation. I invited her to join the two of us for a beer but she politely declined—stating that she was in town from Texas to visit her sister and brother-in-law and was returning to Texas the next day. I was sorry that there did not seem to be an opportunity for the two of us to get better acquainted. She continued on her exercise walk and Jimbo departed for his home—I continued to sit outside and enjoy the late afternoon spring weather. Just as I was getting ready to call it a day and go inside, the lady appeared again. This time she stopped and invited me to join her for a drink at her sister's home at five o'clock. Of course, I was delighted to say yes! After a shower and a change of clothes I was pushing their doorbell at 5 PM with a bottle of wine in my hand. I did not know the people who lived there but it turned out that the two were a fun couple about my age—the visiting sister from Odessa, Texas was named Susan. We socialized over a few drinks and I was invited to join the three of them for dinner at a local restaurant where they had already made reservations. Susan and I drove together to the restaurant and had a chance to talk alone. She was married and had two sons in grade school but it was obvious that the marriage was on the rocks and she was trying to make a decision as to the future direction of her life. When she heard that I was an Airline Pilot, she said that she had always wanted to become a stewardess but had gotten married after college and became a housewife/mother instead. I also found out that she was Miss Texas in 1972 and made it to the final ten in the Miss America beauty pageant that same year.

After a very pleasant dinner, I suggested that the four of us go to a nearby night spot where dancing was available. Susan was wearing a long white dress with a plunging neckline and when she entered a room—any room— heads started to turn. When we stepped out onto the dance floor it was as though everyone else stopped and we danced all alone. She was the most beautiful lady that I had ever met. When we danced it was also obvious that she wore nothing under that clinging white dress. I was the envy of every man in the room—I liked that feeling!

After several dances we both felt that it was time to leave—sister and brother-in-law decided to stay. Susan and I drove to my place, built a fire in the fireplace as the evening was now a bit cool, and made ourselves comfortable. We began to kiss but I wanted more. She stopped my advances by saying, "I have never been unfaithful to my husband and as long as the marriage is still valid, I just can't go all the way." I respected her feelings and slowed down my amorous behavior. We continued to kiss, however, and the kissing became more intimate. Suddenly she said, "We can go a bit further if you wish, but only from the waist up." I was trying to figure out exactly what she meant when she untied her top and the dress fell to her waist. I was now looking at the most beautiful and amazing breasts that I had ever seen—even in a Playboy magazine! She was rightfully proud of those beauties and I simply stared. When I caught my breath I stammered, "Are they real—or have you had some surgery?" She indignantly replied, "Of course they are real—it runs in the family—my sister has perfect breasts too, she will show you if you don't believe me!" I began to fondle those perfect breasts—they definitely were the real things—when she said, "You can kiss them if you want." I could have spent all night kissing and licking those breasts, but I wanted more. Somehow my pants were now down to my knees and I wanted to go further than "waist up." We were both panting out loud and trembling when she pushed me away and said, "No further, we have to stop now."

I walked her the two blocks to where she was staying and the cool night air calmed us both down. After a lingering kiss at the door she went inside. She was leaving the next day and I knew that the probability of us ever getting together again was very slim. I slowly walked back to my place, took a cold shower, and climbed into a very lonely bed—it was just after midnight. I was awakened by the ringing of my door bell—the clock showed that it was not yet 6 AM. Who in the hell could be at my front door at this ungodly hour? I slipped into a bathrobe and answered the door—there was Susan, looking bright and cheerful in a jogging outfit. She said, "Can I come in?" I stood aside and she started in—taking off her sweatshirt as she came through the door. There were those beautiful breasts again, looking straight ahead. By the time I closed the door she was shedding her jogging pants—there was nothing underneath. I looked at her and said, "What's going on, have you had a change of heart?" She smiled and said, "That's the lady's prerogative, isn't it?" She was now running up the stairs to the master bedroom—her naked rear end was just as spectacular as the view from the front! She jumped onto my unmade bed and beckoned for me to join her. I told her to hold her thoughts as I needed to brush my teeth and throw some water on my face—I wanted to be wide awake for what was about to happen! When I returned to the bedroom I dropped my bathrobe and looked down at her lying on the bed—what a beautiful sight. She had such an even tan that it was evident that she sunbathed in the nude. Her pubic hair was carefully trimmed to the shape of a very small triangle that could be covered by the tiniest of bikinis. I noticed a small area by her right hip bone that was very white—not deeply tanned like the rest of her body. Later she told me that she always placed a small patch on that particular spot when she was tanning herself so that she could tell what her real skin color was.

I joined her on the bed and asked, "What made you change your mind?" She said, "I had a long talk with my sister after you dropped me off last night, I told her how unhappy my marriage was and how I needed to move on with my life. My sister gave me some good advice—she told me to seize the moment and do what my heart told me to do. That's why I'm here—now, no more talking!" We began slowly—kissing and touching each other until we were both at a fever pitch. I reached between her legs and tested her wetness with my fingers—suddenly I felt something that should not have been there, something was sticking out of her vagina—like a wire or a stem! I stopped, looked at her and asked, "What's going on—is there something that you need to tell me?" She giggled and replied, "Why don't you take a good look down there and find out for yourself." I quickly obeyed and moved down the bed to where I could see just what this obstacle might be. There was a small stem slightly protruding from her labia. I grasped it with my fingertips and gave a gentle pull—on the other end of the stem was a CHERRY! I held it up like a trophy and we both began to laugh. She said, "Now that you have my cherry, what are you going to do with it?" I did what any red blooded, sensible male in that situation would do—I ate it!

We enjoyed incredible sex—no, lovemaking, for the next several hours until she reminded me that she was scheduled to catch a plane to Texas before noon. I took her to the airport and it was indeed sweet sorrow to see her leave—she did not want to get on the airplane but I knew that she must. We would meet again after she had resolved her relationship with her husband. Our relationship lasted almost one year—she did divorce her husband, took a job as a stewardess with Continental Airlines and moved to Houston. Finally we both moved on in different directions.

The airline was still expanding in the late eighties and I was getting close to a Captain bid. Instead of enjoying my seniority on the B-727 as a copilot until I could move into the left seat, I decided to take a bid as a DC-10 First Officer. I wanted to fly the "wide-body" airplanes that seemed to be the future for the airline. I had never flown anything as big as the DC-10—the only plane larger was the B-747—and I started training with great anticipation. I had started school on the DC-10 almost 10 years earlier as a Second Officer— I hoped that this training would have the same result. Maybe I would be awarded a Captain vacancy before my training was complete. No such luck! I finished my training and reported to the line as a copilot in Denver. My first trip, the IOE, was DEN to ORD and on to DTW. After a layover in Detroit, I flew to LAX for another layover. This was very different flying than what I was used to on the narrow body aircraft, where there were usually three or four legs each day. The longer legs on the DC-10 were not yet boring as there was plenty to keep a new copilot busy, but I felt that eventually it would become less of a challenge. The DC-10 was much more automated than the

727 and ninety percent of the time the autopilot was in charge. To complete my IOE, I continued from LAX to HNL and on to LIH (the airport of Lihue on the island of Kauai). That short leg from Honolulu to Lihue was the only fun part of the trip. We were assigned to fly the DC-10-30 model on that short segment—an airplane with bigger engines and longer range than the other model, the DC-10-10. We took off from Honolulu with only about 50 passengers—a very light load for such a big airplane. We were airborne very quickly and I knew that I had my hands full with this powerful, light machine. We were cleared to 15,000 feet and the nose attitude to keep the speed at 250 knots was about thirty degrees—I felt like I was flying a rocket, not a passenger carrier! I leveled off at the assigned altitude and before I knew it the airspeed warning was going off—we were exceeding the speed limits of the aircraft! The check pilot was roaring with laughter—he knew that I was not prepared for the performance of this plane on such a short flight. By the time I had caught up with the plane it was time to descend—the airport of Lihue was straight ahead. The Captain pointed to a lighthouse and said, "Head for that point and you will be lined up for the runway." I was high and fast and still behind the power curve as I called for gear down and reached for the speed brake handle. The Captain said, "Let's see if you can make it without using the speed brakes." I raised the nose to dissipate some airspeed and called for flaps when we were slow enough. As I turned toward the airport the nose of the plane was so high that I could only see the last part of the runway. I felt like I was making a carrier approach! We touched down on the first third of the runway and comfortably made the last turnoff—but I was not very pleased with my performance. The Captain debriefed me later and stated that he had tested me on that last flight to see how I would handle such a situation. He commended me on my airmanship but gave me some advice that I remembered for the rest of my career. He said, "Never let the airplane get ahead of you—if you feel rushed or uncomfortable, take it around and get yourself set up better for the next approach." I also gained a lot of respect for that big old DC-10!

The fourth engine failure that I experienced in my career with United occurred on the DC-10. The most senior trip in Denver was a nonstop to Honolulu, layover for about thirty hours and fly back nonstop. The only down side was that the return trip was an all-nighter that departed HNL in the evening and arrived in Denver shortly after dawn. I was never senior enough to fly that trip on a monthly schedule but was occasionally assigned to it on reserve. The Captain I was with on this particular trip was a friend and someone that I had flown with many times before. Usually the Captain flew to HNL and the copilot flew the return redeye. He asked me if I would fly the first leg and I was happy to say yes. We were departing to the north from Stapleton International Airport, using the longest runway as we were quite heavy that day. The engineer or Second Officer was none other than old Howard, the father of the nympho Mary Ann and a scab during the strike. He was now over the age of sixty but refused to retire so he was now flying as a non-pilot or S/O. I could never personally understand why a pilot would want to continue flying after the age of sixty as a flight engineer, but quite a few chose that path. Most, with a few exceptions, were worthless. They had been flying as Captain in command of the crew and now were relegated to being the junior man in the cockpit—the one who ordered the coffee for the pilots from the stews, the one who had to go fix the movie projector or unplug the toilet, the one who had to do the walk-around in foul weather. Needless to say, most of these "retreads" were not happy with their job and consequently were borderline incompetent. They abused the sick leave policy and had no motivation to do a professional job in the cockpit. Howard was a typical retread—he sat at his engineer's desk and read a book or worked a crossword puzzle—when he was not taking a nap.

I started the takeoff roll on runway 35R and everything looked normal. Rotation speed was about 135 knots on this day and I was rapidly approaching that speed when I felt a heavy "thud" and the aircraft veered sharply to the right. I pushed in full left rudder and glanced at the engine instruments. I noticed the number three engine gauges spinning down and at the same time the Captain called, "Engine failure!" As my left hand was still on the throttles, I pulled them to the idle position and immediately placed the number two engine into full reverse. My feet were on the rudder pedals and I began moderate to heavy braking—we were more than halfway down the runway and still over 100 knots. The Captain was completing the engine shut down procedure as we reached the last turn off and was able to take control of the aircraft and taxi clear of the runway. Not a word had been heard from "Howard" during the entire event. When we were clear of the runway I looked back at him and he was just sitting there, staring straight ahead and shaking! I said to the Captain, "Charley, I don't thing we're going to get much help from Howard!" The Captain looked at Howard and shouted, "Howard, shut the fuel off and do your part of the checklist, then call the company and tell them that we've had an engine blow!" Howard finally stammered, "Which engine failed?" I almost laughed but the Captain was now really pissed at poor old Howard and started barking orders for the exact procedures that were expected from the Second Officer. When we arrived back at the gate, Howard was trying to record the problem in the maintenance log book but his hands were trembling so badly that he could not write legibly. The Captain was justifiably fed up and told Howard to leave the cockpit. Then he looked at me and asked, "What the hell should I do with that worthless asshole?" I could only shrug and say, "That's your decision, Captain, that's why you get paid the big bucks." We both laughed.

I flew the DC-10 for one year only and frankly that was long enough—it was definitely a boring type of flying. From Denver we flew into only ten or so major airports and the flights were generally long and tedious. Although the DC-10 flew at fast speeds—mach .86 was pretty much standard—it seemed to me to always be too nose high. I felt that the aircraft was not flying at the correct angle of attack for best fuel efficiency. It was definitely not the best aerodynamically designed aircraft that I flew. Most of the layovers were in large cities such as New York, Chicago or Philadelphia. The only interesting layover I recall was one in Philadelphia—we were at that time staying at the Belleview Stratford Hotel, one of the classiest hotels on the east coast. This was, of course, before the notorious episode of "Legionnaire's Disease" that almost put the hotel out of business. Our scheduled departure from PHL was very early in the morning which necessitated a pick up from the hotel before it was daylight. I usually was the first in the crew to arrive for the limo and on this particular morning I decided to step outside and get a breath of fresh air while waiting for the other crew members. Suddenly a taxi pulled up to the curb and the driver got out, opened the trunk and took out two large items. One was a really big "boom box" and the other was a huge tennis bag—more like a duffel bag—that contained at least six tennis rackets and what appeared to be nothing else but dirty clothes. The driver set these items on the curb and opened the back door for the passenger, who was fast asleep. The cabbie shook the passenger until he awakened and sleepily crawled out. I immediately recognized the passenger as John M., at that time still one of the top tennis players in the world, although his career was slowly on the decline. Mr. M. stumbled over to me, gave me a bleary-eyed stare, reached into his pocket and handed me a crumpled up twenty dollar bill. He blurted out, "Don't just stand there, take care of my bags, you jerk!" Perhaps I should have taken the twenty and helped carry his bags into the hotel, but I could only laugh and handed him back his tip. At first he looked like he was going to take a swing at me—then he blinked and apologized, "Sorry, I thought you were a bellman." About this time the real bellman arrived and took care of the famous tennis pro's luggage. As he was walking through the door into the lobby, John M. could not resist one last insult. He said, "Shit, you airline pilots look like doormen—you just get paid a lot more!"

Every twelve months all airline pilots (at least with United) were required to have a proficiency check, a three day event at the Denver training center. As my first PC was coming up on the DC-10 I started to study the books, a ritual that we all went through in order to refresh ourselves on all the numbers and procedures that were committed to memory. Just when I was beginning to feel that I was ready for my check ride I was notified that I had been awarded a CAPTAIN BID on the B-727! I would start training for that assignment before my PC was due on the DC-10. I was elated to finally get a bid to the left seat on my favorite airplane. After almost 21 years with the airline, surely I was prepared for those "heavy responsibilities of command!" The only downside was that my assignment was to Chicago, still the most junior domicile with the airline, and it appeared that I would be on reserve for quite a long time. At that time nothing could dampen my enthusiasm.

Due to the fact that it had been over a year since I had flown the 727 as a First Officer, I was required to take the whole transition course—this would be the fourth time that I had been through that particular school. The only difficult part was getting used to flying with my RIGHT HAND on the throttles! Every airplane that I had ever flown, both in the Navy and with the airline (as a copilot) had the throttle(s) on the left side! The other big change was that my headset, called a minitel, was now plugged into my left ear! The school went according to schedule and my check ride, called a rating ride since an FAA inspector was required to be present, was thorough and fair. The only unpleasant part of the rating ride was the fact that the "check airman" conducting the check was a "scab" who had been hiding out in the training center since the strike of 1985. What should have been a most pleasant event was somewhat degraded by that individual. The overall atmosphere in the Training Center had dramatically changed since the strike of 1985. As I left the training center after that final check, I began to think about how we might make the overall training program a more enjoyable experience. I was in deep thought as I walked to my car in the employee parking lot. It was nearly dark on a late fall afternoon and the temperature was starting to turn quite cool. As I approached where my automobile was parked, I noticed a small table and two tiny chairs sitting next to my car. Sitting on one of those tiny chairs was my girlfriend at the time, Barbara was her name, and she was dressed to the nines! On the table, which was covered with a small linen cloth, was a bottle of Dom Perignon in a silver ice bucket. There were two crystal champagne glasses filled to the rim with the chilled bubbly. My somber mood turned to one of surprise and glee as Barbara rose and made a toast to the NEW CAPTAIN! I'm sure that we were a strange sight as we embraced and then sat down at the tiny table and drank our champagne in the failing light, all alone in the parking lot! I was dressed in my finest suit as that was the custom at the time. A new Captain getting his rating ride tried to look better than the check airman or the FAA inspector. I hope that tradition continues to this day. As we finished the bubbly, Barbara told me that she had made reservations at one of the finer restaurants in Denver for that evening—it was a great night of celebration!

Chapter Eighteen

"The Only Thing Worse Than a Captain Who Never Flew as Copilot is a Copilot Who Once was a Captain!"

I decided to make my stay in Chicago, regardless of how long it might be, as painless as possible. I had no intention of leaving my residence in Denver, but I knew that I needed to rent a place near O'Hare while on reserve. Commuting (living somewhere different that your assigned domicile) was becoming more and more popular with the pilots and many carried it to unbelievable extremes. I knew a pilot who lived in Scotland and flew out of New York—another who lived in New Zealand and was domiciled in Honolulu. Because United did not fly from New Zealand direct to Honolulu, that pilot had to fly first to the west coast (LAX) then connect to another flight to Honolulu! It took an entire day for that pilot to get to work!

I found a nice apartment complex in the Chicago suburb of Wheeling. It had all of the amenities I wanted, plus the most important of all—a heated underground parking garage! I was familiar with the severe winters in the Chicago area and I wanted to have every advantage possible for my stay. I drove my "old trusty Chevy Blazer" from Denver to Chicago and hoped that it would last for the duration. No such luck. It froze solid during the first cold snap when it was parked out in the open in the employee's parking lot at O'Hare. I was forced to trade it in on a new Jeep Cherokee—suitable not only for the Chicago climate but just the vehicle for Denver—called by some the "Colorado Cadillac." The winter of 1989-90 was one of the coldest on record in Chicago, with one bitter storm after another. The bad weather caused massive delays at O'Hare and this affected the entire system. Reserve crews were worked to the maximum and it finally resulted in the necessity of having "field standby" crews at the airport. This meant that if a reserve pilot was not assigned a specific trip, he/she would be required to report to the field and "stand by" for the unexpected. Every single time that I was called out for field standby, I was used! Since you never knew if you would be assigned a one, two or three day trip, you packed for the maximum. Once I was given a two day trip but reassigned so many times that I was actually away for a total of six days!

At this time reserve pilots were given ten days off each month—three periods of two days off and one four day off period. Often you worked into your "scheduled days off" because of weather delays and reassignments. In reality the only time that you could make any sort of plans was during that four-day off period. Generally, that was when I returned to Denver. I needed that time to rest, but usually spent it skiing during that first winter. The trips that I flew during that first year in Chicago were varied, to say the least. Often I flew with a new copilot and a new flight engineer—we were all a bit green in our assigned positions. Since the B-727 was such a versatile aircraft, we flew to all four corners of the continental United States and every place in between. In addition we even had a few trips north or south of the border. Flights into the Canadian cities, such as Toronto or Vancouver, were routine—but trips down into Mexico were a whole different story. There were two aircraft in the entire United fleet that were equipped with a special navigation system called OMEGA. These two airplanes were used to fly from Chicago to the Mexican resort of Cancun, on the Yucatan Peninsula. The Omega navigation system was basically a poor man's version of INS (Inertial Navigation System) and was sufficient to legally fly across the Gulf of Mexico—where there were no navaids. Although I had many years of experience flying the B-727, I had never flown one of those two Omega equipped planes. During training that system was skipped with a lame explanation that "you will probably never see one of those planes in your career." There was a special section in the flight manual that covered the procedures to follow with the Omega system—it was about thirty pages long!

One night I received a phone call from the crew desk (not unusual) that I was desperately needed to fly an early morning trip due to the scheduled crew being stuck in a snow storm in Buffalo, NY. The trip that I was assigned was from ORD to Cancun and return—the departure was about five hours from the time I received the call. I really needed to study those Omega procedures right now! Since my flight bag was at operations, I got up (after less than three hours sleep), packed my bag, donned my uniform and headed to the airport.

The roads were icy and slippery in the Chicago area that night—the only cars on the road were driven by cops, drunks or AIRLINE PILOTS at such an ungodly hour! When I arrived at United Flight Operations it was three hours before scheduled departure—plenty of time to review the procedures for the Omega system. While I was studying those procedures, the copilot assigned to the trip arrived, introduced himself and announced that this was his very first trip as a new copilot. He had never flown to Cancun and had no idea what Omega was all about. We both started studying the book when the Flight Engineer arrived—he did not even know where Cancun was located! We all laughed and tried to prepare ourselves as rapidly as possible. Thankfully the trip was delayed for over one hour—all flights were delayed that morning, many were cancelled. I silently hoped that one of the cancelled flights would be ours—no such luck. The copilot and I looked over the flight plan and the weather report for Cancun. Neither of us was able to read the weather sequence or forecast. I knew that international weather reports were somewhat different than those for the domestic stations but this looked like gibberish. I sheepishly approached the dispatcher—the guru of weather reports—and admitted that I was not able to read the weather for Cancun. The dispatcher looked at the piece of paper that I handed him and laughed. The report had gotten garbled in transmission—no one could read it! He printed out a new report and it too was garbled—something was wrong with the system in Mexico. Then the dispatcher assured me that the weather was fine in Cancun and would remain so for our arrival. He requested that I contact him while enroute and he would provide an accurate weather synopsis. The copilot and I agreed on one condition—increase the fuel! We finally agreed to add as much fuel as possible before our departure. Since it was planned as a full load of passengers (Chicagoans escaping the winter weather for a nice vacation in Cancun) there was not room for very much fuel unless I chose to offload baggage. I did not want those vacationers to arrive in Cancun without their SCUBA and snorkeling gear, so I opted to add fuel without restrictions on passengers and baggage.

Finally we departed on our flight to Cancun—almost two hours late. The copilot and I had figured out the workings of the Omega system sufficiently so that we felt safe to fly across the gulf. Once we departed the Chicago area the weather improved rapidly and it appeared to be a fine day to fly to the Yucatan Peninsula. Unfortunately we were not able to contact United dispatch before we were over water and out of radio range. There was not a cloud in the sky as we left the gulf coast and headed out to sea—everything seemed just fine. When we were about 100 miles from our destination we noticed that there appeared to be some major buildups ahead—soon they would show up on our weather radar as severe thunderstorms. We were monitoring the approach frequency for Cancun and started to pick up a lot of chatter—sounded like things were getting exciting down there. When we checked in with approach control we were given terse instructions: "Hold over the airport at 20,000 feet." This was certainly not a legal holding clearance in the U.S. where we would have been issued a specific navigation point to hold, direction of turns and an expected approach clearance time. "When in Rome, etc"—we headed toward where the airport was located. It was directly under the largest thunderstorm in the area and the tops were over thirty thousand feet! I decided that I could hold at 20,000 feet if I flew a pattern that circumnavigated the storm and remained in the clear. Suddenly I noticed other aircraft in the area doing exactly the same! I spotted a Northwest Airlines 727 as it went by very close to our aircraft and since we were all on the same frequency I gave him a call: "Northwest, this is United—what is your holding clearance?" He responded, "Same as yours, I guess, hold at 20,000 over the airport!" There were at least three other American planes holding in the same pattern as well as an unknown number of Mexican airliners—they were being given instructions in Spanish so I was not able to follow their progress. Basically we all watched out for each other and eventually we were allowed to enter the landing pattern once the storm had passed.

Our plane was one of the very last to land and fuel was becoming a major concern. I was very happy that I had added as much fuel as possible—actually I was beginning to feel that I really did not care if the passengers had their baggage or not! I breathed a sigh of relief as we rolled onto the runway and taxied to the parking area. I hoped that the other crew members did not notice that there was a small trickle of perspiration slowly making its way down my face! As I approached our assigned parking slot I spotted the taxi director giving me signals—everything seemed normal. Suddenly the tower controller shouted, "United, stop! Hold your position!" I came to a halt even though the taxi director was urging me to come forward into the gate area. After a minute or two of silence I transmitted, "What's the problem, we are under control of the taxi director—can't we continue to park?" More silence. Then I glanced around the cockpit, hoping to find something that would explain the problem. Oh shit, the copilot had not retracted the flaps after landing—one of the basic procedures that are usually automatic. One of the "secret" signals that were worked out between pilots and controllers after hijacking began was to lower the flaps while on the ground—indicating to tower personnel that there was a problem in the cockpit that could not be transmitted in the open. Obviously the Mexican controllers were "perplexed" when they noticed our flaps extended and they did the proper thing—telling us to stop. I reached over and raised the flaps—the copilot was terribly embarrassed that he had failed to do his procedure; I was embarrassed that I had not noticed, and the flight engineer was oblivious to the whole situation! After the flaps were retracted, I asked the copilot to request that we continue our taxi. We were quickly cleared to our gate with the subtle remark, "Glad that everything is okay, senor!"

We had been scheduled to spend almost three hours on the ground in Cancun, but because of our late arrival we were rushing to turn the aircraft as quickly as possible and depart on time for the return to Chicago. I asked the copilot to program the Omega system for our flight to ORD while I went inside the terminal to contact the dispatcher. United maintained only a skeleton staff in Cancun and we had actually been released for the return trip when we departed O'Hare early that morning. I needed to check on weather and decide if the fuel we had planned was still adequate. Everything was as planned and the weather was improving in the Chicago area with only scattered clouds forecast for our arrival. When I returned to the plane the passengers were aboard and all was ready for an on time departure. I did not take the time to double check if the copilot had properly loaded the Omega system—the last time that I would make that mistake! It was the copilot's leg and I would handle the communications and navigation systems. After we were airborne we were cleared to our first fix, geographical coordinates for an imaginary spot in the middle of the Gulf of Mexico. All we had to do was follow the guidance of the Omega system which was interlocked with the autopilot. The copilot engaged the autopilot and selected NAVIGATION on the control panel. Immediately the aircraft began a turn back towards Cancun! I took over the controls, disengaged the autopilot and returned to a northerly heading. Then I gave the aircraft back to the copilot and told him to hold his heading while I checked out the Omega system. He had loaded the navigation fixes into the computer backward! We could not use the system for navigation across the Gulf! I had to make a quick decision: Dump fuel and return to Cancun to properly program the system, or; fake it and hand fly the aircraft using dead reckoning across those few hundred miles where there were no navigation aids. I personally had no problem with plan 2—the skies were clear and we knew what the winds aloft were from our trip to Cancun earlier. The other crew members went along with my decision and we continued northward—obviously not legal as far as the FAA was concerned, but logical in my way of thinking. In reality we had a lot of fun working as a crew and planning what headings to fly—navigating like the trans-ocean pilots of thirty years earlier! The copilot hand flew (he needed the practice) and I gave him headings to follow. Our first real navigation fix was a VOR located at Grand Isle, just south of New Orleans and I hoped that we would be within five or ten miles of our planned track if the Omega had been working properly. I figured that our aircraft would appear on the US radar screens about the time that our VOR would lock on Grand Isle. If we were too far off track we would have a bit of explaining to do to the controllers in the US. When the needle swung to home in on Grand Isle we all breathed a sigh of relief—we were right on track!

Once again I had learned a valuable lesson—always follow the proper procedures, even when they seem redundant or cumbersome. We came out okay on this occasion but I did not want to press my luck in the future. I also found that it was proper to think of what was best for the passengers—what would I want to happen if I were sitting in the back of the cabin. If what was best for the passengers was SAFE, then it was probably the best decision—even if it stretched the "legalities" and FAR rules just a bit.

The only telephone that I had while in Chicago was a cell phone—a fairly new device at that time and mine was about the size of a quart of milk. Nevertheless it gave me a lot of freedom as I did not have to sit in my apartment waiting for a call from the friendly crew desk. Generally, I was used so much on reserve that I was often assigned a new trip when I returned to Chicago from an earlier assignment. One evening when I returned from a trip, I was indeed given a new sequence that departed the next morning. Just as I was retiring for the night, the crew desk called and stated that I was not legal for that assigned trip as it would give me too much time without a legal break. These were contractual legalities and the individual pilot could not keep up with each "legal" requirement—that's where the computers at the crew desk came in. The scheduler in this case told me that he did not have another assignment for me at the present but I could count on getting a trip sometime the next day. At least I got to sleep-in that next morning. I had not heard from the crew desk by ten AM—very unusual—so I decided that I would go for a jog. About the only time that I could not carry my cell phone was when I was on a run, so I called the crew desk to tell them that I was going to be away from the phone for thirty minutes or so. When I identified myself to the crew desk I was told that I had been WOPed for the day! This meant that I was With-Out-Pay for missing a trip assignment! The scheduler stated that he had personally called me twice earlier that morning, about six AM, and both times received a recording that the number dialed was "not in service" at the time. He went to the next name on the reserve list and reported me as being "unavailable." I started to argue with the controller but was told that I needed to talk with the Duty Flight Manager—a management pilot who was assigned the dubious duty of being in charge of all flight operations. Each week the Duty Flight Manager was changed—one week of that stress was enough for anyone!

The crew scheduler transferred my call to the Duty Manager and it turned out to be an old friend of mine from Denver whose name was Mack. Before I had a chance to explain, he started ribbing me about missing a call, asking if maybe I was out chasing women instead of listening for the phone. I replied, "Mack, I never chase women at six AM and they sure as hell are not interested in me at that hour!" He laughed and said that when the report crossed his desk with my name on it, he figured that something was not right. I assured him that I "slept with my cell phone" and it did not ring that morning. Then I asked if the report listed the number that was called to contact me. After checking the report, Mack repeated the number that the crew man called to contact me—the last two digits were transposed! Mack asked me to hang up and stand by the phone for a few minutes. After about five minutes he called back. He said, "I called the number in the report and got a recording that that number was not in service, then I talked to the crew man. You are back on call, you won't lose any pay, and the scheduler will be talking to you soon." The scheduler did call me later with an apology. He stated that he was very busy that morning and was a bit stressed. When he dialed my number and heard the recording, he did not recheck if he had dialed correctly, instead he hit the redial button and got the same message. He needed a warm body quickly so he went to the next name on the list and reported me as unavailable—which was what he was supposed to do. Then he assigned me a trip later that day— I still had time for my run before departure!

My cell phone was a great convenience—but it also gave me a few humorous moments. One evening I was having dinner at a local bistro—a TGIF restaurant that was near my apartment—when the phone rang. Since the crew desk was the only place that had my cell number, I always knew who was calling. On this occasion I was eating at the bar as all the tables and booths were busy and it was very noisy—sounded just like a bar in a rowdy bistro! When I answered the phone I had to practically scream to be heard. The crew scheduler asked several times for me to identify myself before he was sure that he had the right party. Then he could not resist asking, "Just where the hell are you? Sounds like some beer joint with a big party going on!" I'm sure that almost all calls to pilots were made to their home phone and were answered by the pilot or spouse in a quiet environment. Since the crew desk had no way of knowing that my number was a cell phone, they were always surprised to catch me at unusual places. After the scheduler assigned me a trip for the next day, he said that when he got off his shift he was going to stop by that TGIF's for a cold beer. Unfortunately I was long gone before he arrived.

In spite of the lousy weather in Chicago, in spite of working almost every day that I was on call, and in spite of flying some pretty rotten trips with junior copilots and brand new engineers, I was having a real blast that first year as a Captain. As an old saying went: the best part of being the Captain is that you already know who the asshole in the left seat is! Although I did not notice any extra respect from the crew schedulers—they treated everyone the same, whether you were a new hire Second Officer or a grizzled senior Captain—I did notice that flight attendants, gate agents, mechanics, and ground personnel were a bit more attentive when they were listening to a pilot with four stripes on his sleeve. The Captain was also treated with a bit more respect from hotel personnel and waiters in restaurants—maybe it was just that those people were more respectful to "older" people, but it made me feel good to have the "scrambled eggs" on my uniform cap.

United was still expanding in 1990 and I was beginning to hope that my stay in Chicago would not last more than one year or two. At least time was really flying since I was staying so busy with reserve trips—many months I ran out of time a week or so before the month ended. The worst scenario was when I would "almost" run out of time, i.e. I was eligible for a very short trip of only one or two hour's duration. Most scheduled trips involved more time than that but there was always the slim chance of a ferry flight or even a test hop. These types of trips were infrequent but it was not worth taking a chance and leaving town while you were still on call. I tried it one time only and was a nervous wreck. I had less than one hour of legal time remaining for the month with three days to go and I decided to take a chance and catch an early flight to Denver. I boarded my flight and placed my carryon luggage in the overhead bin above my seat—my cell phone was in that bag. The flight departed the gate and started taxiing to the runway when my phone started to ring! Cell phones were still rare then and passengers were looking around to see what was going on as my phone kept ringing—I could not (would not) get out of my seat to answer that phone. I had to sweat it out until we landed in Denver, and I did indeed do a bit of sweating! I contacted the crew desk after arriving in Denver and they assured me that they had not called and I was not needed for a trip, at least not at that time. I caught the next flight back to Chicago and sat in my apartment for the next two days. I was not called but at least I was available!

Finally summer arrived in Chicago and the weather turned from cold and miserable to hot and miserable! Spring and fall seemed to last about one week each. United decided that summer to start a new service from Chicago to Greensboro, North Carolina and began this service in the middle of the month, after bids were posted, bid and awarded. These trips were now to be flown by reserve crews. However, I was somehow assigned a series of those trips and it was almost like flying a real line—I knew when my next trip was and I flew with the same crew for the whole series. The trip was a real piece of cake—it departed ORD in the evening, flew nonstop to GSO (Greensboro), a flight of about two hours, and departed the next evening back to Chicago. We flew that schedule three times in a row for a six-day-on, two-day-off pattern. It looked bad on paper but was really a very easy trip with a nice long layover in a beautiful city. The copilot that I flew with was a real hustler named Bob who propositioned every female he came in contact with—especially flight attendants. He would walk up to three stews and ask the closest one if she would go out with him that evening. When she turned him down, he asked the next one the same question without a pause! Rejection was not in his vocabulary! His theory was that perhaps one in a hundred would say yes and so he simply moved to the next female and tried again, and again, and again! Bob had no luck with the flight attendants that we flew with on those trips so he began to hustle the lady at the reception desk of our lay over hotel—actually a motel, like a Ramada Inn. She was an attractive lady who appeared to be in her late thirties and was evidently single. By the third trip Bob convinced her to go out with him. She agreed on one condition, that her girl friend who worked the switchboard in the back room go along too. I had noticed a very attractive pair of legs that were sometimes visible from that back room when we checked in each time but had not seen the rest of the person that belonged to those great gams. I agreed to go along to make it a foursome and the switchboard operator stepped out to the desk—she was a real knockout! The two ladies were due to get off their shift at eleven PM, about an hour away, giving Bob and I time to change into civvies.

At eleven on the dot, Bob and I were there in the lobby to pick up our "dates." Before we left in the receptionist's car, my "date" said that she needed to call her husband to ask him if it was okay for her to go out that evening. I was taken aback a bit but decided that I would at least go along for the ride. We drove to a nightclub several miles away—the type of club that was "members only" (you could buy a temporary one night membership for five dollars) and you were expected to bring your own booze. The lady who drove had a bottle of scotch in her car and I found that I could buy beer by the bottle—we were all happy. The place was not at all crowded as it was in the middle of the week and there were only about a dozen couples around a rather large dance floor. The entertainment consisted of a man and his wife who played musical instruments and sang—actually they were quite good and joined our table during their break for a drink or two. We all had an enjoyable evening and it appeared that Bob had finally found his "one in a hundred." My "date" and I had been dancing the fast numbers—she was a much better dancer that I—and finally we stepped onto the dance floor to some slow music. She pressed her body against mine and began a very seductive grind. I kept thinking about her husband whom she had called before leaving the motel. She suggested that we go to her friend's car in the parking lot for a bit of "private time!" I asked her if she had told her husband where she was going after work—she said yes but not to worry as he was home taking care of the children. I asked her how many children, she said two, and then I asked her what her husband did for a living. She said, "He's a bodyguard for some Teamster Union officials who are involved with the mafia in the Greensboro area." I immediately lost any interest in romance and said, "Goodnight!" I returned to our table and said that it was time for me to call it a day. We returned to the motel and I fought off the advances of my date in the back seat as best I could—she was a real handful! I thanked her for a lovely evening and quickly made my way to my room. Five minutes later as I was brushing my teeth, I heard a soft knock on the door—I knew that the person outside was spelled TROUBLE! I reluctantly opened the door and my "date" stepped inside, just to "talk."

The "talking" part lasted only a very few minutes. I was clad only in my under shorts and suddenly she started to take off her clothes—promising all the while that I was in for a treat that I would never forget. She said, "My breasts are small but so incredibly sensitive—I want you to kiss them and I will show you just how it turns me on!" I was starting to get desperate. My bad side was telling me to take advantage of the situation and enjoy a fun romp in the sack with this attractive female. My conscience was telling me to get her out of my room as soon as possible. My common sense was telling me that her husband could burst into the room at any moment and beat the crap out of both of us! I knew that if she continued to take off her clothes I would succumb to the weaknesses of the flesh! I needed to tell a huge lie. I said, "I need to warn you that I have a SEXUALLY TRANSMITTED DISEASE that has not responded to treatment and I don't have any protection tonight." She looked me in the eye and I saw her lust turn to dismay and then disgust in a few seconds. She began to put her clothes back on and I helped her out the door. Her last remark was, "Thanks for nothing, you prick!"

Twenty years earlier I would not have passed up such a one night stand. Was I getting older or was I getting wiser—perhaps both. At least I felt good about my decision the next morning. My copilot, Bob, had a different outlook—he had "scored" with his date and I had to hear all the details several times during the next few days! I was beginning to feel like a Captain—an old Captain!

Most of the trips I flew as a junior Captain were filled with more light-hearted events. When the weather was good and the skies were not too crowded, there was a lot of good humored dialogue between the controllers and the pilots. We enjoyed putting "one over" on the controllers every chance we got and they in turn loved to get the best of the pilots—all in fun and with safety in mind, of course. One morning I departed Newark Airport enroute to Denver at about the same time that a United DC-10 departed Philadelphia, also destined for Denver. The DC-10 was in front of our 727 and climbing to a higher altitude. We could see the DC-10 about ten miles ahead and when he leveled off at FL350 (35,000 feet) he was leaving a visible contrail that was easy for us to follow at our altitude of FL310. The DC-10 was equipped with

INS—a navigation system that would allow him to fly point to point instead of following the airways as we were required to do in our old 727. We were on the same frequency when the DC-10 leveled at his cruise altitude and requested direct to Iowa City, a navigation point about 800 miles away that was not available for us with our equipment. By going direct the DC-10 would cut the corners on the airways and save time and fuel. New York Center cleared the DC-10 to proceed direct. The copilot was flying that particular leg on my aircraft and I was handling the communications. I decided to pull the leg of the controller just a bit and transmitted, "New York Center, United 403, request present position direct Iowa City." There was a short pause—I'm sure the controller was checking my "strip" to see what navigation system I had—then the controller responded, "United 403, what navigation system are you using to go direct?" Since a couple of our planes were equipped with Omega, it was possible that we were indeed able to navigate direct—the one we were flying was not one of those! I transmitted to the center, "United 403 is equipped with the latest technology called LAR." After another pause wherein I envisioned the controller asking his co-workers if anyone had ever heard of "LAR" he reluctantly cleared us to proceed direct to Iowa City. Obviously he did not want to admit to everyone listening on the frequency that he did not know about this new system called LAR! I told the copilot to simply follow the DC-10 ahead and above us as he was navigating direct. I had recognized the pilot's voice as one of my friends flying the DC-10 and he had figured out what we were doing—following him to Iowa City! Soon we were switched to Cleveland Center and then Indianapolis Center. Each new controller seemed hesitant to query me about our navigation system but I could sense that they were all trying to figure out if we were legitimate. Since we were heading direct to IOW, thanks to our friends in the DC-10, it appeared on the radar screens that we were navigating normally.

When south of Chicago, the DC-10 climbed to FL390 and we followed with a climb to FL350. Unfortunately the DC-10 now encountered stronger headwinds at his altitude and we began to pass underneath his airplane. We were now having a bit of trouble with our headings as we still could not navigate to IOW with our systems. The DC-10 pilot recognized our problem as we got into the lead and began to discretely transmit headings for us, such as, "Left two degrees." The controllers had been patient with this whole farce for about two hours and finally they had had enough. A new voice contacted us from Minneapolis Center—the deep voice of a senior controller or supervisor—who said, "Alright United 403, we give up down here, no one has ever heard of this new system called LAR—just what does it stand for?" After a pregnant pause so that all aircraft on the frequency could listen to my response, I transmitted, "LAR stands for Looks About Right—we've been following the contrail above to Iowa City!" After several guffaws from other pilots listening in, the supervisor responded, "Good one United, our compliments on your sense of humor. Fly your present heading for a vector to the end of runway 26L at Denver—now we will show you how accurate we are down here." Indeed he was a very good sport and gave us headings right to the runway—we all enjoyed that type of professional cooperation between the pilots and controllers.

My first year as a Captain was coming to an end and I was still not close to getting a bid to Denver. I really did not look forward to another winter in the Windy City. Thankfully, an opportunity arrived that would change the direction of my career in aviation. I reported to Denver in October, 1990 for my annual proficiency check, or PC, a three day event that every pilot endured once each year. Many pilots dreaded this "bet your job" check ride and the whole experience had become more stressful since the strike of 1985. The training center was still filled mostly with pilots who had been "loyal" during that strike and the animosity between them and the regular line pilots was still quite elevated. However, there was now a movement toward improving those conditions and a few striking pilots had volunteered to "enter the lion's den" and take jobs as pilot instructors, check pilots and managers. The manager of the B-727 training program, his title was Fleet Captain, was a friend of mine named Dick—a leader of the striking pilots in 1985. He asked me to stop by his office when I finished my proficiency check.

Dick described to me a new program that was beginning to take shape in the training center. The TCA's (Training Check Airmen) were to be replaced with Pilot Instructors (PI's) who would be recruited from junior pilots with training backgrounds. A new position would be created called a Standards Captain, whose duties would be to conduct proficiency check rides, rating rides, and enroute checks. This would be a management position. Dick asked if I would be interested in such a position. I asked him what the requirements were. He answered that they were looking for Captains with at least two years of line experience. I admitted that I only had one year as a Captain under my belt. Dick and I had flown many times together when he was a Captain and I was his copilot. He grinned and said that he was sure that the second year could be waived in my case—I had twenty years with the company and most was flying the B-727 from all three seats. It took me only a few seconds to decide. It would mean that I would be in Denver, not Chicago, and I would have more control over my life than ever before. I made two requests, that I be assigned to the 727 fleet and that I could return to line flying after two years if I chose. Dick agreed and we shook hands. I would start training to be a Standards Captain at the start of the new year. Two more months in Chicago did not seem so bad now!

Chapter Nineteen

"A Male Pilot Is a Confused Soul Who Talks About Women When Flying, and About Flying When With a Woman!"

I reported to the Denver Flight Training Center in January, 1991 to begin my training to become a Standards Captain. It was necessary that B-727 Standards Captains (SCs) were proficient in all three seats on the aircraft so my training began with Second Officer procedures. My instructor for this training was none other than the "good old boy" who had been my teacher in new-hire school, an ex-Air Force pilot named Andy. We were to spend three days together to reacquaint me with the flight engineer's panel and most of the time was spent talking about those earlier days. Andy said that he remembered me from 1968 because I was one of his very first students—I certainly remembered him because he was quite a colorful guy—tall and skinny with a southern drawl that obviously came from somewhere in Texas or Oklahoma. Now Andy was an old pro who had been doing exactly the same thing for the last twenty plus years, instructing new-hire pilots to be flight engineers on the B-727. He knew everything there was to know about the Boeing 727 aircraft and could probably have built one in his garage if he was so inclined!

It had been many years since I had "flown sideways" but I quickly became comfortable in the engineer's seat after just a few hours at the panel. Next I was checked out at the copilot seat by another instructor—not a problem as I had spent many years there not too long ago. Then I began to learn all about the simulators and how to operate them when conducting proficiency checks. This was a lengthy training process that ended up with an FAA inspector giving me a check ride while I was giving a check ride to another Standards Captain! Like every other airline pilot, I had received many check rides in my career, both in simulators and in the real airplane. I had also given many check rides to other pilots while a Navy instructor, but conducting a proficiency check to an entire crew in a simulator was a new experience. Those sims were marvelous machines that were so realistic that it was easy to believe that you were in a real airplane. You could feel the cracks in the pavement during taxi and the sense of sustained acceleration during takeoff was truly amazing. There were also some fun things we could do in those sims—like fly under the Golden Gate Bridge or join up with a military tanker to "take on fuel."

There would be a total of eight SCs in the 727 fleet. Six of us were new to the training center and the other two were holdovers from the TCA program that was being replaced. The two ex-TCAs had been in the Training Center since before the strike of 1985 and did not want to go back to flying the line. They were both nice men, even though they had both been scabs during the strike, and they did a great job of getting the other six of us up to speed in the simulator procedures. The other five of my fellow SCs were really a talented group who impressed me with not only their flying skills but their dedication to the new job at hand. We worked well as a team and formed lasting friendships that endured well beyond our flying days. Soon I settled into a routine schedule of conducting proficiency checks in the simulators, giving rating rides to new Captains or certification rides to new copilots, and, my favorite job—conducting enroute checks. Each Captain on the line was required to be checked once each year while flying a normal trip. These check rides had been conducted by Flight Managers previously but were now to be part of the SC responsibility. The check pilot could show up unannounced and give the Captain and crew an impromptu check ride. My personal program was to contact the Captain at least one day in advance to let him/her know that I would be conducting an enroute check. Thus, there would be no big surprise and the Captain had a chance to make sure that his manuals were up to date and his crew was ready for a check ride. I felt that it was enough pressure on a crew to know that at any time, at any airport, under any conditions, an FAA Air Carrier Inspector could show up and conduct his own check ride. I usually planned my checks so that I would conduct the enroute check on an outbound leg and then displace the Captain on the return leg—that way I had a chance to fly myself. After the check ride was completed I would hand the Captain a First Class seat assignment, tell him/her to go back and relax, and I flew the next leg. I would apologize to the copilot because I would fly a segment that was normally his—I never had a single complaint!

Part of the Standard Captain job was to handle special projects and resolve fleet problems such as complaints from line pilots about certain procedures. Some of those projects involved lots of paperwork—not a lot of fun. On the other hand, some of the complaints that were assigned to me were quite humorous. One complaint was from one of our more notorious Captains—one who wrote a letter almost weekly to complain about almost everything. I requested from the Fleet Captain that I be permitted to respond to that particular Captain personally—assuring my boss that I would not do anything to reflect discredit on management. The Captain who was writing a letter of complaint was none other than my old "friend" from Miami—the furloughed pilot who purloined several beers from my delivery of Coors Beer each week! His latest complaint was about a particular departure procedure from San Jose airport. It was indeed a complex departure that required some serious planning in order to execute properly—especially if the departing aircraft was really heavy, which was usually the case. My response to "Captain Jim" was that Standard Instrument Departures (SIDs) were predicated on average piloting skills from average pilots. If he was having trouble with that departure or any other procedure, perhaps he should notify the Training Center and we would be happy to schedule him for some "remedial training." I ended my letter with the fact that he "still owed me several cases of beer!" The Training Center never ever received another complaint from "Captain Jim."

Standards Captains were paid handsomely—much more than I had ever been paid—but we earned that pay through hard work. We often worked six days a week and the days were sometimes very long. The rewards, in addition to fat paychecks, were certain perks. Our group of SCs worked well together and when one needed some time off, the others were always there to help out. We were also allowed to pick our own trips on the days that were designated as "line flying days." We could select those juicy charters to New Orleans or Bermuda or simply displace a Captain who was flying a nice trip in his awarded line of flying. Once I displaced a Captain on a nice three day trip that involved a beautiful layover in Seattle the first night and a long layover in San Diego the next night. I almost felt guilty when I called the Captain the night before that trip and asked if he minded if I flew his trip for him—of course he was paid as though he had flown the trip himself. He readily agreed—no pilot in his right mind ever refused the chance to be displaced (me being the only possible exception). Another Airline Pilot saying: **THE BEST TRIP IN A PILOT'S SCHEDULE IS NEVER AS GOOD AS DAYS OFF!**

After enjoying another great layover in SEA, our crew departed late the next day for San Diego. One leg per day was a rare treat in the normal 727 schedules where you usually flew at least three legs each day and had duty periods as long as sixteen hours. It was a beautiful evening up and down the entire West Coast and as we passed by the Bay Area we looked in awe as we could see all the way from northern California almost to Los Angeles on a rare perfectly clear night. My copilot was relatively new in his position but was a well qualified ex-military pilot with many flight hours. The Second Officer was a young lady who looked like she could have been my daughter (or granddaughter) and weighed less than one hundred pounds. Everything was going exceptionally well and we were all enjoying some incredible views from our altitude of 37,000 feet. When things are going so smoothly in aviation—look out! Suddenly the autopilot disengaged and lots of yellow warning lights started to appear in the cockpit. Red lights are more serious as immediate action is required, but sometimes those yellow lights can mean that there are some real problems at hand. We had lost our primary hydraulic system (called the "A" system on the 727) and that caused many restrictions. First we had to descend to an altitude of 25,000 feet since we now had lost one of our yaw dampeners—those systems that were so important to the B-727 type aircraft. We requested an immediate descent from air traffic control which triggered the usual inquiry—what is your problem and what are your intentions. We were now working as a team and things were happening quickly and in a most disciplined sequence. I flew the aircraft, the copilot handled communications with the center and the S/O contacted our company dispatch. We were well aware of the restrictions caused by the loss of that hydraulic system—the landing gear would have to be manually cranked down, landing flaps were restricted to only fifteen degrees (normal landing flaps were 30 degrees) and there would be no nose wheel steering once on the ground, meaning that we would have to be towed from the runway. This last problem would mean that the airport runway where we landed would have to be closed for probably 30 minutes. We were now faced with several options. We could turn to our right and land in San Francisco or we could continue to LAX and land there. Or we could continue to our original destination, San Diego! There were problems with each option. If we landed in SFO, our passengers would never get to their destination that evening due to the fact that SAN had a 10:00 PM curfew. If we landed at LAX, the passengers would have to be bussed to SAN and arrive after midnight. I requested to personally speak with our company dispatcher to arrive at the decision that would be best for all concerned.

The dispatcher properly told me that the decision was strictly up to me, the Captain in command. I asked if we had personnel in SAN who could tow the aircraft from the runway and fix it overnight. The answer was yes and no—we had qualified personnel who could tow the plane in but we did not have maintenance people in SAN to fix the problem. Then he stated that our maintenance people could be flown from LAX to SAN and arrive about the same time as our ETA. My decision was made. I told the dispatcher that we would continue to SAN and plan for an on time arrival which was shortly before the curfew. We would burn up a lot more fuel enroute as we were now at a much lower altitude but would still have sufficient reserves when we landed. Then the dispatcher threw in a real zinger! He stated that the weather in SAN was 1000 feet overcast with good visibility underneath but that the conditions were probably going to deteriorate before we arrived. I conferred with the other two crew members and asked them for their candid opinions as to my decision to continue to SAN. If either one had protested I would have decided to land in LAX. Both the copilot and second officer agreed with my decision—hopefully not because I was a Standards Captain, but because it was the proper thing to do. We decided that when we flew by LAX we would re-evaluate and make a final decision.

We had lots of time to prepare for the landing and brief the flight attendants as well as the passengers. I explained as best I could to the passengers that our landing would be the same whether we landed in Los Angeles or San Diego—we would still have to be towed from the runway to the gate and there would be lots of emergency vehicles around with flashing red lights. This was normal procedure. We were well into our descent as we passed just to the east of LAX. We could see the runways clearly and it was a bit tempting to simply land there and not worry about the passengers. I stuck to my belief that if it was SAFE, then the best decision was what was best for the passengers! I now began to set up the cockpit for what we were preaching at the Training Center. I assumed the role of Cockpit Manager and passed control of flying to the copilot. Now I could be in overall control of what was happening without having to actually fly the aircraft—a new thought process that many old time Captains were not yet able to accept. They felt that in emergency situations the Captain was supposed to fly the plane and make all the decisions at the same time! Too many accident reports indicated that the

Captain was severely overloaded while the other crew members were mere spectators!

When I contacted San Diego Approach Control I asked that all other airplanes scheduled to land that night at Lindberg Field be placed in front of us as we would probably close down the airport until the curfew took effect. As there were only two planes in the sky destined for SAN, it was not a problem—we would be the last aircraft to land that evening. The weather was still overcast, bottoms of the clouds about 800 feet, but the visibility underneath was more than three miles. I asked for a long straight-in approach to give us time to manually crank down the landing gear. I was a bit concerned about the Second Officer's ability to accomplish this chore—she did not appear to be very strong and the process was not physically easy. When the time came, she grabbed the crank handle that was attached to the bulkhead, opened the doors in the cockpit floor and started to turn that crank like she was a three hundred pound gorilla! I was amazed and delighted at her strength and skill. Soon we were in position to land. As we started to enter the overcast I asked the copilot to give the controls back to me—it would be my landing and I needed to get a feel of the flight controls (without proper hydraulics) before the landing maneuver. All of the checklists were completed as we entered the clouds. As I usually did, I turned off the landing lights as we entered the clouds—the reflections were a bit disconcerting and it also ruined your night vision. Soon we popped out of the clouds and the runway was about three miles directly ahead—everything seemed to be happening just as we had planned and I was thinking that we had performed a textbook perfect emergency procedure. As we crossed the threshold of the runway, however, I had a feeling that something did not look right. I decided that it was the different angle from the cockpit as we were landing with only fifteen flaps, giving a more flat attitude. Just before touchdown I remembered that I had turned out the landing lights as we entered the clouds and had forgotten to turn them back on—that was what was giving me such a different view! I reached up and slapped the gang bar that controlled those lights—at the same instant we touched the runway! That was one of my worst landings ever on the 727! No one said a word in the cockpit and the passengers were happy to be safely at their destination. The final insult came from a mechanic who met me as I left the airplane. He walked up to me and said that he had just flown in from LAX and watched my landing. With a twinkle in his eye he asked, "Tell me, Captain, is that a new procedure to turn on the landing lights right at touchdown or did the landing itself jar the switches to the on position?" We both had a good laugh about my ugly landing. I suppose that the moral of this story is: Don't pat yourself on the back for a job well done until you are safely in the hotel or in your own bedroom!

United Airlines was still expanding during the early nineties and beginning to concentrate on overseas travel. UAL had always been primarily a domestic airline but the acquisition of the Pan Am routes in the mid-eighties had given an international flavor to the airline. The Pacific routes were very profitable and United was now trying to become a main contender in the highly competitive North Atlantic routes to Europe. The decision was made by upper management that we would establish a hub in London's Heathrow Airport and fly from there to other cities on the continent. In theory the plan seemed sound. United would fly large aircraft, primarily B-747s, from major hubs in the states to London. Generally these flights would arrive in the early morning after an all-nighter. Then the passengers could connect to other airports on the continent via smaller aircraft, all with United's colors. It was decided that the B-727 aircraft would be best suited for those flights. At the time there were still three different types of 727 aircraft in United's fleet; the original 727-100, the stretched version of that plane called the 727-200, and the advanced model with bigger engines called the 727-222. The underpowered stretched version was chosen for the London hub and eight of those airplanes were reconfigured for what was expected to be an upscale operation. The First Class section contained 24 leather seats and the coach section had additional leg room and fewer seats than the domestic version. Meals would be served on fine china and drinks poured into crystal stemware—it would be a first class operation!

Shortly after the announcement about the London hub, all of the Standards Captains were scheduled for a day long briefing about the differences in international flying—and there were many, many differences. The only international flying I had ever done in the airline consisted of flights to Canada and Mexico which were only slightly different than domestic flying. Only one of our SCs had international experience as he had flown for Pan Am before the merger. His name was Jeff and he was the one who conducted that initial briefing. As I took my seat for the special briefing I began looking over the many handouts that explained the special rules for our new London flights. In the middle of this stack of papers was a schedule of briefings to be held at every domicile for pilots who would be sent over to

London on temporary duty one month at a time. The first domicile briefing was scheduled to be held in Chicago the next day—the Standards Captain conducting that briefing was none other than yours truly! Surely there was some mistake, how could I learn everything about the London operation today and brief pilots tomorrow in Chicago? I jumped up and went directly to the Fleet Captain who was getting ready to call the meeting to order and start the briefing process. I said, "Dick, what's this all about? No one told me that I would be doing this brief tomorrow and I am certainly not prepared!" Dick frowned and replied, "You should have been told by Jeff at least a week ago." We both turned to Jeff who mumbled an apology about the fact that he had been so busy lately that he simply forgot to tell me! Needless to say, I paid very close attention during the briefing, took lots of notes and asked many questions. At the end of the day I packed up the briefing materials into two boxes and sent them to Chicago. Then I went to my home and packed a small suitcase. I departed to Chicago later that night, spent the evening at the Hilton Airport Hotel—mostly preparing for the next morning brief—and after very little sleep, conducted an international brief to a large group of pilots in the flight operations briefing room at the airport. After several more of these briefings during the next few months, I almost felt that I knew what I was talking about!

It would take several months from the planning stages before the London flying actually began. Finally it was time to ferry the airplanes to London and check out the new routes. We would soon find out if our briefings were adequate to prepare our domestic oriented pilots for this type of flying. I was delighted to be chosen to fly one of the first aircraft to London—it would be the highlight of my airline career! I had never dreamed that I would some day fly my favorite airplane across the ocean to far away places in Europe. Four crews were sent to San Francisco to pick up the first four planes—later four more would be ferried to Heathrow. These planes had been reconfigured for the European operation and equipped with a "Rube Goldberg" navigation system that would be suitable for the overwater portion of the flight. Basically it was an old INS that was placed in the first class section of the aircraft with a large cable running into the cockpit to provide power to one small instrument. This small instrument would tell us if we were on track or not! We departed SFO for the first leg to Chicago, a test of the INS equipment with FAA inspectors aboard. Once airborne we asked the controllers to let us fly to ORD with our navigation systems to see if they worked—maybe the same controller was on duty that day that had encountered my LAR joke! We were given mostly vectors to our waypoints and we never really found out if the INS system worked properly or not!

From Chicago we next flew to Bangor, Maine where we spent the night. The next morning we planned our flight to London with a refueling stop in Iceland. We were advised that the weather at our refueling airport in Iceland was not good—not unusual at all—and we decided that we would stop in Goose Bay, Newfoundland for fuel before continuing on to Iceland. After getting fuel at Goose Bay we continued our flight to the airport in Reykjavik, Iceland where we found the weather to be as bad as advertised. Somehow I was now in the first airplane leading the pack of four to England and I had to pass the weather conditions to the other three planes that were following. We had enough fuel that we could return to Goose Bay if a landing was not possible in Iceland. As we approached REK, the second officer, a very talented pilot instructor from the training center, advised us that the weather was 400-1, meaning that the ceiling was 400 feet and the visibility was one mile. Not a problem as the ILS minimums were 200 -1/2 and we had room to spare! Then we got the bad news—the ILS approach was not available and we must execute a VOR approach. Minimums for that approach were—you guessed it, 400-1! The approach was oriented to an offset heading that was thirty degrees from the runway and I knew that the runway, when and if it appeared, would be off to my left when we broke out of the overcast. Thankfully, the approach was over water and we were sure that there were no obstacles or terrain features to interfere with our arrival. We dipped below the published minimums a bit and finally caught sight of the runway—exactly where it should be. I advised the other three planes of the situation and we all arrived at the airport without incident.

We spent several hours in Reykjavik while our planes were refueled and serviced. Meals were boarded for the crew (three pilots) and I signed the bill for the charges: $2100.00 for our three dinners! Without a doubt that was the most expensive meal I ever had! There were no McDonalds or fast food choices so we had to pay whatever they charged—actually the food was quite good! When we took off again we knew that it would be quite late when we arrived in London's Heathrow Airport. This was in reality good news as there would be fewer traffic delays and we should be able to be in our downtown hotel before dawn. I landed in Heathrow well after midnight and our crew was taken directly to a downtown hotel. After a few short hours of sleep I was eager to see what London was all about. The crew of three gathered in the hotel lobby the next morning and we went in search of our first meal in England. When we found what appeared to be a nice restaurant it was almost time for lunch and I ordered what I had always looked forward to if ever in England, FISH & CHIPS. My circadian clock said that it was time for breakfast and I should have listened. When the English style fish & chips arrived I took one look at that big greasy fish wrapped in a newspaper with some potatoes thrown in and decided that I would pass on this first meal! I love the English people but found that their weather is rotten, their food is not healthy and their beer is too warm!

Our crews spent about two weeks in London flying all of the new UAL routes to European cities like Brussels, Amsterdam, Paris and cities in Germany such as Hamburg, Berlin, Frankfort and Munich. We also started service to Geneva and Athens—parts of the world that I had never seen and never thought that I would fly into as a pilot with United Airlines. The other Standards Captains and I found this new type of flying to be a bit challenging at the start but the fun and excitement made it a wonderful experience. It was amazing to me that the legs were so short—we were going from one country to another faster than passing state boundaries in the northeast U.S. In a way it was the airline pilot's perfect schedule—almost all flights departed Heathrow around ten AM, flew to a city on the continent such as Berlin, then after a twenty hour layover, flew one leg back to London. The only leg that was over one hour long was the one to Athens, Greece which was about three hours in duration. We stayed in first class hotels not only in London but in all of the cities that we visited on the continent. It did not take long before the word was out to the pilots in the states that this was an exceptionally rare good deal and the most senior pilots in the 727 fleet began to bid for this temporary duty in London.

Our little group of Standard Captains checked each other out on the new routes so that we would be able to "speak from experience" when we were introducing new crews to this part of the world. For the most part the FLYING WAS FUN but there was, as usual, an interesting twist or two. I was assigned to fly our first trip from Heathrow to Paris's Charles de Gaulle Airport one morning and when I arrived at the airport I found that the weather in Paris was lousy and the CDG airport was closed due to fog. France was the only country in Europe that required airline crews to have a VISA on their passports. As I waited in London dispatch for the fog to lift in Paris, I was notified by one of our dispatchers that I had a phone call. When I answered the phone I found that it was my girlfriend calling from my hotel in downtown London. She casually informed me that my passport was on the dresser in our room—did I need it for my trip that day? Oh s***! Of all the places to not have a passport (with my French Visa)—how could I have been so absent minded? When I hung up the phone the dispatcher informed me that the weather was breaking and we should be able to depart soon. I quickly made the decision to fly the trip without my passport—to do otherwise would have meant canceling the trip. We were not scheduled to layover in Paris but to return to Heathrow after a very short turn around. I decided that I would not leave the cockpit in Paris—hopefully there would not be anyone at CDG brazen enough to come to the cockpit to check if I had my passport.

The short flight to Paris was a nightmare! The weather was still bad and traffic was backed up with long delays. We were placed in a holding pattern with several other flights and were told to await our turn for an approach. Although English is the official language for aviation, the French do not subscribe to that rule. The controllers spoke French to most of the aircraft arriving into CDG and their instructions to us were very difficult to understand. Although I had three years of French in college and thought that I had at least a rudimentary grasp of the language, I was not able to understand most of the transmissions from the controllers without asking them to repeat their instructions. My copilot and flight engineer were unable to help with this language barrier. Eventually the controller cleared us for a particular arrival. There were several arrivals on our charts that could be confused with one another and we needed to be certain about which one was our clearance. The approach controller, who happened to be female, was very busy and quite stressed with all of the traffic that was backed up because of the weather delays. My copilot asked her three times to repeat the name of the arrival— each time she spoke more rapidly and with more accent than previously. It was becoming embarrassing for us to keep asking for the controller to repeat herself—and it was tying up the frequency needlessly. Just when I was starting to think that we would have to ask for a different controller, we were saved by a most astute pilot from British Airways who was also on our frequency. In his most clipped British accent, he said, "United, I will translate for you so that we will all be able to land today!" He related the proper pronunciation for the approach, we acknowledged, and everyone cheered! I thanked "Speed Bird" for his help and we continued to a routine landing at

CDG. Luckily, no one asked me for my passport or visa during my short stay in Paris and we soon departed for our British sanctuary. Never again did I leave my hotel without my passport!

Before any crew member could be assigned the temporary duty in London, he/she had to attend the international briefing, receive the proper maps and approach plates, have a current passport and visa (for France of course) and have current inoculations required for certain areas. It was also a requirement that each Captain would be accompanied by a check pilot (Standards Captain) on his first trip from London. This meant that at least two SCs were required to be in London for the first week or two of each month when new crews arrived. I volunteered for this choice duty and managed to make at least a half dozen trips across the Atlantic just to conduct those check rides. Most of these "shotgun rides" were routine, as the Captains were well briefed and motivated for the new challenges of that type of flying. Only once did I encounter an obstinate Captain—a very senior gent from the Chicago domicile whose name I cannot remember. We were to fly from Heathrow to Berlin, enjoy a nice layover, and fly back the next day. I occupied the copilot seat to help in whatever way the Captain wanted—of course I signed the release as the pilot in command. Before we even left the blocks at Heathrow, this Captain had written three "Captain's Reports." A Captain's Report is in reality a complaint about something that should be fixed—usually a problem that could cause a delay or create an irregularity. This particular Captain found fault with everything—he did not like the fact that his coffee was served in a porcelain cup (he wanted paper), he did not like the way the Customer Service Agent boarded the airplane, etc., etc. By the time we arrived in Berlin, late of course because of his complaints, we were all worn out and more that just a bit exasperated. When we reached the hotel I asked the Captain to join me for a beer after we changed clothes. He informed me that he did not drink spirits of any kind and would not join me for any alcoholic beverages—he was going to take a nap! I decided that it was time for me to earn my management pilot pay. I informed him that we would debrief the flight in my room—now! Reluctantly he accompanied me to my room and I had him sit down while I remained standing. I explained that neither he nor his crews would have a "good time" with this type of flying unless he loosened up a bit. He insisted that United should be the same in London and Berlin as in Chicago and Des Moines. I explained that the Brits invented bureaucracy and were quite good at it—neither he not anyone else with UAL could change that. Either we did it their way or we would be in for a ton of trouble. He did not seem to be persuaded until I gave him an ultimatum. Either he became more flexible or I would not allow him to continue with his assignment in London. He looked at me with confusion and anger and said, "You can do that?" I said, "Tomorrow we fly back to London—consider that a check ride. If you do not perform properly, you will be given an unsatisfactory grade and sent to Denver for special training. After that you will be placed on special tracking and be required to have a check ride with a Standards Captain or Flight Manager every six months." He said, "I'll see you tomorrow."

The next day we flew back to Heathrow. The problem Captain was a completely different person—congenial, cooperative, and downright pleasant. The second officer told me, "I don't know what you did, but it sure worked—thanks." The vast majority of the crews who came to London were, thankfully, not like "Captain Grouch" but ones who truly enjoyed the unique experience. Unfortunately, mainly due to poor management decisions, our experiment with the B-727 aircraft in London lasted only about one year. I often wondered exactly how much money United lost on that operation. I doubt that anyone in the know will ever come forth with those numbers.

Standards Captains, because we were considered "management pilots" were assigned the dubious honor of being the System Duty Manager— usually once a year for a week long stay in Chicago. I was assigned this duty after almost one year at the Training Center. I noticed that my fellow SC's looked at me with sincere sympathy when they knew that it was my time in the barrel. The Duty Manager was on call 24 hours each day for a solid week—a week in hell, we all thought! United's corporate headquarters, called EXO (Executive Offices), were located near O'Hare airport in a large, rambling complex built in the fifties. The Duty Manager or DM was housed in a dorm-like room near the operations center, where he could be reached at all hours. Since United was now a "round the world" airline, there were hundreds of our airliners in the air at any given moment. There were dozens of incidents—problems—that occurred every day that were brought to the attention of the DM. It always seemed that the more serious ones happened in the middle of the night, Chicago time! It was the responsibility of the DM to solve these problems as best as possible with the least disruption to schedule integrity. Often it meant ordering a crew to do something that they did not want to do—such as waiving a certain legality in order to complete the trip. All the Captain had to do was use the magic word, SAFETY, and he/she would get what the crew wanted. Most of the line pilots did not know or take advantage of this loophole and often were forced to fly when it was in their best interests to not do so.

Each morning the DM was required to brief the Senior Vice President of Flight Operations about the incidents during the previous 24 hours. During the time that I was the DM, the VP was an ex-Pan Am pilot by the name of Hart. The first time that I briefed him I had a long list of significant incidents to cover. Before I was halfway through he interrupted me with a question, "How many delays were blamed on flight operations yesterday?" I looked at the last page of my brief and found the number that he wanted—six. He then said, "Contact each Captain and see if the blame for the delay can be placed on maintenance, cabin service or the gate agents—that will be all." I was dismissed. Hart did not care one whit that there had been a political coup d'etat in Caracas, Venezuela the night before and I had to evacuate our crew with armed guards to get them out of the country unharmed. He did not care that one of our airplanes departed Chicago with a new tire that blew on rotation, causing the loss of one engine and at least one million dollars damage. I was beginning to realize why problems with United were never solved—the game was to put the blame on another department, not try to fix anything. Each morning's brief after that first one consisted of how many delays were able to be blamed on other departments.

The Duty Manger's station was on a raised platform surrounded with all the latest technical equipment in the middle of a huge room on the top floor of the Executive Offices. On one side were the crew schedulers and on the other were the dispatchers and technical people who "knew all the answers." The DM could contact any flight in the air, call any crew at their hotel, and keep track of every significant trend taking place in real time. In a way it was a fascinating power trip to have such control over all the flight operations that were taking place at any given time. There were also times of great levity, humor being the best medicine for stress. Most routine crew problems were supposed to be handled by the flight office at each pilot's domicile—that was the job of the Chief Pilot and his subordinates. On weekends and after normal working hours, pilots with special problems or requests would call on the Duty Manager. Late one evening I received a call from a B-747 copilot who was based in New York—his flight office was closed for the night. He sounded exuberant as he related that his wife was on the way to the hospital to give birth to their first child. He was scheduled to depart on a six day trip the next morning and he wanted to drop that trip so that he could be with his wife. That sounded like a reasonable request to me, but a small alarm bell was going off in my head. I asked him to stand by for a few minutes while I checked on reserve availability to cover his trip. In reality I was checking his history over the last several months. Lo and behold, this very same copilot had dropped three trips in the last six weeks for—you guessed it—his wife giving birth to their first child. Each time he was paid for the trip and charged with vacation days. It appeared that he was maximizing his vacation—30 days vacation would cover five such trips, giving him the equivalent of two and a half months off! I returned to the conversation with the copilot and asked him if his wife had given multiple births in the recent past. He stammered that each time it had been a false alarm, but this time it was for sure. I agreed to let him drop his trip but he would not be paid for it—if he wanted to recoup his pay he would have to try to pick up open flying on his days off. As he had no choice, he reluctantly agreed. As I hung up the phone I began to wonder if I had been too harsh on the young man. I decided to call his flight manager, a pilot from New York that I did not know. I reached that man at his home and explained the situation. He started laughing as soon as I mentioned the name of the copilot. He said, "That guy has pulled every stunt in the books—we are not even sure that he is married. If I could find a good reason I would fire him on the spot!" This particular copilot was one of the "fleet qualified" scabs that were hired during the strike of 1985. Less than a year later he was discharged for child molestation!

One night I was awakened by a phone call from one of our 727 pilots in the London operation. He was unable to land at Heathrow due to fog and had diverted to his alternate of Glasgow, Scotland. I recognized his name and his voice as one of my Marine pals but he was oblivious as to whom he was speaking. All he knew was that he was in a bit of a jam and needed to talk to the Duty Manager. I listened to his tale of woe—basically he needed to back up the aircraft in reverse from the gate because the diversion airport did not have the proper push back gear. After he explained it all to me—I was still half asleep—he asked, "Do I have permission, sir, to use reverse thrust to get the plane away from the gate?" After a short pause, I replied, "Walt, you can back that plane all the way to London if you wish—just don't call me again in the middle of the night!" There was a pregnant pause then Walt said, "Is that you, Bill?" I laughed and said, "Call me only if you can't get the plane to go in reverse—I'm sure that you Marines can handle such a simple operation!" Several hours later—when I figured that my buddy had reached his hotel room in London and was deep asleep—I called Walt. After several rings, he picked up the receiver and mumbled hello. In my most cheery voice I said, "Walt, this is the Duty Manager—just checking to see if everything turned out okay." His sleepy-voiced reply was: "You got even with me, Bill, can I go back to sleep now?"

Since the company had centralized the crew schedulers into one location, EXO, some years previously, most pilots never knew the person who controlled their working lives. The crew scheduler was the one who called you in the middle of the night with a reserve assignment, the one who called you at the hotel at 3 AM to tell you to go back to sleep as your flight was delayed. He or she was also the one that the pilot called first with problems involving layovers, transportation, meals, etc. Once a male dominated profession, the crew schedulers were now just as likely to be female. The ladies did a far superior job in my estimation as they were more sympathetic to the pilot's personal problems—and, what kind of pilot could turn down a female who seemed on the verge of tears when stating that you were the only one available to fly the most important mission in the history of United Airlines! There were still a few legendary males within the crew scheduler group—the most notable being a gruff old guy by the name of Malone. No one knew if that was his first or last name. He answered the phone with a single word—"Malone"—making it seem like a challenge to continue the conversation. Many pilots hung up the receiver when Malone answered and tried their call later, hoping to find a more pleasant person to listen to their request. Many pilots complained about Malone and his lack of tact and he had been sent to "charm school" several times—all to no avail. One day I received a call from a pilot who wanted to complain about his treatment from Malone. I decided to have a little talk with the notorious figure whom I had never met. At my fingertips I could contact any crewperson with a touch of a few buttons. I looked up the number for Malone, called it and waited for him to pick up his phone. Shortly I was rewarded with the usual gruff voice that growled, "Malone, what do you want?" I said, "Is that the way you are supposed to answer the phone?" His response was, "That's the way I answer the phone, now what the hell do you want?" I answered, "I want you to hold up your hand and keep it up high until I get there, and this is the Duty Manager." Then I hung up the phone and looked out onto the floor below where there were about twenty cubicles for the schedulers on duty at the time. Slowly one hand came into view. I walked to Malone's work station and found a man who looked exactly like he sounded. He was a large, rough guy who appeared to be in his mid fifties and was even more menacing because of a huge scar that ran from just below his right eye to his chin. I'm certain that it was made by a jagged beer bottle in a bar fight some years ago. I looked at Malone and suddenly felt sorry for the poor guy—obviously he could not help being the abrasive person that he was. I introduced myself, he extended a large meaty hand without getting out of his seat, and I stated that he needed to work on his people skills just a slight bit. He grunted and then we both laughed—we both knew that he was not going to change and I knew that there was not a damn thing that I could do about it. He looked away for a moment and then said in a softer voice, "I'll be taking early retirement in less than one year—got a small spread in eastern Colorado where I won't have to deal with fucking airline pilots ever again!" I told him, "Good luck and keep up the good work!" I would be willing to bet that to this day, on his ranch while pushing around horse shit, he thinks back to those days when he was a crew scheduler and sincerely misses all of those damned airline pilots.

After my week as the Duty Manager, I was literally exhausted. I talked with my boss at the Training Center and had a few suggestions. Mainly, I felt that the job of Duty Manager was too overwhelming for one person and that it should be assigned to two pilots who could share twelve hour shifts. Dick felt that my suggestion was worth some merit but as usual nothing happened. Fortunately it was time for me to take a little vacation. I usually requested my vacation in the month of October—first, there were very few pilots who wanted a vacation during that month and—second, I usually played in the Airline Pilots Association Tennis Tournament that was always held during October. This year, 1991, the tournament was held, as usual, in Palm Desert, California. The tennis tournament was becoming more of a social event than a competitive one and each year we all gathered to have fun, talk about our individual airlines, and play some decent tennis. It was about the only time that pilots from other airlines could get together and compare notes. In a way it was the equivalent of the Tailhook Convention for Naval Aviators—pilots from Alaska Airlines, U.S. Airways, Delta, TWA, Flying Tigers, United, Northwest, etc. were together for a week of fun and competition.

On a Monday night during that October tennis tournament I was with a group of pilots watching the Monday Night Football game at a place called The Elephant Bar in Palm Desert. It was a game in Denver between the Broncos and their perennial enemies, the Oakland Raiders. As we watched the game in our shorts and tee shirts it began to snow in Denver. Soon it was a blizzard. I looked around at our group in this environment and decided that perhaps I should look for a second home in this desert paradise. Less than six months later I purchased a small condo at The Lakes Country Club in Palm Desert—perhaps the second best decision I ever made. The first best decision was to come about two months later. While playing tennis with a group of my new pals at the tennis facility I noticed a group of ladies heading to their courts. There were the usual assortment of females, some short, some tall, some older, some fatter—but one stood out. She had the best looking legs I had ever seen. I blurted out, "Look at those legs!" Evidently I said it loud enough that the lady in question overheard my remark. I was embarrassed as she looked over her shoulder to see who would make such a callous remark. When our eyes met, I knew that my impolite comment would be forgiven— she had a most kind and compassionate look in her eye and I was instantly smitten!

Donna and I were married on the center court at our tennis club two and a half years later. That was definitely the best decision I ever made in my life!

Chapter Twenty

"Never fly in the same cockpit with someone braver than you!"

As I had planned, I resigned from the Standard Captain position after two years and returned to line flying as a B-727 Captain in Denver in January, 1993. The next four years were perhaps the most rewarding in my airline career. First, I was flying Captain on my favorite airplane; second, I was based in Denver where the flying was great and the living was easy; and third, my personal life had reached a plateau that I had only dreamed about. I was now senior enough that I could hold good schedules and by being willing to work weekends and holidays was able to maximize that seniority. I was also designated a Line Check Airman (LCA) which meant that I conducted IOE (initial operating experience) flights for new Captains and copilots. These IOE flights were richly rewarding as it was always a pleasure to work with pilots new to a different cockpit seat, and some were VERY INTERESTING!

Checking out new Captains was never a problem. Every Captain that I took out on his/her IOE was well prepared, very experienced, and eager for that new assignment. Many had been flying in the left seat on the B-737 and were used to being in command—others were finally reaching the ultimate goal for airline pilots, they were now the CAPTAIN IN COMMAND! Some of the new copilots that I checked out were a bit less experienced—some had been flight engineers for many years and had lost a bit of their flying skills, others were fairly new with airline flying and were suddenly now able to fly in the right seat after just a year or two with the company. Despite their inexperience they were well motivated and eager to learn. One of the first copilots that I checked out was a seasoned ex-Air Force fighter pilot who had been with United less than two years. These were very good times for new hire pilots as the airline was expanding rapidly and there were not too many second officer positions available—the airline, like all airlines, was transitioning to a fleet of "glass cockpit" types of aircraft and they would all be flown by only two pilots. Soon even the newest of pilot hires would go directly into the right seat of an aircraft without spending those lost years as second officers. It was the best of times and the worst of times!

Marv was the copilot's name and he had many credentials as a pilot with the Air Force—he had flown with the Thunderbirds during his last tour. Even though he was based in Chicago (still the junior base for new copilots and Captains) he deadheaded to Denver to fly a three day trip with me for his IOE. As usual, every other leg was into Denver so I mixed up the sequence so that Marv could fly into other airports. He was a very sharp pilot during approaches and departures but I soon noticed that he became a bit lax when the work load was more mundane. Evidently he was used to more stressful flying as a fighter pilot and was not so attentive when things became routine. His flying was precise—when cleared to a new altitude, he executed it promptly. If climbing, he jammed on full throttle and jerked back on the yolk; when descending, he slammed the throttles to idle and dumped the nose over. When he reached his assigned altitude he pushed or pulled the controls to level at the exact foot! Great for military flying but the poor passengers were choking on their drinks or watching their ties fly out in front of them. I explained that he needed to be a bit smoother to accommodate the passengers. He did not seem to take this advice seriously—he was more intent on impressing me with his flying skills.

On day two of our IOE trip I talked with the senior flight attendant on one leg into Denver. She was one of our more "crusty" stews and I knew that she could help me handle the problem with the fighter pilot. After one of his abrupt level-offs during a descent she walked into the cockpit and loudly asked, "Who is flying this fucking airplane like a dive bomber?" When the copilot glanced over his left shoulder to look at her she was standing in the middle of the cockpit with her pantyhose and panties down around her ankles! We all started to laugh and the light went on in the copilot's head—he began to fly the airliner like it was supposed to be flown!

The B-727 flying from Denver was the best in the system. We flew to all corners of the mainland but the best flying was always to the northwest. I tried to get those trips in my schedule that ended up in places like Boise, Spokane, Eugene, Portland, Seattle, etc. Many of those trips, late at night, were spectacular. We witnessed the most incredible views of the Aurora Borealis, or Northern Lights, and often invited the stews into the cockpit to watch. Many were non-believers—they thought that what we were seeing was nothing other than thunderstorms with lightning flashes. On many occasions I witnessed such displays that I too doubted were real. Sheets of green clouds would reach out to engulf the airplane, smoke rings would pass over the aircraft, and sometimes we seemed to be in the middle of some sinister celestial storm. Only pilots flying along the upper reaches of the US-Canada border were treated to such incredible views.

Another phenomena was watching the SUN RISE IN THE WEST! I personally observed this unique occurrence at least three times in my flying career—all, I believe, happened when departing from the Denver airport. Due to the proximity of the mountains just to the west of Stapleton Airport, the sun would set while we taxied out to the runway. If the timing was just right, we would take off on runway 35 after dark and climb fast enough to catch the sun and watch it rise over the Rocky Mountains—then set again shortly thereafter. I would turn the airplane so that the passengers could see the sun rise as we climbed out—telling them that soon they would see the normal sunset. Only a few passengers were appreciative of this unique experience—those passengers always stopped to talk to me after we landed.

Flying into and out of the Denver airport could be a challenge for pilots of all types. Due to the high elevation (perhaps one could join the "mile high club" during taxi?) Denver was subject to severe but usually fast moving winter storms that could dump lots of snow on the airport and leave icy runways. The summers were often even more troubling for aviators due to the frequent thunderstorm activity, usually in the afternoons. Meteorology was becoming a more exact science, thank goodness, and forecasting these powerful storms was no longer guesswork. Frequent fliers were becoming more knowledgeable and concerned about the weather phenomena that might affect their flight and would often stop by the cockpit when boarding and ask questions such as: "Any microburst activity or windshear reported today, Captain?" I always replied that since the pilots were the first ones to arrive at the scene of an aircraft accident, we were not going to take unnecessary chances—ever! Denver Stapleton and DIA (the new Denver International Airport) were both equipped with what was called TDWR (Terminal Doppler Weather Radar) and the pilots were advised of the winds at various points on the airport—IF WE ASKED FOR IT! Normally arriving and departing flights were given the centerfield winds by the tower. Only when one or more of the other sensors sets off an alarm will the tower provide those sector winds.

One afternoon I was scheduled to depart Denver to the northwest during one of the more severe thunderstorms that I had ever seen. The airport had been closed for over one hour due to hail storms, windshear, and microburst activity. When departures were once again permitted we queued up for departure and my aircraft was second in line for takeoff on runway 35L. Ahead of me was a Continental flight and I was happy to let him go first. It was now after sunset and the visibility to the northwest was dropping rapidly due to the approaching darkness. In the distance we could see many thunderstorms with visible flashes of lightning. The tower cleared the Continental flight onto the runway—"position and hold." The Continental flight moved slowly into position and finally the tower cleared him for takeoff. I knew just what was going on in the cockpit of that airplane—the crew was looking intently at their weather radar as they were now pointing directly down the runway and could get a clear picture of what lay ahead. The pilot acknowledged their takeoff clearance but nothing happened. After about one minute the tower repeated the clearance: "Continental, you are cleared for immediate departure—either start the takeoff roll or depart the runway!" After a lengthy pause, the Continental pilot stated, "Tower, we are not going to take off into what we see on our radar." The tower responded, "Taxi down the runway to the first available exit, then contact ground control." We all knew what would happen next—that airplane would now go to the rear of the line for takeoff. Instead of being number one for departure he was now number 23! My turn was next.

The Denver tower cleared my flight into position on the active runway. I lined up the airplane and looked at what was ahead, both on the radar and visually. There was still enough light to the west that I could see a few breaks in the line of storms—the weather radar agreed with what we had visually. It looked like we could slip through the bad stuff without too much effort. When the tower cleared us for takeoff, I looked at the other two crew members and asked them if they had any problems with us taking off in these conditions. Both said no. We started our takeoff roll and when the copilot called out Vr (rotate speed) I started to gently lift the nose wheel from the runway. As the nose came up I glanced at my airspeed indicator. It seemed to be stuck at the rotate speed for a few seconds and then it began to drop! I eased the nose wheel back onto the runway and jammed the throttles to full forward.

Indicated airspeed had dropped over twenty knots and we were now more than halfway down the runway—stopping would not be easy! I glanced at a wind sock just off to my left around center field. I was pointing straight out—at least a forty knot wind—but it was pointing the same direction we were taking off! Our headwind had turned into one hell of a tailwind. Slowly the airspeed on my indicator began to increase. I waited until I had at least twenty knots ABOVE normal rotation speed and pulled back on the yoke as we approached the end of the runway. As we lifted off and began to climb normally the tower controller shouted, "Microburst Alert!" I keyed my mike and asked what the Doppler radar at center field was reporting. The controller answered, "The microburst alarm was triggered by a reading of almost 50 knots from the south at midfield just as you were taking off. We are now stopping all further departures." I confirmed that assessment and added that we had at least a thirty knot airspeed loss at midfield. The tower then cleared us to contact departure control for our climb out.

I had been at the controls during the takeoff but now passed the flying duties to the first officer as we had briefed. While he hand flew the aircraft, I served as the flight director. I handled communications with ATC, worked the radar, and looked out the windshield to find the best path through the storms ahead. The copilot merely followed my directions—it was the best was to fly through rough weather. When I checked in on departure control, I knew that all of the aircraft on the ground were now listening on that frequency to hear what conditions we reported on climb out. The departure controller gave us carte blanche—deviate as necessary to avoid the buildups—and requested pilot reports as we climbed out to the northwest. With a few "S" turns we were able to avoid all of the diminishing buildups and experienced a remarkably smooth ride. When we reached FL 180 we were now in the clear and able to resume our normal climb profile on course. The departure controller, before he turned us over to enroute ATC, requested a "ride report" which I had not given to this point. I could not resist saying what I had always wanted to say over the air: "PILOT REPORT FOLLOWS—LOOKS BAD, FEELS GOOD!" Several guffaws and chuckles were heard before we were passed on to the next frequency.

During these "good years" with the airline, the early nineties, United decided to become the only airline to serve all 50 states. For several years we did just that, until the next down cycle when the airline did its inevitable shrinking act. Because the B-727 was still the most versatile aircraft in

United's fleet and due to the central location of Denver, our crews now began to fly into cities that were completely new to all of our pilots. When a new city would show up in our schedules we all tried to be the first to check it out. It was exciting to fly to new locations such as Little Rock, AR, Portland, ME, Jackson, MS, and Rapid City, SD. One month I was able to hold a line of flying that included a nice layover in Rapid City, a place I had never been. The pattern was from DEN to SAN, back to DEN and then to RAP on the first day. Early the next day we flew from RAP to DEN then to BOS for a layover. The third day involved several legs before ending in DEN late at night. The early morning flight from RAP to DEN was usually very light. We would average only about 50 passengers for the short flight to DEN—most of those passengers were businessmen. Mount Rushmore National Memorial was located just to the southwest of the airport and each morning as we took off we could get a fleeting glance of those famous carvings. On the second or third trip of the month I asked the tower controller before takeoff if we could do a "Mt. Rushmore departure." The controller responded that there was no such thing as what I was requesting. Then I admitted that I wanted to take a short tour around that famous mountain to show the passengers those notable faces carved into the stone. The controller responded, "Sure, United, you are cleared for a 360 degree turn over the Monument, stay above 2000 feet AGL." We took off, leveled at 2000 feet above ground level and gave the passengers (and crew) a magnificent view of the area before departing on course to DEN. The flight attendants enjoyed the tour and reported that "most" of the passengers did also. For the rest of the month we took that scenic departure each time we took off from Rapid City, and each time we arrived in Denver on time or early. At the end of the month I received a phone call from my Flight Manager, a nice guy whose name happened to be Bill. After the usual pleasantries, he asked me if I knew anything about a "Mount Rushmore" departure from RAP. I laughed and admitted that I flew that "departure" each time out of Rapid City. He then stated, "I'm sure that 99 percent of the passengers enjoyed the tour, but it's the one percent that we have to worry about. We have received a letter from one passenger complaining about the waste of time and fuel. I checked the records and see that your flight was always on time and the fuel burn was less than planned. Good job. Now promise me that you won't do that departure again. You can keep your fingers crossed if you wish—I can't see them anyway!" I made the promise and we turned to more important matters, like: Did you hear the one about…

Cockpit crews spent a lot of time telling jokes—I miss that part as much as anything. I found that the Captain's jokes were always a lot funnier than any other crew member. I was starting to think that I was a great joke teller until I began to recall how I always laughed at the "Old Man's" jokes no matter how many times I had heard them previously or how corny they were. Nevertheless those long hours of boredom, especially at night, were broken up by lots of stories and jokes. Many of the flight attendants joined in—they would come into the cockpit during their slack times and ask if we had heard any new jokes. They too contributed by telling some of the funniest (and raunchiest) jokes of all. One month I flew with two of the wittiest and best joke tellers ever—and they were both cute as buttons, one a blonde and the other a redhead. Yes, they told lots of "blonde" jokes, but they loved to startle the cockpit crew (usually all male) by telling some very risqué anecdotes. One afternoon as we were flying up the west coast enroute to Portland, OR, I was the pilot flying and we had just been issued a discretionary descent— meaning that we could start down whenever we chose as long as we made a certain crossing restriction, in this case 11,000 feet at a point 30 miles from PDX. We were still at our cruise altitude of FL 350 and I was mentally computing my point to start descending when the blonde entered the cockpit. Usually she had another funny joke, but this time she said that she had done a really bad thing the other night after having too much wine. She continued her story that on a dare she had gone to a tattoo parlor and had a small tattoo of "Tweety Bird" placed on her lower abdomen. The three pilots were listening intently to her tale, wondering if she was pulling our collective legs or if she was actually telling a true tale of woe. At this time flight attendants had several different uniforms and the blonde was wearing slacks, very appealing in this case, I might add, as she had a very nice figure. Suddenly she said, "Would you all like to see my Tweety Bird?" Of course we all rapidly nodded, like those little plastic puppies in automobile rear windows. Slowly she pulled down her slacks to her knees and then started to slip down her panties. At this time we were all enthralled and probably salivating a bit. As her panties were dropped to just barely expose the beginnings of her pubic hair she exclaimed, "Well, darn, it's gone, I guess my pussy ate it!" She pulled up her panties and her slacks and departed the cockpit. We were all three roaring in laughter when I heard the center ask, "United, are you going to be able to make the crossing restriction or do you need to execute a 360." I looked at the instruments that I had ignored for the past few minutes and found that we were now only thirty miles from the fix that we had to cross at 11,000 feet. I had 24,000 feet to lose, usually requiring about 70 miles. I turned on the seat belt sign and told the second officer to tell the passengers to strap in immediately. I told the first officer to tell the center that we were descending and inquire if there was any speed restriction at the crossing altitude. The controller recognized our predicament and gave us a break, saying, "No speed restriction but the crossing altitude is hard." This meant that we MUST be at 11,000 feet at the 30 mile fix, no exceptions! I had closed the throttles and eased the nose over—I didn't want to make the passengers too uncomfortable due to my error in concentration—and I pulled out the speed brakes to their full deployed detent. We were coming down like a rock. We made the crossing restriction, indicating over 350 knots (about 100 knots faster than normal) and the controller said that he was impressed. I felt badly about any discomfort to the passengers but received not a single complaint. We were still laughing in the cockpit when we landed in Portland—the blonde had pulled the best one yet!

During the winter months the most senior trip for Denver based B-727 crews was a three day trip that included a 33 hour layover in Palm Springs. I was not senior enough to hold that line of flying except in the summer, when it became very junior due to the extremely hot temperatures. One December, however, (I believe it was 1994) I managed to be assigned the PSP trip only because it included a layover on both Christmas Day and New Year's Day. I was scheduled to arrive in Palm Springs late Christmas Eve and depart early in the morning on the 26th. This was the perfect trip for me as I was living in Palm Desert during the winter months and I would be just where I wanted to be for the holidays. My copilot for the month was a really fun guy by the name of Bernie—who had just gotten married. He planned to bring his new bride on the Christmas trip so that they could be together. Our layover hotel was the Spa Resort in downtown Palm Springs—a very nice hotel within walking distance of fine restaurants and upscale shopping. Of course my wife would pick me up at the airport and we would spend the layover at our home. The Palm Springs airport was considered a "special airport" by the FAA because of the terrain just to the west of the field. A "special airport" designation created some significant restrictions. The Captain or First Officer had to be airport qualified, meaning that he/she had to have made an entry to that airport within the preceding 12 months or had viewed a special video about the airport. Both Bernie and I met those qualifications. The weather in Palm Springs was VFR about 99 percent of the time and there was not a precision approach into the field. The only instrument approach was a VOR approach that was flown from the Thermal VOR—located about thirty miles to the southeast. The minimums for this non-precision approach were quite high—again due to the "special airport" designation.

When Bernie and I looked over the weather reports for out trip on that Christmas Eve we discovered that the weather in the area was not good, with low clouds, rain, and poor visibility. Our alternate was the airport at Ontario, CA only fifteen minutes away by air. I requested additional fuel so that we could hold in the Palm Springs area for at least two hours if necessary. The passenger load was very light, less than fifty people including Bernie's new bride. When we arrived in the area the weather was indeed below minimums and we held as long as possible. At one time the visibility lifted briefly and we executed the prescribed approach—only to find that at our lowest legal altitude we were not able to see the runway sufficiently to land. Finally we departed to our alternate and landed normally in Ontario. The passengers were bussed back to Palm Springs but the crew remained overnight to ferry the aircraft to PSP early the next morning. That next morning we arrived at the airport to ferry the aircraft, the pilot and flight attendant crew plus Bernie's wife. The Ontario airport was, at this time, a very small operation for United Airlines, used primarily as a diversion airfield for LAX. The entire station crew was housed in a temporary trailer parked outside of the terminal and quite close to the tarmac. When we arrived to flight plan the next morning for our short flight to PSP, Bernie's wife was with the crew, but she stuck out like the proverbial sore thumb as she was dressed as a passenger. Since she was an employee traveling on a pass she was actually dressed much nicer than most of the paying passengers. One of the operations personnel asked me about her and I honestly admitted that she was the wife of the copilot and would accompany us on the short flight to PSP. That person, a female load planner who was making out the manifest, went directly to a telephone and called United Dispatch in Chicago. Shortly she handed me the phone and indicated that the dispatcher needed to talk to me.

The dispatcher said, "Captain, I understand that there is a passenger that you want to take on the crew ferry flight to PSP—is that correct?" I explained that the "passenger" was the copilot's wife and would be stranded in Ontario on CHRISTMAS DAY if we did not take her with us to PSP. The dispatcher was sympathetic but added that a crew ferry flight, by definition, did not allow anyone but the authorized crew to be on board. After this phone conversation I called the crew members, both pilots and flight attendants, together outside the operations trailer. I explained the situation and the consensus was: This is bullshit, let's take her on this flight! I reentered the operations trailer and made a phone call to the Duty Manager. I recognized the name of the duty man and I think he recognized my name also, but we did not personally know each other. I explained the situation as best I could, hoping that he could give me authority to deviate from the regulations—on Christmas Day! He responded in a most appropriate way. He said, "Captain, it sounds like you are going to take that 'passenger' with you no matter what I say. Do whatever you think best but don't tell me about it—and we never had this conversation!"

We boarded our airplane and departed for the short flight to Palm Springs—three pilots, three flight attendants and one blushing bride. It was now a beautiful morning and the weather from ONT to PSP was VFR. I invited Bernie's bride to ride in the cockpit and told Bernie that it was his leg. He was delighted to fly the plane to PSP while his new wife sat on the jump seat and watched—her first and probably only flight in the cockpit of a commercial airliner. We kept the cockpit door open and the flight attendants gathered around as we flew through the pass into the Coachella Valley and I pointed out the sights along the route. It was one of the most rewarding trips of my career and one of the shortest. I also knew that technically I could be fired for violating the federal regulations. I felt then and still feel today that it was certainly worth it! Bernie and his wife thanked me profusely—with hugs and handshakes, followed later by thank you notes—and the flight attendants were all grateful as well. We all enjoyed a nice Christmas Day in the Palm Springs area and departed the next morning for our scheduled flight back to Denver, a full load including one bride!

One month I had the pleasure of flying into one of those small towns that had a most unique personality, Fort Wayne, Indiana. Many towns really did have character and they somehow assumed an identity that kept them separate from the mundane. It was easy to confuse the two towns of South Bend and Fort Wayne, but they were really worlds apart. South Bend (SBN) seemed to have a church or ornate cathedral on every corner, perhaps influenced by the presence of Notre Dame University. Fort Wayne (FWA) on the other hand, had very few churches and seemingly at least two WIG SHOPS in every block. Did that mean that people who lived in SBN were more religious than those residing in FWA, where most of the people were bald?

This particular trip that I was flying departed FWA early each Saturday morning for ORD and continued on to DEN. At the time there was an Air Force Reserve squadron that was based at the airport and they operated on weekends. Each morning as we taxied out for takeoff we passed a small shack to the left of the taxiway that was used when the AF planes were operating. A Runway Duty Officer, probably the most junior officer in the unit, occupied this shack. His duties, which I am sure he considered very boring, consisted of checking over planes taxiing out and ensuring that they had their landing gear down when landing. When our 727 taxied by his shack he would stand outside and wave. I also waved to him and then extended a salute, which he always returned. By the end of the month our crew, which consisted of two ex-Navy pilots and a Marine flight engineer, had formulated a plan to have a little fun with the Air Force. We had figured out that if I moved my seat full forward the Marine could squat down on the observer seat and MOON the AF officer as we passed by! That morning as we approached the RDO shack and the Marine was getting into position, I made my usual "welcome aboard" announcement over the PA system to our passengers. Then I added: "Those of you seated on the left side of the aircraft will get a chance to wave to one of the Air Force's finest—I'm sure that he will wave back." Sure enough the young officer stepped outside his shack and waved to me as we passed. Instead of saluting, I pointed to the window just behind my seat as the Marine dropped his pants and pressed his bare butt to the glass! When the AF Officer saw this he did what any red-blooded military man would do—he extended his arm toward us with his middle finger fully extended! I keyed the PA system and said to the passengers, "Well, I guess that the Air Force is not having a good day today!"

During the early nineties I began to notice some subtle but profound changes in the makeup of the new pilots being hired by United Airlines. When I had been hired in 1968, it was definitely a white male dominated profession with the majority of the pilots being ex-military. The only question posed to a new pilot when he introduced himself to the other crew members was: "Air Force or Navy?" Once that question was settled the conversation would revolve around types of aircraft flown, fighter or attack. Every now and then a pilot would arrive who had flown in the Army, Marines or Coast Guard. These guys were always interesting to talk with because they had some different stories to tell. Only occasionally would we meet a new pilot who did not have a military background. This pilot got a lot of respect from most of us because he had to pay for his flight experience—Uncle Sam paid for the rest of us. When I started there were probably only three or four black pilots and zero female pilots on the seniority list of just over 5000.

In the mid-eighties United came under increasing pressure from the EEOC (Equal Employment Opportunity Commission) and other rights groups to hire more females and minorities as pilots. We began to have special training about "diversification" and other buzzwords to prepare us for the inevitable influx of females and minorities into the cockpit. By the mid nineties it seemed that at least half of the new hires fell into those classifications—ex-military white males were becoming the minority. For the most part these new pilots, whatever their background, were well qualified and readily accepted into "the brotherhood." The only down side was that we all had personal knowledge of pilot applicants from the military who were turned down by the United selection process. We began to suspect that there was a "quota system" being used by United. Most of us felt that pilots hired to join us in our cockpits should be selected because of their qualifications and experience, not because of their race or gender. Pilot hiring for all of the major airlines was a cyclical process. There were many years when zero pilots were hired, and then suddenly the airlines needed more pilots than were available in the pipeline. For instance—United experienced a major expansion in the early sixties, before my time, and there were not enough applicants from the military. What did United do? They hired a large number of Canadian pilots from the Canadian military! Then they hired low time pilots from the corporate and private fields of aviation. Everything worked out just fine and these pilots performed as well as any of the ex-military American pilots. It was simply a case of supply and demand. Now the situation was completely different. There were literally thousands of ex-military pilots in the United States (mostly white males) who were lined up to take airline pilot jobs. There was definitely not a lack of supply. Then why were those well qualified applicants being turned down and a low time female hired? Like most of my contemporaries, I could not answer that question—but I was more than just a bit curious.

Suddenly I was given the opportunity to find out those answers myself. One day the Denver Chief Pilot invited me to his office. Usually this meant only one of two things: One—it was time for the pilot to receive his new seniority pin (given each five years with a small diamond added each time). Most pilots never wore these pins on their uniform—instead we wore our ALPA wings of gold. Two—the pilot had done something wrong and it was time for the Chief Pilot to chew him out. In this case it was neither—my "boss" wanted to ask me if I would be interested in conducting new pilot interviews. I jumped at the chance. Now I could find out for myself how this pilot hiring process actually worked.

When I first reported to the "Human Resource Center" which was in a separate building from the Training Center, near Stapleton International Airport, I was impressed with how shabby the whole operation seemed. The carpets were dirty, the furniture looked like it had been purchased from Goodwill, and the place seemed to be quite disorganized. This department was tasked with hiring new pilots who would be carrying millions of passengers over their careers. These newly hired pilots would spend most of their adult lives in the employment of United Airlines. This was a major event for prospective pilots trying to fulfill their lifelong dream—getting hired by a major airline. I noticed that almost all of the employees here were female and more than half were black. Where was this "diversity" that had been drilled into us underlings for the past year or two?

I met with the head of the pilot hiring department, her name was Doris, and was informed that I could start my intensive indoctrination process the following week. I inquired as to what was the length of this training and why was it even necessary. She rolled her eyes, put her hands on her rather large hips and said, "I hope that we won't have any problems with you, Captain, we know what we are doing here!" I agreed to report for my training the next week. I met several of the other Captains who conducted interviews and found that most were very junior. Then I found out why. They were not able to hold a schedule or else they were flying only lousy trips due to their lack of seniority. By participating in the interview process they were able to drop (and get paid for) a bad three day trip by conducting interviews for one or two days. They all wondered why I, a fairly senior Captain and ex-Standards Captain, would be there at all. I was beginning to wonder also.

After my indoctrination, which lasted over two weeks, I began to conduct new applicant interviews. During these interviews I was the PR, or Pilot

Representative, and the major domo was the ER, or Employment Rep. My role was simply to ask a few (very few) questions to the candidate of a technical nature to ascertain his/her knowledge about aviation. I assumed that the ER was a highly qualified person chosen for her interviewing skills and probably held a degree in psychology. I was very wrong. The ER was more likely a clerk who had applied for the job and been accepted. I never met a single ER who had an aviation background; most had never been inside the cockpit of an airliner. They made their decisions based on how the applicant answered "trick questions" such as: "Tell me what you would do if your boss gave you an illegal assignment." Most pilots would have a bit of trouble answering such an asinine question. I recall one interview with an ex-Navy pilot who held a degree in aeronautical engineering, had many medals and commendations from the service and was an exemplary citizen in his community—I was very impressed with this candidate. When the interview was over, the ER turned to me and said, "We only have about five minutes before my lunch break. Shall we wait until after lunch or make our decision now?" I replied, "Well, there doesn't seem to be much to discuss about this candidate, let's do it now." She said, "I agree, he is completely unacceptable. Now I can get my lunch a bit early." I'm sure that my jaw must have dropped to the floor. I stammered, "This is one of the most highly qualified candidates I have ever met—what do you mean that he is unacceptable?" She looked at me and said, "He reminds me of my father, and I hate my father!" I was speechless for a minute or two. Then as she collected her papers together and started out the door so as not to miss her all important lunch break, I found my voice. I stated, "I completely disagree with you, what is the procedure now?" Normally the ER and PR arrived at a mutually acceptable decision—either the candidate was up or down—and I did not know what was required if we disagreed. She looked at me and said, "I heard that you were going to be a trouble maker, you write up your report and I will write mine. I'm going to lunch now."

I wrote my decision on a piece of paper and submitted it to one of the secretaries—I found out later that the ER wrote her decision on her word processor and the two recommendations were submitted to the proper channels. I was scheduled to conduct another interview early the next day. As I was dressing the next morning prior to leaving for the Human Resource Center, I received a phone call from one of the other Captains who was also conducting interviews. He said, "Bill, I'm just giving you a head's up—you are getting a check ride this morning." I started to laugh; this was going to be a very interesting day. Sure enough, the head of the department, Doris, sat in on the interview that I conducted that morning. I was with an ER that I had never met and she was very nervous, as though she was the one getting the "check ride." I felt that the interview was completely unfair to the applicant, but I held my thoughts and conducted the interview to the best of my ability. After the process was over, Doris invited me to her office. She explained that she had sat in on my interview because she had received a complaint from the ER of the previous day, who reported that I was not "a team player." I related the "hate my father" incident and asked Doris what had happened to the candidate that I had wanted to accept. Doris said, "He was turned down, of course. He has the right to reapply in one year." I asked Doris, "Did I pass my check ride this morning?" She looked at me and said, "Of course, but you need to be more in tune with our procedures here. We are committed to getting the best pilots from the candidates that are available. The decision comes from above as to which ones are accepted." I asked her to explain.

Doris began to look a bit uncomfortable, but to her credit, she explained the process that United used to hire new pilots. It seemed that the candidates who successfully completed the interview were then placed into six different "buckets." The largest of these buckets contained over 1000 applicants, white males who were primarily ex-military. Another bucket contained only females—blacks were in another. Then there was a bucket that contained those who were ALPA recommended—usually pilots from union airlines that had gone out of business, such as Braniff, Eastern and Pan Am. The next bucket contained the names of those who were sons and daughters of United employees. The last bucket was for "other minorities" such as Arabs, Chinese, Native Americans, etc. Each week the word came from "upstairs" as to how many applicants were to be chosen from each bucket, depending on how many pilots were needed for a new hire class that was scheduled to start usually at least a month away. For instance; 30 pilots were needed for a new class—5 were to be picked from each of the six buckets. Sounded reasonable until one looked at the numbers. Perhaps bucket five only contained ten names—all with lower qualifications than the thousand candidates from bucket number one. If you were in bucket five you had a 50-50 chance of being hired. If you were in bucket number one your odds were 1 in 200! Sure sounded like a quota system to me regardless of United's explanation. I realized that I could not change the system and if I continued to conduct interviews it would be an exercise in futility that would only add to my personal frustration. I told Doris that I was "resigning" from my assignment. She gave me the usual BS about how much I had contributed to the hiring program but I could tell that she was breathing a big sigh of relief that I would no longer be a thorn in her side.

Most of those interviews that I conducted over a period of approximately six months were routine. The applicants were well prepared and had usually been prepped by some of the "interview experts" who were now in the business of coaching the candidates before they checked in for their processing. They were told how to dress, how to have their hair cut, and how to sit while being interviewed. Most of the pilots that I personally interviewed looked as though they came from an assembly line. Occasionally, however, there were the few mavericks that brought a smile to one's face. One gentleman that showed up for an interview was in his late fifties, had worked for Pan Am until it went out of business, and had no idea why he was there to compete for a job with United Airlines. He had not flown an airplane for almost 10 years and was presently happily employed with a Pep Boys auto parts store in Miami. If he "passed" his interview he would be placed in the bucket of ex-ALPA pilots that consisted of very few candidates. Most Pan Am and Eastern pilots that were looking for a flying job had been hired years before. He was a very nice man who told me that he received a letter from UAL asking him to apply for a pilot position. United paid for his trip to Denver and simply asked him to bring his flight logs. He had not gone through one of the prep schools prior to reporting for his interview and it was obvious. He did tell me that he had purchased a new suit and was wearing a tie for the first time in many years—he looked very uncomfortable. When he walked into the interview room he carried a large brown paper bag, the type that one would get at the local grocery store. After we exchanged pleasantries, I could not resist asking, "What's in the bag?" He placed it on the desk of the ER and stated, "These are the only flight logs that I could find." This huge disorganized pile consisted of monthly records from his service in the Air Force many years ago and computer printouts of his flight times with Pan Am. I asked this gent only one question: "Did United put you up in a nice hotel here in Denver?"

He responded, "Oh yeah, I'm having a great vacation! My wife is with me and we're enjoying a fun time here in Colorado. Wish we could stay a bit longer." I said, "I'll see if I can get United to pay for a couple of extra days before you have to leave." I turned to the ER and said that the interview was complete as far as I was concerned. I walked the ex-Pan Am pilot out of the room and we chatted for a short while. He admitted that he had no hopes of being hired and confessed that he had busted his last check ride with Pan Am and was in the process of applying for early retirement when Pan Am folded. When I returned to the interview room, the ER was not happy. She said, "What was that all about? We don't have many candidates in his category— it should make you union pilots happy to have him hired." I responded only reluctantly to her question. I said, "It would be a waste of United's money to try to train that gentleman—it will be a lot cheaper to pay his hotel bill for a few more days and let him return to Miami with fond memories of his vacation." It took several phone calls but I was able to extend his stay at company expense.

Another interview that I conducted, this time with a young lady, was almost as poignant but certainly more humorous. She happened to fall into the category of being both female and the daughter of one of United's Captains. She was well prepared for the interview and it was obvious that she had been coached. The problem was with her log books. She had very low time—easily overlooked because she was female and a company relative. She could go into two buckets if approved by the interview process thereby doubling her chances of being hired! She had worked for a small non-sked cargo carrier for the past year and that is where she had accumulated the majority of her flight time. I noticed from her log books that she listed most of that flight time in the small prop planes as PIC, which stood for Pilot in Command. I asked her if she flew from the left seat during those flights and if she signed the flight plans as the Captain. She looked a bit confused and said that she always flew from the right seat, and no, she never signed the flight plan or the log book. Then I asked her, "How were you able to list this time as PIC?" She replied, "PIC stands for Pilot in Control, and I was always in control when the Captain let me fly!" I hate to admit it but she was a BLONDE—and a very cute one! I tried to keep a straight face as I explained that she could not count that time as Pilot in Command flight time and it was necessary that she have her log books corrected. She still looked perplexed and asked, "What is the difference between being the Pilot in Command and being the Pilot in Control?" I could think of several responses such as, experience, seniority, training, etc. but merely replied: PAY! Rather than turn down this lady pilot I suggested to the ER that we consider that the interview never happened. That way the candidate could get more experience and more flight time and apply again in the future without having it on her record that she was turned down previously. After some discussion we agreed on this solution and informed the candidate accordingly. She had a great sense of humor when she was told of our decision. She frowned and said, "And I bought this nice business suit just for the interview. I'll keep it in a special place until I return—hope it will still fit!" Then with a big smile she thanked us profusely and went on her way. I hope that she did return after getting more experience and that she is happily flying the Friendly Skies to this day!

During these years of growth within the airline I was keeping very busy as an LCA conducting IOE's for new Captains and copilots. After a while it seemed that I was being used almost every trip as an LCA. Although it was interesting, challenging and rewarding to check out these new pilots, there was always a certain amount of stress involved and I was getting a bit weary. I decided that I would only accept one LCA assignment each month— maximum! I had started to discover that the most senior copilots in Denver were bidding to fly with me on a monthly basis—not because they loved my company, but because they knew that they would be displaced frequently because I would be conducting IOE's. I missed flying with regular crews on a routine trip that was fun and uneventful. One day I received a phone call from the Chief Pilot with a special request. It seemed that a new copilot had just completed her IOE with another LCA. The problem was that the LCA had released her to fly with one condition, the condition being that she be assigned to fly with a Line Check Airman for her first month on the line! This was highly unusual—either the pilot was OK to fly with whatever crew he/she was assigned or was scheduled for further training or perhaps special evaluation. The Chief Pilot was not happy with the situation and justifiably so—she had been dumped on his doorstep so it seemed. I agreed to have the "problem child" fly with me but decided that the trips would be conducted as though they were regular flights—I would not be conducting a check ride.

Before that first trip I received a second phone call, this one from the Fleet Captain at the Training Center. He wanted to also give me a head's up with what was going on with this particular copilot. He explained that she was a very low time pilot who had been "taught to fly" by her husband in his small private airplane. Her husband was currently a B-767 Standards Captain at the Training Center. He needed to go no further, I knew the person in question. What I did not know was the extensive training and retraining that had transpired to get her qualified as a copilot. After her normal training and several additional periods in the simulator, she busted her check ride. She was then scheduled to go through the entire school again and received extra simulator time. She could not pass the check ride the second time. At this point any other pilot would have been washed out, or relegated to fly as a Second Officer or non-flying pilot for the rest of his/her career. For reasons that I could not understand, she was allowed to go through the entire training process a THIRD TIME and finally passed her check ride in the simulator. She had accumulated over 100 hours in the simulator to complete training that normally took less than 20 hours! She flew her IOE with a contemporary of mine, an LCA who I knew very well. He could not sign her off at the end of the IOE and she was sent back to the Training Center for additional training. Eventually she went out on the second IOE, this time with a new guy who signed her off "conditionally."

The copilot's husband was a friend of mine and I had been to their home several times. I had also flown with his wife when she was a flight engineer. She was very competent in that position—frankly I would say that she was one of the very best Second Officers I had ever worked with. She knew the aircraft very well, performed her duties to perfection and was great with the passengers and flight attendants. She had been with the company for several years and had passed up many chances to bid up to the copilot seat. She had decided that she would wait until she was senior enough to get a bid in Denver, where she lived with her husband and two small children. Then she waited another year or two so that when she moved into the copilot position she would be able to hold a decent schedule—she did not want to be on reserve. During these stagnant years, over five, she only flew at the controls of her husband's airplane on rare occasions. She had her hands full with her multiple jobs of flight engineer, wife and mother.

I did not look forward to this "special assignment." Had I known who the copilot was I would have refused to fly with her when asked by the Chief Pilot. Now I was stuck—it appeared to be a no-win situation. When we met in dispatch for our first trip together she had a hang-dog expression and appeared to be resigned for another check ride. I did my best to assure her that it was not a check ride—but admitted that I was there because of my status as an LCA. We would be flying a great three day trip with decent layovers and the weather was forecast to be absolutely beautiful. I would fly the first leg and then we would alternate—it would be a normal trip.

She performed her duties as the PNF (pilot not flying) superbly on that first leg—now it was time for her to be the flying pilot back to Denver. The weather was indeed perfect and she was flying into an airport that she was completely familiar with—what could possibly go wrong? After takeoff she engaged the autopilot as soon as it was legal—a bit unusual but there were lots of pilots who preferred to let the AP do the work. She flew the entire trip with the autopilot engaged and did a commendable job. I had always found that flying the autopilot in the B-727 was a skill that was more challenging than hand flying. With the AP engaged, the pilot flew by maneuvering a small knob on the center console with three fingers. She was one of the smoothest operators I had ever seen with the minute movements required to fly the aircraft with this knob. When we arrived in Denver from the northwest we were vectored to the south to make our landing to the north—this required a left turn to get lined up with the runway. The weather was good, the winds were calm and we were cleared to land visually on runway 35L. She started her left turn with the autopilot still engaged and made a very nice 15 degree turn. Making a left turn on final is difficult for a copilot as the visibility is restricted—he/she can only see the Captain's profile. This copilot was not looking out; she was flying on instruments with inputs to the autopilot controls. As I looked out the left side I realized that she was going to overshoot the runway and would be in the flight path of aircraft landing on runway 35R. Luckily there was no other traffic but the controller noticed that we had overshot and asked if we wanted to land on the right runway—this was usually a bit embarrassing for a pilot. Up to this point I had not volunteered any flight instructions, although I had given my advice when asked. Now I asked her, "What do you want to do, land on the runway we were cleared to or land on the parallel runway to the right?" She seemed completely confused and continued in her 15 degree bank—we were now going to overshoot the right runway. Finally I said, "You've got to tighten your turn or we will have to go around." When she rolled out onto the runway heading I asked her to look outside—the runway was way off to our left. She spotted the runway and meekly asked, "What do I do now?" I asked her, "Do you feel comfortable to land?" She replied in the negative. I told her to execute a go-around or missed approach and I informed the tower of our intentions. Of course the tower controller inquired as to what were our problems—making a missed approach on a clear day with no apparent weather problems. I informed the controller that we were not comfortable with the approach and requested vectors for another landing. We were cleared to an altitude that was rapidly approaching and given a heading assignment. The copilot was completely overloaded and still trying to fly the plane via the AP. We overshot the altitude assignment and were now exceeding the maximum speed of 200 knots in an airport zone. I had no choice but to take over the controls—otherwise I would have a flight violation.

I flew the plane around the pattern and made an uneventful landing. We still had another leg to fly that day after our usual two hour layover—time to get some popcorn. My copilot looked completely dejected—I thought that she would start crying at any moment. We arrived at our pilot's lounge and went our separate ways, agreeing to meet one hour before the next departure to flight plan. I purposefully did not want to get involved in a lengthy debrief. When we met later she seemed to be resolute—I found out that she had called her husband and had received some words of comfort and encouragement. That was fine with me.

We departed on the next leg and it was my turn to be the PF (Pilot flying). Again she did a great job as the pilot handling the communications and other non-flying duties. When we arrived at our layover hotel she asked if we could go to dinner together. At the restaurant she inquired as to the probable outcome of this trip—was she going to make it as a copilot? I tried to be as tactful as possible but admitted that unless she performed better it did not look good. After a glass or two of wine she admitted that she really did not want to be an airline pilot, she was perfectly happy to be a wife and mother. She had been pressured into the airline pilot job by her domineering husband. I felt sorry for her but felt that the decision as to her future was mainly up to her. She did not want to be a quitter—that would be unacceptable to her husband.

The next day we departed again for Denver. Then we would fly to Albuquerque, back to Denver and then on to somewhere in the Midwest. So that she would not always have to fly into DEN, I asked her to pick her two legs that day—the first two or the last two. She chose to fly the first two legs. Again we were arriving from the northwest into DEN, with a landing to the west. We were cleared for the profile descent over the northwest gate. This meant that we had to cross a certain fix to the northwest between the altitudes of 23,000 feet and 17,000 feet, a rather large window. Usually the pilot tried to remain on the high side if landing to the west and needed to be on the low side if landing to the south. This copilot started a gradual descent when cleared for the profile by reducing the throttles to about 90%—usually we planned the descent so that we could close the throttles completely as we started down. We were descending at a rate of around 1000 feet per minute when we needed 3000 FPM. Again she was flying with the AP engaged and making very minor but smooth inputs. Soon it became apparent that we were not going to be below 23,000 feet by the fix which was a maximum crossing altitude. Finally I told her that she needed to increase her rate of descent—otherwise we would receive a flight violation. She seemed very confused about how to get down faster. I waited as long as possible and finally pointed to the throttles which were only halfway retarded. She glanced down and took action—she PUSHED THEM FORWARD! Now our rate of descent was reduced to about 500 FPM and our airspeed increased substantially. Once again I had to take over the controls, close the throttles, extend the speed brakes and dive so as to meet the crossing restriction. Once we had complied with the clearance I turned the controls back to her. With a lot of coaching she was able to get the airplane onto the runway—but it was far from a thing of beauty!

The next leg was into ABQ—one of my favorite airports. The weather in Albuquerque was almost always VFR, similar to Denver, and the prevailing wind was usually from the west. Normally we arrived from the northwest and made a left turn to the east to be in position for a right turn back to the west for landing—this day was no exception. Due to the mountains to the east of the airport, it was necessary for the pilot to slow down the aircraft and descend rapidly enough so that the plane was not too low when over that high terrain. I decided that I would not coach her for this approach and see what happened—the weather was perfectly clear and we were the only traffic arriving at the time. When we were eastbound and cleared for a visual approach, she continued toward the east instead of making a right turn to the airport. I bit my lip. Eventually the tower asked, "United, where are you going? You are cleared to land on runway 26—start your right turn." She started her turn and soon we were pointing toward the runway—3000 feet too high! As the runway disappeared beneath our airplane, the controller said, this time in a more gentle tone, "United, would you like to make a 360 to the left or the right?" I looked at my copilot and shrugged. She had absolutely no situational awareness as to where the airport was and how to get there. Finally she stammered that she needed a 360 degree turn to the right. She then executed a beautiful circle without losing a single foot of altitude! We were now exactly where we started, 3000 feet too high for a landing! The controller had a bit of trouble controlling his laughter as he stated, "United, let me know what you are planning next, we'll keep the runway clear until you land!"

The rest of that three day trip was not much better. When we finally arrived back at our domicile the next day, she knew that her performance was not acceptable. My only concern was: How in the hell did this person get through the hiring and training process to start with? Was it because she was a female? Was it because she was the wife of a Standards Captain? Was this the future of aviation in America? Too many questions and too few answers. I made my report to the Chief Pilot and the Fleet Captain. They both thanked me for my opinion and assured me that she would not fly as a copilot with United again. She returned to her position as a 727 Second Officer.

I wish that this story ended with the above paragraph. A few years later, I received a phone call from an LCA who was with the B-737 fleet—now a glass cockpit airplane that was flown mostly with the fingertips (computerized) as opposed to the "seat of the pants." This LCA, whom I did not know, informed me that he was scheduled to conduct an IOE with the person that I had flown with some two years previously. He wanted me to brief him as to what happened earlier—he knew that this person had some "history." I pleaded the "fifth" and refused to defame that copilot—it would be up to him as to whether she should be allowed to fly as a pilot in control with UAL. To this day I do not know if she passed her IOE as a 737 First Officer.

Chapter Twenty-One

"No Pilot Can Fly Forever Without Getting Killed!"

The last three years of a pilot's career are, unfortunately, the years that one is forced to "chase the flying." Because of the structure of the pension plan, the retired pilot receives a pension based on the salary he/she received during those last three years. As I approached the age of 57, I began to look toward that inevitable future. I was tempted to remain on the B-727 and enjoy those final years flying my favorite commercial airliner as a senior Captain in Denver. But I also had to crunch the numbers. Suddenly I was senior enough to get a Captain bid on the B-767—a fairly large raise in pay. I passed up that opportunity because I decided that if I waited another six months I could get a DC-10 bid, a bigger pay raise. Then I looked into the future another six months and thought—maybe I can get a B-747 bid in the junior domicile of Honolulu! That flying had always been beyond my wildest dreams—I figured that I would retire on the DC-10. Captain bids in HNL were going fairly junior for several reasons. Most Captains in their last three years were established in a domicile near their home and Honolulu was not an easy commute. To move to the Islands was not easy—and the cost of living there was the highest in the nation.

When I brought up the subject of transferring to Hawaii for those last three years to my wife, Donna, she showed her flexibility and accommodating nature when she said, "Let's go for it!" In 1996 I successfully received a bid on the big bird, sometimes called the aluminum overcast, and was scheduled to train so as to be based in HNL in January, 1997. I would spend a few months flying the 727 from DEN before my training and I decided to enjoy it to the fullest. I refused to accept any LCA assignments the last two months and flew some of the most fun and rewarding trips of my career. When I had a nice layover, Donna would accompany me and we enjoyed those layovers together. Finally I arrived at my last month on the 727, the last month that I would be based in DEN, the last month that I would fly domestic trips. My flying partners that last month were two of the best—I could not have chosen a better copilot or flight engineer. The engineer was an ex-Air Force pilot named Jim who was also an excellent tennis player. We took our tennis rackets on each trip and played some really fun tennis—I believe that Jim always won, but he tried his best to make me look good! The copilot was a great gal named Betsy, also an Air Force product who happened to be one of the best pilots I ever had the pleasure of flying with. She was also one of the "boys" who loved to go out on layovers and drink beer, eat pizza and even shoot pool. Her husband was also a pilot who had his own flying business, quite successful I might add. My two cockpit crew members made that last month a most enjoyable one.

I tried to make the last trip that month as routine as possible but Betsy and Jim had other plans. I was treated like a king and I loved it. Betsy insisted that I fly every leg and she graded me on each landing. I tried my best to make every one of those last landings better than the previous one. On the second day of our three day trip I was flying an early morning flight from Phoenix to Denver. We were landing in Denver under perfect conditions—arriving from the south and landing to the north at DIA, runway 35L, 12,000 feet long with the last turn off being the closest one to our assigned gate. As I rotated the nose for the landing the S/O, Jim, shouted, "Power!" Later he confessed that he did that just to make my landing a bit more complicated. I ignored Jim's command and eased the power off. I thought that we should be on the ground by now but nothing seemed to happen. Then I noticed the speed brake lever starting to move rearward—this only happened when the tires were spinning up—we were on the ground! I stopped the progress of the automatic speed brakes—they often screwed up a good landing—and held the nose in the air until it slowly fell to the runway. I reached for the reverser levers and decided not to bother—we had plenty of runway remaining and there was no need to make a lot of noise. We slowed gradually and I turned off of the runway at the end. Not a word had been said in the cockpit. Then we could hear cheering from the passengers—probably prompted by the First Flight Attendant, who knew that it was my last trip on the 727. Betsy and Jim both began to clap and cheer—it was without a doubt the best landing of my career! When we arrived at the gate and the cockpit door was opened, the First Stew entered and said, "Captain, I've been flying over 30 years and that was the smoothest landing I have ever witnessed!" That was quite a compliment from such an experienced professional. As the passengers streamed by they too gave me some wonderful compliments. Even the seasoned business travelers shook my hand and said that it was the best landing they had ever witnessed. That would have been the perfect way to end my 727 flying career—but there were two more legs to go.

After our usual two hour layover in DEN we continued on to Boston. I insisted that Betsy fly that leg—knowing that I could never make a better landing than the one I had just made in DEN. As usual she did a remarkable job and we enjoyed a fun layover with a great seafood dinner at one of the best restaurants in town, Bookbinders, located in the basement of our hotel. The next day we flew back to Denver—this was to be my very last flight on the 727 and I was feeling a bit nostalgic. I wish that I could say that the last landing was as good as or better than the one the day before—it was a *good* landing but I realized that the one on the previous day was THAT ONE IN A LIFETIME!

The next month I started training for the B-747. I found that school to be truly a "gentleman's course" and perhaps the most fun training ever. There was only one other pilot in the class, a very senior engineer who was upgrading to the copilot position. He had years of copilot experience with another airline and remained as a 747 engineer with United until his seniority allowed him to move to the right seat. Since he was currently on the airplane he was excused from the two weeks of ground school and enjoyed a little vacation until we started simulator work. As I was now the only pilot in the class the instructor and I set our own schedule—I think we spent less than three hours each day in the classroom and worked only three or four days each of those two weeks. The rest of the instruction was equally relaxing and soon I had my type rating and was ready for my IOE.

My IOE started with a flight to Honolulu with a good friend named Mack. We had both been Standard Captains in the 727 fleet some years previously. I was scheduled to deadhead from DEN to SFO early in the morning to arrive in San Francisco in time to do the flight planning for the trip to HNL. It was a tight connection in SFO in light of the fact that UAL dispatch was located remotely from the terminal and it required catching a crew bus each direction. I had asked the crew desk to let me deadhead the evening before and stay in a local hotel to ensure that I had sufficient time. The crew desk, being penny wise and pound foolish, refused. When I arrived at the airport for my flight the next morning the gate agent gave me some bad news. My assigned flight, a DC-10, had a serious mechanical problem and would be at least three hours late! Many of these flights to major hubs such as SFO had what were called "wing-tip flights"—which meant that there was also a smaller plane leaving at basically the same time for the same destination. In this case there was a B-727 flight scheduled to depart 30 minutes later. I asked the agent if I could catch that flight. He laughed and said, "Captain, that flight is completely full with full fare passengers, your only chance would be to ride in the cockpit."

Strangely enough, there was a small clause in the pilot's contract that prevented me from riding in the cockpit when deadheading to fly a revenue trip that was scheduled for over four hours in length. Pilots were required to be accommodated only in First Class when this was the situation. I now went to the gate for the 727 flight and found that it too was running almost one hour late. The poor gate agent was really stressed—passengers from the DC-10 flight were streaming to his desk to try to get a seat on a flight that was already completely full and the scene was a bit chaotic! I knew the agent and really did not want to add to his workload but had no choice. When I told him that I REALLY NEEDED to get on that flight he repeated what I had heard from the other gate—no way unless I rode in the cockpit! Then I used his telephone at the podium and called the Duty Flight Manager. After explaining the situation to the Duty Man I handed the phone to the gate agent. After several nods and "yes sirs" he hung up the phone. He looked at me and said, "I don't know what's going on but I have to pull a full revenue passenger from first class and give you that seat. This is not going to be fun!"

I didn't like the situation any better than the gate agent. I told the agent to wait until the flight was ready for departure before pulling someone off— maybe we could work something out. Finally the flight was ready for departure—it would arrive in SFO about thirty minutes before my flight to HNL was scheduled to depart. I contacted the IOE crew scheduler and gave the bad news—no way could I arrive in SFO in time to do the flight planning. I was advised that I was the only pilot available and the trip would depart whenever I arrived—otherwise it would be cancelled. It appeared that my only choice was to bump some poor soul from his/her first class seat and feel like a real jerk. Finally I came up with an alternate solution. It seemed that the flight was going to depart with one empty *stew jump seat!* Although certainly unusual, there were no rules that said I could not sit on the flight attendant seat for the flight to SFO!

I waited until all passengers were boarded before I walked down the jetway with my two bags. I stepped into the cockpit and introduced myself to the Captain, noticing that there were two junior pilots occupying the observer seats. The most junior started to get up, thinking that I would be bumping him from the flight, when I motioned for him to keep his seat. I told the Captain what I was doing and he just rolled his eyes. I asked if I might leave my bags in his cockpit and of course he agreed. Then I introduced myself to the First Flight Attendant and asked if I might share her jump seat. She gave me a hard look and stated, "We're short one stew, I might need you to help with the service."

All I could do was grin and say, "Okay, but only if I don't have to wear an apron." The next two hours were really busy—I worked much harder that I had ever expected on an airliner. With my uniform jacket off most of the passengers thought that I really was a flight attendant, and a very incompetent one at that. Mostly I worked in the galley making drink orders that were given to the head stew and getting meals out of the ovens. When we landed in SFO I was a bit tired but really happy that the hardest part of the trip was now behind me!

When I arrived at the departure gate for my first flight in the 747 it was about twenty minutes before pushback. The Check Pilot, my friend Mack, had completed the flight planning and was busily loading waypoints into the INS computer when I entered the cockpit. The engineer helped me stow my bag—I had never been a crewmember on a 747 and did not even know where to put my overnight bag! After I strapped into the left seat I looked toward Mack and asked, "Ready for the checklist?" He started laughing and merely answered, "Yes Sir, Captain." We departed on time.

It was a fun flight to HNL although there were thunderstorms and heavy rain when we arrived. We actually landed on runway 26—the first and only time I can recall that a flight I was aboard was forced to land in that direction. Normally the winds were easterly and all landings and departures were in that direction. I managed to make a very smooth landing that first flight and Mack gave credit where it belonged. He said, "You were lucky, the wet runway cushioned your landing!"

We spent the rest of the day and the next talking about the idiosyncrasies of the B-747. Mack had been flying as Captain for several years and knew the aircraft quite well. He gave me lots of tips and pointers about flying that huge aircraft. He stressed that the pilot needed to pull back on the yoke very hard to initiate the flare just before landing. I had not done that when I made my first landing—again he insisted that my smooth landing was mostly luck because of the wet runway. I promised that I would do what he suggested on the next landing, which would be in SFO at dawn the next morning. We departed HNL late in the evening after our 33-hour layover and arrived on schedule just before daylight in the bay area. The weather was a bit foggy as usual but the approach was basically routine. Just before touchdown, Mack reminded me once again that I had to pull back on the controls with more force than usual to ensure a smooth landing. I trusted my mentor and gave the yoke a mighty tug just when I thought the wheels were ready to meet the runway. WE LEAPED INTO THE AIR! Mack started laughing aloud and the engineer commented, "He does this to every new 747 Captain."

Now I had my hands full—the power was off, airspeed was decaying and we were now starting to come down like the proverbial rock! I jammed the throttles almost full forward to lessen the impact and almost salvaged the landing. We came down hard, but not hard enough to awaken the most sound sleepers. My second landing on the 747 was certainly not a thing of beauty, but again I learned a valuable lesson. Mack was still laughing as we parked the airplane and I was calling him some choice names. When we deplaned, I asked him, "Do you think I pulled back a little too hard?" His only comment: "NO SHIT!"

My wife and I moved to Hawaii in January 1997. We thought that we would spend the rest of my flying career based in the Honolulu domicile, almost three years. We had vague plans of spending one year on each of three different islands. We decided to spend the first year on the island of Oahu, but live as far away as possible from the city of Honolulu and its tourist trap called Waikiki Beach. We would not give up our residence in the desert, but needed a comfortable place while spending time for work and play in Hawaii. We chose to lease a very nice condo on the North Shore at Turtle Bay, adjacent to the Hilton Hotel Resort of the same name. It was perfect—our own little piece of Paradise! We were situated on a golf course overlooking the beach—within easy walking distance to all of the amenities of the resort. Tennis was available every day and the snorkeling was the best on the island. The first time I played tennis there I discovered that seven out of eight of the players on our two courts were current or retired Airline Pilots! It was a really fun group.

The pilot domicile in Honolulu was the smallest in the system, consisting of roughly 50 crews or 150 pilots. The Chief Pilot was a friend of mine—also named Bill—and the flight office was probably the friendliest in the system. The domicile culture mimicked that of the island—very laidback. The pilots based in HNL only flew westward; they were not responsible for trips to the mainland, which were flown by SFO crews. There were only four departures each day, two to Narita and two to Osaka, Japan. These flights continued on to other cities in the Far East. Before I completed my IOE, it was required that I fly to Japan and on to China. Flying into the Chinese cities of Shanghai and Beijing was so unique it was mandatory that each new Captain in HNL be accompanied by an LCA to complete his qualification.

After getting settled in Hawaii it was time for the final portion of my IOE. The LCA was a senior Captain named Felix. I did not know Felix personally but was aware of his reputation—a good one I might add. He had been a leader and officer in the union, ALPA, as long as I could remember. He was near the end of his career with United and it was a pleasure for me to be assigned to fly with this gentleman. He assumed the role of the First Officer for the trip to Narita and Shanghai. The flight to NRT was pretty much routine, although I was once again amazed at the primitive navigation systems still in use when flying across the vast reaches of the Pacific. Once out of radio range of the Hawaiian Islands, we used HF radios for position reporting—the same frequencies that were used over thirty years ago. Our navigation depended on the INS systems. We were equipped with three independent INS systems—they were *"intermixed"* before departure and the aircraft followed the guidance of the best two of the three inputs! The permissible margin of error was an astounding THREE MILES PER HOUR! This meant that after a seven-hour flight to NRT, it was okay to be 21 miles off course! Keep in mind that R-Nav and GPS—the next generation of computerized navigation systems—were not installed on the older model 747's. The newest version, the 747-400, was a glass cockpit type and was starting to replace the older versions. I would not get the opportunity to fly the 400.

During our layover in Narita, Felix introduced me to all of the "crew hang-outs"—places called the Flyers Club, the Cage and the worst of all, the Truck. The Flyers Club was located down an alley and up a long flight of rickety stairs. It was always full of pilots and crews from every airline that flew into NRT. Peanuts were free and as usual the shells were thrown on the floor to add to the "atmosphere." The best part of this place was the fact that *crash movies* were played over and over on the closed circuit TVs scattered around the bar. We had all seen those graphic flicks of planes crashing onto aircraft carriers, spinning into the ground and/or colliding in flight many, many times and we collectively groaned or cheered with each crash. The Cage was another dump that catered mostly to flight attendants who spent their time doing karaoke routines on the small stage. After a few too many beers, some of the more adventuresome pilots would make feeble attempts with the microphone—usually to a lot of boos from the crowd of FAs who were certainly much more talented. The Truck consisted of two semi-trailers that were joined together on a small lot within walking distance to the layover hotel. It was usually the last stop on the bar circuit and was the hang out for the younger crews who still liked loud, loud music and warm drinks. The only bathroom at the Truck was a binjo ditch arrangement shared by all. It was easily located by merely following the stench.

Felix and I met the following morning and he gave a thorough brief of our next leg to Shanghai. My first landing in China would be at night and I was warned about the fact that many of the navaids would probably not be working. Every approach to the airport was started from a single VOR—Felix related that it had been out of service for over six months. Then he told me that most of the Captains flying into China set up the INS for each fix on the approaches. Considering that the flight to SHA (airport designation for Shanghai—later changed to PVR) was almost six hours (due to the fact that the Chinese would not allow us to fly direct because we were not permitted to fly over Korea before landing in China) I calculated that the INS could be as much as 18 miles off when we arrived! I was also told that many of the Captains flying into China carried a hand held GPS that they had purchased from Radio Shack and relied on those inputs instead of the INS! This was one hell of a way to carry 450 passengers into a primitive airport on the Chinese mainland!

When we arrived in the vicinity of Shanghai, we were informed that the radar for approach control was "out of service." Felix commented that this was normal—their radar was so primitive that they were embarrassed to attempt to guide us to the airport. I also knew that the Chinese Military controlled the airspace and armed fighters would meet with any deviation from prescribed arrival routes! The weather was not too bad—visibility was reported as three miles in "haze"—basically smog. I was cleared for a non-precision approach to the runway. Pilots all know that the most precise flying that they will ever be required to do is to fly the dreaded *non-precision approach!*

When I rolled out on final with gear and flaps extended I peeked out over the glare shield—nothing was visible and we were only three miles from the field, as far as I could guesstimate. Felix calmly asked if I had the runway in sight. I squinted again and finally saw two very dim rows of lights directly ahead. I reported that I had what appeared to be taxiway lights. Felix laughed and said, "Those are the runway lights—electrical power is so poor that they are probably only the equivalent of sixty watt bulbs in the US." I landed between those two strings of dim lights and taxied to the gate with a sigh of relief. Flying into China was certainly exciting and also a bit of a challenge! I was beginning to like flying this huge bird into exotic places!

When we arrived at our hotel it was after ten PM local time. Our layover was about 14 hours so I had time for a beer before the twelve-hour rule came into play. The other crewmembers opted to pass on my invitation for a drink. I, on the other hand, had never been to China and at least wanted to walk around a bit before retiring for the night. I was amazed at the number of employees at the hotel—it was impossible to walk more than a few steps before someone offered his/her assistance. All of the employees spoke acceptable English and were literally tripping over each other to be of help to an American. I had the impression that the Chinese people were genuinely "in love with Westerners" and wanted to extend every courtesy. After a short walk of a few blocks from the hotel, I returned to visit the one bar that I had noticed just off the main lobby. When I entered the room it was almost pitch black—I paused to let my eyes adapt and finally located the bar where all the seats were empty. I could tell that there were people sitting at the small tables throughout the room but the darkness prevented me from making an estimate of how many customers were there. Behind the bar there seemed to be a bartender every three feet—the closest one took my order for a Budweiser and asked if I would like some popcorn. Never one to turn down my favorite snack, I said yes. Quickly I was given a can of beer that looked to be Budweiser—but it sure tasted different. I found out later that it was brewed in China and their process was evidently quite different from that in St. Louis. Then I was presented with a tiny cup of popcorn, about one handful. At the same time the band returned from a break and took their positions on the small stage.

As I tossed a few kernels of popcorn into my mouth the band began to play. I don't know which was worse! The popcorn was burnt and very greasy and the band was incredibly loud. After I took a few swigs of the lousy beer to wash the bad taste of the popcorn away I decided that this was just not my kind of place! I asked the bartender for a check and was soon presented with a tiny piece of paper—of course I could not read the Chinese writing and had no idea how much the bill was. I showed the barman my room key and asked if I could sign the tab to my room account. He nodded and I scribbled my name and number on the paper and quickly left the room. The next morning when I checked out I found that the bar tab was almost $40.00 in American currency. When I complained, I was told that the "night club" charged for the entertainment as well as a substantial cover fee! Capitalism had certainly taken over in this Communist nation!

When we departed the next morning I was able to take a good look at the airport—basically only one runway that was narrower than the standard width of those in the U.S. The taxiways were also very narrow—the outboard engines extended beyond the pavement and we created a cloud of dust on both sides as we taxied to the runway. Even more disconcerting was the incredible amount of pedestrian traffic all around the airport. People walked or rode their bicycles nonchalantly along the runways and ramp areas and often disappeared beneath the nose of the plane as we moved along. As our 747 neared the departure runway I was required to make a 180-degree turn to line up on the runway. Due to the narrow taxiways I would have to make square turns that would require additional power on the outboard engines. I was concerned about those pedestrians getting jet blast during the turns and advised the tower about my concern. The tower controller responded, "No problem, sir, cleared for takeoff." Evidently, they had people to spare in China and no one cared if a few got blown away!

After my IOE was completed, Felix asked me to become a Line Check Airman. He would soon retire and LCAs were hard to come by in the 747 fleet, mainly because it meant many more trips into China than the normal line Captain would expect. I felt entirely too green to take on that responsibility but agreed to give it some thought after about six months. After more coercion from the Chief Pilot, I did become an LCA after six months and enjoyed checking out new Captains and copilots on this fabulous machine. It was far different than IOE work on the 727. All 747 Captains were highly experienced; most having flown in the left seat on several different types of equipment, and the transition was a relative easy one. The same applied to new 747 copilots—they all knew how to fly!

Being a reserve Captain in HNL was a bit different than being a junior Captain in Chicago. It was very rare to not receive at least 36 hours advance notification for a trip. The very first day that I was on reserve after my IOE was an exception. I checked with the crew desk the previous evening and was advised that there were no open trips. I scheduled myself for a tennis game and was halfway through the second set when my cell phone rang. Only the crew desk had that number. I answered the call and the first words out of the scheduler's mouth were the dreaded: "How fast can you get to the airport?" Suddenly I felt that I was back in Chicago some twenty years previous. I responded, "One hour, maybe an hour and a half at the most."

The crew scheduler let out an audible gasp! He said, "Really? Every other Captain I call in Hawaii needs at least three hours, usually four, to get to the airport!" After telling him that I needed to get home to shower and pack, I asked him how long would I be away? He related that an inbound crew from LAX had been delayed and would be out of duty time before flying their scheduled flight back to the mainland. I would only fly one leg, lay over and deadhead back the next morning—a piece of cake. I rushed home and was about out the door for the airport when the phone rang again. It was the same crewman. He said, "Forget it Captain, I was not able to find a copilot or second officer for a short callout—the trip is cancelled. You can go back to your tennis game."

The trips flown from the HNL domicile were all at least five days long and some were as long as nine days. Generally you flew only two or possibly three trips each month. This meant that there was a lot of time off between assignments—time to enjoy all the delights of the Hawaiian Islands. We generally returned to the mainland once each month and Donna sometimes returned by herself when I departed on a long trip. Often she would accompany me on some of the better pairings and it was like a mini-vacation. When Donna did not go along she would drive me to the airport and pick me up when I returned. The return flight from the Far East was always an all-nighter that arrived usually an hour or two after sunrise. No matter how you prepared for that all night flight; sleeping late that morning, taking a nap in the afternoon, etc., you always felt like crap when you made that last landing looking into the sun at Honolulu. Donna knew how tired I would be and she always brought a present for the drive to our condo on the North Shore. As we started down that last small hill and caught sight of the ocean near the town of Haleiwa, I breathed a sigh of comfort and opened that ice-cold can of Coors Light that Donna brought. A beer never tasted better—even if it was only 9 AM!

My favorite trip of all was one that included a Guam turn. All other airports in the Far East had very structured arrivals followed by a precision instrument approach, regardless of the weather. It was not only boring but it was wasteful—wasteful of time, fuel and money. Even if your airplane was the only one in the sky arriving at NRT, you were still required to fly a very circuitous approach in order to arrive at the runway that was visible from fifty miles away. In Guam, the controllers were American—most ex-military. My first arrival in Guam was typical. We contacted the controller about 100 miles away from the airport. His first response was, "Do you have the airport in sight?" I answered, "I have the airport in sight, I have the runway in sight and I have our gate in sight!" The controller laughed and in his southern drawl said, "You're cleared to land and cleared to the gate—call me when ready to taxi out for takeoff." Unfortunately, a few months later a KAL 747 crashed just short of the runway and thereafter we were required to execute a lengthy instrument approach on every arrival.

Chapter Twenty-Two

"The Optimist Invented the Airplane, The Pessimist Invented the Parachute!"

My next favorite airport in the Far East was Manila. The airport itself was not particularly efficient but the layover more than made up for what was lacking from the bureaucrats that controlled the airdrome. This airport had long been on the "Black List" due to its lack of proper security. When international pilots complained long enough about security concerns, an airport was placed on the so-called Black List and the pilots threatened to stop flying there until the situation had been corrected. Now the airport officials had over-reacted and the levels of security were among the strictest in the world. Armed guards, actually active duty military, seemed to be everywhere. The pilots were escorted to and from the airplanes by those soldiers who carried fully loaded machine guns. The first time I landed there, late at night as usual, those guards met our crew as we departed the cockpit. We were escorted into the main terminal where we were now on our own. The terminal was bedlam! It was almost impossible to push through the masses of people who seemed to be trying to go in every direction but getting absolutely nowhere.

Thankfully the copilot was familiar with the local procedures and he told us to stand still and wait for a tall man in a white uniform. Very soon such a person appeared and led us through the throngs of humanity. As he strode through the crowds, it was like the parting of the Red Sea. When we arrived outside the terminal, it was even more chaotic. Vehicles were bumper to bumper and each driver tried to honk his horn louder than the others. Again the crowds parted and we were led to a long white limo parked in a restricted area. As we sank into the soft luxurious leather in this air-conditioned limo, the driver said to me, "Captain, there are drinks for you and your crew in the bar refrigerator." I found the fridge to be well stocked and passed out ice-cold San Miguel beers for the three of us. The Flight Attendants, all 23 of them, were transported to a different hotel in a large bus. They were surely not getting the treatment that we were now enjoying. The driver weaved masterfully through the traffic, mostly consisting of thousands of WW II type jitneys, colorfully decorated and outfitted with every imaginable device for making noise! Even though it was after ten PM local time the streets were teeming with people and traffic. Manila was alive and well!

When we arrived at The Westin Manila the driver took my bags personally and requested that I follow him into the Hotel. As we passed by the front desk, the copilot and second officer stopped to check-in. The driver escorted me to a private room where I was met by a concierge who stood at attention as I entered the room. I was handed a large golden key and profusely welcomed to this fine hotel. I was asked to choose from a large selection of beverages what I would like to be delivered to my room. I selected bottled water.

When I arrived at my suite my luggage had been carefully unpacked and my uniforms hung in the spacious closet. My accommodations consisted of a corner suite with a wrap-around balcony with magnificent views of downtown Manila on one side and the beautiful bay on the other. There were three large rooms and two baths in this suite that probably had over 1000 square feet of space. There were three large TVs and of course a well stocked bar. The master bath was all marble. This was definitely the way Airline Captains were supposed to be treated! As I was changing clothes in order to meet with my fellow pilots for a beer in the lobby bar, there was a soft knock on my door. The hotel employee handed me a wrapped gift and asked if there was anything—*anything*—else I wanted. I had the feeling that he would be happy to provide booze, drugs, women, or anything else I desired! I had never been treated so lavishly in my life—this was the way it should always be! When I opened the "gift" I found it to be a very nice bottle of the local rum. I kept it as a souvenir.

The next morning I departed the hotel in my running shorts and t-shirt for a little jog. When I reached the front lobby door the doorman stopped me. He said, "Captain, let me show you where to jog and where not to jog." How did he know that I was the Captain the way I was dressed? The copilot was in his forties and the second officer was in his sixties—like most of the engineers, he was a "retread." Maybe the doorman called all of the crew members "Captain" or maybe it was one of those mysteries of life! I was so impressed with the accommodations and the treatment I had received that I brought Donna on the next trip that I flew into Manila. It was like a mini-vacation.

Donna and I took advantage of all of the amenities at this Five Star Hotel. We played tennis on the roof top courts with a ball boy in attendance. He kept score and made sure that we never had to bend over to pick up a tennis ball—quite a treat. I tipped the ball boy two dollars American. Donna insisted that I should give more—so I increased the tip to five dollars. The young man was extremely grateful. The next day when I checked out I found out why. My account was automatically charged $5.00 for his services—he had made a small fortune! There was a golf driving range at this hotel where the guest could hit balls out into the bay. Again, one never had to bend over to tee up the ball—an attendant placed it there. When the balls were hit out into the water there were young men in kayaks (with hard hats) who picked up the floating golf balls and returned them to the range. This was the way all layover hotels should be!

Our flight from Manila went to Seoul, Korea and after a short layover continued to Narita for a longer layover before returning to Hawaii. The flight from Seoul was always full and I was a bit concerned about Donna being able to get on as an NRSA (non-revenue space available) employee. When I boarded the flight I kissed Donna goodbye and gave her options for returning to Narita if she did not get boarded on my flight. The Chief Purser, a rather crusty flight attendant from Chicago, noticed my concern. She came into the cockpit as the passengers were being boarded and said, "Captain, your wife will be boarded—I took care of it!" I wasn't sure how she "took care" of it but thanked her and held my breath. Just as the doors were closing prior to our pushback, Donna entered the cockpit. She was laughing as she said that she had been seated in First Class and was being treated like royalty. Later she told me the whole story. The Korean gate agent had told her that the plane was full and she would not be boarded. Then the Chief Purser walked up to the agent and said, "This lady is the wife of the Captain and this airplane will not depart until she has been seated in First Class." Before the agent could protest, the Purser continued, "The flight attendants are going to be out of duty time shortly and we will all walk off the plane and go to a hotel if we do not depart on time with this lady onboard!" Donna was instantly presented with a boarding pass and we departed on time! Once again I had been

368

reminded that the Flight Attendants were the ones who actually controlled the airline. The Captain was only in charge after the flight had departed the gate!

The fifth and final engine failure of my career happened on a flight from Honolulu to Osaka, Japan. Donna dropped me off at the airport that morning and the flight departed on time and seemed to be routine. As usual the plane was full with 450 passengers, 23 flight attendants and a cockpit crew of three. There were also 28 infants sitting on laps. Our total souls on board (SOBs) were over 500—a small city flying through the air! The Captain was the MAYOR! At such heavy weights our climb speed was quite high and we were routinely given permission to exceed the 250-knot restriction below 10,000 feet. We were programmed for a step climb as usual—as we burned off fuel and became lighter we were able to climb to higher and more fuel-efficient altitudes. After almost four hours enroute we were finally able to climb to 35,000 feet. We were very near the "coffin corner" as we struggled to FL 350 and leveled. Just as I started to retard the throttles to cruise settings I noticed a "low oil pressure warning light" start to flicker. I turned to look at the engineer's panel and at the same time the copilot said, "We're losing the number two engine!" The S/O chimed in with, "Oil pressure dropping to zero on number two!" With a 25% loss of thrust the airplane simply could not fly at this altitude and I felt a shudder start in the airframe. I pushed over on the controls and started a descent—at the same time starting a gradual turn to the left. This was the normal procedure when making an emergency descent in uncontrolled airspace over the ocean. I gave the orders to shut down the engine and follow the prescribed checklists as I continued to descend. We had not yet reached the "Point of no Return" (actually called the PET or point of equal time) which meant that we would have to return to HNL instead of continuing to Osaka.

I continued to fly the aircraft and the rest of the crew handled communications and checklists. Without referring to the charts in the flight manual, I thought that the aircraft should fly okay at about 27,000 feet and I started to level as we approached that altitude. The three operating engines were set to max continuous thrust settings. The airframe started to shutter as I attempted to level—obviously I needed a lower altitude or less weight. I told the S/O to start dumping fuel so as to arrive for landing at HNL at the maximum permissible landing weight. As he started dumping fuel I continued to descend. I also briefed the passengers as to our "problem" and advised them that we would be returning to HNL. I descended to 17,000 feet before reaching a comfortable altitude—much lower than the charts indicated. We were probably heavier than we thought—maybe they should weigh the planes when empty to find out how much dirt had fallen into the cracks?

We were given priority to land on the longest runway in HNL and everything was textbook perfect. When we were switched to tower frequency the controller asked if we could slow so that some departures could be accommodated—obviously he had not been advised that we had an engine shut down! The copilot angrily responded with a few expletives and the tower controller apologized—we were now cleared to land without restriction.

After completion of the usual paperwork the crew was taken to a local hotel for the night. We would start over again the next day—same flight, same pairing, just one day later. I contacted my wife and she joined me at the hotel for dinner, which we enjoyed via room service. The next day we returned to the airport to flight plan and I discovered that the aircraft that we were scheduled to fly was the same as the one from the previous day! How could this be? I knew that United did not have spare engines or maintenance personnel in HNL to accomplish an engine change—and there was a brand new engine installed where the failed engine had been! I contacted system maintenance in SFO and was given the explanation. After we reported our engine failure to the company via radio, a special crew from SFO flight test was alerted and booked on the next flight to HNL. They arrived early that evening, flew the aircraft to SFO on THREE ENGINES—empty of course— where a maintenance crew waited. The engine was replaced in a matter of hours and the aircraft was then ferried, again by a test crew, back to HNL! This all took place in less than 16 hours. I was amazed at the efficiency of United's maintenance department. Then I remembered that a single B-747 could generate as much as one million dollars in revenue every 24-hour day—miracles were possible when large sums of money were involved!

There's an interesting postscript to this engine failure event that borders somewhere between a strange coincidence and something outright eerie. A week or two earlier I had ordered a wooden model of a 747 from a Filipino artisan in Manila. This skilled craftsman could construct a beautifully detailed scale model of any airliner being flown at the time. I commissioned him to build a model of the 747-100 with United Airline colors. A month or two passed before I returned to Manila and found a large wooden box with my name on it at flight operations. It was packed for shipping and I did not open it until several months later at my home in southern California. As I assembled the model, I was impressed with the accuracy and detail that had gone into this work of art. Then I noticed the aircraft number on the fuselage—N153UA. I said to Donna, "What a coincidence, this is the number of the aircraft that I was flying when the engine failed."

Donna then looked over the model and asked, "Wasn't it the number two engine that failed? You better take a good look into the intake of number 2 on this model!"

I looked at the front of the number two engine and noticed that some of the compressor blades were missing! Obviously the blades were only painted on and the artist had missed a few strokes of the brush. Nevertheless, the engine was flawed. Perhaps that's why it failed!

Somehow I had managed to avoid flights into the Chinese capital of Beijing the first six months or so after being based in HNL. I was almost used to the idiosyncrasies of Shanghai by now, but the tales I heard from other crewmembers about PEK (code for Beijing, once Peking) were alarming. The facilities there were as bad as SHA and the controllers were even worse! It really seemed that the Chinese government did not want foreign carriers such as UAL flying into their country and they were sometimes less than helpful to the pilots. Finally I was assigned a trip that included a PEK layover. In a way I looked forward to the challenge and I also really wanted to visit the Great Wall, not accessible from SHA. As usual, the flight departed HNL for NRT and after a long layover we would fly to PEK. The layover there was only about 12 hours. During the long layover in Narita, I spent a great deal of time studying the route to PEK and the layout of the airport—I wanted no surprises. We would depart NRT after dark and land in PEK shortly before midnight local time. That afternoon I accessed the computer provided for the pilots at the hotel to check the weather and details of the flight. The weather forecast was for scattered rain showers with periods of reduced visibility at times—no real problems. Then I checked, via the computer, the planned load and the proposed takeoff gross weight. There I had a big surprise!

The aircraft I was scheduled to fly was one of only two in the fleet—hybrids that were completely different from all other 747's in United's fleet. I had never flown that type! During my training for the 747, I was told that there were three different types of planes in the fleet: The 747-100, basically the original 747, called the "rope start" or the "Jurassic Jet" by the pilots; the 747-238, an advanced version with better engines and avionics; and a strange breed, the 747-200B. The 200B was an intermediate step from the analog generation of aircraft to the new "glass cockpit" types that would soon replace their dinosaur predecessors. These two airplanes were the longest-range planes in the world at the time and were kept in a closed loop between New York (JFK) and Tokyo (NRT). They were specially configured with over 100 first class leather recliner seats and a small coach section that was more like business class than economy. Access to the upper deck and cockpit was via wide stairs instead of the narrow spiral staircase on the other types. These differences were of no concern to the pilots—the major differences that were of concern to us were many and profound!

During my training for the 747 I was told by my instructor, "Don't even worry about the 200B—you will never see it in your career unless you transfer to New York. We have a special three day course for those pilots." There was an entire chapter in the flight manual explaining the differences and procedures for this aircraft—this chapter was over 40 pages long! I had never opened the pages of that chapter. The main concern was the special navigation system, called, appropriately, PMS, which stood for Performance Management System. It was mandatory that the aircraft be flown with this system engaged—it linked flight directors, auto pilots and auto throttles together to fly the plane more efficiently than a mere mortal! It required lengthy programming before departure—in addition to the normal cockpit setup.

After I discovered that we would be flying this strange beast to PEK that evening, I contacted the copilot and second officer. The copilot, a fairly senior type who was a native Hawaiian of Japanese descent (great to have on layovers to translate the menus) had flown into PEK before but had never flown the 200B. The Second Officer, who was almost 70 years old and approaching senility, was taking his afternoon nap and not available for our brief. Yukio, who was the F/O, and I spent several hours studying the chapter about the plane we would soon be flying and felt that we could manage the new systems. When we met in the lobby of the hotel for the ride to the airport, I asked the S/O if he had ever flown the 200B. Of course his reply was, "What's a 200B?"

Since the S/O would not really be involved with the flying or navigating, I did not feel concerned about his lack of knowledge. My only concern for him was that this aircraft had a completely different communication system, called SATCOM, which was the cutting edge for long-range flights that enabled the pilots to contact controllers and company dispatchers via satellite versus HF frequencies. This was something that the pilots had been wanting for a very long time. I asked the S/O to review those procedures and he mumbled that he could handle this new challenge. Yukio and I had our hands full with the different avionic and navigation systems but managed to at least stay up with the airplane as we approached PEK. Control areas in that part of the world were very narrow. At our cruise speeds we passed from one controller to another very rapidly with each new controller speaking a different dialect than that of the previous controller. Often we were given a new frequency, checked in and were immediately handed off to another controller on a different frequency. When less than one hour from landing we were passed to our first Chinese controller. We had to pay special attention as these controllers spoke very rapidly with heavy accents and did not like to repeat their instructions.

That first controller said, "United, Beijing cannot accept you, return to base." I looked to Yukio and said, "Did he say *return to base*?" Yukio asked the controller to repeat—we were met with silence. After several more requests for the controller to repeat his previous instructions, the controller merely gave us a new frequency to contact the next controller! After Yukio checked in, the new controller said, "No can land at Beijing—return to base." I had never heard such a clearance and asked the controller if the airport was closed. Again my request was met with silence. We were still hurling through the skies at nine tenths the speed of sound and rapidly approaching a point that we either had to descend or make a decision to return to Narita. Our alternate airport was Shanghai and I asked the Second Officer to check the SHA weather and also contact UAL dispatch to relate our predicament. Several minutes passed without a response from the flight engineer. I looked back over my right shoulder and found him thumbing through the FOM (Flight Operations Manual) trying to look up the procedures for operating the SATCOM system. He was still in the index section! I realized that there would be no help from him for the rest of this flight. I told Yukio that I would handle the communications with the Chinese controllers if he would try to contact our dispatch for instructions. I felt that we were starting to get a bit BEHIND THE AIRPLANE at this time.

Trying to put as much authority in my voice as possible I told the controller that we either needed to continue to PEK or proceed to our alternate of SHA. After a long pause he replied that I could not go to SHA. I then requested to hold at my present position until I had contacted my company dispatch. He replied, "Cannot hold, return to base." Then I asked for clearance to NRT. This was met with a long silence. We were now less than 100 miles from the airport at PEK and my radar showed only a few rain showers in the area. About this time Yukio reported to me that he had been able to contact United dispatch and they were not aware of any problems, weather or otherwise, in the PEK area. I made my decision.

I told Yukio to tell the Chinese controller that I was starting my descent and turning to the airport for landing and needed no further assistance. The only response from the controller was a terse, "Okay." As I circumnavigated around a few buildups (in the Midwest in the summer these would have been called light rain showers), I told Yukio to contact PEK approach control. When the controller answered, Yukio looked at me and asked, "What do I tell him?"

I said, "Tell him that we are starting our approach for landing." The controller's response again was, "Okay." Once we were lined up for the runway I told Yukio to contact the tower and report that we were landing. He did so and the tower response was, "Okay." Then as though it was an afterthought he added, "Cleared to land." Visibility was at least ten miles and the showers had ended. The runway was wet but as usual that helped make a smooth landing. As we exited the runway, the controller—a different voice, ordered: "United, stop and hold your position!" I slowly brought the big bird to a stop on the taxiway and looked around the airport. Not a single airplane was moving. After several minutes, I keyed the mike and asked, "Why are we not allowed to continue to taxi?" After a long delay the controller said, "Other traffic has priority."

I looked far into the distance and noticed a small airplane under tow to a hanger. That was the only movement on the entire airport—and he had priority! This was the Chinese way of "saving face" and I was being punished for my arrogance! Finally we were cleared to continue taxiing but were directed to a remote parking area that was not even on my charts. Eventually I picked up a taxi director who had a tiny flashlight and followed his guidance until he disappeared under the nose of the aircraft. I decided that this was far enough and set the brakes and shut down the engines. This had been a trying day to say the least!

The passengers were deplaned to buses that arrived after a short wait and driven to the terminal, which we could see in the distance. There were many empty gates at that terminal. Since we were the only plane in town with United colors we (the pilots) left our flight bags in the cockpit and deplaned with the flight attendants. We were loaded onto a tiny bus, which appeared way too small to accommodate our 26 crewmembers. When all the seats were filled, the driver went to the back seat and pulled down a small jump seat on each side of the aisle. He then directed two F/A's to those seats. He continued to do this for each row until there was exactly the right number of seats. As the last person to board I would be sitting next to the driver. I looked at all of the personal bags sitting beside the bus—26 bags—and asked the driver where they would be boarded. The driver spoke no English but knew what I was trying to say. He started to pass each piece of baggage down the aisle— over the heads of those on the jump seats. Each person had to place a bag in his/her lap for the drive to the hotel. Welcome to Beijing!

When we reached the hotel, Yukio and I arranged for a car and driver early the next morning to take us to the Great Wall. In order to climb to the top of the Great Wall and return to the hotel in time for our departure back to NRT, we needed to leave by 4:00 AM—we would only have about four hours sleep. Not knowing if I would ever return to Beijing (silently hoping that I would not) it was worth losing a little sleep. The hotel concierge assured us that we would have a modern vehicle with an English-speaking driver.

Yukio and I showed up at 4 AM, a bit sleepy but eager for our adventure. Our driver spoke absolutely no English and his vehicle was little more than a wreck! I had hoped to get a bit of sleep during the two-hour ride to the Great Wall but spent the entire trip absolutely terrified! The driver drove like a maniac and his headlights were the equivalent of 40-watt bulbs. Pedestrians, bicycle riders, rickshaws, and other motorized vehicles were forced to the sides of the streets as we sped toward the Wall. It was still dark when the driver arrived at a large, empty parking lot and parked his vehicle. The driver immediately curled up in the front seat and fell asleep. Yukio and I wandered around in the parking lot until we located some steps—seemed a logical way to begin our climb to the top. As we neared those steps two figures appeared out of the shadows and approached. I was not sure if they were friends or foes. When they held out their hands for money, Yukio remembered that we were supposed to pay a fee to visit the Great Wall. After exchanging some funds, about two dollars each, we were on our way to the top. It was now getting light and the climbing seemed to be easy. Almost two hours later we were drenched in perspiration as we struggled up the last steps and stood on top of this remarkable landmark—one of the very few man-made objects recognizable from outer space by our astronauts.

After an hour or so on the wall we started back down—there was now a steady stream of visitors climbing upward but we were all alone on the downward trek. When we reached the parking lot we were met with vendors trying to sell their wares. Two women were very persistent in their efforts to sell us a Panda blanket. We were not interested, especially at the asking price of $150 American. The closer we came to our vehicle the faster the asking price was lowered. Soon it was only $50. We awakened our driver and prepared to leave. The ladies were still in tow as we started to drive away. The last words I heard as we left them behind were, "Ten dollars, okay?"

Traffic was a nightmare on the way back to the hotel and when we arrived we barely had time for a quick shower and change into uniforms for the trip to the airport. At the airport I was met by United's Airport Manager who was extremely apologetic for our treatment the previous night when we arrived. How did he know that we had been mishandled on our arrival? After flight planning we were taken to our airplane, still parked in the remote area where I had set the brakes. When I reached the cockpit I was amazed at where we were parked. The nose of the 747 was extending over a boundary wall that was about eight feet high. On the other side was the small back yard of a Chinese home. I was looking directly down into the back door of this home. The residents and their neighbors were all smiling and waving to me in the cockpit! I smiled and waved back.

Yukio and I once again programmed the PMS for our departure, setting in the expected routings and altitudes from our flight plan. The departure clearance was rather complicated and our altitudes were once again given in meters. Normally it would have been the copilot's leg as I had flown in the previous evening but Yukio and I agreed that I would make the takeoff and climbout. He was better with the communications and I felt more comfortable at the controls. The passenger load was light that morning and we had not boarded any fuel in China. For reasons that remain unclear, we landed the previous night with over 100,000 pounds of extra fuel just so that we would not have to buy fuel in China. I suspected that United felt that the Chinese fuel was not up to their usual standards.

The weather was overcast with light rainfall as we started the takeoff roll. Due to the light load and cool air, the aircraft performed like a fighter as we roared into the air and pitched up to the maximum angle of climb. This was the way to leave Beijing—quickly! I engaged the PMS after we were established in our climb and sat back to watch the auto systems perform their magic. Everything was working beautifully—always a sign that something was about to go wrong! The first thing that happened was the departure controller changed our routing. Not unusual, but it created more of a workload for both the copilot and myself as we had to reprogram the computer that was now in charge. Before that was complete we were given a change of altitude and told to switch to another frequency. We had originally been cleared to 7000 meters (22,966 feet) and the airplane was rapidly approaching that altitude. The new clearance was to level at 6500 meters. Everyone else was busy with other tasks so I looked at the conversion table that I kept in my flight bag and set the new altitude (21,325 feet) in the altitude alert box. Immediately a warning started to go off—we were rapidly going to bust that altitude and the autopilot was not able to correct quickly enough with the rate of climb that had been established. My only choice was to override the AP—which caused another alarm to sound! I managed to level the aircraft at the proper altitude and now had to assume manual navigation—things were getting very busy! Soon I had maps and charts all over my side of the cockpit. Yukio was still trying to contact the next controller and the Second Officer was busy with a minor fuel transfer problem. Then the Chief Purser entered the cockpit to inform me that two flight attendants were ill and she suspected there was something wrong with the airplane air conditioning system. Suddenly she stopped with her rambling, looked at the three of us frantically handling multiple problems, and merely said, "I guess you aren't listening to me with all those alarms going off! I'll come back later."

Just as I felt that things were coming under control, another alarm sounded. This was the overspeed warning, called the "clicker-clacker" that sounded when the airspeed was exceeding the maximum speed as determined by what was called a "barber-pole" on the airspeed indicators. At that time a speed warning was the least of my concerns and I chose to ignore that warning. Our clearance was changed again and Yukio was struggling to program the computer. I told him to not bother, as I was hand flying the aircraft at the time. He looked at me and said, "Captain, I'm having a hard time trying to communicate with all the alarms going off!" We both started to laugh and I turned to the S/O and told him to silence that overspeed warning. For the very first time the S/O acted quickly—he located the circuit breaker for aural warnings and pulled it out—the noise stopped and everything became dead silent. I was about to breathe a sigh of relief when Yukio shouted, "Look at the airspeed, we're about to go supersonic!" When I had disengaged the AP, the auto-throttles remained engaged at max climb power settings and we were now level and hurling through the air at ever increasing speed! We were indicating .98 mach—then it switched to .99. I was tempted to let it go and see if we could break the sound barrier in a 747, but my better judgment took over and I slowly reduced the thrust levers to normal settings. We were now out of Chinese airspace and cleared to resume our original routing. Everything was soon back to normal. It had certainly been an interesting departure—and, in a way, quite exciting. Even the Second Officer was laughing as he said, "That's the most fun I've had in years!"

I contacted the Chief Purser and asked her to come to the cockpit so that we could resolve the problem with the sick flight attendants. She said, "Is it safe to come up there now?" I assured her that everything was under control. When she entered the cockpit she reiterated her report of two of her crew being sick. I asked if any of the passengers were showing symptoms also. When she replied in the negative, I asked her to send one of the sick F/As to the cockpit. The young lady did appear to be a "bit green around the gills" when she reported to the flight deck. I asked her if she had eaten anything the previous evening that might have caused her sickness—she replied that she had not eaten anything during the 12-hour layover, not even breakfast that morning before departure. I told her to sit down on the jump seat behind me— then I ordered breakfast from the Chief Purser. After the young lady had consumed a rather large meal, I asked if she was felling better—she smiled and said yes. I repeated the process for the other "ill F/A" and the problem was solved!

After returning to Honolulu, I spoke with the chief pilot and expressed my concerns about the way we were handled by the Chinese controllers. He agreed that their procedures were not acceptable and we composed a letter that was sent to the Chinese equivalent of the FAA. We both doubted that we would ever receive a reply as the Chinese bureaucracy was notorious for its inefficiency—especially in aviation matters. To my surprise, I received a copy of a letter from the CAA in my company mailbox about two weeks later. In very formal language the Chinese apologized for the way my flight had been handled, and blamed everything on a new, inexperienced controller. The letter concluded with a terse statement that "the controller will be dealt with severely!" I often wondered if that meant that he had been sentenced to face a firing squad—I hope not!

I flew many more trips into Beijing during that year in Honolulu and thank goodness they were all less stressful—never routine, but at least manageable. Almost all of the pilots who flew into China during those years felt that we were lucky to avoid a catastrophic accident. Those pilots are to be commended for a safety record of ZERO accidents.

Chapter Twenty-Three

"No matter which seat a Pilot occupies in a three Pilot aircraft, the other two seats are always occupied by idiots!"

The end of that first year in Honolulu was rapidly coming to an end. Suddenly I was now senior enough to hold a 747 bid in SFO—an option that had never entered my mind when I took the bid to HNL. Donna and I quickly decided to spend my last two years with UAL on the mainland—we had all the ALOHA we needed to last a lifetime! Life was soon to become much more simple—no home in Denver, no residence in Hawaii, and soon, just one residence in the desert. It became a *fait accompli* on January 1, 1998.

The flying from SFO was very different than that in HNL—more variety because of a mixture of domestic trips with the international flights. This was a welcome change. The downside was that I was once again on reserve and the commute from Palm Springs to SFO was not convenient. United did not fly direct, so it involved a trip to LAX followed by a shuttle to SFO. I discovered that Alaska Airlines was a better alternative. That airline flew non-stop PSP to SFO and they treated pilots from other airlines very well. Due to the fact that most of the 747 flying departed early in the AM from SFO, I ended up spending lots of nights in hotels/motels in the proximity of the airport. Fortunately, my status as an LCA improved my seniority and whenever I was assigned an IOE I was provided with positive space tickets to and from PSP.

Another benefit to being based in SFO: NO MORE CHINA TRIPS! The long haul flying across the Pacific always started with a non-stop to Narita. These flights were scheduled for less than 12 hours, although often the actual flight time exceeded that twelve hour rule. As usual, the rules applied to *scheduled times,* not actual times, and we always flew as an "un-augmented crew," meaning that an extra crew member (a long range First Officer) was not required as part of the crew. Sitting at the controls for almost twelve hours with only short breaks for "physiological necessity" was not a lot of fun. Obviously, we all took short rest breaks individually to be ready for the more demanding parts of the flights. Like most Captains, I insisted that at all times two of the three crew members were awake and fully alert. On the all-nighter return flight from NRT to SFO, it was sometimes quite a challenge. For instance, one night the F/O announced that he was going to close his eyes for a few minutes. The S/O and I became more alert—then I noticed the Engineer's chin falling to his chest. Not a problem, I could keep an eye on everything myself. The next thing I remember is the Chief Purser, who had her own cockpit key (thank goodness), tapping me on the shoulder and asking politely if I would like a cup of coffee! I hope the sleep drool was not too evident on the side of my face!

From Narita our trips continued on to different destinations on the Asian continent—airports that were different than what I had flown into when based in Honolulu. Two of the more interesting destinations were Singapore (SIN) and Bangkok (BKK). The longest trip in the domicile was a nine day affair that included layovers in both of those exotic cities. That trip was about four days too long! The first time that I flew to BKK was an interesting journey back in time as it required flying across Vietnam. When we approached the coastline in the vicinity of Da Nang, we were told to contact Ho Chi Minh control. The last time that I had flown into this area, I was carrying a load of ordnance to be dispensed over the area that Ho Chi Minh controlled! It was a nostalgic feeling to think that some 33 years ago, my main concern when in this area was to deliver my weapons successfully and get back to the ship for an arrested landing! Now I was transporting over 400 passengers to their destination in Bangkok—most were not even born when I was there last.

On one of those trips to Bangkok I had the pleasure of flying with one of the few female copilots on the 747. She was a real hoot—an ex-Air Force pilot who was a very sharp pilot and a real pleasure to work with. It was her leg into BKK and the weather was not good when we arrived. It was a challenging approach with a strong crosswind and she did a remarkable job. After the landing I took the controls to taxi to the gate—she breathed a sigh of relief and contentment after a job well done, as any other pilot might do. Then she said, "After that landing I'm ready for a LBFM!"

I did a double take. The last time I had heard this acronym was over 30 years ago. In my vocabulary from the Navy days of flying into these areas we used the term "LBFM" as a description of some of the bar girls in southeast Asia which stood for "Little Brown Fucking Machine!" I looked at the young attractive female copilot and asked, "What do you mean when you say LBFM?" She looked at me like I had asked a very stupid question, and then responded, "LBFM means Lite Beer From Miller, everyone knows that!" Suddenly I felt old enough to be her grandfather.

Every departure from SFO to NRT was a maximum take off gross weight nightmare. With a full load of passengers and full fuel tanks (332,000 pounds of jet fuel) the aircraft usually grossed out at the max weight of 812,000 pounds. I am still amazed that an aircraft weighing that much could actually get into the air and FLY! Quite often we were forced to offload cargo to accommodate passengers and their luggage to stay under the max weight limit. I always thought about the amount of dirt in the cracks as we roared down the runway at the MTOGW! We could only use the longest runway at SFO—28R—which was almost 12,000 feet in length. When we rotated for liftoff, the end of the runway had long ago disappeared—we hoped that there was enough asphalt under the wheels to get us airborne. As we maneuvered through what was called the Gap Departure, the engines were at the maximum rated thrust and we cleared the rooftops and hillsides with very little to spare. Since SFO was a "noise sensitive" airport, we usually rang the bells on every heavy departure. A Flight Manager would call me a few weeks later to inform me that once again I had made too much noise and people were complaining. I never made an excuse for those violations.

Those long trips were not a lot of fun—but there were other flights that were almost like the good old days of 727 flying. Every morning there was a scheduled flight from SFO to Kona, on the big island of Hawaii. This flight was supposed to be flown in a DC-10. For reasons unknown to me, there was a two month period that the KOA trip was flown by reserve 747 crews—called an "equipment substitution" by the crew desk. The flight departed early in the AM, around 8 o'clock, but it never showed up as a 747 trip until about five hours before departure. Most of the 747 reserve crews were aware of this "catch 22" but occasionally a pilot was caught on a short call-out and was not able to get to the airport in time for departure. This looked bad for the reserve crews. I was assigned this trip several times on reserve and it was one of the most fun trips I flew on the jumbo jet. The little airport in Kona still had a distinct flavor of Hawaii—there were, at the time, no jumbo jets scheduled into that quaint field. The weather was always VFR and the controllers gave the pilots clearance to land without restrictions. On my first arrival into Kona, I decided to fly down the runway at 1000 feet, break left and fly a Navy pattern for landing. The tower gave their approval. In reality it was the best way to look over the airport before landing and assure that one was lined up to land on the proper runway. In Kona, there was only one runway.

I entered the break at 250 knots indicated and rolled into a 30 degree bank, calling for gear and flaps as the speed dissipated. When abeam the landing end of the runway I called for the final landing checklist. Both the F/O and S/O were enthralled at the type of approach I was flying and were grinning from ear to ear. As we rolled out on final, only about half a mile from touchdown, the checklist was completed. We touched down as the wings were leveled. The tower controllers were elated and the passengers were oblivious. Only one flight attendant commented that it was a very "different type of approach." After we parked our giant aircraft at the gate we were aware of large crowds of people watching. Most of the local people had never seen a plane as large as our B-747 at their tiny airport. I believe that our airplane was larger than the entire terminal at Kona!

After about two hours, enough time to refuel and load new passengers, we departed for the return trip to SFO. That leg seemed very dull and routine!

Generally I was still too junior to hold a scheduled line of flying until near the end of my first year in SFO. Sometimes I would be awarded a "partial line" or a move-up into a line held by someone senior who was on vacation. The first real line I held consisted of non-stop flights from SFO to IAD (Dulles airport in Washington, D.C.) with a non-stop return the next day. It was a very easy trip but was considered not desirable because it operated with two trips back to back—four days on and three days off. That meant lots of trips to the airport—not good for many of us who chose to commute to SFO from our homes far away. I was happy just to have a schedule even if it did mean that each week I had to spend two nights in the Bay Area and two nights in Washington. The layover was almost 24 hours at a nice hotel in Georgetown—close enough to enjoy the usual tourist attractions in the nation's capital. To my delight the Second Officer assigned to the same line was a gentleman named Bob who I had worked with some 20 years earlier when he was a senior Captain and I was a junior copilot. He was now almost

70 years of age. I wondered why he had chosen to continue working after age 60—most of us were ready to retire when that number came up.

Bob and I went out to dinner together that first night in Georgetown and I found out why he made such a decision. It seemed that his wife of many years had died unexpectedly when he was 59. His plans for a wonderful retirement with his mate had disappeared. They had no children and now his whole life was United Airlines and his many friends in aviation. He had been one of the most popular Captains with the airline and he continued to be one of the more personable souls I ever knew. He loved to be around the crews and the flight attendants really enjoyed visiting the cockpit when he was the S/O to listen to his many stories. Unfortunately, Bob had been a long time smoker and he was now paying the price. He no longer smoked but he had emphysema so badly that he could only walk about one block before he had to stop and rest. He usually departed for the airplane about one hour before departure to ensure that he had sufficient time for his duties. On our layovers I enjoyed visiting the Smithsonian Institute and touring some of the national attractions. He would accompany me only if we took a cab for our sojourns— if any walking at all was involved.

Bob was a delightful and sweet person, but he was also starting to lose his short term memory and was starting to become a liability in the cockpit. In other words, I had to watch his panel quite a bit and gently remind him of discrepancies that I noticed. Usually these were minor problems that would cause a problem only if ignored for long periods. One day we were flying from IAD to SFO and Bob was entertaining two young flight attendants with his colorful tales. Everyone was laughing and a good time was being had by all! As I casually scanned his engineer's panel I noticed that he was in the process of balancing the fuel—trying to even out the fuel loads in the many tanks that were part of the complicated fuel system designed by Mother Boeing. Instead of turning off fuel boost pumps to the tanks that were *receiving* fuel, he had turned off the pumps to the tanks that were *transferring* fuel! These fuel pumps also fed the engines!

Bob was in the middle of a long winded story and I really hated to interrupt. He was also very hard of hearing. After I called his name several times, he looked to me and asked, "What do you need, Captain?" I merely said, "Check your fuel panel, Bob."

Bob took a look at the panel and said, "Oh yeah, I should have turned off the other pumps." He then turned off the only pumps that were still operating and turned to the young ladies and resumed his story! The copilot was out of the loop because he was flying the airplane and could not see the engineer's panel from his seat anyway. Now I looked at that fuel panel and every warning light was on—all the pumps had been turned off. We were not in immediate danger of flaming out the engines due to fuel starvation because of the engine driven fuel pumps—nevertheless, it was a bit disconcerting to see the panel lit up like a Christmas tree! A change of attitude could cause an engine to flame out—also the fuel balance problem was now not being corrected, it was getting worse. I called out Bob's name again several times to get his attention—no reaction as he was into the best part of his story. Finally I yelled, "Bob, Goddamnit, look at the fuel panel!" He swiveled to face his panel and breathed those two most used words in aviation: "Oh shit!"

Bob started flipping switches as the two F/As quietly departed the cockpit without hearing the conclusion to his last story. Soon the problem had been solved and Bob gave me a sheepish apology, admitting that he should have been more vigilant. I apologized for yelling at him. He admitted that he needed to be "yelled at" because he sure couldn't hear for beans anymore! I only laughed as I asked him to continue with his story—even though I had heard it at least a dozen times. Perhaps the FAA knew what they were doing when they set the arbitrary age of sixty for airline pilots to retire!

Every airline pilot looks forward to that FINAL FLIGHT that will conclude his or her career in commercial aviation. Some approach that day with joy, looking forward to new adventures without ever having to worry about another check ride or maintaining those cumbersome flight manuals. Some approach that day with sadness, feeling that they are being cheated out of several more productive years (usually the prime earning years) because of the mandatory retirement age dictated by the government. Others approach that day with indifference—it's just the end of another chapter in the book of life. My personal feelings leaned toward that first group—it was time to move on. I knew when I took the job that I would be retired on that day that my chronological age turned that magical 60, regardless of my mental, physical and spiritual health. In my career I had flown with so many pilots that were near the end of their careers. Many were certainly able to continue flying without restrictions, but just as many were simply past their peak. Almost all of the Second Officers I flew with on the 747 were over the age of 60—only a very few were fully competent!

United Airlines treated retiring Captains quite well—if the Captain requested special treatment. The company would allow the Captain to pick a final trip of his choice and allow him to take his spouse with a positive space ticket on that last flight. Other family members could go along only on "space available" tickets. Some Captains went out with a big flourish—paying full fare for all the seats in First Class to take their family and friends along. Some Captains wanted no such fanfare and were happy to settle for a small cake at Operations after the last flight was completed.

I was awarded a very nice line of flying for my last month consisting of the most senior trip in the domicile. It was what the pilots called a "W-pattern" type of flying. The flight departed from SFO in the morning non-stop to HNL. After changing planes in Hawaii, the crew then flew to LAX for a 36 hour layover at a nice hotel in Redondo Beach. After the second night there the crew retraced their steps by flying back to HNL and after switching planes once again, continued on to SFO. These were very long days of flying, usually over eleven hours in the air both days. The good news: There were only four trips in a monthly schedule, equating eight days of actual flying. I planned to take my wife for sure on the last trip and my two children were also to be invited. One of the Flight Managers in SFO, my good friend, Tom, would fly as my copilot to HNL where my family and I would get off. Tom would fly on to LAX as Captain with the regularly scheduled copilot. After the layover he would return to HNL and I would join the crew to fly the last leg to SFO as my final flight! I would have about 48 hours to enjoy the beach in Waikiki to insure that I was completely rested up for that last leg! Tom was happy with that arrangement as he actually lived in southern California and would get to spend two nights at home. It seemed to be the perfect FINAL FLIGHT.

As the saying goes, "The best laid plans…" Before the second scheduled trip of the month the crew desk called and asked if I would conduct an IOE flight for a new copilot. This would be a five day trip to the Orient. I did not want to do another IOE, especially on my last month but the crew desk supervisor pleaded with me and I finally agreed. I would not fly the next two trips in my schedule but would still fly that FINAL FLIGHT as planned. As a reward for agreeing to conduct the IOE, I would be provided with positive space tickets to and from SFO for the rest of the month and my family would all be guaranteed positive space for that last trip. It seemed to be a win-win situation for all.

That trip to the Orient turned out to be a lot of fun. The copilot was a delightful young man (about 30) who had been a Naval Aviator fighter pilot. He had been flying as copilot with United for several years on smaller equipment and was an excellent aviator. He also had some interesting stories to tell about his flying during Operation Desert Storm. I was amazed at the changes in Naval Aviation since my tour some thirty years previously. Catapult shots from the carrier were "hands free"—the pilot was not allowed to touch the controls until the aircraft was safely airborne! Completely automated approaches and "hands off" arrested landings were in the near future. During the copilots short career with United he had only flown new generation aircraft with the so-called glass cockpits. He had never flown an aircraft with a Second Officer before—his airline experience was only in a two-person cockpit. He really felt that he was taking a step back in time by flying the "rope-start" 747—which was what the new pilots called our plane. He had bid to fly the 747 because he wanted to fly by the seat of his pants one more time—he knew that these airplanes would soon join their ancestors parked on some lonely desert strip. He reminded me of myself so many years ago when I chose to fly the AD Skyraider prop plane instead of the new jets.

That last IOE trip consisted of the usual non-stop to Narita, and then the next night we flew to Singapore. SIN was one of the most modern airports in the world—far superior to most of the US airfields. After landing on their well-lit runway we were cleared to "follow the green lights" to our gate. These green lights were recessed in the centerline of the taxiways and as we moved along they were programmed to stay about 100 meters ahead of our position. As we taxied over them they were extinguished. What an ingenious way to get to your parking spot!

After a very nice layover in SIN we flew back to NRT. As usual I flew the first leg and the copilot flew to SIN and back to NRT. The final leg, the all-nighter to SFO, we would split in half. I ended up flying the first part and the copilot took over half way across the ocean. Before we departed Japan the dispatcher had briefed me on the presence of a very strong jet stream that would possibly be along our route of flight. The winds in the core of that stream were forecast to be up to 200 knots. If we were to find just the right spot we could get the benefit of a huge increase in our groundspeed. I selected a route and altitude that would take advantage of such a boost.

We were lucky and found that right spot. Suddenly our ground speed jumped to over 700 knots—roughly 805 miles per hour! This was probably the fastest that I had ever moved across the ground in a commercial airliner. My indicated airspeed was greater on the PEK departure but the ground speed was much lower. I took a picture in the cockpit of the INS indicating 702 knots—I still have that photo. We would arrive over one hour early in San Francisco.

After the halfway point where I passed the controls to the copilot, I went for a "walk-about" through the cabin, which was my habit during these long night flights. I left my hat in the cockpit and slipped a sweater over my uniform shirt so that my epaulets were not visible. I enjoyed these 20 minute walks consisting of two or three laps around the cabin incognito. It broke up the monotony of the long flight, gave me some exercise, and I had a chance to see how things were going on the other side of the cockpit door. All 450 seats were filled, almost exclusively with Japanese citizens, and the vast majority of these passengers, who had willingly chosen to be trapped in this huge aluminum tube, were sound asleep as we sped across the Pacific faster than a "speeding bullet" some seven miles above the surface of this planet. The wonder of it all never ceased to astound me—even after some forty years of flying all types of aircraft over almost every part of the world.

When I returned to the cockpit I was once again filled with contentment that I had been blessed with such a wonderful career—never once did I feel like I had to "work for a living"—it was just the opposite. Every time I donned my flight suit or wore my airline pilot's uniform, it was with real pleasure. I would certainly miss these feelings.

As we approached SFO, almost one and a half hours ahead of schedule, we were advised that the airport was socked in with early morning fog that usually lifted around dawn. It was still pitch black and first light was more than an hour away. We had the capability to perform an auto-coupled, auto-land approach with auto-throttles in this particular aircraft—the ultimate "hands-off" landing. Only once before had I flown a completely auto-land approach, a year or so earlier in Seoul, Korea. On that occasion, I had to disengage the autopilot just before touchdown because of excessive crosswind drift. This time the wind in SFO was dead calm—the perfect setting for such an approach. This would be good experience for the new copilot who had performed these landings before with glass cockpit aircraft. It would also be a test for me—could I keep my hands off the controls as we touched down in this huge airplane full of people? Did I have enough confidence in the aircraft's ability to land in conditions that were beyond the legalities of mere mortals? We would see.

There was very little other traffic in the Bay Area so we were cleared for our "auto approach" without delay. It was a complex procedure to couple up the flight directors with both autopilots; select the auto-land function, and then engage the auto-throttle feature. It was a very structured approach that most pilots found to be a bit awkward—mostly because it was so seldom used. I had only practiced the entire procedure to a landing in the simulator. Once we were on final approach and all systems were hooked up, I was once again surprised at all of the green lights in the cockpit—much better than amber or red! At 100 feet on the radar altimeter there were no runway lights in sight. Normally this was as low as one could go except in the present situation where all systems were in the green—we were allowed to continue. I was literally sitting on my hands at this time, trying my best to not grab control of the aircraft. At 50 feet another green light came on indicating that the flare had been initiated. I felt a very slight rounding out for the landing. Then at 30 feet the throttles were automatically retarded. Dim runway lights were now visible but I could not tell if we were on the center line of the runway. We were at the mercy of those computers that were now in charge. Suddenly we touched down and the brakes were automatically applied. At last I could touch something! All that was remaining was for me to put the engines into reverse and disengage the auto features. Quickly we were at taxi speed and I turned off the runway to proceed to the terminal. My hands were as sweaty as they had ever been during the most challenging landings in my career. The copilot was cool as a cucumber—just a routine event for him! Aviation was rapidly changing—the computers were the future. I asked myself as I taxied to the gate—could I have hand flown that approach to a landing in the center of the runway with visibility less than one quarter of a mile after being at the controls for almost ten hours, in the middle of the night? The sad but realistic answer—NO! It was time to retire.

Due to an unfortunate and untimely accident I was not able to fly that scheduled FINAL FLIGHT—I was on sick leave with my arm in a cast. That automatic landing in San Francisco would be the last time I would sit at the controls of a commercial airliner. In many ways, it was truly a fitting ending. I have never had any regrets. I flew during those years WHEN FLYING WAS FUN!

Epilogue

To the best of my knowledge there is nothing on the drawing boards to replace the airplane as the safest, fastest and most efficient means of transporting people and goods over long distances. As long as there are airplanes, there will be pilots. The question is: Will the pilots of the future be true aviators or will they be computer operators? It seems that the only logical conclusion is the latter answer. The limiting factor in future aviation is the human one. Military aircraft can be built to sustain 20 or 30 G's—no human in any g-suit can survive that type of punishment. The UAV (Unmanned Aerial Vehicle) will eventually be the fighter/bomber of the future, controlled by grounded pilots who operate their flights across front lines or continents via computer inputs.

Commercial airliners will continue to be flown by two pilots—eventually one—who basically monitor the computers that have been programmed by other computers! The only fun type flying will be that flown by adventuresome aviators daring enough to fly their own frail machines in places that are not controlled by controllers! That uncontrolled airspace is getting smaller every day.

I will dearly miss the days when passengers dressed up in their Sunday finest to board an airliner that would take them on the adventure of their life. I will miss those relaxing trips to the airport where passengers and crews breezed through the terminals to their assigned gates with merely a nod and smile from airport employees.

I believe that we have truly reached the end of an era in aviation. Airliners are now Greyhound buses with wings. Even the major aircraft builder in Europe admits to that reality by naming their plane the "AIRBUS." The legacy carriers in America are struggling to remain solvent, being forced to conform to the low standards of service provided by the new "low-cost carriers." My friends who are still in the cockpits of today's airliners do not have a lot of enthusiasm for their careers—will there be a pension when they retire? Will their airline even be in business when they reach retirement age? I do not see a lot of smiling faces on flight crews when I make my infrequent trips in the Unfriendly Skies of today's airliners. Flight Attendants know that they will not get help from the pilots when confronted with drunken passengers, hijackers or terrorists on today's flights. Their profession is no longer the glamorous job that it once was.

Additional security brought on by the terrorists has added considerable stress to the traveling public. Hopefully this will pass and commercial aviation will once again be the comfortable and elegant way to fly that it once was. In the meantime, I will always be proud to say that I was a Naval Aviator and an Airline Pilot and I flew during those days WHEN FLYING WAS FUN!